'Forget the study of politics! Forget methodologies of data management! This nonsense is foisted on us by an unholy alliance of science and the market whose only aim is to put a stop to thought. In this passionately argued book, Arpad Szakolczai ruthlessly exposes the insanity of reason eating at the fabric of our world. The anthropological task, he argues, is to search for a way – a method – that opens to the inner truth of life for the political animals we humans are. At once mischievous and erudite, contrarian and humble, Szakolczai speaks from the heart. His words should matter to us all.'

– **Tim Ingold**, *Emeritus Professor of Anthropology, University of Aberdeen, UK*

'The title, *Political Anthropology as Method*, gives nothing away. Knowing a little of Arpad Szakolczai's previous work, I anticipated a challenging, wide-ranging, multilingual, and enormously erudite discussion of genuinely fundamental questions in social science, philosophy, and theology. With such a guide no reader can be disappointed. *Political Anthropology* is a way of doing academic/scholarly/research work in order to understand political reality. This is not, however, a handbook on how to do things. Rather, it illustrates by way of examples. As F.R. Leavis used to say, it is a conversation that takes the form 'this is so, isn't it?' And expects by way of response, 'Yes, but ….' Such an understanding is already both personal and participatory – initially as a conversation, but also in what the conversation is about, namely understanding reality, the reality where the sun comes up in the east and sets in the west. Humans can never transcend such a participatory perspective. Political Anthropology thus provides the greatest contrast to what, conventionally, we call science, methodological, universal, professional, and especially quantitative, science. As for *Method*, it refers first to a path, a way, on which we, bipedal creatures, walk. Quadrupeds also rely on paths – they are motile, after all – to traverse both the undergrowth and the open prairie, but theirs are more beaten paths, game trails, than personal or new ones. The way is also spiritual and reflexive, from the Tao of Lao-Tzu to the Gospel of John (14:6). These paths imply movement, along the right way, which is already there, and they reach an end. One needs a trusted guide, not a map, to find the end of the road. *Political Anthropology as Method* shows that Szakolczai is such a person.'

– **Barry Cooper**, *Professor of Politics, University of Calgary, Canada*

'*Political Anthropology as Method* will transform the reader's view of methodology in understanding social life. It demonstrates how the social sciences went astray when they tried to imitate the natural sciences. It debunks the idols, the delusions, and the alchemy of so-called scientific research designs. It invites the reader to step back from objectivity, variables, and hypothesis-testing by which the dictates of methodology bend reality. Rather, it encourages researchers to trust their intuition, walk the unfamiliar ways that can be illuminated by trustworthy guides and, most of all, exercise one's own personal judgement. The rewards of reading this outstanding book will be many. Perhaps the most important one is that understanding social and political life is a long-winded journey, sometimes risky and often onerous. If we want to get a chance to illuminate reality and approach 'truth', it will demand the wholesale participation in the complexities of historically grown life.'

– **Harald Wydra**, *Professor of Politics,*
University of Cambridge, UK

'Arpad Szakolczai and his circle have been developing political anthropology over the past couple of decades. *Political Anthropology as Method* provides an account of this school of thought. One would be tempted to call it the School of Cork (Ireland) if its members were not so spread out across Europe. But its lack of settled place is fitting because, as Szakolczai shows, political anthropology is less a reductionistic 'methodology' than a *met'hodos*, a 'way' that traverses what Eric Voegelin, following Plato, called *metaxy*. Political anthropologists follow the way not only *across* various genealogies and an eclectic combination of disciplines, but also *up* from the Anaximanderean *apeiron* to the divine. Szakolczai invites the reader to join in their quest along the way.'

– **John von Heyking**, *Professor of Political Science,*
University of Lethbridge, Canada

'*Political Anthropology as Method* is a bold and breath-taking attempt to approach politics and humans differently. The usual methods of modern anthropology, based upon the Cartesian paradigm, are not only wrong but rather fatal, Arpad Szakolczai argues. A misguided understanding of rationality and science has made nature uninhabitable, and a dehumanized understanding of humans has made our social and political world hostile to a meaningful, good life. We seem to be substitutable parts of soul-less machinery. In this way, the history is read against the grain by Szakolczai; modernity appears as a genealogical drama. Even those who see modernity in a brighter light and who have more faith in the enlightenment and contemporary science must read this challenging book. With immense erudition and subtlety, hidden connections are revealed and examined critically. A completely different history of ideas dawns that radically turns our common interpretations upside down. At the same time, the outlines of a new (and partly rather old) humane anthropology emerge. Szakolczai's suggestions will undoubtedly experience as much admiration as harsh rejection. However, to echo Kant's remark about David Hume, this ingenious book is suitable to awaken everyone from the dogmatic slumber of too naïve a belief in modernity, whose terrible consequences we can experience everywhere.'

– **Christian Illies**, *Professor of Philosophy,*
University of Bamberg, Germany

'Political Anthropology as Method is a guidebook to explore vast and complex territories of contemporary philosophical, anthropological and political thinking, through an original and stimulating approach that starts from the experiences encountered by those who in our days take up an academic career in a humanistic field, moves to the critical analysis of scientific methodology, and reaches finally the theoretical, symbolical and mythical foundations that characterise its origins. Through such analyses there appears ever more clearly the methods used by the author whose principles are not announced, abstractly, beforehand, but rather emerge through a critical confrontation with important protagonists of modern thinking like Heidegger, Foucault, Voegelin, Mauss, and many others. The work of excavation is guided by a genealogical inquiry, which is separated from the historical: if this latter turns around the idea of process and advances universalistic claims, the other is guided by the idea of participation and is marked by movements of recognition. Participation is one of the central categories of the book, connected to the experiences of real life and its languages, but also having analytical significance. Experiences of participation are connected to gift-giving, a central anthropological term that has, however, remained marginal within the mainstream. The term liminality, also central for the book, is linked to the emergence of scientific thought and marks its limits, even in a mythical sense. The reconstruction of lines of meaning traced by the author, apart from the suspended and dilated liminal moment that characterises modernity, converge in outlining a political anthropology elaborated in a philosophical key. This renders the book a stimulating contribution to reflexions on contemporary society, of certain interest to philosophers, anthropologists, and scholars of politics.'

– **Giuliana Parotto**, *Professor of Political Philosophy, University of Trieste, Italy*

'*Political Anthropology as Method* guides our attention to some of the most intriguing parts of academic research. This book presents nothing less than an outlook to the world, and ways of researching real problems in the world we are inhabiting. Indeed, Arpad Szakolczai paves the way for personal and invested engagements with our contemporary predicament without prejudice but with bold clarity. Any scholar will benefit enormously from Szakolczai's graceful treatment of these fundamental issues.'

– **Andreas Bandak**, *Associate Professor, Anthropology, and Head of Centre for Comparative Culture Studies, University of Copenhagen, Denmark*

POLITICAL ANTHROPOLOGY AS METHOD

This book explores considerations of method in the field of political anthropology, contending that this constitutes a distinct approach within the broader area of the human, social, and political sciences. Faithful to the basic guiding ideas of anthropology, it nonetheless challenges and rejects the pretended stance of scientific neutrality and advances a position that engages with the notion of participation, recognising its value and arguing that participation is essential to the development of a proper social and political understanding. An outline of what political anthropology can offer by way of methods, this invitation to consider the development of methodological ideas beyond the presumed 'scientific' and 'universalistic' approaches that dominate in the social sciences will appeal to scholars of anthropology, sociology, and politics with interests in questions of method and methodology.

Arpad Szakolczai is Emeritus Professor of Sociology at University College Cork, Ireland. He is the author of *Sociology, Religion and Grace: A Quest for the Renaissance*, *Comedy and the Public Sphere*, *Novels and the Sociology of the Contemporary*, *Permanent Liminality and Modernity* and *Post-Truth Society: A Political Anthropology of Trickster Logic*. He is the co-author of *Walking into the Void: A Historical Sociology and Political Anthropology of Walking*, *From Anthropology to Social Theory: Rethinking the Social Sciences*, and *The Political Sociology and Anthropology of Evil: Tricksterology*.

CONTEMPORARY LIMINALITY

Series editor: Arpad Szakolczai, University College Cork, Ireland.
Series advisory board: Agnes Horvath, University College Cork, Ireland; Bjørn Thomassen, Roskilde University, Denmark; and Harald Wydra, University of Cambridge, UK.

This series constitutes a forum for works that make use of concepts such as 'imitation', 'trickster' or 'schismogenesis', but which chiefly deploy the notion of 'liminality', as the basis of a new, anthropologically-focused paradigm in social theory. With its versatility and range of possible uses rivalling mainstream concepts such as 'system', 'structure' or 'institution', liminality by now is a new master concept that promises to spark a renewal in social thought.

While charges of Eurocentrism are widely discussed in sociology and anthropology, most theoretical tools in the social sciences continue to rely on approaches developed from within the modern Western intellectual tradition, whilst concepts developed on the basis of extensive anthropological evidence and which challenged commonplaces of modernist thinking, have been either marginalised and ignored, or trivialised. By challenging the taken-for-granted foundations of social theory through incorporating ideas from major thinkers, such as Nietzsche, Dilthey, Weber, Elias, Voegelin, Foucault and Koselleck, as well as perspectives gained through modern social and cultural anthropology and the central concerns of classical philosophical anthropology *Contemporary Liminality* offers a new direction in social thought.

Titles in this series

Making Sense of Diseases and Disasters
Reflections of Political Theory from Antiquity to the Age of COVID
Edited by Lee Trepanier

Political Anthropology as Method
Arpad Szakolczai

Liminal Politics in the New Age of Disease
Technocratic Mimetism
Edited by Agnes Horvath and Paul O'Connor

Art and Enchantment
How Wonder Works
Patrick Curry

For more information about this series, please visit: https://www.routledge.com/Contemporary-Liminality/book-series/ASHSER1435

POLITICAL ANTHROPOLOGY AS METHOD

Arpad Szakolczai

NEW YORK AND LONDON

First published 2023
by Routledge
605 Third Avenue, New York, NY 10158

and by Routledge
2 Park Square, Milton Park, Abingdon, Oxon OX14 4RN

Routledge is an imprint of the Taylor & Francis Group, an informa business

© 2023 Arpad Szakolczai

The right of Arpad Szakolczai to be identified as author of this work has been asserted by him in accordance with sections 77 and 78 of the Copyright, Designs and Patents Act 1988.

All rights reserved. No part of this book may be reprinted or reproduced or utilised in any form or by any electronic, mechanical, or other means, now known or hereafter invented, including photocopying and recording, or in any information storage or retrieval system, without permission in writing from the publishers.

Trademark notice: Product or corporate names may be trademarks or registered trademarks, and are used only for identification and explanation without intent to infringe.

British Library Cataloguing-in-Publication Data
A catalogue record for this book is available from the British Library

Library of Congress Cataloging-in-Publication Data
A catalog record has been requested for this book

ISBN: 978-1-032-21778-9 (hbk)
ISBN: 978-1-032-23002-3 (pbk)
ISBN: 978-1-003-27513-8 (ebk)

DOI: 10.4324/9781003275138

Typeset in Bembo
by Taylor & Francis Books

CONTENTS

Preface *xi*

PART I
The Meaning of Method **1**

1 What is a method? And a methodology? 3

2 The importance of participation 17

3 Participation on the road 27

PART II
The Troubles with Scientific Methodology **35**

4 The absurdity of a scientific methodology 37

5 Some matters of historical context 60

6 The idols of scientific methodology 83

PART III
Some Methods of Political Anthropology **97**

7 Words 99

8 Images 116

9 Understanding through authors 149

10 Understanding through novels	157
11 Historical methods	161
12 Anthropological methods	194
Conclusion	205

Bibliography *210*
Name Index *217*
Subject Index *221*

PREFACE

Be lowly wise.
Think only what concerns thee, and thy being;
Dream not of other worlds, what creatures there
Live, in what state, condition, or degree,
Contented that thus far hath been revealed
Not of Earth only but of highest heaven.

John Milton, Paradise Lost, *VIII.173–8*

her mind, brooding solitary, had grown diseased, as all minds do and will and must that reverse the appointed order of their maker

Charles Dickens, Great Expectations, *338*

If it had ever been meant to be lived in, I might have thought it small, or inconvenient, or lonely; but never having been designed for any such use, it became a perfect abode.

Charles Dickens, David Copperfield, *29*

This book, as indicated by its title, will not present the methods of Political Anthropology – this will be offered in its third part –; rather Political Anthropology as method.

Political Anthropology – a term that will be capitalised in the book, to distinguish it from 'political anthropology' as a subfield of social or cultural anthropology – offers an outlook on the world, a way of doing research, and a mode of bringing together various academic disciplines in order to promote understanding.

Thus, to start with, Political Anthropology offers an outlook which, in line with the term 'anthropology', starts not with 'science' and 'objectivity', but with us humans, who furthermore do not live in the 'universe', but here on Earth, and even further not just 'on' Earth, but immersed inside its Nature. It is therefore 'political' in the classical Aristotelian sense of man being a *zoon politikon*, or a 'political animal', and it is in this capacity that we need to understand our involvement in and with Nature, which is given to us and in which we all participate, starting from recognising both this givenness and its beauty, and being grateful for it – recognition and gratitude being the same words in some languages, also rooted etymologically in *charis*, or grace, with fundamental classical-theological implications. Starting with participation also implies that scientific neutrality cannot offer the last word; quite the contrary; such neutrality and universality, far from being unquestionable assets, are rather dangerous liabilities, threatening us in our very humanity.

Second, Political Anthropology is also a way of doing research. The aim of this book is to bring out what this means, by reflecting on how work in Political Anthropology was conducted in the past, on what method-logical principles this was based, and to promote this further by doing it at the same time, based on the idea that the best way to present Political Anthropology as method is not by establishing some kind of prescriptive canon to be rigidly followed, but by showing it in working, and explaining how it works. While this book is personal, mostly informed by my own way of proceeding, it will also try to incorporate my understanding of how this work was done by others. Thus, far from trying to prescribe my own way for the others, it is doing rather the opposite: it incorporates the experience with Political Anthropology of others into my own method-related investigation.

Third, Political Anthropology is not being offered as a new (sub-)discipline, rather as an interdisciplinary field, bringing together historical-genealogical sociology, social and cultural anthropology, classical political philosophy, art history, comparative archaeology, classics, and comparative mythology, even elements of theology. Its focus is on comprehensive understanding, which is not possible to pursue within the limits of a single modern academic discipline.

Political Anthropology as an undertaking is not my initiative, but originates with a single person, Agnes Horvath, who also brought it into fruition. In my life I never encountered another person whose ideas come even close to the radicality, originality, and determination of Agnes' – not to mention that she also gave birth to and brought up five boys, by now all having finished university. She first developed the idea in conversations with József Lőrincz, a classical philologist-ethnographer-political sociologist from Sepsiszentgyörgy with an EUI Florence PhD, who sadly passed away last year, shortly after having taken the second dose of the COVID 'vaccine'. A central part in the project is played by the peer-reviewed journal *International Political Anthropology* (IPA), which she founded in November 2007 with Bjørn Thomassen and Harald Wydra, and of which she was chief editor until the end of 2021. She managed to convince me, over the years, that pursuing the combination of Weberian historical sociology, as continued by Voegelin, Elias, Borkenau, Koselleck, and others, with the Nietzsche-Foucaldian genealogy is not sufficient. My role was limited to contributing my share in bringing forward the idea.

Still, this book is also much based on my 1987 Austin, TX, PhD thesis, built around the person and the work of Henri di Saint-Simon (see Szakolczai 1990, for its Hungarian published version). Saint-Simon is mostly known as an obscure figure in the history of thought, discussed by Marx as a utopian socialist, precursor of socialism. However, my PhD thesis argued that he is much more than that, actually just as important for a genealogy of the absurdities of modernity as Marx himself. This is because, as Durkheim already realised – and it has been decisively argued that Saint-Simon was more important for Durkheim than Marx – he was also a founding figure of sociology, mentor of Comte; and, even further, and much more than Comte actually, he pioneered the strict, mechanical, mimetic application of the methods of the 'natural sciences', *in particular medicine*, for social and human understanding, and thus was a direct precursor, apart from the untenable idea that the social sciences must mechanically follow the methods of the 'natural' sciences, of the excesses of the current quasi-totalitarian sanitary politics. Even further, and making him even more relevant for our times, he championed at the same time entrepreneurialism and the managerial technocratic state, thus envisioning their fusion. In his ideas the distant roots of the European Community were also recognised, while at the same time he had a pioneering insight, way before Tocqueville (and paralleling, actually, Hegel), about the inescapable rise to dominance of the United States – exactly because, in his views, the US is less held back by the forces of 'tradition' – the main enemy for Saint-Simon.

In his life, Saint-Simon tried to promote his ideas by writing to all kind of potentates, prominently including Napoleon, just as writing public letters, founding associations, and ending his life by trying to re-found Christianity – his last book is entitled *Nouveau Christianisme*. For all these reasons, his contemporaries considered him as a lunatic. Thus, today, we have only two choices, in a typical Kierkegaardian situation: either recognise in him a unique prophet, the brave hero of the coming modernity – or, on the contrary, we have to admit that we are now living in a real-ised, lunatic absurdity.

Writing this book implied a perpetual struggle to keep it inside an assigned word limit. Sections were significantly shortened, and planned sections were cut or remained unwritten to comply with this obligation. Still, there are some good reasons why an academic book of 100,000 words is preferable to one of 200,000 words, and I'm perfectly happy with the way it turned out, within its allotted limits.

The book has three parts. The first shows, starting from the most basic method-related requirements of a PhD thesis, and even a Third Year Research Project, what is wrong with the basic tenets of the 'scientific methodology' now imposed practically everywhere in the social and human sciences, following the prescient – or lunatic – ideas of Saint-Simon, and how and why Political Anthropology offers a better way to reach meaningful results. Part Two offers a detailed philological and historical genealogy of 'scientific methodology', while Part Three offers a few basic method-logical guidelines about doing research in Political Anthropology, through showing the way by analysing the work of some particularly important guides inside the field, around some of its central tools and orientations.

The book, evidently, is based on my previous books, including especially those co-authored with Agnes Horvath and Bjørn Thomassen, and also on other works around the *IPA* group,[1] but I tried to avoid, for evident reasons, repetitions, especially in the Bibliography, as much as possible, so 'ideally' those works should be consulted when reading this.

Note

1 For some representative publications, see Horvath (2013, 2021), Horvath and Szakolczai (2018a, 2018b, 2020), Horvath and Thomassen (2008), Horvath, Thomassen and Wydra (2015), Szakolczai (2022), Szakolczai and Thomassen (2019), Thomassen (2014), Wydra (2015), and Wydra and Thomassen (2018).

PART I
The Meaning of Method

1
WHAT IS A METHOD? AND A METHODOLOGY?

> The most valuable insights are gained last of all; but the most valuable insights are the *methods*.
>
> Friedrich Nietzsche, The Will to Power, 469

> He and some one hundred and forty other schoolmasters, had been lately turned at the same time, in the same factory, on the same principles, like so many pianoforte legs. He had been put through an immense variety of paces, and had answered volumes of head-breaking questions. ... If he had only learnt a little less, how infinitely better he might have taught much more!
>
> Charles Dickens, Hard Times, 14–5

> only in destroying I find ease
> To my relentless thoughts
>
> John Milton, Paradise Lost, IX.129–30

Let me start by resuming, as clearly and concisely as possible, the standard, mainstream approach to the way a research project should be conducted. This is the manner in which we are supposed to teach our students, in most if not all fields of the social sciences about how they are supposed to write a final year undergraduate Research Project, a minor thesis, or a PhD; but this is also how one is supposed to formulate a postdoctoral research application, just as any other application for research funds, from the most mundane local funding bodies up to the 'blue sky' horizons of ERC.

Such activity must start by specifying, as clearly and concisely as possible, the research problem or question. It can be just a sentence or a paragraph, in more complex cases – where more money is searched for – up to a full page, but certainly not more. It should then continue by offering a review, as comprehensive as possible, though of course tailored to the circumstances, of the existing literature on the field to which the research question belongs. Such tailoring means that of course one cannot expect a final year undergraduate Research Project to offer a comprehensive review, only a selection of it – supposedly the most important ones; such literature review should be more extensive for a minor thesis, but a PhD 'really' should offer as comprehensive a review as possible. It should then continue, on this basis, to build up the theoretical framework of the project – the *own* theory of the student or researcher. Such theory should indeed be a personal, quasi trademarked effort; using the theories of others is a second-rate endeavour. A 'doc' method for theory-building is to use only one work by every theorist, avoiding even the shadow of mere imitation.

This, however, is only the background, as here comes the key moment for any research project: the specification of *methodology* (here the kind reader should imagine the tingling of bells and odour of incense). The definition of research problem goes without saying; the literature review is simple homework; the theoretical framework is important but in general consists of a few concepts in their relationship which is to be applied in the research; but the really crucial issue is *how* this research is to be done. Any funding body now specifies that the numerically greatest and for the evaluation most important part of any research proposal is its *methodology*. Such methodology implies, in the most prestigious cases, where quantitative methods are used to test hypotheses on empirical data, the operationalisation of theoretical concepts into measurable variables, the specification of the hypotheses; the description of the population on which data are to be collected, the method of data collection, the techniques of statistical analysis, and so on. It is not so different for the so-called 'qualitative' methods, and various mixing of quantitative and qualitative techniques, only there, instead of operationalisation and quantification, the specification of methodology will involve other techniques.

Concerning the way this 'methodology' is to be specified, three preliminary considerations are offered. To start with, theory and methodology are supposed to be strictly separate. Theory has to do with general, universalistic, decontextualised concepts, following the neo-Kantian logic of concept-building, modelled on Platonic 'ideas'; while method is restricted to applying these general concepts to an empirical field. From this perspective, there is a clear sequential order between theory and method, and there is no feedback from method to theory. Second, while theory-building is supposed to be personal, in the sense of connecting previously decontextualised general concepts in a new way – this is *my* theory, says the proud researcher who follows this mainstream-establishment process; questions of methodology are strictly *not* personal. 'Ideally' – meaning: from the perspective of funding bodies, high-level university administrators, policy makers and jetsetter academics who travel from one global city to another, evaluating research projects according to 'best practice' standards – such methodology should follow the tenets of a 'scientific methodology', imitating the 'natural sciences' – at least, imitating the way the natural sciences were supposed to work, some decades or centuries before. Third, such methodology again is supposed to be comprehensive, which means not just a general specification of the methods to be used, quantitative or qualitative, in considerable details, but a prior description of the *entire* research process. Thus, again ideally, which so far has reached its apex in the Horizon 2020 projects to be submitted to Brussels, implies a kind of detailed, prior, step by step specification, comparable to writing a computer programme, even better an algorithm, of more or less *everything* the research project will try to accomplish, so that actual research will be nothing else than the mechanical performance of these steps. So, if funds were granted, the researcher can go to the field and (another telling word) 'execute' the research activities 'planned' in advance.

I hope I have given as precise and concise a description as possible of the research steps into which we as academics are supposed to instruct our students, and which we ourselves are supposed to follow when applying for a research funding. I was not trying to give an exaggerated, caricatural description of the process, as that would serve no purpose. Still, now I must continue by saying that I consider that this standard approach is wrong basically in every single one of its precepts and suggestions.

I hope I can demonstrate this convincingly in the present book, and for now, in a preliminary manner in the following paragraphs.

To begin with, and as it is always the case in similar situations, the first step, and indeed the skeleton of the entire process, seems to be simple common sense. Of course, there is need to clearly define a research question, to review the way others approached it, to look for conceptual tools and approaches by which the question can be examined. So, in a way, all this is quite fine in so far as a final year undergraduate Research Project is concerned. The trouble is that the moment we deal with something less trivial and basic, such clarities break down.

As an authoritative example, I refer to Max Weber's *Protestant Ethic*. The original title of the first essay, running to about 40% of the whole work, excluding footnotes, Part I of the book as published in English, is 'The Problem'. This means that Max Weber, founding father of sociology, spent almost half his most important research book on specifying the research problem he was trying to tackle. The inevitable corollary is that, had Weber submitted his work to any contemporary university, it would have been rejected without appeal.

This is absurd; so, what is going on? To start with, and most evidently, Weber's research was 'complex'. This, however, is not a sufficient explanation, as complexity usually refers to the answer and not the question. At any rate, even a complex question could be formulated in a page or so. Second, beyond complexity, there emerges the related question of simultaneity. Weber's first essay, or the first part of the book, does not merely deal with the 'problem', but at the same time offers considerations on what is considered as literature review, conceptual framework, and method, even some results, in a simultaneous and non-recursive manner. All this is because, beyond complexity and simultaneity, the essays also involve reflexivity, even self-reflexivity, taken further in one of Weber's most important works, published as the 'Author's Introduction' to the *Protestant Ethic*, but originally written as the Introduction to the comprehensive five-volume collection; and which starts with a self-referential statement.

Thus, Weber is not offering an external, neutral, objective definition of a straightforward research question (say, 'What were the historical origins of modern capitalism?'); rather, from the inside, as member of the culture that developed this capitalism, as *participating* in this process, being inside it, poses the question of how could we overcome this involvement and participation, the taken for granted of our modern world, dominated by 'capitalism', exploring how this could have become possible.

Returning now to the claim, certainly stunning for many, that *everything* is wrong with the standard research project methodology, let us review, one by one, all the other steps.

Problems continue with the next step, a 'comprehensive' literature review. In one sense, again, the underlying reason is trivially true: before doing research, one must be aware of who else did similar studies, and with what results. However, in our days a major concern is the exponential growth and limitless escalation of publications. As anybody knows (who indeed knows), much of this, whether as empirical research or theoretical commentary, is simply meaningless, the conducting of research to prove trivialities, or making endless comments on writings where already endless comments were made, with the sole reason of improving one's publications record and getting an employment, so students of the next generations are saturated with commonplaces. Thus, what research *really* needs is *guidance* concerning what is important to read and what not – or, a thesis supervisor, or research director, who is capable of discrimination; and on the other hand, not any theorist accepted by the 'discipline', but genuine authors who can offer guidance through their life-work.

Concerning the first point, in our days this idea, on the one hand, is considered 'not democratic' enough (this is nonsensical, as academic quality is not a matter for democracy); on the other, as too 'intrusive' on the student; so the usual solution, propagated explicitly by related books and teachings, increasingly done not by academics but HR departments, is that given the large number of publications, a very short and narrow research question should be selected, a theme on which one should read *everything*. This, however, is another non-solution, as it only results in hyper-specialisation, offering incremental improvement without any significance, while the reading of a large number of already hyper-specialised works without any proper sense of discrimination ensures intellectual mediocrity and the resulting boredom of students eventually taught by such persons.

The second point will be discussed extensively in Chapter 9.

All these considerations apply even more for 'theoretical framework'. Here the standard textbook approach is blatantly wrong. One certainly needs to consult more than one theorist or theoretical approach, but it does not mean consulting only one concept, or book by a single author, so that one could build one's 'own' theory. What one needs are *guides* who help to direct one's thinking. A guide is a person whom one trusts as a person; thus, from a thinker whom one considers as a guide, one must read as much as possible. What really matters, instead of building up one's own theory, is sensitivity to various approaches; and then, through in-depth familiarisation with the writings of several thinkers, develop a specific world vision and intellectual style.

Thus we arrived, after these preliminary considerations, through the broader issue of formulating a research proposal, to questions of method.

Method, methodology, method-logic

The first question now concerns the distinction between 'method' and 'methodology'. This book will consistently talk about 'methods', avoiding the term 'methodology', which will be shown to systematically promote intellectual corruption, except for pointing out the reasons why the current, dominant, almost taken for granted use of this word is problematic. However, given the need to use a word that expresses a sustained concern with method as the way, it introduces the term 'method-logic'.

One might claim, using an argument popular in establishment circles, that it does not matter what word one uses, only how one defines it, but this is a fallacy, belonging to the same (neo-)Kantian semantic universe and its problems. Kant famously argued that words are mere instruments for thinking, and any concern with their etymology and history is sophistry; every thinker is not just free but is obliged to develop his own terminology. This is why neo-Kantian social theorists, like Parsons, Habermas, Giddens or Bourdieu, require their readers first to familiarise themselves with *their own* distinct terminology, so that readers could understand their works – but what this really means is that the very reading of these works implies an implicit ideological indoctrination, through the amount of time and effort it requires to go through the obscure and in the worst sense scholastic terminology used by their writers. However, as always with Kant and Kantianism, the opposite is true: words *do* matter, both through their etymology and semantic history. As Foucault (2002) argued, words are not neutral tools for scientific categorisation, as it came to be assumed in the 'classical age', but have their own reality; are part of the real world. No writer and thinker is 'autonomous' to use and develop them, but must take up these words as they exist, respect their meaning, which is the condensation of centuries and millennia of human wisdom, as left over or transmitted for us; and one should develop a new word only if it is absolutely necessary, as no existing word can express the specific meaning. Furthermore, instead of developing one's 'own' theoretical vocabulary, one should rather collect and take up those terms that were developed by other, innovative and in a way necessarily maverick thinkers and social theorists, as one can be sure that, just as there are no private languages, no single thinker can develop an entirely new terminology. Any such effort can safely be assigned to modern scholasticism or – even better – to sophistry.[1]

Words, therefore, *do* matter, and there are good reasons why the word 'methodology' will be systematically avoided in this book. Some of the reasons are connected to the present, while others are historical. Concerning the former, the word 'methodology' in our days, through its various uses, inside different disciplines, and magnified through funding bodies, gained a very specific meaning, implying a presumption of 'scientificity'. All prescriptive discussions of methodology, whether in textbooks, course outlines, advice of funding bodies, and the like, presume that the methodological considerations they advance are superior and exclusive, because they have a high degree of 'scientificity'. This pretence is unacceptable, as the problem with the 'natural' sciences is exactly that they are *universalistic*, while we are not universal beings, but *humans*, who furthermore live not directly in the *cosmos*, but on Earth. This is a serious issue, as much of our current problems, in nature just as in society and personality, derive from the presumption that anything that is *universally* valid must be directly applicable in our own lives, which is a fallacy. What it implies is that the *truth* of our concrete lives and existence can be quite different than the *truth* as professed by the 'sciences'.

Let me illustrate the point by a simple example. It is a truth of astronomy that the Earth is rotating around our sun. From this perspective, our evidence that the sun starts by rising in the East, then moves towards the South, and eventually sets in the West, is an illusion. However, this is only true if we assume the *universalistic* perspective. Actually, in so far as it matters for our lives, and for Nature, the sun indeed rises in the East, and so forth, and this is what we should take as indication guiding our lives. Thus, this is also a truth.

The methodology which is imposed on us – as members of an academic staff, researchers applying for grants, students studying at any level of academic life – is therefore not 'scientific'; such pretence has no sense whatsoever. Which leads to the second key word by which methodological streamlining and standardisation is justified, 'professionalisation'.

Professionalisation

> Enlighten your children,
> The brigands are just men,
> Witches just female vendors
> (Barking dogs are not wolfs!)
> […]
> Perhaps mumble a new tale,
> of fascist communism
>
> *Attila József,* Enlighten!, *1936*[2]

> It has been death to many, but it is a joke in the profession.
>
> *Charles Dickens,* Bleak House, *6*

This term seems just as if not more authoritative than 'scientific methodology', the two being often deployed together to educate and enlighten (read: indoctrinate and intellectually sterilise) students. In selecting one's methods (and theories), one must follow the guidelines of the 'profession', those established the 'field'. The problem here is the opposite of universal scientificity: it is the narrowness and hyper-specialisation of academic disciplines, thus professions. Sociologists need to develop and follow a sociological methodology, anthropologists an anthropological one, and so on for economics, political science, history, archaeology, you name it; except that all these disciplines deal with the same human beings, communities, and cultures, thus have shared method-logical concerns. This leads to the well-known circle, impossible to square, preoccupying persons dealing with 'method-teaching' at any university: there should be common courses to all students, especially post-graduate or PhD students, in a faculty; but for all sorts of reasons it is impossible to harmonise the method-related approaches of the different disciplines, except for courses about mathematics and statistics, further animating pretences about a universally valid and applicable 'scientific method'. Professionalisation is not a solution, just a further justification of ideological streamlining and compartmentalisation in academic enclaves.[3]

However, and in line with the significance of words, 'professionalisation' has its relevance. The term comes from Latin, meaning an open declaration, gaining in the Middle Ages the sense of vows taken when entering a religious order. Due to the close connection between the development of universities and the monastic orders, 'profession' gained an academic connotation (see the word 'professor'). It is this sense that became secularised, modernised, and democratised, first of all – and this is an interesting aspect! – in various trades and skills, also called as 'vocations', while the *university* preserved its original *universal* (meaning: non-fragmented, non-specialised, non-'professional') character. The slogan 'professionalisation' in academic life is therefore strictly speaking anti-academic, and much contributes to downgrading the pursuit of academic knowledge to the kind of fragmentation characteristic of various mechanical and other trades, confirmed by HR Departments looking for 'skills' and not 'understanding'.

Still, concerning 'methodology', there is a further issue to be mentioned. Around the pretence of 'scientificity' the religious overtones of 'profession', meaning a solemn public declaration of one's convictions is maintained. I encountered several people in my academic career, in particular teachers of 'methodology' or of microeconomics, who in their mode of speaking and behaviour, especially when teaching, manifested the same solemn attitudes as priests when preaching. For them the basic principles of 'methodology' or micro-economics were not just technical issues to be taught and discussed, but indeed solemn declarations of what they believed was the very *essence* of human being and of 'scientific education'. These are not just personal idiosyncrasies, but bring out the underlying justification for pursuing such narrow and streamlined approaches, further supporting Eric Voegelin's claim that modernity is a secular Gnostic religion; reasons why such perspectives, though clearly wrong and untenable – just as most of the basic tenets of rational choice and economic theory – are impossible to dislocate, as no argument showing that they are wrong can shake such ideological convictions.

But what exactly is wrong with 'methodology'? It is quite simple, and this is what makes it so convincing and universalistic: it suggests, and teaches, a fixed set of procedures that infallibly produce a uniform result. These can be taught in a course, students can write it down, memorise, follow the steps in their project or

10 The Meaning of Method

thesis work, receive the results, which confirm the mechanical technique they followed, and all is fine. They can teach in this manner the next generation, and it continues until the end, until every remaining independent thinking and meaningful academic work is exterminated, through the procedures of 'scientific methodology' and 'professionalisation'. Even better (or rather, worse), such a procedure can be put into a computer algorithm, which can perform the steps on its own, so even more results can be 'gained' or 'produced' (note the economistic terminology) through the same steps.

Still, what exactly is wrong with this? How can it be demonstrated that such a streamlined, 'scientific', professionalised procedure is wrong, and does not produce the truth it pretends to offer? In a way, the whole of the present book is written to argue, and show clearly and in detail, why this is wrong, and how something better and more meaningful can be put into its place. Here I can only suggest, as a preliminary position, that it is the presumed simplicity and easy following of such a mechanical process that reveals it being wrong. Throughout the book I will compare the principles of such methodology to the way alchemy operates; and here the parallel is particularly strong with the 'magic wand' of alchemists. Alchemists of all ages tried to find a 'magic wand' by which, through the application of the same mechanical techniques, everything could be turned into gold – actually or metaphorically. This was impossible, but the efforts of alchemists were not without effects. These include technology and the scientific method, where the *exact* same idea was offered, though now inside the mainstream, inside the universities, and as unquestioned wisdom of European culture or Western civilisation: that universal knowledge and truth can be gained by following a set of simple and prescribed steps, by taking apart and reunite.[4]

This, however, is simply wrong. This book will not search for a 'scientific' and only-saving 'professional method', rather will offer reflections concerning various 'methods' that can be followed in order to gain understanding and meaningful truths.

In line with such considerations, I'll start with the *word* 'method'.

Method as the way

> The lasting element in thinking is the way
>
> Heidegger, 1982: 12

Starting from etymology, an always privileged starting point, 'method' comes from Greek *met'hodos*, meaning 'according to the way, path, or road', immediately confirming Heidegger. 'Way, path, or road' are one of the most important words in any language, having an almost inexhaustible yet quite precise range of meanings, starting from the most concrete, and ending at the most general. A path or a road, to begin with, is on which we humans can walk, or exert our most specific activity, as we are bipedal, became humans due to our walking on two legs,[5] in contrast to using four legs, or flying on wings. Without a path, we can hardly walk, as we would either be continuously upheld by overgrowth, or be lost in an open land. But the 'way' is at the same time one of the most spiritual *and* reflexive words possible. 'Tao' in Chinese means 'the way'; the book of Parmenides, a key presocratic philosopher, of which only fragments survived, was called 'The way'; and in one of the most quoted passages of the Bible Jesus says that 'I am the way and the truth and the life' (Jn 14: 6). But the way or the path in many languages is identical with experience – not surprisingly, as experience can be gained by starting to walk, by taking up the road, instead of staying put in one place (the curse of settlement).

The word used in the Biblical passage above is *hodos*, defined in Liddell-Scott as 'way, path, track, road, highway', so related to traveling, but also having the most important specific sense of 'threshold'; important, because of the direct links between 'threshold' and 'liminality', and thus experience. In this sense the word is a version of the more general term for 'threshold', *oudos* – aspirated 'h' in Greek is not really a letter. Thus, the term in John has a very clear allusion to a particular aspect of the 'way', the liminal passage, as the start or the end of the road, where there is a door or gate which one must traverse, thus evoking a central role of Christ as mediator or door (see further in Chapters 8 and 11). As none of the two terms have an etymology, it is not possible to progress here. However, there is another Ancient Greek term for way, *patos* 'trodden or beaten way, path', which is particularly close to the specific sense of experience, the recurrent 'passage through' the same area, which then forms a road through the beaten track, just as repeated experiences form a human being. It is just this sense of the 'beaten track' or the trail that was discussed by Victor Turner (1992), including an etymological excursion.

In its written form *patos* is strikingly close to *pathos*, Greek for experience. While philologists staunchly refuse to consider any connection between these terms, lingering doubts remain, as through history the 't' of *patos* could easily become a 'th' (as in English 'path'), while the 'th' of *pathos* became 'ss', as in 'passion', and still further, in Ancient Greek the Ionic 'ss' and Attic 'tt' were equivalents. Human languages do not work like rigid algorithms, and human beings in history do not act like neo-Kantian philosophers, as most linguists, or even sociologists as Durkheim, seem to assume.

There is further evidence strongly suggesting that possible links between *patos* and *pathos*, theoretically unsupported until the discovery of liminality, should be taken seriously. To start with, 'pat', evident root of *patos*, is an onomatopoeic word, just as its reverse 'tap', with the additional, not negligible point that such 'patting' or 'tapping' is first of all connected to *feet*, regarding walking on a *path*. But it also applies in Hungarian, where *tapos* means 'tread by feet', and *tapint* 'touch by hand'; while *pattan* means jump forward, *pattint* 'snap' (e.g. flints) and *pattog* 'cracking fire' – not surprisingly, all words connected to the most archaic activities of humankind. Furthermore, the Hungarian word for experience is *tapasztalat*, derivative of *tapos/ tapint*.

Even further, Greek, English, and Hungarian can be complemented by Latin, where the root of a crucial word for experience, **sent* (see sense, sentiment, sensation), has as its original meaning 'path, trail', still visible in French *sentier*.

In sum, a 'method' is a way, a way is a mode of experiencing, and in the social and human sciences experiences are the 'way' to follow, as experiments there are impossible. But 'experience' and 'experiment' are also clearly related words, 'experiment' being a derivative of 'experience'. In sum, there is absolutely no point for social and human understanding to imitate the derived and limited techniques of the 'natural' (rather universalistic) sciences, all the more as they, due to their specific assumptions, are not applicable or helpful for our world.

It is in this sense that we can make use of Heidegger's reflections about the way, in contrast to reified 'method'. The way does not belong to a rigorous and formal set of governing rules, rather – in the sense of participation, as it will be also explored soon, in Chapters 2 and 3 – 'the way belongs in what we here call the country or region.' It is a 'clearing that gives free reign' for thinking and exploring, instead of limiting it in advance; and '[t]he freeing and sheltering character of this region lies in this way-making movement, which yields those ways that belong to the region' (Heidegger 1982: 91). This country, where we are and participate, instead of reducing it to an object of study, and thus of conquest, 'offers ways only because it is country. It gives ways, moves us' – or, the ways are *gifts* which are offered, spontaneously, naturally, to all those who participate; and these gift-ways, in the spirit of Mauss (2002), or of the Three Graces (Wind 1967), are not just lying there, but serve as inspiration, as *ways* of inspiration: they also move us. Furthermore, continues Heidegger, exploring further the links between 'way' and 'gift', even offering a definite formulation, '[w]e hear the words "give way" in this sense: to be the original giver and founder of ways' (1982: 92). After a few sentences focusing on German meanings and dialects, omitted from the English edition, Heidegger turns to a broader linguistic interpretation of 'the way', considered as an 'ancient primary word [*ein Urwort der Sprache*]', identical to Laotse's *Tao*, which can be further translated as 'reason, mind [*Geist*], *raison*, meaning, *logos*' (92; 1985: 187). The relevance and power of the word thus becomes practically limitless, as '[p]erhaps the mystery of mysteries of thoughtful Saying conceals itself in the word "way" '; even

> [p]erhaps the enigmatic power of today's reign of method also, and indeed pre-eminently, stems from the fact that the methods, notwithstanding their efficiency, are after all merely the runoff of a great hidden stream which moves all things along and makes way for everything
>
> *(1982: 92).*

The inevitable conclusion is that '[a]ll is way' (92).

After these still rather preliminary considerations, let us now see what exactly it means to follow a way (or the path), in terms of a method, in social or human understanding.

What does it mean to follow a 'way'?

A method as a 'way' implies that such a way does not simply exist in the mind of a researcher, but is something that concretely and truly exists, which is out there in the world. When one is doing research, what one wants to discover is what are the 'ways' that are out there in the social world; what are the paths that humans, we all use when we conduct our lives. Here we immediately bump into a major Kantian injunction, the distinction between what the things are in themselves (which supposedly is unknowable); and what they show for us. Such distinction, however, on the one hand reproduces a major aspect of Eastern mysticism, particularly strong in the Vedas, and has Gnostic affinities; on the other, is a fallacy, as it ignores the fact that the way 'things' are, in so far as they have to do in any extent with human activity, not to mention that it applies to *any* aspect of human and social life, are themselves formulated through words and language, thus words and language, our major tools, are perfectly applicable to reach into what they are, and are not necessarily doomed to produce only illusions. This latter, however, is true exactly for the kind of social research that is conducted by a slavish imitation (presumed literal following) of the 'natural sciences', like survey research methods, which rarely have produced any other result than reproducing illusions human fabricate to hide their essence (thus, returning to our previous example, survey researchers know that Danish respondents reproduce the illusion that they are all most happy, while Sicilians the illusion that they are all miserable – even, according to perceptions registered by surveys, Sicilians see hardly more sun than the Danish!).

Anybody who is Danish or Sicilian, or who knows the Danish or the Sicilians, would tell this, without requiring the EU to spend yearly hundreds of thousands of euros on such trivialising research, conducted at the supposed coincidence of the public interest with advances in science and scientific methods. So, instead of such Kant-inspired Gnostic undertakings, the true way, or method, for research is to start by trying to find out what are the ways *out there*, in the real world. We must understand *this*, instead of imposing on it our own theoretical and methodological framework, and then analyse the extremely meagre and meaningless 'information' we gained by such standardised, real-world-alien techniques.

Second, to find the *real* ways out there in the *real* world, we need guides. Here the metaphor of the way, derived from the etymology of 'method', turns out to be helpful at a second level (also showing how everything hangs together if we start to pay attention to the 'world', itself of imposing ourselves on it, hubristically, our own predilections, manias and fixed ideas), as on the road, on any road we have not yet taken – and writing a PhD, a model case to which this book is written, is certainly such a 'first road', or 'first experience' – one needs guides. This does not mean the supervisor alone, but all those thinkers, writers, academics, who touched upon the theme and can offer some guidance concerning how this is to be understood. These thinkers should be considered, indeed, as *guides*, instead of selecting some of their ideas as parts of a 'theoretical framework', trademarked to the writer, which then can be 'operationalised'. Understanding the ways 'out there in the world' must start by understanding the guides – once they are selected. This is the meaning of education: getting familiarised with various aspects of the real world, and at the same time getting familiarised with various thinkers, where comprehensiveness – meaning: reading as much as possible *from the selected guides* – is way more important than the 'comprehensive' literature review, and the similarly 'comprehensive' familiarisation with the concrete field of study (which should be rather done in its historicity, in its concrete context, using as much as possible comparative perspectives).

The third aspect of the way is that it also must be personal. What is important is not to develop one's 'own' theory (this is to be avoided at all costs), rather one must be personal *exactly* where standard, 'scientific' methodology prescribes strict neutrality and objectivity: in the 'methods' (understood: ways of proceeding) one selects. The aim of a research is to understand the ways *out there*, in the world, as closely as possible. For this, one needs guides that are understood as closely as possible (see Chapter 9). While here research must search for objectivity, the way a research quest is pursuing cannot but be personal, following an approach that at every moment is concretely guided by the continuous judgments of the researcher: what to read, what to study, which hint to pick up and how, and so on. The metaphor of guiding a car, with dozens of judgments one must make every minute, depending on the other cars, the roads, and the surroundings, is appropriate concerning the *method* a research project must follow. Such judgments are inevitable, as education means to prepare students for making properly such judgments, instead of indoctrination into a narrow set of techniques, or ideological statements, that supposedly are universally applicable.[6]

Concluding comments

A method is not the application of a universally valid 'scientific methodology' that one must scrupulously learn, and is not a blueprint, scenario, or algorithm either, which must be defined in advance and whose steps one must rigorously follow. A method is a way, which helps to formulate and conduct proper research, and in this sense it is indeed necessary, as without finding a right way one becomes hopelessly lost, not knowing what to do.

The right way is already there, inside the theme or object of study, which must be recognised and not forced by some artificially developed research technique or methodology. The key term is *recognition*, with its semantic horizon, including acknowledgement, appreciation and gratefulness, as the most important intellectual operation is to identify in what is already there, in the 'world', the way along which everything falls into its place and becomes intelligible, and – again – not the forced arrangement alongside the preconceived theoretical or methodological scheme. If we knew in advance what the results of our research are, we evidently wouldn't bother to perform it. Yet, the rulers of research funding, just as increasingly the powerbrokers of academic life, require us to pretend that this is exactly what we'll do, as setting up *a priori* the main research steps in a methodological section is all but identical to claiming that we know the results. As otherwise, or what is the *actual* situation of any meaningful research, it is only once the first step of the research is completed that one gains a clear idea what to do in the next step. The same is true for any genuine PhD research, where original titles and outlines are changing and *should* change at every step, after every draft chapter. Yet, the various administrative committees that are mushrooming in any university increasingly make stricter and stricter rules against changing the original PhD title, as if a PhD title would be identical to a 'contract', and so its change a kind of betrayal and failure to honour the terms of a contract. I am not joking and exaggerating here: this is the spirit and increasingly the word of what is going on in any contemporary educational establishment and research funding agency. But this is counter-productive and simply absurd, a way to destroy innovative research and academic integrity, in line with the general and programmatic destructiveness of modernity (see 'creative destruction'), the generation of a situation in which everybody doing serious intellectual work, which implies a continuous change in direction and ideas, could be reprimanded for 'breach of contract'.

Still further, finding such a path, and reaching its end, requires the use of proper guides. Such guides are and must be and can only be not concepts or theories, but concrete human beings, whether as colleagues, supervisors, or authors, classical or contemporary, with whom the researcher has thoroughly familiarised oneself. The way is out there but it is not easy to find for somebody who is searching it for the first time, so without good guides one is easily lost. Finding the right guides with whom one can work, both in real life and concerning broader readings is the most difficult but also most important part of any research work.

Finally, though the road is out there, in the real world, independently of us, and guides similarly have their concrete existence and works that we must understand and follow, the path of a research is profoundly personal at its every step. The research theme must be personally selected and considered as meaningful and important, just as guides who must be personally trusted. Any research, from the conception of its outlines to its writing must be conducted personally. Otherwise, the results will certainly be meaningless and irrelevant; mere application of concepts and techniques; pushing certain buttons.

There is one word that so far was hardly mentioned, though assumed as being central. This word is 'participation', and so this book now must turn to study the meaning and relevance of participation.

Notes

1 These considerations will be developed further in Chapter 7.
2 'Világosítsd föl gyermeked/ a haramiák emberek;/ a boszorkák kofák, kasok./ (Csahos kutyák nem farkasok!)/ [...]/ Talán dünnyögj egy új mesét,/ fasiszta kommunizmusét' (Attila József (1905–1937), *Világosítsd föl*)
3 For further discussion, see Tim Ingold's recent book on education (2017), also Ingold (2011: 155), using the term 'compartmentalisation'. It is taken from Paul Nadasdy, who analyses the distortion of the knowledge of wayfarers into abstract classificatory schemes by the twin processes of 'distillation' and 'compartmentalisation'; particularly interesting due to the evident alchemic terminology.
4 As Gandalf states to Saruman, the science-magician wizard, during Elrond's Council: 'He that breaks a thing to find out what it is has left the path of wisdom' (Tolkien, *Lord of the Rings*). On the importance of Tolkien for social understanding, see Curry (2023).

5 A particularly good way to illustrate the path 'out there' that must be recognised and followed, instead of imposing on the 'world' our own concepts, is pilgrimage. For details on walking culture, see Horvath and Szakolczai (2018a), Gros (2014), Ingold (2004).
6 According to Wilhelm Hennis (1988), such education of judgment was at the centre of Max Weber's methodological essays (see also Sam Whimster and Keith Tribe).

2
THE IMPORTANCE OF PARTICIPATION

> The worship of truth apart from charity – self-identification with science unaccompanied by self-identification with the Ground of all being – results in the kind of situation which now confronts us. Every idol, however exalted, turns out, in the long run, to be a Moloch, hungry for human sacrifice.
>
> *Aldous Huxley,* The Devils of Loudun, *326–7*

> let it be remembered that most men live in a world of their own, and that in that limited circle alone are they ambitious for distinction and applause.
>
> *Charles Dickens,* Hard Times, *336*

It goes without saying that any researcher in the social and human sciences participates in the world of his investigation. It is so evident that there seems to be no reason to waste time and paper on it. Yet, this must be explicitly brought out to the surface, as a central and mostly unquestioned aspect of 'scientific methodology' is that the researcher must be 'objective' and 'neutral', so should downplay as much as possible such participation, which implies the worship of idols, mentioned by Huxley and connected to the par excellence non-participatory ritual, sacrifice. The reason for this obsession in the field of the 'natural' sciences would require an investigation on its own, as part of any reflection on 'method', given that the current environmental crisis is much due to the 'natural' sciences indeed managing to overcome such participatory aspect, helping to produce on a mass scale objects which are incompatible, or incommensurable, with life on Earth. The limits of neutrality have been reached even in 'pure' science.

It should thus be revisited how and why participation came to be excluded from the social sciences as a consequence of a slavish imitation of the 'natural' sciences.

DOI: 10.4324/9781003275138-3

The unpardonable deeds of Hegel and Durkheim

The problem can be illustrated through the two perhaps most important instances through which participation came to be excluded from social thinking.

The first was the debate between Hegel and Schleiermacher, which ended with the victory of the former. Hegel went on to become the philosopher king of Germany, Europe, and the entire modern world, fully recognised by the Prussian state, though whoever has a minimal understanding of the modern state, in particular Prussia, would recognise immediately that such an official celebration is most revealing. The outcome was not self-evident from the start, as at the time of their debate, in 1817, Schleiermacher, last major figure of European philosophy who was at the same time Professor of Theology, was much more widely known. Hegel, on the other hand, had the incredible fortune of sharing a flat in his first university years with two absolute geniuses, Hölderlin and Schelling, compared to whom his abilities were second rate. His most famous and indeed important idea, the master-serf dialectic, heart of his *Phenomenology of the Spirit*, was derived of his experience of 'overcoming' Hölderlin and Schelling, just as another famous idea, *Aufhebung* (preserving while cancelling), central for his logic. All this has crucial method-logical implications.

Hegel won with a simple trick – and *indeed* trick: making Schleiermacher look ridiculous by turning him the butt of a joke. The centre of Schleiermacher's work was concerned with capturing the nature of participatory experience, beyond the Kantian reduction of experience to sense perception – as Schleiermacher quite rightly perceived that there was something fundamentally wrong with the approach of Kant, and so he wanted to start from the experience of participation. Such participation, according to him, implied a profound belongingness, or the dependence of all our experiences from the actual realities in which we participate. This allowed Hegel to crack the joke that for Schleiermacher the model philosopher was the dog. It stuck, in an environment where – joint legacy of medieval (Byzantine) scholasticism, court society mentality and French Enlightenment – ridiculing was a major mode to settle debates and scores. Schleiermacher lost his students, and the road was made for Hegel to become – a perfect example for the master-serf dialectic – the philosopher king, a position he was much striving for, given his mediocrity. The corpses of Schleiermacher, Schelling, and Hölderlin – his one-time close friend who survived him by a few years, though with his mind clouded decades ago – served as both metaphorical and literal springboards to achieve such fame. Hegel is fundamental for modern 'thinking' – understand: sophistry – in demonstrating how mediocrity can be hidden behind developing a complex private language, with a series of all but unintelligible terms, generating the impression of profound originality.

The second main debate on participation has as its protagonist Émile Durkheim, a thinker even more mediocre than Hegel. Durkheim was a most narrow-minded neo-Kantian neopositivist, offering as his main work a book on the Rules of Sociological Method which nobody ever took up, thankfully – though, strangely enough, this never inspired sociologists to question his status as 'founding father' of the discipline.

Durkheim waged three debates around participation, which he won, due to rationalistic academic power politics, together with his main heirs Lévi-Strauss and Bourdieu, against Tarde, van Gennep, and Lucien Lévy-Bruhl.[1] In the debate with Tarde, the central issue was the importance of imitation as an aspect of participatory experience, which Durkheim misunderstood as mere mimicking. Durkheim 'won', as Tarde died soon after the debate. The debate with van Gennep was even more momentous, as it concerned liminality. According to van Gennep, the most important ceremonies (celebrations, feasts, rituals) of cultural life are rites of passage, rites celebrating transition, or the passage of time: whether between seasons, or as marking the major moments of the human life cycle. According to Durkheim, the foundational ceremonies are rather rituals of sacrifice: rituals that involve the killing and eating of the otherwise untouchable bodies of the sacred animal of the clan, not to mention those even more violent but historically important rituals of human sacrifice and cannibalism.

Van Gennep, who was a trained anthropologist and ethnographer, considered Durkheim's ideas as a non-starter: hardly more than incompetent ramblings of a neo-Kantian legal philosopher who re-trained himself following the tritest approaches of French and German positivism. Durkheim, however, had the last word, as he spoke from a position of academic power. The most important judgment in this debate is indirect and is contained in the work of Marcel Mauss – implicitly, in its entire fate. For a combination of evident reasons Mauss, who in his 1898 essay on sacrifice, written together with Henri Hubert, laid the groundwork to Durkheim's approach to sacrifice, and who was a close university colleague and friend of van Gennep, did not engage in a direct criticism of his uncle, thesis advisor and mentor, but after WWI, and seven years after Durkheim died, did offer his dissent but laying the ground of a completely different approach to anthropology and attitude to social life. In 1924, instead of reasserting the centrality of rituals of sacrifice, he rather argued that the foundations of social life are constituted by gift relations.

The third debate was against Lucien Lévy-Bruhl's interest in participatory experience, to which he was jointly led by his dissent from Cartesian rationalism (theme of his dissertation), and his explorations the archaic mind. His work was strongly criticised by the Durkheim school, with the significant exception of Marcel Mauss, who supported and appreciated him till the end. His expulsion from social thinking was completed by Claude Lévi-Strauss, who certainly cannot be accused of intellectual mediocrity, but whose mind was bereft of any concern with human emotions and genuine experiences, thus had no sympathy for the experience of participation. He finished Lévy-Bruhl off at the height of his own fame and influence, in a series of unjust remarks that aimed strictly below the belt.

It has its own, and quite considerable, importance that the two main modern theorists who literally expulsed any consideration of participation from social thinking were Hegel and Durkheim – the two most problematic figures of modern social theory, and who did so much in turning classical academic life into Prussianised professional compartmentalisation, institutionalising, at the heart of philosophy and the social sciences, an academic power politics, ruthlessly doing away with those more worthy who became their opponents in the drive for unlimited and unconditional power. In Germany, Hegel's path was imitated by the neo-Kantians, who in turn served as model for Durkheim's neopositivistic neo-Kantian academic power politics.

The reassertion of participation as central for social theory, even for understanding rationality, is due to the work of Alessandro Pizzorno, who in a series of articles has shown, starting from inside the tradition of Western rationalism, that considerations of participation and presence cannot be ignored.

Alessandro Pizzorno: Participation as the precondition of rationality

Alessandro Pizzorno (1924–2019) is one of the most distinguished social scientists of the past long half century – certainly without a peer in Italy. Having studied at the University of Torino, as well as in Vienna and Paris, he taught both in Italy and at the University of Teheran before taking up a series of most prestigious appointments at Nuffield College (Oxford University), at Harvard University, where for years he was Head of Department, at the State University of Milan, where he built up the Department, and finally at the European University Institute in Florence, where I had the great privilege of having been his colleague for five years, until his retirement – and where he stayed on as Emeritus professor until 2017. If his work is not as known as it should be, this is partly because it is situated outside the beaten tracks, and partly because he was a perfectionist who had great reluctance in letting any written work out of his hands, especially in English.

Pizzorno's work was woven around the nature of identity and recognition, with a focus on the meaning of rationality. This is also a main reason why his work, in spite of its scope and depth, lacks a decisive book publication, as 'rationality' is a theme that is almost impossible to treat in a full monograph. In the modern world 'rationality' is something inside of which we all exist, and so its specific nature has become invisible for us, can only be studied through a series of short explorations into its depths, much helped by questions from others. Thus, his two arguably most important investigations were a response to his commentators in his 2000 Festschrift, and an almost 100-page-long essay (Pizzorno 2007), though these assume familiarity with his earlier work (see especially Pizzorno 1986, 1987, 1991; also Pizzorno 2008, a shortened English version of the arguments). In these Pizzorno demonstrates, from inside mainstream rationalism, that participation is necessary for any explanation, in particular for assessing whether a particular course of action is rational, so it is of exceptional value.

Pizzorno's ideas on participation and rationality are based on his work on recognition. The starting point is the Hobbesian idea of 'self-preservation', which for him is not a solution but a dilemma. In order to be preserved, the 'self' must be worth preserving. This assumes that it is *recognised* as valuable. Self-preservation can't be achieved in isolation from others: 'I need other human beings to judge that I am worth preserving' (Pizzorno 1991: 218). Recognition is mutual, circular, shared, providing a mirror for others in which, through the others, the self can be seen (218–9). In a 1994 conference paper recognition is defined as 'the will and capacity to enter in communication with somebody else, keeping in mind, even competitively or malevolently, the value of his presence' (Pizzorno 1994: 6). One accepts the recognition of his/her own worth only from others who are recognised by the self as valuable, and vice versa. 'The "original resource" a human being can offer to another human being is the capacity to recognize the worth of the other to exist – a resource which cannot be produced if it is not shared' (Pizzorno 1991: 218). Instead of assuming an 'original agreement' that the premises of the theory cannot explain, Pizzorno only assumes the 'presence of other people' (221).[2] The key step is the move from 'recognition' to 'circles' of recognition. Given their 'mutual recognition', human beings 'have received an identity, and they may count on being recognised by some circles of others. These circles make recognition durable and, hence, trust rational. Individual interests grow out of different positions in the networks and circles of recognition' (Pizzorno 1991: 219).

Furthermore, acts of recognition (of the worth of others) assume criteria applied in such acts that are shared by others. It is in this way that 'the process through which reciprocal recognition, giving names, and forming identities produce social stability and continuity', while at the same time it 'generates individuation and distinction' (Pizzorno 1991: 221).

The aim of social research is to explain what is going on in social life, what actions are taken and why, and who are those acting. Explanation thus must start with the assignment of identities to social actors, through some classificatory schema, naming and identifying actors. Such identification, however, claims Pizzorno – and perhaps this is the best way to introduce his ideas – is always arbitrary (2000: 235). Who tells us who is actually acting? In what capacity? For Pizzorno, there are three such possibilities – three modalities of arbitrariness, which must first be identified, so that we can start our search to reduce arbitrariness. First, such identities are assigned by the actors themselves – but this, while certainly important, cannot be accepted at face value. The second option, assigning such identity by the researcher, however, is equally unacceptable – and the importance of this point cannot be exaggerated, as Pizzorno throws into the wastebasket any neo-positivist, neo-Kantian, or neo-Marxist mode of social research and theorising. This is because, and fully in line with Weber and Mauss, main sources Pizzorno's sociology, the central aim of social research is to assign *meaning* to the acts performed, so starting with preconceived categories precludes a serious study of meaning. One must search for a third way, outside full involvement and complete detachment.[3] This is offered by others who are also *present*, so also *participate*, thus can assist us assigning meaning to the actions by reconstructing the situation in which the acts took place, and also to assign a meaningful identity to the actors.

In order to explain what is going on it is not enough to give an account in terms of intentions, which only the actors can offer, in case they are honest; and neither is it sufficient to be well-versed in theoretical frameworks – this would only enclose the researcher inside his/her pre-existing mental framework. Explanation must start with mapping the situation in which the actors find themselves, so must prepare a map of experiences, akin to Koselleck's 'horizon of experiences'. This is because – and here comes one of Pizzorno's masterstrokes valorising participation – social research has a particular possibility, and duty: the investigator cannot be satisfied with finding an explanation to the events with which one is happy, but must test his ideas by explaining them to those who carried out the acts. This does not mean that we must repeat their explanation. The researcher's explanation must be different from familiar accounts. But it must be *linked* to internal meanings, opening them to a broader area of participation (243).[4] The researcher cannot remain outside, coming up from the height of his theoretical sophistication or critical position with a supposedly objective, universalistic explanation; must come down,[5] become involved, gain the meaning of the events in concrete situations and contexts; and furthermore, once this understanding gained, must test whether he can explain to participants this understanding, making them face how their actions look to somebody who took the trouble of trying to understand what was going on. The corollary is that social research, instead of enforcing a supposedly 'omnipresent rationality' (243), rather opens up and comes to recognise and valorise diversity. Genuine explanation lies both beyond taken for granted familiarity and external objectivity; it offers the risk, and also the pleasure, of a kind of understanding that previously was not accessible, either to the participants or the researcher.

Pizzorno took the theme further in the most important essay of his 2007 collection, that had 'diversity' in its title, while the essay title is 'Rationality and recognition' (2007: 109–197). This is the only chapter of the second part entitled 'The difficulty of rationality'; while the first part, containing three chapters, has the much-related title 'Explaining in front of an audience'. All this alludes to the central theme of this long essay, fundamental for questions of method in social research: what it means to explain a particular set of social acts in terms of its 'rationality'. While for an economist, and those influenced by theories of 'rational choice', it is plainly evident what rationality means, for Pizzorno this is by no means the case. This is not a refusal or criticism of rationality: what he demonstrates is that the standard, taken for granted meaning of rationality is based on accepting the meaning of a situation given by partisans of economic rationality, participants of a certain sector of academic life, the 'natives'; but if we start to scratch the surface and go beyond the unquestioned acceptance of such rationality, we soon are forced to realise that the emperor is without clothes; the theory of rational choice cannot give an account of itself, so it is by no means 'rational'. Or, as Pizzorno claims in the title of the first and longest section of the chapter, this theory is nothing else but 'common sense [meaning: what in our modern societies has become (mis)taken as the common sense] theorised'; and so it is simply an 'insufficient theory' (109).

The 2007 chapter goes into further details concerning the meaning of participating in a given situation as a precondition of understanding the meaning of what is going on, especially in so far as the assessment of the 'rationality' of a particular course of action is concerned. Even further, such clarification, while still staying inside the modern European tradition of rationalism, not only manages to pin down the social foundations on which such an idea of rationality is based, but also, and beyond the concrete concerns of Pizzorno, exposes the bases of such tradition in theatricality. So, while modern rationalism has social foundations, such foundations are rooted not in genuine social life, but its theatricalisation.

The chapter starts by an extended critique of rational choice theories, a slightly modified version of the 2007 Handbook article against 'rational choice'. The central argument is presented at the end of the second section where Pizzorno, after discussing, through nine quite different cases, whether the behaviour of participants could be considered as rational, draws the theoretical inferences. The perhaps most important, highly Platonic inference – recalling the *Theaetetus* – is that there is no universally valid criterion of rationality; rationality simply cannot be defined: 'we are not enabled to give a definition of rationality that is valid for every case' (171). The observer does not have a privileged, universal, Kantian position from which it can assess and evaluate, from the outside, whether a certain action is rational or not. But this does not mean that the actor is in full control, as rationality is irreducible to intentions. Here Pizzorno offers, if not a paradoxical definition of rationality, after claiming it impossible, but a specification of what it means when one assesses the rationality of an action: it is a *judgment* (171); moreover, it is primarily a judgment over a *person*, and not just an action (176); a judgment that can be safely made only once the observer controlled this judgment through its reception by the participants; and, even more, that such assessment of rationality itself is judged by an audience that moves beyond the circle of concrete participants, and which possibly involves – introducing another key term – a new 'grammatic of the situation' (171–2).

The argument is summed up in the penultimate paragraph of the 'excursus' that must be quoted almost in full and commented extensively:

> the judgment of the rationality of an acting is relative until the observer, reconstructing the grammatic of the situation observed, transmits to the audience the interpretation of the participants and opens the discourse which the circle that posed the question of the need for an explanation expected.
> *(172)*

The assessment of rationality is thus negotiated between two circles: the circle of the actor and the other participants of the action (context of the action, locals or 'natives'); and the circle of the observer and his colleagues, or a broader, second order audience, who at the end assesses the rationality of the actions, and also the rationality of the explanation, but only after incorporating the assessment, in so far as it is possible, of the first order audience. In this way 'a new conception of rationality is born, which can offer itself as valid only once the modifications in the expectations of this second circle are taken into consideration' (172). However, the validity of an assessment beyond that cannot be decided in advance, as that depends 'on another event, and thus on another theoretical investigation that will again pose the question of what was meant there by rationality'. Beyond such limits, it makes no sense to assert rationality – any such claim will be merely ideological.

This is as far as the thinking of Pizzorno goes in problematising the theory of rational choice and the connected idea of instrumental rationality, perspectives that simply regurgitate as universally valid explanation the contemporary common-sense attribution of intentions to participants, and which are thus woefully inadequate as scholarly explanation. At this point, and in the spirit of his inferences, in the third section entitled 'Recognition as sociality' Pizzorno spells out in further detail the meaning of the two circles introduced above: the meaning of the situation or context of the participants, or the social nature of rationality; and the situatedness of one's own arguments, or the researcher inside the broader tradition of social theoretical understanding. While incorporating classical social theory, the central figures are Hobbes, Adam Smith, Rousseau, and Hegel. The discussion on Hegel adds little new to his previous, sustained discussions in his articles on recognition, but his ideas on Hobbes go well beyond his classic 1991 article, as while there Hobbes was considered a methodological individualist, focusing on self-preservation, here Hobbes is presented as a theorist of recognition.[6] However, the most important part of the section is its discussion of Adam Smith and Rousseau, both in terms of Pizzorno's analysis of their ideas about the inherently social aspects of recognition, but also by implication, in bringing out the inherently theatrical character of modern sociality *as a problem*. This adds a further layer of problematisation to that of positivism, instrumental rationality, and analytical philosophy: these approaches not simply reproduce the 'common-sense' practices of modernity, but such practices are inherently theatrical, thus deeply unreal. The real, effective, social bases of instrumental rationality unearthed by Pizzorno at the level of foundations, using the most classic figures of modern political and social philosophy, are themselves unreal, merely theatrical.

His position is expressed in the title of first subsection, 'Recognition as sociality' (172). The social basis of instrumental rationality can be traced to the works of Adam Smith, who therefore was 'the first modern thinker who emphasised the importance of the judgment of others for the individual choices' (177) – strangely enough, the same thinker most associated with modern economics. Given that Adam Smith is considered for well over two centuries as the undisputed founding father of modern economic thinking, it is difficult to say something new about his ideas and work. The last time this happened in the late 1970s, when his Glasgow lectures were rediscovered, and in this context his *Theory of Moral Sentiments* was revalorised, especially concerning his ideas on sympathy, as the foundation of his economic theory.

Pizzorno takes this development further in two significant respects. According to him, the central issue concerning sociality for Adam Smith was not simply sympathy as an internal, inner, psychological predisposition shared by every human being, but that the aim of an action was not just 'to satisfy one's own autonomously formed needs, rather to obtain a favourable judgment from the others' (177). The second is the character of those others who were supposed to provide such judgment. These were not 'the usual *everyday spectators* whose gaze is upon us for a thousand reasons in every second', rather the proper judge of our actions, whose approval we desperately need, must be an '*impartial* spectator' (178–9). Thus,

'Smith built an entire system of "moral sentiments" on this concept of an "impartial spectator" whose judgment the actor would keep in mind while making his choices, and which would reinforce him in his capacity of *self-command* [*sic* in original]' (177). It is thus this 'impartial spectator' which, through its gaze, assures the stable identity of the self over time, leading Smith to an 'unexpected "anti-robinsonade" ' (177–8). The resulting 'I', or 'self', however, will not just be 'social', in the sense of incorporating the others through the judgment of the 'impartial spectator', playing a 'role' according to the judgments and expectations of such an omnipotent spectator, but his mind, and even the person himself, will also be inherently schismatic, split between the judge and the actor. We can add that it is this position and perspective of the 'impartial spectator' that will be taken over by Kant and placed at the heart of his moral philosophy as the very foundation of personal autonomy.

It is also the same problem, in particular the terror of being judged, the fear of the gaze of the others, that is a main driving force of Rousseau's thinking, leading him to a dramatic fight against the powers of that gaze (179–81), and so a similarly schismatic vision of the self.

In the previous pages, following Pizzorno's thinking, we have travelled across a rather peculiar path. It was started by problematising the modern 'scientific' perspective excluding the idea of participation, which was transmitted to the social sciences through the logic specific to economics, instrumental rationality. It was then shown that the very assessment of the rationality of a particular act assumes incorporating the perspective of participants, as from the outside it is impossible to adjudicate whether a particular action was rational or not. One must know the identity participants attribute to themselves, through those who participate in the concrete situation, understanding the role they play. However, then, through Pizzorno's reading of Adam Smith, it was shown that participants themselves, at least in so far as the modern world goes, incorporate an external judgment – not of 'observers', rather spectators, especially the 'impartial spectator'.

In this process it became increasingly evident that the terminology used is theatrical. This is quite surprising, as the starting concerns were not theatrical. 'Participation' is not a theatrical category, and neither is 'rationality'. Still, when trying to demonstrate the untenability of a purely external, rationalistic perspective, and the need to incorporate the perspective of the participants, Pizzorno was forced through his own approach, as if surreptitiously, to take up a theatrical language. The method-logical implications will be discussed in Chapter 10.

Conclusion

Through the work of Alessandro Pizzorno it was shown that neither the attribution of identity, nor the assessment of the rationality of an act can be done without paying attention to participation. However, inside the tradition of modern rationalism, participation is inherently tied to theatricality and theatricalisation. We need to go back to square one and reconstruct the meaning of participation.

Most evidently, participation means that any scholarly investigation and search for understanding must start by situating the subject matter, and the object of study, on the field to which they belong, or where their protagonists participate. Such participation is both manifold and structured. It is manifold, as everyone participates in a series of fields, networks or realms: family, relatives, friends, colleagues, native language, village, town, city, region, country, continent; ultimately, planet Earth, and then the solar system, our galaxy, the entire universe. It is also structured, taking cues from Norbert Elias (1978), as a series of concentrical circles: at the core is the family, relatives, friends, and then the broader surroundings, in an ever widening circle. One's own circles are intermingled with the circles of others, in an ever more complex but still fundamentally structured manner. Networks of workplace and profession add further, 'non-linear' complexity.

For a further investigation of participation, the book will turn to hermeneutics.

Notes

1 For details, see Szakolczai and Thomassen (2019).
2 On the importance of 'presence' for political theory, see Hoppen (2021).
3 This implies close affinities with the approach of Norbert Elias.
4 Pizzorno's ideas were developed further, in the direction of the experience of 'home', by Paul O'Connor (2018).
5 This is the meaning of Nietzsche's famous *Untergang* in his *Zarathustra*.
6 The emphasis is on Chapter 16 of *Leviathan*, about the person and the mask, and on Hobbes' interest in theatre, centre of Pizzorno's great unfinished book on Hobbes, on which he worked until his last years.

3
PARTICIPATION ON THE ROAD

> none of the old rooms were ever pulled down, no old tree was ever rooted up, nothing with which there was any association of bygone times was ever removed or changed.
>
> *Charles Dickens,* Nicholas Nickleby*, 768*

We do not participate in something static, fixed, unchanging. We participate, first of all, in life on Earth, which is undergoing in every moment of its existence various, manifold, even exciting changes, though at the same time, with these very changes, offers a stable and meaningful background to our existence.

Such participation – and one cannot emphasise it strongly enough – is fundamentally experiential (ontological-sensual) and not merely cognitive (epistemological-normative). We now know that at a certain, universalistic-cosmological level, the Earth moves around the Sun, the entire solar system moves around the centre of our galaxy, and so on, but this has precious little relevance for our everyday existence, as those dimensions, true and real as they might be, are *incommensurable* with our lives. What matters for *us*, not simply as modern individuals living right here and right now, but as humans living on Earth, is that the Sun rises on the East and sets on the West, it rises earlier and sets later in Summer, in a contrary manner in Winter, and so on. These are the changes that are commensurable with our existence and our experiences, and these data (certain not 'facts', as we have not made them, we have nothing to do with their existence) are not just pieces of evidence we must know about, but are the points of orientation for our existence,[1] as ignoring them, or acting against them, makes our life, even our survival, simply impossible – except as being part of the very peculiar form of life which is called modernity; a form of life, however, as we are now increasingly and evidently realise, is demonstrating not only its absurdity, but its unsustainability. As life on Earth, which is

DOI: 10.4324/9781003275138-4

much bigger than us, and which we can only destroy not reproduce, is rendered possible and follows these movements: the movements of the seasons, in manifold and different, yet stable ways, as such changes are perceived and experienced in the different locations of the planet.

Apart from following and adapting itself to these movements, life on Earth, in all its forms, also follows a type of movement that originally must have grown out of such seasonal changes, and in many instances still imitates these changes: the cycle of life that starts with birth and ends with death. The basic details are so well known that there is no point in giving a detailed account; however, here and now, in this book about social science research methods, it is important to evoke them and signal their importance.

This is because human culture, as far as it is possible to follow it backwards, always and everywhere was based on these movements. The distinguishing feature of human culture is that around the seasonal changes (rhythm) of nature and life, and around the crucial events of life, growing up, conceiving new life, and death, thus on the basis of participating in nature and life, certain rituals were developed which both celebrated these events and accommodated humans to their necessary givenness. It is by collecting these rituals and reflecting on their features, that Arnold van Gennep wrote his foundational book *Rites of Passage*, introducing the crucial term 'liminality', and emphasised that human culture grew out of and is attuned to such cosmic cycles of nature.

Everything always is in context; there is never a 'new start': Hermeneutics

Modern rationalism starts with radical distancing, both in time and space: a questioning of and separation from any historical tradition, just as a dislocation from any concrete place, and furthermore with the urge of not simply observing and describing aspects of reality, but penetrating them from the outside, to break and decompose them, dividing them into ever smaller elements so that they can be reintegrated into a system that supposedly is more rational, useful, and accommodating; that increases 'our' power, control, and money. In contrast to this, which was a radical break with the European tradition, there emerged a kind of philosophising that attempted to recover the tradition, questioning revolutionary rationalism at its core: its break with tradition and the presumed exteriority and objectivity is neither possible, nor desirable. These philosophical efforts do not attempt systematic-building neither do they form a single school, but have been cultivated by a series of thinkers over the past centuries, outside the mainstream rationalistic tradition. The perhaps most significant term capturing these efforts is 'hermeneutics'.

The starting point of modern hermeneutics, and related approaches, is so self-evident, even trivial, that one might think that it is not even worthwhile mentioning. And yet, it is explicitly denied by modern rationalism; even further, it is by such a purported escaping of such trivialities that it can start its radical revaluation of values, establishing itself out of the blue, even literally out of nothingness, starting with pure (self-)consciousness, the imaginary situation of the single, isolated thinker in face of the world: 'everything'. Instead, hermeneutics starts with the plain *given* (not a fact, as it was not 'made' by anyone) that we, all of us, not just the 'thinker' who does *not* have a privileged position from the start, are 'situated' somewhere; belong to, or participate in, a context which simply is there.

It is the conceptualisation of this taken for granted background horizon, the condition of possibility of any knowledge, understanding and experience, that is at the centre of interest of the hermeneutical tradition, at least since Schleiermacher. Bacon and Descartes pretended to start anew, marking a new and better beginning. But this is simply not possible, say Schleiermacher and his followers; somebody is always already somewhere. The search for knowledge cannot be established on itself, in absolute certainty, as it is always already based on something, on pre-reflexive foundations.

Such situatedness of literally everything, both concretely and historically, or participation in a background horizon as a necessary starting point, while trivial and self-evident, also poses as an insoluble problem, as such overwhelming background is partly invisible, and partly impossible to capture and describe in its wholeness. The hermeneutical tradition offers an answer, though it somehow remained underemphasised and under-theorised. This is that the background horizon out of which everybody by necessity speaks might become visible through an uncertain, transitory, in-between situation. Serious thinking and search for truth always starts in-between: '"Beginning in the middle is unavoidable"' (as in Schleiermacher 2007: xxvi; from 1814–5); it involves an oscillation between the determinacy of the particular and the indeterminacy of the general (xxviii-ix). Every thinking takes place in a moment, thus is transitory – though leaves something solid behind (125). Dilthey takes a further step and connects the in-betweenness of thinking to consciousness about one's own transitory times (Makkreel 1975: 4), just as the possible in-betweenness of a concrete place, formulated with particular force for Germany, this 'country of the middle [*Land der Mitte*]' (in Rickman 1976: 38).[2] Heidegger even connects the background as Beyng and transitoriness in his notes written at a particularly liminal moment in modern history, the explosion of WWII, claiming that 'this "between [*Zwischen*]" ' – which he previously characterised as the 'abyss' – 'is beyng itself' (2017, XIII: 7); that it is uncanny; and that the key feature of the abyss is that it is forcing an oscillation 'in between [*Inzwischen*]' (8).

The in-between evoked by Schleiermacher, Dilthey, and Heidegger can be expressed, in the terminology of Political Anthropology, as liminality, an affinity already recognised by Victor Turner.[3] Concerning the emergence of the modern scientific world view, this has the further importance that in Political Anthropology liminality is theorised as a void experience, combining void, nothingness, and flux. A liminal moment, a passage or transition between two stable states, implies a temporary encounter with the abyss or the void; or, as again Victor Turner already realised, it is a kind of death experience, facing complete emptiness. If we return to Bacon and Descartes (and also Newton, Locke and Kant), we can see the full significance of the previous discussion, as the pretence of an absolute new start, a zero point in history, a *tabula rasa* is nothing but the extension of their own specific historical condition, the transitoriness and liminality of their own times, into an absolute starting point in thinking, the establishment of true and universal science.[4]

Yet, in order to close the picture, one element is still missing, the application of 'rationality' for human conduct. *Ratio*, just as *logos*, originally means harmonious proportionality and graceful order; a world of beauty. A chaotic world, a culture in collapse, a transitory time in between two stable states certainly cannot show up such features. The mind cannot search for harmony in chaos – rather must attempt to *create* some order out of this liminal void and chaos; or, which is not the same thing, but which somehow became combined in the period, to discover how in 'nature', or in 'the world', order emerges out of chaos, and how this could be imitated in returning to order in human life as well.

Humbleness, arrogance, and judgment

These two concerns, though connected, are by no means identical, rather stand in a considerable tension, and furthermore can be situated on the polar opposition of arrogance (hubris) and humbleness. At one extreme, there is the humble scientist, subordinating his life to the task of discovering the laws of the universe; at the other, the hubristic social engineer who pretends to create a new order. However, even this version is too simplistic, as the would-be humble scientist also demonstrates considerable arrogance in trying to know and explain everything; not to mention that, as evidenced by Bacon, the pursuit of science also promises power, and such power/knowledge combination implies the transformative use of science, beyond humble exploration.

What it already alludes to, and what Goethe explored in his *Faust*, after toying with the *Prometheus* fragment, is that somehow the arrogance dimension would gain the upper hand over humbleness, and almost inevitably.

We still need to make the connection tighter between modern hubris and modern rationalism. Hubris is characteristic of a single individual who fails to recognise his own limitations, and at the same time does not respect the limits of the community. Such problems with limits bring in another crucial figure, the anthropological trickster, and indeed Prometheus has been identified as a trickster figure of Greek mythology. Even further, the other key trickster figure of Greek mythology is Hermes, and Hermes is the main Greek deity connected to boundaries and limits, just as the link of Hermes to Gnosticism, and also alchemy and Hermeticism is also evident. Promethean technology and Hermetic knowledge jointly allude to the hubris characteristic of modern rationalism and science.

But how can we move from this instructive metaphor to *demonstrating* the hubris of modern rationalism? Only one step must be made, and it is the precise identification of the kind of judgment implied by an individual making a judgment about something as being rational. The problem is very close to the one discussed concerning the ideas of Pizzorno, but not identical: as, even if all the strictures raised by Pizzorno are taken care of, there still remains the point that a modern enlightened individual cannot accept a position unless he can be convinced about it by rational means; and that this is simply identical to a serious problem of hubris; in fact, a kind of hubris that renders communal life impossible, and that in the long run is bound to destroy our world. This is because authority, just as judgment, is first of all *personal*, and this cannot be subordinated to discursive rationality.

For us moderns, accepting an authority outside reasoning power sounds immature; almost the definition of childish immaturity. Yet, one of the most interesting examples for authoritative judgment outside reasoning is constituted exactly by children. To be sure, children by definition need, and accept, authority. However, anyone intimately familiar with children knows well that children, even quite young children, can arrive at very sound judgments without any reasoning. Gaining the confidence of children is not simple, and children can recognise problematic and dangerous people much better, and earlier, than 'reasonable' adults. In fact, one of the consequences of modern, enlightened, rational education is to undermine this sense of judgment in children. Dickens's novels are full of examples about this phenomenon – the perhaps most evident is the contrast between Sissy Jupe, the uneducated and – in the modern rational sense – uneducable child of a circus clown, and the children of the education luminary Mr Gradgrind, in *Hard Times*: with Sissy managing to come up with sound judgments not only better than the other, educated children, but even above the schoolmaster.

Still, the most evident examples of sound judgments concern people with established and recognised authority. Judgments made by such people are not and cannot be arrogant, as they are not coming to a judgment or a statement (significantly, both covered by the word 'sentence'), by their own individual reasoning power, but are *entitled* to make such judgment because their sense of judgment was *recognised* by others – whether such recognition was official, traditional, or simply 'interpersonal'. Such judgments are not arrived at by rational deliberation, but by a weighing of the situation and the characters involved, and thus cannot easily be explained – in fact, such 'explanation' is unnecessary, possibly even misleading, as the person arriving at a judgment might not be able to translate the manner in which he arrived at such judgment in the terminology of deliberative reasoning – as it was indeed *not* made through such means.

The measure of a judgment is not the reasoning offered about it, but its soundness, which only becomes evident much later – when the justification used for it, if any, is long forgotten. But those involved will not forget who made the right judgment – and who made repeatedly wrong judgments – and such memories develop into a sound recognition of the sense of judgment of various people. Note that in this important expression 'sense' has the same form, and etymological root, as 'sensation', the 'senses', and even 'sensuality', different from 'reason', though in the sense of a very strong 'power of reason': more empirical, experiential, and most importantly more sound. It conforms to the Pascalian uses of 'sentiment', and also the similarly Pascalian 'reasons of the heart'.

In this way we got closer to capturing the hubristic arrogance of modern rationalism, and its *tabula rasa*. Starting from zero, a new beginning, is not only disruptive and destructive of all cultural traditions, as well as of nature, but it deprives people of whatever certainty and stability they still had. Instead of such certainties, measures, limits and guideposts in their lives, they are offered the fake and illusory combination of free choice and reasoning power: they are free to choose, and have, whatever they wanted, using their means through the sovereign powers of their reason. This is not only the underlying guiding principle of modern rationalism, but also of free market economies and democratic polities – showing the tight connections, indeed complicity of the three. We moderns can hardly even imagine what is wrong with it, though our global situation unmistakeably reveals that the principles did not bring the panacea they promised – so we must understand what is wrong with them.

Conclusion

Participation and historicity are indeed fundamental, the central, basic concerns of human life. Participation will be revisited in the last chapter of the book, as one of the key methods of Political Anthropology. As participant observation, it is central for standard anthropology; however, there it will be shown that a better method, developed by Colin Turnbull on the basis of the ideas of Lévy-Bruhl and liminality, is 'total participation'; while participation, in the form of *metalepsis* or *methexis* were already central for Plato and Aristotle. Historicity will be discussed in the penultimate and in a way most important chapter of the book, as another central method of Political Anthropology; but the idea that historicity and not scientificity should be the foundation of social and human understanding will be the basis of the discussion already in Part Two, or the problematisation of 'scientific methodology'. This is because not only participation is historical, but the ignoring and denying of participation, precondition of 'scientific methodology', is also based on certain historical conditions, as Chapter 5, another central chapter of the book, will show in some detail. One cannot repeat enough: *everything* in life and even in reality is based on history.

Finally, just as importantly, and stating the same from a different angle, *everything* in life and even in reality is based on participation. Even the increasing acceptance of *non*-participation as a starting point is based on participation: instead of starting from the self-evident fact that we all participate in our lives, in our families, native languages, home cultures and so on, in the Eliasian concentric circles, but *also* in the similar circles of Nature, as argued among others by Bateson and Serres, we now, moderns, accept participation in the 'economy', assuming – falsely – that everything in our lives always depended on the 'economy' – are *forced* to accept it, as otherwise we could not make a living; accept participation in the 'state', are similarly *forced* to accept it, as otherwise, without passports and other documents, we could not live – and which, whether through the hyper-modern buzzword-trick of citizenship, or the classical-modern buzzword-trick of nationality, abuses our need for belongingness and home to lure us identifying with it; and finally, most central for accepting 'scientific methodology', we 'men of knowledge' (Nietzsche, *Genealogy*, Preface) no longer live an *academic* life, inside our home universities, while belonging to the world of *academia*, but participate first of all in professional associations, which set up their 'states within the states', define their agenda, canon and methods, guarding them jealously, instead of searching for a genuine understanding about genuine participation.

Political Anthropology is different; it tries to bring together all ways of genuine understanding, so much needed in our world going so desperately wrong. Thus, in Part Two, the book will show how and why 'scientific methodology' became accepted, and why is it wrong; while Part Three will be devoted to the methods, or *ways*, through which Political Anthropology suggests to promote understanding.

Notes

1 Note that 'orientation' is from 'orient' (East), meaning that we 'orient' ourselves to the rising sun, with then our right hand pointing to sunny South, and the left, pointing to cold North, by implication being 'sinister'; every single 'trivial' aspect of our language has deep meaning.
2 See also Schleiermacher in *Life of Jesus* on Christ as a historical turning point.
3 See Szakolczai (2004). See also Foucault on problematisation.
4 See Argyrou (2013) for a similar problematisation of Locke and Kant.

PART II
The Troubles with Scientific Methodology

4

THE ABSURDITY OF A SCIENTIFIC METHODOLOGY

> science oscillates between two opposed attitudes: on the one hand, vainglory, an excessive and often indecent pride; and on the other, when it becomes necessary to silence critics, a false humility that consists in denying that one has done anything out of the ordinary, anything that departs from the usual business of normal science
>
> Jean-Pierre Dupuy,
> On the Origins of Cognitive Science: The Mechanization of the Mind, xvi-xvii

> Narrow rationalism has a tremendous capacity for reducing the most interesting questions to a few resounding platitudes
>
> René Girard, The Theatre of Envy, 67

> All other swindlers upon earth are nothing to the self-swindlers
>
> Charles Dickens, Great Expectations, 192

> the word analysis as opposed to synthesis, is thus defined by Walker. 'The resolution of an object, whether of the senses or of the intellect, into its first elements.' As opposed to synthesis, you observe. *Now* you know what analysis is
>
> Charles Dickens, Dombey and Son, 196

Introduction: Methodology as idol

In contemporary academic life, 'methodology' is perhaps the single most important word. It is considered to have unique, almost magical powers. The value of a PhD proposal or a research project lies in its methodology. In postgraduate education, methodology courses increasingly are considered as most important; research proposals, by all funding bodies, but especially in the most highly coveted ERC grants, are primarily assessed on their methodology. This is known by everyone, and is written in plain words on advertisements in websites or in packages sent to prospective applicants.

DOI: 10.4324/9781003275138-6

Thus, using the terminology of Francis Bacon, certainly against his words, but in a significant sense even against their spirit, methodology can be considered as the major idol of modern science – the kind of undertaking whose spirit is captured in the quotes above from Dupuy and Girard.

'Methodology' is almost taken for granted today, and it is considered as *scientific* methodology not just inside academic life, but the wider world. Scholars, according to politicians, businessmen, journalists, the media, the wider public, should not just use and follow a rigorous and well-defined methodology, but a *scientific* methodology. Disciplines are evaluated according to their scientificity: according to this mode of evaluation economics is more scientific than politics or sociology, in fact than any other social or human science, as a Nobel prize is only offered in economics. The other social sciences, especially now political science, desperately try to follow economics, which currently means first of all to apply rational choice theories, in order to gain the supreme recognition and be offered a Nobel prize.

Yet, as it has already been argued in the first part, and as will be specifically discussed in this chapter, this is seriously wrong. What today in the social sciences is considered as a prioritised, presumably 'scientific', methodology is usually nothing else but the slavish and mechanical imitation of methods and means that are presumably used in the natural sciences, but that are hardly used by scientists now, and which in any way are profoundly inapplicable for genuine social and human understanding. The use of such methods are highly problematic even in the 'natural' sciences, as they contribute to the technological destruction of our home-world, Nature, due to their universalistic pretences. Or, in other words, the problem with even a genuine scientific methodology is not that it is not universal, but rather that it exactly *is*. Thus, taking over such a perspective for our own social and human existence is simply an unpardonable error, and only contributes to the ideological justification of deeply intrusive and destructive policies and practices.

By our days, the need for the application of a scientific methodology is almost considered as a truism, ignoring its tragically destructive impact on our lives, culture, and traditions. It is therefore absurd. So we must try to reconstruct, as far as it is possible to do so in a book chapter, following the words and spirit of the major problematisers of the 'will to knowledge' and technologised scientism like Nietzsche, Mumford, Yates, Voegelin, Wittgenstein, Heidegger, Toulmin, Foucault, and many others, how such an erroneous perspective could have insinuated itself into the heart of European culture.

The current chapter will focus on the two main sources of the modern rationalistic scientific method: Francis Bacon and René Descartes, trying to capture, in a detailed study of their best known works, what exactly was new in their attempts to give a rigorous methodological basis to the search for knowledge.

Francis Bacon

it's a fine thing to understand 'em [instruments]. And yet it's a fine thing not to understand 'em. I hardly know which is best. It's so comfortable to sit here and feel that you might be weighed, measured, magnified, electrified, polarized, played the very devil with: and never know how.

Charles Dickens, Dombey and Son, *46*

Francis Bacon (1561–1626) is widely considered as the founder of 'scientific methodology', source of the claim about the close connection between power and knowledge to which the enormous influence his ideas had could safely be attributed. His most influential work, *The New Organon*, laid the foundations of 'scientific methodology'.[1]

Bacon the rhetorician

Bacon, to begin with, is quite rhetorical, and in a very particular way, and right from the start. This is, to say the least, problematic for someone pretending to break new ground in truthfulness and knowledge. His rhetorics has two main features. First, and at the very start of the Preface, he sets up two opposite extremes – both hardly sound or realistic – between those who claim to know everything, and those who claim that nothing can be known, so that he could present himself as the rational arbiter between such extremes. Second, and repeatedly, he offers two opposite positions: one, which was believed so far, and which is simply erroneous; and the other, his own, the evidently and clearly right one. What is common to both rhetorical tools is that they are dichotomising and dualistic; thus, they clearly reveal Manichaean and Gnostic influences.

Bacon the critic

Apart from being rhetorical, Bacon also offers a critical stance. He does not criticise everything; first of all, he does not even make critical hints concerning God, religion, or even the Church. But this is practically the only area he leaves intact – everything else is subjected to a quite thorough and evidently devastating critique. This starts with nature, where Bacon pursues a subtle rhetorical strategy, perhaps in line with his view that nature itself is quite subtle in its ways. He starts from the position that man is a mere servant and interpreter of nature, in harmony with his pious attitude towards God and religion; but such piety would soon yield to an ever more intrusive and violent terminology, where the mere servant of nature, as if anticipating Hegel's master-serf dialectic, is transmogrified into the master of nature, whose aim is, or rather should be, to conquer it, and then, at the start of the second book, this rhetoric is replaced by the even stronger rhetoric of *transforming* nature. One again cannot help but be struck with the Gnostic/ alchemic implications of all this.

His criticism becomes stronger and more direct concerning human nature. The expression is present in the very first sentence of Aphorism 41, about the Idols of the Tribe, where the famous critique of the four idols start. Bacon asserts there that '[T]he idols of the tribe have their foundation in human nature itself' – and the tribe is identified with mankind itself [*gente hominum*]. This is because such idols are due to the weakness and unreliability of the most important human organs: the senses and the mind (intellect).

The evidence produced by the senses, the sensations or experiences are fundamental for Bacon's purposes, offering the starting point for any search for knowledge (Preface, p.2; I.19). Yet, they have fatal weaknesses, as it 'is the fact that the human senses are dull, incompetent and deceptive' (I.50). They fall in prey to what strikes them immediately and strongly, thus overlook what is more important but less perceptible, and in this way they mislead the intellect, giving rise to the idols of the tribe. Thus, as we'll see, they need to be complemented by various means, methods, and instruments. It is in this way that we can be conducted back to the facts (I.36). While here the Latin word used by Bacon is *rebus*, not *factum*, in a later passage where he claims that the proper scientific question to be posed is not to look up existing theories, but ' "What are the facts about this matter?" ' (I.112), the Latin term used is *de facto naturae*. Thus, and not surprisingly, according to the Online Etymology under 'fact' the '[m]ain modern sense of "thing known to be true" is from 1630s', thus can be assigned to the influence of Bacon.

The main target of Bacon's critique, however, object of a genuine wrath, is the other part of human nature, the mind. What conventionally is considered as knowledge is the mere outcome of operations of the intellect; products of the imagination of the mind. The main problem is that the intellect is not working properly. Instead of paying close attention to reality and facts, the intellect is rather preoccupied with dialectic, or logical argumentation, using the powers of the mind (I.9–10, 20, 29), based on notions instead of the search for truth (14–8), but these notions themselves are merely pale impressions of nature, not giving justice to its subtlety (23–4), as usually the mind commits errors in its very first steps (30), and anyway '[t]he human intellect is like a distorting mirror' (41). This is because the very powers of the mind mislead it, as 'the mind loves to leap up to generalities and come to rest with them', instead of following the empirical road of experiments to truth (20). The sections about the idols of the tribe offer a detailed critique of such illusory 'false notions' (38) of the human intellect. The conclusive inference is that, while one is not to despise the intellect, instead of us relying upon the powers of the mind, the intellect should be regulated ([*intellectum non contemnimus, sed regimus*]126).

This passage immediately requires two comments. First, instead of congratulating Bacon for not despising the intellect, one should rather pose the question how on earth a philosopher dealing with questions of knowledge *could* arrive at all at such an idea. Second, and in a closely connected manner, Bacon not only mistrusts the senses, which for a philosopher might be understandable, even if not acceptable, he also mistrusts the mind, revealing the same Gnostic life-hostility.

If the errors of the mind are partially laid to the weaknesses of the senses, Bacon also finds fault with language itself. The notions that mislead the intellect, away from the truth, are not only consequences of an erring mind, its precocious jumping to generalisations, but also to the words themselves, which are vulgar, products of everyday perceptions and interactions, and not suitable for a proper scientific interpretation of nature. Bacon calls this the third main idol, the idols of the marketplace. The two main versions of such idols are names given to non-existing entities, and ill-defined names given to real things. He singles out for attention qualitative, imprecise names, like 'heavy' or 'light', which prevent exactness – or exactly the terms central for everyday participatory understanding, which he intends to replace by a life-alien exact, quantitative terminology.[2]

This is the reason why, in fact, the introduction of this third idol is preceded by the identification of the second idol, called the idols of the cave, by which Bacon means the errors that are due to being enclosed in concrete, particular settings, taking these particularities for granted and extending them to the foundations of all knowledge. Philosophical understanding, the interpretation of nature since many centuries attempted to break out of this error but, as it started by using the words which were themselves developed out of this vulgar, particularistic perception, it did not manage to accomplish this task. Or, if the very first step taken is wrong, inevitably the entire path that follows will be in erring (I.30).

However, here again, one immediately must make a counter-point, which in a way could have been evident even in Bacon's time, but which can rely on the most recent evidence made available by archaeological research, and which in general should be the starting point of *any* serious understanding in our own days, shedding a completely different light on previous interpretations of history. The name Bacon gave to his second idol is particularly revealing, as it indeed reflects two connected prejudices which are widely shared, in spite of much better archaeological understanding of our own historical record, up to the present. One is the mistaken idea that in distant prehistory humans were cave-dwellers, while the second, and the origin of this prejudice, is that human culture started with settlement; or, that living inside an enclosed place was what gave birth to civilisation – the idea that gave the occasion for Nietzsche's critique of civilisation and morals in the *Genealogy*, following up on Rousseau. Archaeological research demonstrated that human culture, at the very highest peaks, existed for tens if not hundreds of thousands of years, without settlement, as part of a walking culture. It was during that period that language was developed, which now is traced back, through Atapuerca, to almost half a million years ago. The words of language which indeed offer a starting point for any understanding (see Chapter 7) were not developed out of a limited experience of primitive barbarians who lived in a cave, but were developed by people who walked over vast areas, gaining thorough familiarity with if not the entire planet, then a quite significant part of it, and developing the words by which their experiences could be transmitted through countless generations. Thus, criticising the idols of the cave and of the marketplace, combined, does not lay the foundations of a genuinely scientific understanding of our world, rather succeeds to alienate us at the same time from our surroundings (Nature) and our own historical background (culture), or laying indeed the foundations for our current situation and plight.

The fourth idol is a corollary of the previous three, completing Bacon's critique of not simply knowledge and understanding as it existed before his work, but even of the very features of human beings (man as created – presumably on the image of God …). These idols are contained in the existing books, and philosophical systems, and are called the idols of the theatre. This, in one sense, is a criticism of scholasticism, which existed before Bacon and would be repeated countless times; yet, Bacon's account both gained a paradigmatic status and has some specific distinguishing features.

First, medieval scholastics were identified as sophists before, for e.g. in the famous debate between Erasmus and Luther, and calling an adversary sophist could be considered a simple rhetorical trick. However, Bacon's point here has interesting and important features, as he is not labelling adversaries, but rather argues that the entire history of philosophy, after its earliest phases (I: 86), is dominated by Sophists. He does not specify what exactly he means by such early beginnings, but it is evident that he implies those Greek philosophers who wrote before Plato and Aristotle, and who are now called Presocratics (I.71, 86). This is most interesting, partly as these thinkers called themselves physiologists, or students of nature (*physis*), and not philosophers, a term that was only invented by Plato. While occasionally Bacon is respectful of Plato and Aristotle, focusing his critique on their followers, the Neoplatonists and the scholastics (I: 89), who built philosophical systems on their ideas, he accuses 'Plato and his school' of superstition (I.65), while in another passage he summarily condemns all schools of philosophy, starting from Plato and Aristotle, as Sophists (I.71). This actually is quite an important point, and is close to the ideas of Heidegger, in contrast to the perspective on the history of philosophy as codified by Hegel.

However, and second, Bacon extends his critique of generalising philosophical systems to a more or less unconditional critique of books (I.61–8. 78, 85). While it would certainly not be right to consider his ideas as the source of the various modern campaigns of book-burning, together with his critiques of 'schools', or universities, it certainly forms the background for the modern hostility to universities and books by political-technological-industrial-business circles. Universities and books are practically unique to European culture, indeed constitute its backbone, and such hostility to culture, based on presumably more important practical and utilitarian concerns, is the heart of the systematic destruction of European culture. Bacon's ideas by no means are alien to this undertaking, as he repeatedly asserts that knowledge should serve practical and utilitarian purposes. Due to the impact of books and philosophical systems, knowledge did not progress in the past in the sciences as in the mechanical arts (I.74).

The third central distinguishing feature in Bacon's position concerns the title word of the fourth idol, theatre. There are a number of extremely important and revealing aspects of this naming. To start with, it is by no means self-evident that the idols identified with philosophical systems should be associated with theatre. For us, the idea is all but unintelligible, as philosophy supposedly has nothing to do with theatre; but was also not present in medieval thinking – indeed, similarly unimaginable. Such connection could only have been made in the 16th and early 17th centuries, much due to the ideas of Camillo, and its popularity in England, as demonstrated by Frances Yates. It also documents that this mode of thinking was very close to Bacon, and thus the close interpenetration of this mode of thinking with the rise of modern philosophy, recognised by Michel Serres in the theatricality of Descartes' thinking, or later, in the glorification of the 'ideal spectator' by Adam Smith and Kant. Yet, already in these classics of modern rationalism, while theatricality as a mode was present, the term theatre was fully absent. Thus, in spite of such a revealing presence in the work of Bacon, among the idols, the centre of his work, and even in connection with philosophy, the foundational connections between theatre and philosophy were ignored.

It could be objected that Bacon only brought in the term theatre in a critical manner, as an idol. However, a closely connected word was central to his positive proposals: the word 'table'. According to Bacon, genuine, truly scientific knowledge, based on empirical evidence and experiments, elaborated with the proper inductive method and not by vague generalisations, should be arranged in Tables of Discovery (I.92, 102), an idea identified by Foucault as central to the classical episteme. However, such arrangement, focusing on the clear visuality of knowledge, is theatrical in origin, and belongs to the heart of Camillo's project (Horvath and Szakolczai 2018a, Chapter 3). Even further, the very term 'table' is revealing, as its use as a central instrument in gaining knowledge can be traced to the Tabula Smaragdina.

So what does Bacon offer, after all this critique? Nothing less than a full-scale revolution.

Bacon the revolutionary

What Bacon proposes, on the basis of his devastating critique of not only all previous human traditions, but even of human nature – which indeed led to devastation, in the sense of Heidegger – is nothing short of a full-scale revolution. Here again some comments must be immediately made, as while Bacon came after the Reformation, and the Reformation is often considered as the first modern revolution, the Reformation did not have explicit revolutionary aims: it only wanted to get rid of the corruption of the past centuries – a not at all unreasonable aim, given the impact of the Byzantium, especially through its collapse; and return to the presumed purity of the evangelical ways of life.

The aims of Bacon were radically different, and amount to a genuine revolution; and so, after the religious reformation movement and the related civil wars, and before the political revolutions and the increasingly global wars that ensued, it is the scientific revolution inaugurated by Bacon that should be considered as the true model of all later revolutions, genuine gravedigger of our present.

The revolutionary character of Bacon's aims is not a controversial or new claim, as it relies on his explicit assertions.

Bacon submitted the entire way of thinking, even talking, that existed in his times to a very effective critique, as his suggestions became the foundation of our current ways. It is contained in the title of his works, the two most famous being *The New Organon* and *The New Atlantis*, both containing the term 'new'. This is not accidental, as Bacon wanted the new, pursued the new at any price, valued and propagated nothing but whatever was new. Thus, as he states in the Preface to *New Organon*, his aim is not mere rivalry with the ancients; it is rather 'to open up a new road for the intellect to follow, a road the ancients didn't know and didn't try' (p.4). Or, instead of merely rearranging what has already been known, what is needed are new achievements (I.8). As stated in a programmatic manner at the end of the first section of the *New Organon*,

> [i]t is pointless to expect any great advances in science from grafting new things onto old. If we don't want to go around in circles for ever, making 'progress' that is so small as be almost negligible, we must make a fresh start with deep foundations.
>
> *(I.31)*

The preoccupation with the new is repeated with insistence: 'we must make a fresh start with deep foundations' (I.97; the expression 'fresh start' is repeated in I: 92, 97, 115–7, 129), and new experiments 'of an utterly different kind from any we have had up to now' (I.100). Unless someone fails to grasp the significance of the point, he immediately reasserts, and with emphasis, that 'But that is not all. There should also be introduced an entirely different method, order, and procedure'(I.100). Or again, as it is reasserted towards the end of the first part, he has 'the nerve to push aside all the sciences and all the authorities at a single blow, doing this single-handed', adding – using a significant terminology – that a complete censure is better than a partial one (I.122). One could not be a more explicit and self-conscious revolutionary.

The term Bacon uses for this revolutionary undertaking, title of the – unwritten – masterwork of which *The New Organon* was only the second part, is '*The Great Instauration*'. For us today the term 'instauration' is inconspicuous enough, often used for the inauguration of an institutional event. However, it was brought from Latin into English usage by Bacon, and he was not talking about any instauration, but the *great* instauration. Etymology offers a further intriguing insight, one might wonder whether intended or not: the root of 'instauration' is Greek *stauros* 'stake', which is the word used in the Gospels for the cross on which Jesus was crucified. As Bacon studied in Cambridge, he had to be aware of the Greek Bible.

But how such a revolution in science is to be achieved? Bacon is clear and explicit: this requires the pursuit of new methods; through new experiences, to be sure, but most of all new *experiments* (I.70); experiments which follow a procedure that produces certain results. It is here that Bacon lays the grounds of 'scientific methodology', and so we must understand as precisely as possible what does he mean, in what way it represents a radical novelty, and how can he demonstrate the powerful results promised.

Bacon's method: the origins of 'scientific methodology'

The need for new methods, and the manner in which such methods are to be searched, are based on Bacon's anthropology: his views concerning the radically faulty character of human nature. Our senses are weak, our mind easily pursues things in the wrong direction, so the new science to be inaugurated must be based on radically different ways.

The starting point for a new and truly scientific 'interpretation of nature' is that the mind must be constrained to work right, mechanically following procedures; must be forced to work like a machine.[3] This is explained in a programmatic manner in the Preface: there is only one way to overcome the errors of the previous modes: it is 'to start the work of the mind all over again. In this, the mind shouldn't be left to its own devices, but right from the outset should be guided at every step, *as though a machine were in control*' (p.1; emph. AS). This is because problems start with the idols of the cave: human beings are raised and live in particular, limited environments which imprisoned their mind, and so are also explicitly hostile to the advancement of the sciences (I.80). The mind must be forced to disengage from such a limited perspective: it must pursue the way of experiments that are 'firmly regulated' (I: 100), or follow a fixed procedural law; it must be cleansed and purged (I: 69). In order to prevent its erring, the mind must be guided (I: 126), or it is necessary to 'lay out a securely walled road leading to the human intellect directly from the senses and experiment' (I: 81; see also 76). The terminology here is particularly revealing, as Bacon explicitly refers to walling (see Horvath, Benţa and Davison, 2019), or the forcing of the human intellect on rigidly predefined and preconceived ways – instead of considering those ways as being trodden in the past, thus bequeathing on us a secure tradition. The focus of Bacon, unmistakeably, is not on the road, but on the *walls* surrounding it. In order to avoid misunderstanding, he explicitly re-states that science must follow rigid ways, instead of yielding to imagination: 'the stern and unbending search for truth' is incompatible with 'the richness of the array of thoughts and doctrines' (Bacon, I.81). In a related terminology, the mind must follow a proper 'plan' (I: 70).

The argument is reinforced in a series of aphorisms promising hope by such a new science. While in the past discoveries were mostly accidentally made, in the future this should be by 'methodical searching' (I: 108). Apart from forcing the supposedly erring intellect on safe, walled roads, this implies the use of instruments. Here the model for understanding is offered not by previous thinkers, but by the mechanical arts, which Bacon valued way above intellectual traditions. Thus, just as in the practical arts, progress can be achieved, and cooperation secured, 'through instruments and machinery' (Preface, p.2).

Bacon the prophet

Bacon asserts that following his precepts for a scientific methodology brings no small reward, as in this way we can arrive at a genuine Paradise on Earth: 'Entering the kingdom of man, which is based on the sciences, is like entering the kingdom of heaven, which one can enter only as a little child' (I: 68); thus, playing with Biblical support for justifying his revolutionary and radically contrary ideas (the 'kingdom of man' almost advances 'homo deus'). The promises concerning 'the excellence of the end in view' are repeated and detailed towards the end of the first book, amounting to the vision of a genuine Paradise on Earth through science (I: 129). Thus, 'the benefits of scientific discoveries can extend to the whole of mankind, and can last for all time'; and only science can lead us there, not other, merely 'civil' achievements, as 'scientific discoveries bring delight, and confer benefits without causing harm or sorrow to anyone'; such discoveries, of which the three great discoveries of recent times, the printing press, gunpowder and the compass were only preliminary signs, will promote 'mankind's power and control over the universe off to a fresh start'.

At this point, Bacon moves to the second book, where he promises some details about the basic principles of such scientific methodology. From the perspective of the present, these are immediately preoccupying, as they move outside the horizon of a search for truth, discovery and interpretation, getting involved rather with power, effect-producing, and especially *transformation*. The position of the humble seeker of truth and servant of nature is transmogrified into that of not simply a conqueror and master of nature, but one who is set to gain power by any means. The very first aphorism starts by defining and comparing human power and knowledge. The poor state in which knowledge is at the moment can be altered by increasing the power given to the search for knowledge; and this will on its own further enhance human power, as it was already intimated in the first part. This, however, only happens if the ties between power and knowledge are made ever tighter. It is helped by the fact that 'The roads to human power and to human knowledge lie extremely close together and are nearly the same' (II: 4), implying that the knowledge of nature leads to the *transformation* of nature. Thus, the next aphorism starts by saying that 'There are two kinds of rule or axiom for the transformation of bodies' (II: 5). This is most preoccupying, as Bacon quickly makes it clear that the kind of knowledge that would lead us into the promised Paradise on Earth is not some innocent understanding concerning the way things are in nature, but are rather specific techniques about how things can be transformed so that they would be used for certain, presumably better purposes. Understanding is thus replaced by utility, as Bacon already intimated in the first part, when he argued that in matters of science 'truth and usefulness are the very same thing' (I.124), but utility as a measure of alteration is certainly imprecise and unacceptable: utility for whom? Why? And when? Utility is from Aristotle's philosophy, which Bacon is about to dismiss and dismantle, and where the ends are assumed as stable, given, and – for the concrete culture, which Bacon is also questioning as a reference point – also self-evident. The new into which Bacon lured his readers with his promises is thus revealed as the start of a potentially endless process of transformation. The source of such a concern, and method, is immediately revealed through the example offered for the first rule of such 'transformation of bodies', as this is nothing else but gold. The idea of transforming bodies into gold, of course, was identified since time immemorial as central preoccupation of alchemists. Bacon is not engaged in such an undertaking, but the very fact that the first example he brings in concerns gold is most revealing in hinting at the source from where he is deriving his new ideas concerning the aims and methods of science. His example for the second rule is even more revealing, as here he poses the following question: 'For example, one might be inquiring into the origins of gold or some other metal or stone – How does it start forming? What process takes it from its basic rudiments or elements right through to the completed mineral?' Here, apart from *again* referring to gold, Bacon makes a broader allusion to metallurgy in general, or the historical source of alchemy as a practice. While Bacon was certainly not an alchemist in the conventional sense, important studies have identified his interest in alchemy, to the extent that it is probable that he 'seriously believed that gold could be produced artificially' (Linden 1974: 560).[4] Thus, his offering a new scientific methodology as panacea for the future is an attempt to render the alchemical investigation more regular and acceptable, and to make *this* new and improved alchemy into the engine of human progress. As technology, it indeed has become a main engine of our (un)reality.

Hanging the hangman

From our present, we are obliged to pose the question: after all, what is wrong with the perspective offered by Bacon? Given that Bacon asserted that basically *everything* was wrong in the past, one is tempted to say that *everything* was wrong with Bacon's approach – and, actually, this is rather closer to the truth. This is because, while Bacon's 'new start' indeed helped a certain burgeoning of the 'sciences', understood as the explanation of universal processes, without paying any attention to the concrete features of Nature (as on Earth), culture, human history, traditions, the personality, and so on, and the use of such 'knowledge' to transform, beyond recognition, our own surroundings, by now it is evident that such transformative knowledge renders our lives all but meaningless and unliveable, while is about to destroy, through the well-known phenomena of global warming, pollution, and so on, our world.

So – what is so wrong with Bacon's ideas?

It is only proper for a Political Anthropological approach to start with Bacon's anthropology. According to Bacon, both the human senses and the mind are unreliable, therefore must be artificially regulated and normalised, turned into a machinery, and must be complemented by instruments. Left on their own, without being given a rigid directing guidance, and without proper instruments, they are hopeless. However, the actual situation is quite the opposite. The human senses and the mind – and here the mind is understood in its classical sense, incorporating the 'soul', in the sense of Bonaventure, and not reduced to a mere biological brain – are just fine. They might not be perfect, and some senses in some people are faulty, but overall there is nothing wrong with them, if they are left free to develop on their own, and are properly given some loving care and guidance: we as humans can only live if our senses and mental capacities are allowed to develop freely and are encouraged and allowed to trust them. Otherwise, we become hopelessly enslaved to things outside us: machines, laws, experts, politicians, teachers, media gurus, and the like.

It also means that our knowledge, *as* humans, in any of our capacities, can only rely on our own experiences: not because we are all of us so special (which certainly makes no sense), but because *we* only can live our own lives; and that life requires knowledge about every aspect of our world. We can only gain such experience by *participating* in the world, and can only gain knowledge about the world in which we *participate*. Thus, participation, far from being detrimental for knowledge, a kind of 'idol of the cave', is rather the condition of possibility of knowledge as understanding.

Our knowledge, thus, first of all is based on experience; but such experiences have to be elaborated *by our own minds*. To be sure, in order to properly understand our own experiences, we need to gain a distance from the immediate events and our surroundings, but such distancing is a simple fact of life, and was part of the upbringing in any decent human community. Being imprisoned within the narrow horizon of a closed world is not a primordial human experience, rather was brought about by a combination of settlement and sorcery, as it can be followed through the archaeological evidence available about Natufian culture, or Çatalhöyük. Also, we certainly need the ideas of others, first of all those preserved in the tradition, whether in the form of myths, narratives, or books. But all these registered and digested experiences we only need to consult, and not follow slavishly. The only way to gain understanding is to feed our own mind with as many participatory experiences and in-depth readings as possible, train it by loving guidance, and then *to let our own mind work out the results, in terms of ideas and interpretations.* Our talents are different; some people gain more understanding than others. But, under the right conditions, most people can gain a decent understanding. What is certain is that the mechanical application of a set of rules, as it is now being systematically and officially offered in courses about methodology, will not offer *any* understanding.[5] The method might work when making controlled experiments in testing the effects of some medication on rats – with the ethical and other limits of such an approach being also increasingly evident. But they cannot offer any understanding about human life – not even animal or plant life, as life, and nature, is fully outside of the scope of such mechanical manipulations.

But the errors of Bacon that drove a civilisation mad (paraphrasing Auden) go even further. Bacon argued about the insufficiency of the words that were developed out of everyday life, suggesting that scientists should develop their own, unprejudiced terminology, leading generations of philosophers and social scientists to ignore the traditional meaning of words, their etymology and conceptual history, and define their own words and terminology, developing libraries of social science literature that are accessible only to the initiates of the terminology, but which do not offer the slightest understanding, except for reproducing these hopeless approaches through the proliferation of university appointments and the building of schools around individual theorists. But all this is fundamentally wrong, as words matter, they are important; every word and by extension and a fortiori every language is the depository of immense wisdom. In fact, it would do much benefit to genuine understanding if courses about philosophy and social theory would be devoted, instead of the set of sophistic ideas saturating them, to a detailed comparative study of human languages – not in the way linguists study language, which itself is much confused by the approach of 'scientific methodology', but in terms of the wisdom which the basic *semantic* and not merely syntactical structure of language reveals. The scientific terminology proposed by Bacon and developed by modern positivism and analytical philosophy is little better than Orwell's duckspeak.

At this point, one might object that, though the shortcomings of Baconian methodology are indeed evident, it is still impossible to reject all the advances of modern sciences that was made on this Baconian basis, in the last four centuries or so. This is a legitimate point, but also one that goes way beyond the scope of the book, so I can only offer here a few ideas. To start with, the Baconian idea of defamiliarisation certainly helped to promote universal knowledge, but the exact effect and overall relevance of that knowledge for our own lives still have to be assessed. In our days, this is done solely in terms of utility, but such utility is measured by the mediation of markets, money and technology, which reproduces the same distancing, and thus only reinforces the biases of the first. This reached a clearly intolerable state, so just cannot be continued. Second, most research done following Baconian principles in the social and human sciences produced all but meaningless results. Much of what was written over the past decades in economics, sociology, politics and philosophy is all but meaningless. The situation in history is slightly better, as historians must deal with real archival evidence, though hyper-specialisation even there left its mark. The most important recent research in the social and human sciences was produced in fields that are the furthest away from Baconian principles: in anthropology – where the *absence* of any prior participation of anthropologists in the life of the communities they studied required the development of a *participatory* methodology (this will be further studied in Chapter 12); and in the history of the sciences, where the aim was to reconstruct, and thus to problematise, the advance of 'Baconism'. The practically only field where Baconian principles advanced understanding is archaeology.

The special case of archaeology

Archaeology is simply the most important social science of our times. It is a very young field of knowledge – while a certain interest in Roman and Etruscan times in the Renaissance led to some pioneering efforts, hardly anything before Schliemann and Evans can be qualified as genuine archaeology, and even their interests were driven by classical antiquity. Still, over the past century or so archaeology has come up with a series of discoveries that are genuinely earth-shattering, radically altering our understanding about the scope and character of human (pre-)history, except that knowledge about these, apart from a certain journalistic familiarity about the basic discoveries, is still minimal. Archaeology should be taught as key subject in every first year university course.

At the same time archaeology is the most 'scientific', in the traditional Baconian sense, of all the social sciences. Much of what archaeologists now are doing, from the conduct of excavations up to the dating of the results, is simple and pure science. Without the use of such scientific methods and techniques, these discoveries would have been inconceivable.

This is all true; yet, at the same time the character of archaeological research also demonstrate the limitations of Baconian methods. This is because archaeology investigates the results or indeed *facts* of human history through the methods of the universalistic natural sciences. Such techniques and methods are used in a specific and limited sense: to assign a precise *date* and *place* to the findings, in the Bakhtinian sense of chronotope. Second, and as a consequence, the basic drawbacks of the Baconian methods, utility and transformation, do not apply. Archaeological results have no utility whatsoever. They only convey the way in which human beings lived in a very distant past – mostly in such a distant past that they hardly have any contact with our contemporary ways. They help us understand the way we lived – the course of human history *as it really happened*. Also, archaeological research is reconstructive and not transformative. Archaeology is not about advising politicians how to manipulate people, or policy makers about satisfying human needs; it certainly does not promote utilitarian or instrumental considerations.

Third, though using scientific techniques and methods, archaeological understanding also strives for results *opposite* to Baconian science. Instead of trying to arrange knowledge in tables, as pursued by structuralisms of all kinds, archaeology is concerned with reconstructing sequential orders. Thus, while in a way it is positivistic, collecting artifacts and establishing facts, as they happened, it is also historical, while most positivistic research in the social sciences, whether structuralist or not, is radically ahistorical.

The perhaps most important, radically anti-Baconian and anti-positivistic character of archaeological research, at its most empirical, excavating level, however, is that it is as comprehensive, general (though not universalistic) and non-specialistic as possible. The chief excavator of a site – and there must be a chief excavator, as otherwise chaos would reign in such a delicate matter as excavating a place where humans lived many millennia ago – cannot be a specialist in politics, sociology, anthropology, religion, and so on, but must be to some extent familiar with all these aspects, as the excavation of a site is a single event, and as much as it discovers it, reveals it, makes its understanding possible, also hopelessly *destroys* the site as it existed, and so the excavator must immediately and while on the site understand how all aspects of the site hang together, getting a knack for what was going on. All kinds of scientific techniques can be used to preserve the place where the objects were found and to date their exact age, but only the excavator can gain an understanding of how people lived then. For this, the Baconian approach offers no help. Indeed, this is where Baconian education, while at one level made archaeology possible, on the other, with its emphasis on specialisation, renders their proper interpretation difficult, if not impossible.

The most important non-Baconian, even anti-Baconian, aspect of archaeological research is that it paradoxically helps to dislocate us from the modern evolutionary-progressist vision of the world whose chief source was nothing else than Bacon. Bacon's explicit aim was to promote scientific progress, but as a result modern Western culture came to understand itself as constituting unparalleled overall progress, to which it is called to lead the entire mankind. Archaeological discoveries conclusively revealed that in many parts of human history, at least back to the early Palaeolithic, we humans lived in cultures that have nothing to envy us moderns – even in terms of 'quality of life'. Archaeological research demonstrated that the progressive-evolutionary vision of human history is untenable.

René Descartes

Just as Bacon, Descartes started with anthropological assumptions.[6] However, his account included a self-referential and autobiographical aspect, which was also clearly and distinctly theatrical.[7]

Descartes' anthropology focuses on human reason. In this, there is nothing special, here he only follows the most classical tradition, Plato. His most evidently Platonic passage is at the end of Part 5, where he discusses the indestructibility of the soul, or its immortality. The question, however, concerns the exact meaning he attributes to reason.

Here the very first sentence is instructive, though as we'll see – highly misleading. In his very first words Descartes uses the expression 'good sense' for 'reason' and claims that this is the 'best shared-out thing in the world', even 'naturally equal in all men'. Now 'sense' is a particularly good word to use for reason, both etymologically and semantically, as it incorporates both the senses, or the bodily 'extension' of reason, and the sentiments, in a unity of perception, intellect, and emotions. However, this is exactly how Descartes will *not* use reason in the *Discourse*, as reason there is exclusively identified with argumentative and analytical power. Second, good sense is indeed quite equally distributed among adults, in the sense that they are able to move and take care of themselves on their own. Even children have a certain good sense – though it relies more on emotions than on reasoning; and animals also conduct themselves by perceiving and judging what is around them, and what is going on in the environment. However – and here we stumble upon the problem of theatricality in the very first sentence of the work, if we read it for the second or third time and are not satisfied with our immediate impressions and understanding – as analytical reasoning power is one of the *least* equally distributed human faculty. This is what basically is identified today with IQ, and a good approximate measure of this is the speed by which one can resolve simple arithmetic operations.

This leads on to the great theatrical trick of Descartes, which we first must identify, and then assess its significance for his entire work – and the meaning, significance, and impact of this on the kind of rationalism he almost single-handedly inaugurated. As Descartes repeatedly claims that he is not really different from others, only one of those countless people with a good common sense, and thus what he is saying and doing could be done by everybody – indeed, he does no lay out a prescriptive rule, only indicates his ways, and others are free to follow in case they want to do so.

However, this simply could not be true. Descartes' work had momentous effects because it is the work of an extremely powerful mind; a mind that was recognised as such by his contemporaries. And not only that: there can be no question whatsoever that he was well aware of this, and since very early times. Descartes was educated by Jesuits, and Jesuit education was not only particularly thorough and rigorous, but also competitive. Arithmetic was a key subject matter already in medieval universities, and the speed by which one could solve simple arithmetical operations was a central way in which teachers in all times set up a ranking order among pupils. Descartes certainly knew that he was very special; a recognition which also had to be coloured through the meaning of his name ('René' means 're-born', or a bringer of novelty). Thus, under the cloak of an equally distributed good sense Descartes was literally smuggling in sheer reasoning power as the way for anyone and everyone to gain knowledge and understanding – something that before Descartes, and in fact actually always and everywhere, includes also much more subtle perceptions and judgments, involving emotions, aspirations, intuition, empathy, and a whole series of other features of the human soul that would be repeatedly and systematically ruled out of court for understanding by Comtean sociology and Kantian philosophy.

Advancing this as a warning and precaution, let us return and reconstruct the exact way of Descartes' proceeding.

The – false and theatrical – focus on the equality of reasoning power is made immediate use of at the end of the next, very long sentence, as there he claims that thus differences in opinions – which he considers as a main error, source of uncertainty – are solely due to the use of different ways to arrive at the truth. Truth, however, as he would repeatedly state, is only one; and so the use of different paths is the main source of erring. This defines the aim of his work: one must find and follow the right path. His only 'luck' (4), or reason for specialness, is that he somehow stumbled on the right path. This is his *Method*,[8] which allowed him to gain knowledge, and which he is now sharing with everyone, rendering his Method public.

Descartes introduces his Method by a series of qualifications that are both revealing and theatrical. These directly flow into his autobiographical background story which – even by the force of it – is again theatrical. He starts by adding an overarching historical characterisation to his general anthropological premise, and a quite startling one, both in itself and in contrast to his anthropology, as he regards 'the various activities and undertakings of mankind [...] all of them as pointless and useless'. As if to ease the drastic character of such wholesale dismissal, he intimates that he does not have a higher opinion of himself – except for his Method, which gave 'extremely satisf[ying]' results. It is with this double proviso that now he turns to his autobiographical account, with a single key point, repeated again and again, that in spite of being educated in most highly regarded places, his search for true knowledge was always frustrated, leading him to the inference that all such previous forms and modes of knowledge traditions should be discarded, as built on shaky foundations, and the search for knowledge should start again, based on his Method which he accidentally discovered.

The ensuing autobiographical reflections contain various details about his life, and also accounts about the reasons and modalities of his choices – which are revealing also in terms of the errors and shortcomings of his method, though rarely taken into account. Their most important aspect, however, concerns the manner in which the discovery of his Method is interwoven with the autobiographical narrative, as his account is given well after his Method was discovered, interpreting his whole life course in this light, but of course the discovery only took place at a certain moment, or even as a process in time, thus the question concerns the extent to which it is projected backwards, at the start of his 'quest'.

In this regard, the most revealing point is the motivation given for his long travels, and the eventual decision to leave his home country forever[9].

The first of this is presented as a pure exit, from the world of his studies, and also where he lived, but also an entry to the 'great book of the world' at large (4), which led him to the army. Such involvement with the world, however, was both very particular and limited (as much as being a soldier in a warfare goes), and short (as it basically ended with the famous stove-heated room and the discovery of the basic principles of his method; or which at least was assigned there by him).[10] This discovery led him to leave the army and turn to a quite different way of experiencing of the world:

> For the next nine years [implying 1619–28, according to Jonathan Bennett] I did nothing but roam [*rouler*] from place to place, trying to be a spectator rather than an actor in all the dramas that are played out on the world's stage.
> *(13)*

Or, his experiencing of the world no longer meant an involvement, even in the sense of the limited perspective of a soldier, but the purely theatrical perspective of the spectator – another key similarity to Renaissance Magi, here Giulio Camillo.

The Method

So, then, after all, what *was* this famous method that was to solve everything? In the Title, the Preface (to the Preface) and in the very first page of work Descartes makes it clear that the work is about the method, but he takes considerable time to actually describing it – no doubt as part of a rhetorical strategy. Thus, it is mentioned at the start of the first part of the Preface, but no details are given; it is alluded to again at the end of the first part; and then the second part starts by evoking the exact context of his discovery of his method, the stove-heated room in Germany, but details of the method are only offered several pages later. This is because the first part offers the broader autobiographical context which led him to his search, while the second part, before giving the details, first offers some further justification. He felt the need to justify profusely and in advance both the radicality of his approach, and its exact modality. Radicality means that everything in the search for knowledge must be started anew, fresh; that all intellectual traditions, approaches, books, simply must be thrown away, or that, metaphorically, the house must be destroyed, before being rebuilt; while its modality implies that this re-building must be done by one mind (17), alone (27), without any guide, as he could not find one, even without conversation partners, just searching out his own mind – or radicality as if taken to a second power. Note that while Descartes took over some elements from Plato (the indestructibility of the soul), or Aristotle (the desire to know), he rejected their foundational starting points: Plato's participation (*methexis*), just as Aristotle's claim of social being (*zoon politikon*). But his reliance on the conscious mind even reversed the etymological basis of the word, as *con-science* is from Latin *conscientia* 'a joint knowledge of something, a knowing of a thing together with another person'.

After giving all this background, leading the reader to his main points and trying to convince them in advance, Descartes finally offers the heart of this method, the four basic rules, result of a dream-inspired decision. The first is to accept as true only what is *evidently* so; second, whatever is more complex must be divided into as many parts as necessary; third, then must proceed from these simple parts in an orderly manner; and fourth, the process must be complete and comprehensive. Given that all of us, since almost four centuries, are now trained in Cartesian rationalism, these principles seem all but self-evident, just as Benjamin Franklin's maxim about time being money. However, from the vantage point of our present, out of the ruins of a world destroyed by Cartesian rationalism, we must try to understand – it is our *duty* – what is specific and wrong with these self-evident principles. And this can indeed be shown, without much difficulty.

To begin with, the first rule of Descartes, trivial though it might seem is by no means so, and actually gave quite a headache to Descartes as he himself realised in the *Discourse* that it is not so easy to specify, especially outside the realm of mathematics, what the 'evidence' of a truth means: 'this isn't as powerfully simple a rule as you might think, because there is some difficulty in telling which conceptions are really clear' (15). Significantly, he is piling up adjective upon each other, as if they would solve the problem, claiming that the 'evident' truth must be perceived clearly and distinctly (*clair et distinct*), which Bennett, with considerable ingenuity, is translating not as 'clear and distinct', rather as 'vividly and clearly'. But it does not change the fact that considering something as evident, clear, distinct, vivid, whatever, will always remain a *judgment*. And this remains true, even in our days, for any science: we are taught in schools what the *community* of relevant scientists (Thomas Kuhn) accepts as judged being true; many of these 'truths' are very far from being 'plain and evident'.

But here we are jumping ahead, as we are only at the first step of Descartes' four rules; and the second is made for those cases where such immediate, evident certainty cannot be applied. It is this second step which is the most important, the absolute core of the Cartesian method: whenever one encounters a difficulty, when in doubt, one must *divide* or *fragment*: 'divide each of the difficulties I examined into as many parts as possible' (9). This is the heart of Cartesian rationalism, indeed of scientific methodology: divide, fragment, breakdown, simplify, and *then* you might find a solution. And this is where the heart of the problem lies, including our current plight; this is where we must differ, object, and resist, explaining what is wrong with the second rule of Descartes – certainly as a general principle, but almost always, outside the limited realm of mathematics and elementary particles.

This is because division is *violent*. Dividing something, *anything*, takes away the concrete unity of the entity. It infringes intactness. Dividing an entity, breaking it into parts, means *breaking* it, or a modality of *destruction*. Here we return to the starting problem with Descartes's approach, which is to move away from any intellectual tradition. Descartes is supremely oblivious of the violence of his concrete procedure, as his entire stance is based on a previous destruction: ignoring tradition. Thus, one act of violence leads to another – and there is no end to it. Indeed, this is where we are – and I apologise for jumping forward again, but this occasionally must be done, to see where the argument is heading, to our present, as our world is being actively destroyed, not simply in the interest of some or other political or economic power or movement, but through Cartesian rationalism and 'its' science.

The situation is even worse, as the method of division *has* been used, and widely, in politics, as the famous *divide et impera* on which supposedly, since Julius Caesar, the rule of the Roman Empire was based. The politico-military sense of the principle is evident – the more you manage to divide your opponents, the easier it will be to defeat them.[11] The ultimate development was the salami tactics of Mao.

Such military logic has much to do with the 'Method' of Descartes, as he was a soldier, developed his method *when* a soldier, and perhaps even *as* a soldier. Furthermore, the basic principles of Dutch military discipline were developed by the philologist Justus Lipsius, using Roman military history. Thus, when Descartes pulled out of his mind the basic principles of the 'scientific' method, without guides and books, he made use of his immediate personal experience as a soldier involved with military tactics. Serres was dead right with his 'wolf of science' idea.

Still further, division as a mental operation is in radical contrast with proportionality. Here we go into the *difference* between two modes of mathematics – modern and classical. What we call as the operation of division, signalled by the two dots (:), for the Greek represented the setting up of a ratio (or analogy; Greek *logos* is much the same as Latin *ratio*). It did not imply the breaking of an entity into pieces, as it happens with our Cartesian mathematics, rather setting up harmonious proportionality. Here etymology and semantic history is again particularly interesting, as the original meaning of Latin *ratio* is proportion. Cartesian division infringes proportionality, thus strictly speaking Cartesian rationality promotes irrationality in the classical, Greco-Roman sense! This is no small matter – and, to increase perplexity, Descartes singles out proportionality for attention in the commentary to his rules. Thus, the Baconian-Cartesian call for a fresh start, ignoring the concreteness and history of words, produces immediate absurdity – with lasting effects up to our days.

Furthermore, anything divided is not the same as it was before, and so – apart from the problem of violence – it is problematic in a sheer epistemological sense. The idea that if you cannot know something clearly and evidently, you must divide it, simply makes no sense, as if you divide it, *it will no longer be the same thing*, so whatever will be gained in terms of knowledge, will be the knowledge of *something else* – reinforcing the Baconian focus on (alchemical) transformativity.

Thus, apart from empire-building politics and military tactics, the historical precedent of the method of division is the alchemical method, which takes off from metallurgy, and which is based on the idea that in order to create something new, one must destroy, which in metallurgy, the original source model of alchemy, meant that in order to gain metals first the solidity of the rock must be destroyed (Horvath 2021). The method of division was discussed, ironically and as a problem, by Plato in the *Sophist*; though this then, read as being programmatic, was central for the long-standing distortion of his ideas, leading to the affinity between Neoplatonists and Gnostics. Descartes' philosophy is not only the ultimate expression of settlement, thinking for himself closed into a single room, and military conquest, but also of mechanised industrialism.

So, what else could be done, instead of 'division'? This book is devoted to explore such possibilities. Provisionally, one can suggest a look at the matter from a different angle, keeping the intactness of the entities involved; consult other sources; bring in further evidence, talk to people; look for good guides – all possibilities that perhaps were not available to Descartes, in the overall madness of the early 17th century[12] – or he simply did not think about them, overcharging his mind with thinking it all for himself.

Let's return to the path taken by Descartes and trying to understand it, even if we now know that his first rule, far from being self-evident about what is evident, is rather problematic, while his second rule is worse than being false. The third rule, at a first look, seems less problematic, as it merely says that once the elementary and evident parts were identified, thinking should move upward, and in an orderly manner. However, apart from the fact that the real world should not have been broken down into such elements in the first instance, there are two further and quite grave problems with this procedure. Both are concerned with what is meant by 'orderly'. One is that Descartes implies straight line proceeding: first, by dividing things into ever smaller elements; and second, then gradually and increasingly move upward. However, understanding simply cannot move in such mechanical manner. Descartes' mechanical movements can be contrasted with the way a painter is working, according to Foucault, moving continuously back and forth with respect to his image, now moving closer, adding some details, then moving away, so that he could contemplate how the image hangs together. *This* proceeding is indeed natural and rational at the same time, also close to Elias's rhythm of 'involvement and detachment', and can be safely generalised – not as a mechanically universal procedure, but as a rule of thumb. Which leads us to the second major problem, already implied in mechanisation: Descartes not only means orderly in the sense of a straight line, moving ever upward, but also that his rules and at every step must be followed *rigidly*.

This is not an unfair interpretation of his ideas, but is fully conform to his words and spirit. For Descartes, just as for Bacon, the human mind cannot be entrusted to follow its own ways, left to its idiosyncratic erring. It must be *forced* to follow the *one and only* right path; the path of orderly, methodical rigour: 'the Method – *my* method [...] tells us to follow the correct order, and to enumerate exactly all the relevant factors' (Descartes, 10); and he did as he stated, 'constantly employing the Method I had imposed on myself' (10).

The fourth principle adds little new or interesting, as it merely states that the procedure must be complete and comprehensive.

These simple rules, performed with persistence, produce stunning results, according to Descartes,[13] as his method 'contains everything that gives certainty to the rules of arithmetic'; and not only – as his method can be applied 'to the problems of the other sciences as usefully as I had to those of algebra', even offering 'some certain principles in philosophy', which 'is the most important thing in the world' (10).

The proof of the rightness of a method is the results it produces. Descartes' method has proven himself in mathematics, as he is the founder of algebraic geometry, while the book to which the *Discourse* was a preface contained his discoveries in Geometry, Meteorology, and Optics – incidentally, three fields resuming the experiences of a non-participatory traveller. His most famous philosophical discovery, however, is contained in this same Preface, and contained in his famous words 'I think therefore I am'.

For this book, two points need to be mentioned.[14] The first is the starting point of the meditation process that led to the famous claim. In addition of his previous ideas, the break with tradition in thinking and living and the four so problematic rules, Descartes offers a further radical novelty in the form of a *reversal* of the procedure of practical life: instead of acting on the basis of principles that were uncertain, yet accepted provisionally as true, 'to do the exact opposite – to reject as if it were absolutely false everything regarding which I could imagine the least doubt' (14). This implies radically doubting everything that were perceived by the senses, and also every argument formulated by others – as prelude to gain absolute certainty. The mentality is alchemic. The second point, already alluded in the sentence quoted above, is the primacy accorded to radical doubt as the start of the true path towards absolute certainty concerning truth. Descartes discovered his famous maxim 'I think therefore I am' by starting on a path of doubting, rather than thinking, so the statement strictly speaking is wrong, as it should rather be 'I doubt therefore I am'. The difference is not negligible, as when we think we always think of or about *something*: a person or an object, an event or a claim, or try to understand an aspect of reality that presented itself to or inside our life. This might be due to all kinds of reasons. Doubting is something completely different; it is a temporary stop and suspension; a dislocation from views or certainties previously held, and with some evident reason – as we do not have doubts concerning things or people we do not know (we might be suspicious, but that is something different). A doubt involves a loss; it is a pain; it is not really an inspiration for thinking as such, as of reassessment and healing. Thus, to project doubting into a basic principle of method is worse than meaningless; it is self-defeating. Even he, just in the preceding page, expressed reservations about the sceptics 'who doubt purely for the sake of doubting' (13). One might say that Descartes was doubting for the sake of certainty, but it does not alter the fact that he was using doubting as a generalised procedure, and that this is a more than questionable idea.

Such extolling and glorification of doubting can only be compared to Kant's obsession with critique, which again seems to offer a perfect, unshakeable foundation, as whoever criticises a critique is also engaged in nothing else but a critique, thus a critical philosophy seems to lie beyond critique – except, as Tom Boland (2019) has argued, this does not leave us with a sound truth, only a paradox worthy the Cretan liar.

Descartes's doubt and Kant's critique – one cannot even imagine a worse philosophy for life and living.

Conclusion

> From the very beginning of the industrial revolution [Belial] foresaw that men would be made so overwhelmingly bumptious by the miracles of their own technology that they would soon lose all sense of reality. And that's precisely what happened. These wretched slaves of wheels and ledgers began to congratulate themselves on being the Conquerors of Nature. Conquerors of Nature, indeed! In actual fact, of course, they had merely upset the equilibrium of Nature and were about to suffer the consequences.
>
> *Aldous Huxley,* Ape and Essence, *93*

This was the 'rational' 'Method' Descartes discovered, on the basis of a self-analysis (self as *space* and not as substance); and which he offered, as a 'free gift', to the world at large (see Argyrou (2013) about modern thought as gift), added to the similar 'gifts' of Bacon. We now know, and have to understand living in a world thoroughly dominated by this (instrumental) rationality, presumed 'conquerors of nature' (see Huxley), that this gift was highly poisonous. In order to understand this, his supposedly universal method must be situated on its proper context.

The most important feature of this context, both in terms of time and place, was its extreme liminality, to be discussed in the next chapter.

Notes

1 I will use the text translated by Jonathan Bennett (https://www.earlymoderntexts.com/assets/pdfs/bacon1620.pdf, accessed 15 September 2021).
2 Wittgenstein's critique of Viennese analytical philosophy starts right at this point.
3 Bacon's closest follower is Durkheim, for whom 'social facts' are reducible to 'external constraints'.
4 See also Rossi (1968) who offers a series of arguments about Bacon's serious interest in magic and alchemy. Giving only some examples: 'I do not think it is possible to find in Bacon either an explicit or an implicit espousal of these mystical aspects of alchemical tradition, but the influence of the hermetic doctrine of the transmutation of metals is clear. [...] To free a metal from these impurities is tantamount to making it perfect. [...] Bacon's vocabulary bears the distinctive mark of this tradition: he speaks of the assimilation, nourishment, generation, and irritation of substances in the process of conservation or mutation; he makes frequent use of the term fixation with its traditional alchemical connotations. These linguistic affinities reflect an ingrained affinity of

outlook, especially pronounced where Bacon's physics is concerned' (13–4). 'Fixing' is a standard feature of the trickster in the anthropological literature, and other main features of the trickster, stealing and cunning are not missing either: 'We have already seen that the metaphysical aspects of magic and alchemy had little or no influence on Bacon; but he did borrow from this tradition the idea of science as the servant of nature assisting its operations and, by stealth and cunning, forcing it to yield to man's domination; as well as the idea of knowledge as power' (21).

5 It defies belief that in the HR exercises that groomed academic life in most Western countries over the last decades it was formally prohibited to use the word 'understanding' in descriptions of 'course outcomes'. The term was considered too 'vague', so lecturers were required to specify the exact 'skills' student were supposed to gain.

6 I will again use the text translated by Jonathan Bennett (https://www.earlymoderntexts.com/assets/pdfs/descartes1637.pdf, accessed 27 December 2021).

7 About this, see Serres (1982). Theatrical metaphors were also central for Kant, and similarly most problematic, as it is pointed out by Ingold (2010b: S123).

8 'Method' is *always* capitalised by Descartes, in its many uses; and very few other words are. Thus, for e.g., 'religion' or 'state' sometimes is, sometimes isn't.

9 Note the schismogenic complementarity of the lives of Descartes and Kant, the two founders of modern rationalism: one who never left his hometown, and another who roamed all his life. No rhythm between involvement and detachment, intimate participation and dislocating experiences.

10 Note again the importance of walls for the 'scientific method', instead of walking. Note also that his two references to walking are both taken in the very same spirit, and *against* the true spirit of walking: in the first occasion the metaphor of 'walking alone in the dark' is used to illustrate the lonely and isolated character of his work (8); while in the other the metaphor is 'keep walking as straight as [one] can in one direction' (10–1), thus in the sense of strict and mechanical linearity, in contrast to the lineal, as discussed by Tim Ingold (2007).

11 Note that war has no meaning whatsoever, it is purely driven by trickster logic (see Szakolczai 2022).

12 This is captured particularly well by Huxley (1971, 1982), who was not just a novelist turned historian, but one who – just like Bateson – was literally born into a family of scientists.

13 The real problem is that, in a way, he is right. *Any* training of the mind produces certain educational results. If a university course would do nothing but force its students to memorise the phone book of New York City, their mind would be 'trained' by it. This is why ascetic techniques always 'work' – at the price of giving up the chance of living one's own life. Just as rigid team discipline always 'works' – with Roman legions, just as in modern football.

14 For an important commentary, see Elias on *homo clausus*, in the 1968 Introduction to the *Civilizing Process*.

5
SOME MATTERS OF HISTORICAL CONTEXT

> She did not once show me any change in herself. What she always had been to me, she still was; wholly unaltered
>
> Charles Dickens, David Copperfield, 728

> It was a fundamental principle of the Gradgrind philosophy that everything was to be paid for. Nobody was ever on any account to give anybody anything, or render anybody help without purchase. Gratitude was to be abolished, and the virtues springing from it were not to be. Every inch of the existence of mankind, from birth to death, was to be a bargain across a counter. And if we didn't get to Heaven that way, it was not a politico-economical place, and we had no business there.
>
> Charles Dickens, Hard Times, 282

> The earth was made for Dombey and Son to trade in, and the sun and moon were made to give them light. Rivers and seas were formed to float their ships; rainbows gave them promise of fair weather; winds blew for or against their enterprises; stars and planets circled in their orbits, to preserve inviolate a system of which they were the centre. Common abbreviations took new meanings in his eyes, and had sole reference to them. A. D. had no concern with Anno Domini, but stood for anno Dombei – and Son.
>
> Charles Dickens, Dombey and Son, 2

Introduction: The liminality of the early 17th century

Francis Bacon and René Descartes were, without any doubts, fountainheads of the modern rationalistic scientific method. This, also unquestionably, was due not only to the character of their persons and works, but the time in which we lived. We need to move beyond trivialities, and be as precise as possible. Their times was certainly liminal: end of the Renaissance, even of the medieval European world order, and the cusp of early modernity; but this particular situation not just

DOI: 10.4324/9781003275138-7

stimulated their work, but also left a mark on it, which therefore was not simply the 'discovery' of the basic principles of scientific investigation and modern rationality: rather it was *this* peculiar liminality that they fixated as *the* road to 'knowledge'.

This idea, formulated by Agnes Horvath in 2013 by bringing together of Newton and Callot, and reasserted in her 2021 book, has astonishing radicality and far-reaching implications. It goes into the heart of Newton's ideas about the 'flux' and the 'void', as it renders evident and visible, recalling Nietzsche's famous quip about the abyss, that a science which pretends to start from an original chaos, the flux in the void, cannot help but return our world into this chaos, which is currently being done, in the name of science, technology, and progress; and which simply must be stopped, before too late.[1]

The remaining part of the chapter, in line with the scope of this book, will only discuss two aspects of this enormous and most significant issue. First, by using Frances Yates as our guide, it reconstructs the manner in which modern science grew out of certain currents of the Renaissance. Then, and using Joyce Appleby as our guide, it will show, complementing the works of Yates, how the concerns around the rise of the modern economy rhymed with these developments in science, moving outside inane and self-destructive modernist-progressivist accounts. Their analyses should be further complemented by and integrated with the similarly minded works of Toulmin, Foucault, Voegelin, Agnew, and many others, but this cannot be attempted here.

Frances Yates: The birth of the scientific method out of the spirit of Renaissance Hermeticism

> what does all science in general mean considered as a symptom of life? What is the point of all that science and, even more seriously, where did it come from?
>
> Friedrich Nietzsche, The Birth of Tragedy, *Preface*

Frances Yates's work is animated by a perception that seems outdated, but actually is *not*: that modern science, with its rationalism and method, is the eventual outgrowth and successful carrier of old Renaissance hopes about a coming new Golden Age.[2] The idea, taken at face value, is certainly not just naïve but dangerous in our days, as such belief is refuted, and revealed as a dangerous ideology, helped certain vested interests, increasingly every day. But Yates is well aware of the problems, as rendered evident at the start of her 1974 Introduction to the *Rosicrucian Enlightenment*. She evokes a 'profound dissatisfaction with the world of today', felt by many, rooted in a 'distrust in science', based on the recognition that instead of being liberated and empowered, one 'has become imprisoned in technologies, reduced in status as a human being, enslaved by unforeseen results of applied science' (Yates 1975a: 11). Her point is thus that the old, trivial illuminist claim is a double-edged sword, as it can be read in a quite different way: not in the sense that modern science and technology actually fulfils such hopes and prepares for all of us a genuine Golden Age, but that its adherents and protagonists are indeed *animated* by such beliefs. If accent is placed there, then the further question concerns the Renaissance precedents of scientific rationalism and method that made it possible. This leads into all but unchartered territory, as it renders evident the direct, vital, enabling connections between the modern scientist and the Renaissance magi, the obscure backwaters out of which modern scientific rationalism emerged.[3]

A particularly clear formulation of this central aim of her project can be found in the same Introduction. There she continues after the passage quoted above by claiming that while contemporary interest in esoteric religion – in our days called 'new age' – is formulated in contrast to modern rationalism and science,

> the scientific advances of the Renaissance and early modern period arose in the context of a tremendous movement of religious interest in the world of nature as a manifestation of the divine, a movement in which influences which today would be labelled 'Hermetic' or 'esoteric' played a part
>
> Yates 1975a: 11.

Thus, instead of the previous, 'rigorous separation' (11) between scientific and non-scientific, 'the Hermetic tradition touches the rise of science' (14). This Hermetic philosophy, integrated to Neoplatonism, was 'a kind of religious cult of nature, implying religious practices', which 'encouraged the turning towards the world, and the investigations of secrets, as a kind of religious duty' (14). However, as these passages already indicate, this did not imply a respect for nature, nor a way to familiarise oneself with the world in order to discover its manifold beauties and prevent one's own imprisoning into oneself, as argued by St Bonaventure. Quite on the contrary, it implied a divinisation of man 'as the great miracle', an exhortation of its powers and the call for using them, 'plac[ing] man in a dominating position, a being able to operate on nature and bend her to his will', resumed in the call for 'the domination of nature'. This vision of man as 'operating through his magical knowledge paved the way for man as a great miracle, able to operate through scientific knowledge'. Thus, '[t]he Renaissance magus is the immediate ancestor of the seventeenth-century religious scientist' – a clear allusion to Isaac Newton. Indeed, the central, obsessive aim of Renaissance magi is the same as of the modern, technological scientist, including the social and the political sciences: it is the 'power to control' (16) – the only difference being whether it means to canalise the influences from planets, angels, or electromagnetic radiation. Within the (later) Renaissance, this Hermetic philosophy, which incorporated alchemy, Cabala, and elements of Gnosticism, gained a dominant position even over Renaissance Neoplatonism (17), and was centrally concerned with 'the transformation of substances as a whole' as a 'scientific problem' (16), 'turned men's minds in the direction out of which the scientific revolution was to come' (17). In this last phrase, two points are worth attention: that this sentence, written by the way by a woman, is indeed not gender neutral, as Renaissance magi were without exception *men* – trying to gain power over Nature which in most linguistic traditions is *female*; and that the central issue was influencing *minds*, by a new *orientation* in and towards the 'world' – ignoring 'home'. While 'we' tend to consider Renaissance magi as obscure figures representing a minor episode in intellectual history, this is by no means the case: 'This was the tradition which broke down Aristotle in the name of a unified universe through which ran one law, the law of magical animism. This was the tradition which prepared the way for the seventeenth-century triumph' (18) of science.

This tradition, this outlook, this mentality represents a fundamental change both with respect to classical Antiquity and medieval Christianity. The Renaissance is usually considered as a revitalisation of the classical Greek spirit. Yet, if we consider the Renaissance magi and their Hermetic philosophy, *the* direct source of modern rationalist methodology and science, this does not stand. Classical Greece certainly broke new ground in art, architecture, mathematics, law, and science. Yet, 'they never took whole-heartedly, with all their powers, the momentous step which western man took at the beginning of the modern period of crossing the bridge between the theoretical and the practical, of going all out to apply knowledge to produce operations' (Yates 1964: 155). The reason, according to Yates, was 'a matter of the will. Fundamentally, the Greeks did not *want* to operate' (*sic*; 155). The same applies to the Middle Ages, when it was considered that 'any wish to operate can only be inspired by the devil' (156) – such operations (meaning: acts to control and even alter nature) were not dignified for man to make and were also contrary to the Will of God. Thus, beyond the question of a direct descendance of modern science and methodology from Renaissance alchemy and magic – which in itself is not an unimportant matter –

> the real function of the Renaissance Magus in relation to the modern period (or so I see it) is that he changed the will. It was now dignified and important for man to operate [...] It was this basic psychological reorientation towards a direction of the will, which was neither Greek nor mediaeval in spirit, which made all the difference
>
> *(156)*

This Hermetic tradition, in which Neoplatonism, Gnosticism, alchemy, magic, and Cabala all played their contributing role, gained in this period a 'glorious ascendance over the mind of western man', and eventually also 'a strangely important role in the shaping of human destiny' (156).

The character of this new outlook is formulated with particular clarity and force at the start of the same crucial chapter in her pathbreaking book about Bruno from which the previous citations were taken, offering a contrast between the world-picture of Renaissance magi and the medieval world picture. There she states that the novelty lies in nothing less than a new vision of Man and his place in the universe:

> What has changed is Man, now no longer the pious spectator of God's wonders in the creation, and the worshipper of God himself above the creation, but man the operator, Man who seeks to draw power from the divine and natural order.
>
> *(144)*

Here again, and in line with the significant methodological reorientation she takes up from Aby Warburg and his classical school, especially Edgar Wind, she illustrates the point by a monkey man image, so striking in a number of ways, from a work by Fludd (facing page 275). The image, entitled 'Nature and Art', shows a circular design, recalling jointly Leonardo and Camillo, representing the entire cosmos, including the spheres of the planets, the zodiac, and the elements, listing minerals, vegetables, and animals. The centre is the Earth, on which sits a monkey-shaped man, 'or rather Man's Art by which he imitates Nature, with simian mimicry. Man here seems to have lost some of his Dignity, but he has gained in power' (144–5).

The question, at this point, concerns where this new outlook, dominated by a new will-power, came from, and how could it become so successful.

Concerning the direct source, the evidence is clear, but its interpretation most complex, as it has to do with the very meaning of the 'Renaissance'. In the medieval period, much due to the schism between Eastern and Western Christianity, in the West, knowledge of Greek became lost. A central concern of Renaissance humanism, identified with Petrarch, was its recuperation, but this turned out to be a difficult undertaking. Eventually, on the advice of Gemistos Plethon, Cosimo Medici selected Marsilio Ficino to be educated from a young age for the task, but then Ficino was instructed by John Argyropoulos to translate Hermes Trismegistos, before turning to Plato. The consequence of this interference in 'Western' intellectual matters by political authorities (Cosimo) and Byzantine magi (court Sophists, not genuine philosophers) was a hopeless intermingling of Plato and the Hermetic tradition in Renaissance philosophy. This had the crucial effect of lifting the medieval ban on magic, Gnosticism, alchemy, and related thinking, thus rendering this underground tradition, anathema both in classical Antiquity and the Middle Ages, acceptable, eventually producing, *inside Western Christian culture*, modern rationalism, scientific methodology, and technologised science.

A central aspect of this new, 'scientific' outlook concerned 'methodology'. Such concern with method was not an aspect of Plato's or even Aristotle's philosophy, rather emerged in the Second Sophistic, with Hermogenes, source of the overriding modern obsession with methodology and hypothesis-testing.

Here a crucial role was played by the classical art of memory. This art, to be traced back to the poet Simonides, himself connected to the Sophists in many ways, was created to complement and help the natural memory powers of humans, supposedly too weak in themselves, by memorising an artificial image-schema, to which then words could be attached in order to remember them better. The idea is based on the recognition that memory works on two-dimensional images, thus images are remembered better than words, which is indeed true – all powerful tricks have an element of truth behind. However, here again, the tradition was explicitly opposed by both Plato and Aristotle, on grounds that an artificial interference with the way human memory works creates more harm than good. Thus for Plato, as discussed in the *Theaetetus* (191C-D), memory is a *gift*, consisting of imprints made on the soul, and so '[t]rue knowledge consists in fitting the imprints from sense impressions on to the mould or imprint of the higher reality of which the things below are reflections' (1992: 50). Thus rhetorics, as argued in *Phaedrus*, is not an art of persuasion, rather 'an art of speaking the truth and of persuading hearers to the truth', a power which depends on the knowledge of the soul and *its* knowledge, all of which is based on genuine, gift-like memory. Thus, 'from Plato's view, the artificial memory as used by a sophist [is] anathema, a desecration of memory', as 'Platonic memory would have to be organised, not in the trivial manner of such mnemotechnics, but in relation to the realities' (51). All this has a vital link to Plato's general attitude to the Sophists, as Plato's satire on the sophists, including their use of etymologies, could be explained from here (51), and even the main source of Plato's strong objections to the Sophist educational system might have been its use of a 'superficial memorisation of quantities of miscellaneous information' (45). The views of Aristotle are similar, as he warned against the excessive uses of artificial memory (46), and while medieval scholastics used his works for justifying artificial memory exercises, it is 'very doubtful whether this is what Aristotle meant' (49). This position was upheld in the medieval period, and artificial memory constructions again only became popular through the influx of manuscripts and ideas from the Byzantine world, after the sack of Constantinople. Foremost of these was the memory theatre of Giulio Camillo, which also had its share in the new interest in theatre, spreading from Venice.

The third major source of scientific methodology was not in the East, the Byzantium, but in the West, in Spain. The central figure here was Ramon Lull, who integrated aspects of the then emerging Lurian Cabala into his combinations of numbers and names. Lull's ideas were different both from classical rhetorics and medieval scholasticism in three respects. The first is their Neoplatonic and Cabalist focus on divine names. Second, this was combined by Lull's 'effort to excite memory by emotional and dramatic corporal similitudes' (Yates 1992: 177), or a play with 'sensuals' (Agnes Horvath), which on the one hand generated a 'fruitful interaction between the art of memory and the visual arts, and on the other, by designating concepts through letter notation 'introduce[d] an almost algebraic or scientifically abstract note into Lullism' (177). However, the third and 'probably the most significant aspect of Lullism' was that the figures used in his letter notation were 'not static but revolving' (178). While his devices were simple, they were 'revolutionary in their attempt to represent movement in the psyche' (178). Today it needs to be added that all this anticipated contemporary mind control.

Lull was also a pioneer in developing the classical theory of elements towards an 'astral science', by directing astrology into an 'astral medicine through calculating' (1979: 12). Lull turned such calculations and letter manipulations into a 'rigorous method' which would have 'an immense influence throughout Europe for centuries', and so Lullism can be considered as 'a precursor of the scientific method' (16). Apart from Cabala, Lullism also had close affinities with alchemy, as works attributed to Lull that 'added to his reputation' were 'the pseudo-Lullian alchemic works' (1992: 190).

The classical art of memory (in an occultised version) and Lullism became integrated into Renaissance Hermeticism. This was done by a central figure of this tradition, Giordano Bruno, as the art of memory was 'at the very centre of [his] life and death' (199).

Bruno added two new aspects to previous concerns with art of memory as method, with huge historical significance. First, based on misunderstanding a passage in Aristotle, Bruno came to identify thinking with speculating with images, which then became a major source of his magnifying interest in the creative and imaginative powers of the intellect (1992: 289–90). The second was a 'pathological element' of Bruno's work and personality, 'the compulsion for system-forming which is one of Bruno's leading characteristics' (296). Yet, this 'madness' at the same time was the source of 'an intense striving after method', which 'can only be described as a scientific element, a presage on the occult plane of the preoccupation with method of the next century' (296–7). As she would restate in her follow-up work, with another metaphor for liminality, the 'Renaissance was a borderland country, half magic, half emerging science' (1969: 31), combining in one tradition the mystical-magical (Hermetic) and scientific-technological (Vitruvius), and where stage producers, with their use of theatrical machinery, 'were the technicians in an age in which science was emerging from magic' (32).[4]

Thus, Bruno's work has triple relevance, being at the origin of three major preoccupations: the obsession with secret societies (which, to be noted immediately, would always develop in close connection with the public sphere; see Koselleck); the concern with artistic and imaginative powers; and most importantly 'the growth of scientific method' (1992: 297).

A further step towards scientific methodology concerns a slightly older contemporary of Bruno, Petrus Ramus. The approach of Ramus was quite different from Bruno's – Bruno considered him a worse pedant – as Ramus discarded not only the occult aspects of Renaissance Hermeticism but also the art of memory. Yet, and following Melanchton, Ramus was also interested in memorising as an aspect of the Protestant educational reform he promoted, and even further, 'by absorbing memory into logic, Ramus identified the problem of method with that of memory' (1992: 229; Yates here follows Paolo Rossi). Ramus was close to Bruno and Lull in his staunch opposition to Aristotle, while elements of his method closely recall Lull: '[t]he arbitrary manner in which Ramism imposes its "dialectical order" on every branch of knowledge is strongly reminiscent of Lullism' (234). Furthermore, both Camillo's 'memory theatre' and Ramus's method are part of a revival of interest in Hermogenes (235, 419, fn.5; here Yates leans on Walter Ong).

Yates resumes related concerns with the sources of scientific methodology in the concluding chapter, entitled 'The art of memory and the growth of the scientific method'. Her central claim is that while the art of memory was shunned by classical philosophy and so was not important in the humanist part of the Renaissance tradition, it was central for the Hermetic philosophy that became dominant in the late 15th century, after 1453 and 1492, and that it was *this* tradition that, in a transformed manner, gave birth to the scientific method. Bacon, Mersenne, Descartes and Leibniz were explicitly and with a good reason hostile to this tradition, and yet, Yates makes it evident that their work is a direct continuation of the spirit and in several ways even the concrete substance of late Renaissance Hermeticism. Thus, in the 17th century

> the art of memory underwent yet another of its transformations, turning from a method of memorizing the encyclopaedia of knowledge, of reflecting the world in memory, to an aid for investigating the encyclopaedia and the world with the object of discovering new knowledge.
>
> (355)

The question now concerns the exact character of the stamp left by the late Renaissance Hermetic philosophy on the *orientation* and *world view* of modern scientific rationalism and methodology.

The concluding chapter by Yates contains five main points relevant in this regard. The first concerns the very word 'method', a term popularised by Ramus, but also used by Lullism, Cabalism, and Bruno. Yates gives an account of a 1632 meeting of a private academy in Paris, which for its inaugural meeting selected as their theme 'method'. The meeting first discussed, shortly, 'the "method of the Cabbalists" ', then 'the "method of Ramon Lull" ', and spent much of its time by discussing ' "the method of ordinary philosophy" '. These discussions were summed up in a publication entitled ' "*De la méthode*" ' (356), preparing, comments Yates, the publication five years later of Descartes' *Discourse*.

Second, Bacon was not just aware of the art of memory, but used it in his proposal for educational reform, trying to turn it towards 'useful purposes' (357). He even had an interest in the use of 'the "force of the imagination" ', and of gaining power 'through stirring the imagination', illustrating this by a commentary on a story about a card trick (359). Third, the same is true for Descartes, who shifted the focus from the power of imagination to ' "the reduction of things to their first causes" ' (360), Yates adding that '[c]uriously enough, Descartes's suggested reform of memory is nearer to "occult" principles than Bacon's, for occult memory does reduce all things to their supposed causes whose images when impressed on memory are believed to organize the subsidiary images', and thus 'his brilliant new idea of organizing memory on causes sounds curiously like a rationalization of occult memory' (360).

Fourth, Baconian and Cartesian method also have affinities with the work of Lull, as not only did Bacon and Descartes knew about Lull, but their very aims shared a common purpose: they 'promised to provide a universal art or method which, because based on reality, could be applied for the solution of all problems' (361). The great difference with Descartes was that instead of using numbers, he used quantities and calculus to establish a new science, or the 'mathematical method'. However, as Yates kept repeating, mathematics at that time was very much considered as a rather obscure and even occult science, with the great Renaissance magus John Dee writing a Preface to Euclid and mathematics, and one of the main reasons Mersenne and Descartes were so hostile to the Rosicrucians, hiding the commonality of their undertaking, was to avoid suspicions about their interests in mathematics.

Finally, and much connected to this point, Yates discusses the invention of infinitesimal calculus by Leibniz, attributing it to his use of the art of memory. Thus, in his 1667 book on 'New Method' Leibniz discusses the art of memory together with methodology and logics as the three connected modes of making proper arguments (366). Yates concludes the chapter by alluding back to the works of John Dee, Ramon Lull and Giordano Bruno, with their searches for the Great Key being so similar to the 'true *Clavis*' which Leibniz claimed to have found (370–1). Thus, concludes Yates,

> looking back now from the vantage point of Leibniz we may see Giordano Bruno as a Renaissance prophet, on the Hermetic plane, of scientific method, and a prophet who shows us the importance of the classical art of memory, combined with Lullism, in preparing the way for the finding of a Great Key.
> *(372)*

The rise of the scientific method and modern science, a connection that itself cannot be taken for granted and merits further studies, was entangled, in the crucial *Sattelzeit* (Koselleck) of the decades around the year 1600, with a series of further developments, some of which were discussed by Yates, but which also require further guides. These include the rise of the modern theatre, with the work of its main protagonists, Marlowe and Shakespeare falling in between 1587 and 1613; the rise of the modern state, with the main books about reason of state being written in between 1589 and 1613; the rise of the modern economy, with the pioneering French Huguenot works being written in between 1598 and 1615; and the joint rise of modern secret societies and the public sphere, where a central role was played by the Rosicrucian manifestos, written in between 1614 and 1617, culminating in the French Rosicrucian scare in 1623, directly leading to the witch-hunt craze.

The perhaps most evident, but also most problematic, such connection is between science with universalistic pretentions and the imperial idea. The character of such universalism was already evoked above, in the astrological-astronomical-alchemical pretence of a non-Aristotelian, non-geocentric science, which in the name of a unified universe systematically and programmatical ignored the difference between human nature, nature on Earth that has been bequeathed on us as a result of very long processes, the features of other planets and stars, and any possible combination of the elements that can be produced by knowledge. It should be noted here that one of the central disciplines of such a universalising science, geometry, a discovery of classical Greece whose modern synthesis with mathematical calculus was pioneered by Descartes in the very work of which the *Discourse on Method* was the Preface, literally means the measure (*metros*) of the Earth (*geos*), while universalising science not only ignores such measure, but explicitly strives to downgrade the Earth. Such universalisation rhymes well with the imperial idea, formulated in the 16th century as an imperial hope, which is similarly universal, and also fluid – another key word in the terminology of scientism (Yates 1975b: 1).

The close interlacing of the rise of scientific methodology and English imperialism is one of the most important discoveries of Yates, though in properly interpreting it we must move beyond her words. The new importance attributed to geometry and astronomy was much connected to the great maritime expeditions of the times (Yates 1969: 7; 1975b: 48), where just in the late 16th century focus shifted from the Iberian Peninsula to the British Islands. The activities of John Dee, one of the most influential Renaissance magus and Christian Cabalist (Yates 1979: 92–110), who was equally interested in the evocation of demons and angels and in mathematics, can be connected to that Elizabethan moment. In spite of such distinctly non-modern affiliations, his learning was also of a modern kind, with its emphasis on mathematics and technological developments, and it made him equally attractive, for a time, to the Queen and his courtiers and the new emerging social classes, connected to exchange and money-making (Yates 1969: 7–8).

The connection between England's new imperial ambitions and the rise of modern science out of Renaissance occult was for a long time central to Yates's interest, but received a definite formulation only in her 1975 book *Astraea*. For us moderns, just as for St Augustine, secular imperial ambition had an unambiguously negative value, but the like ambitions of England in the Elizabethan period, at least aspirationally, were not secular. In the 16th century England was still a relatively marginal area in Europe, just as it was in the Middle Ages, but the Elizabethan Renaissance, which took place when Italy was already well advanced into the Baroque, not only imitated the Italian Renaissance with a delay, but also took over its main ambitions. Prominent among this was the stance against tyranny, which in the period was not associated with Republicanism, as in Florence, but implied an exhortation against the Empire of Charles V, which united through marriages Austria, Spain, and the Netherlands, accumulating a large realm that had no equal since Charlemagne, and becoming central for the Counter-Reformation, perceived in the Protestant areas as the threat of a new tyranny. It was this threat against which the rising British Empire, in the vision of Renaissance artists and magi, represented at the same time the reassertion of the Holy Empire and the promise of a Golden Age. Science, by promoting useful knowledge, helping technological innovations which occasionally were not shying away from using magic, was supposed to help such aims and thus gained respectability beyond medieval bans against magic and the manipulation of nature, but also usury and theatre.

A crucial role, of revealing importance, was played here by a new vision of the Holy Empire. After the collapse of the Western Roman Empire the institutional structures of the Empire and the city-based civilisation, securing a degree of return to normality, were carried by the Church, led by the Pope and the bishops. In the East, however, the Byzantine Empire survived, and there the Emperor, since Constantine, played a vital role in ecclesiastic matters as well. Stable secular rule was only secured in the West with Charlemagne, whose kingdom however became divided among his heirs, eventually giving rise to the idea of reuniting these territories under the form of the Holy (Roman) Empire. This entity never became a genuine Empire, but played a major symbolic role in the medieval period, and the antagonism between popes and emperors which traversed the medieval period was important due to such symbolical significance. Some main centres of the Holy Empire, like Burgundy, Prague, and Vienna, always had close links to Byzantium.

The Reformation radically rearranged this scenery, as most of the areas associated with the Holy Empire (Italy, Western France, Southern Germany and Austria) became the core areas of the Counter-Reformation, thus closely allied themselves with the Papacy. It was in contrast to this situation that the idea of a Holy Empire was revived, with a strong anti-Pope and anti-Rome bias, in Elizabethan England, and where in the Jacobean period a temporary and rather aspirational alliance developed between London and Prague, which furthermore received a strong Byzantine flavour. It is from this perspective that the role played by Renaissance magi in Elizabethan England becomes particularly important; a link between politics and science that would return with the Royal Society.

With the reassertion of Protestantism after the coronation of Elizabeth, Anglican theologians, in prominent works (Jewel, Foxe), were not only using any Catholic writer who ever criticised the Pope, but 'drew many of their arguments from the Greek, rather than from the Latin, fathers' (1975b: 41), using not only the history of the Eastern Church, but also of the Empire, with a special emphasis on the figure of Constantine, who shifted the centre of the Empire from Rome to Byzantium. Images, especially in such contexts, have as much power as words, and in Foxe's famous *Book of Martyrs*, in the opening sentence of his dedication to the Queen, with which the book effectively starts, '[t]he capital C of Constantine encloses a portrait of the queen', trampling on the pope (43). The image, according to Yates, is 'the climax of the whole book', representing 'the return to the Constantinian, imperial Christianity' (44), a prelude to Puritan eschatological hopes.

These ideas and hopes return in a prominent and influential way in the works of John Dee. Dee wrote a series of works in support of Elizabethan imperialism, of which only one got published, in 1577, connected to the 'Perfect Art of Navigation' (48). In this book a number of authors are evoked to support the importance of ruling the seas, '[b]ut strangest of all is the use which Dee makes of the Byzantine Neoplatonic philosopher, Gemistus Pletho' (48). Thus, through Dee, '[t]he religious imperial theme of Foxe's initial C has here developed into a nationalist imperialist theme' (50).

Another term partially secularised at the same time was 'reform'. Reform originally meant church reform, which had several waves in the Middle Ages, the Reformation being their continuation and in a way culmination. But now and here, centrally associated with Elizabeth, the concern gained an increasingly secular meaning. In commenting another major image of her which influenced a series of cult pictures, Yates argues that an engraving of Elizabeth 'contains a representation of the imperial reform in the form of the Sword of Justice resting on the Word of God, the Bible' (59). Yates locates Shakespeare's *Tempest* in this context, seeing it as part of a never realised London-Prague axis (1975c: 98–9). From this perspective the play is 'one of the supreme expressions of that vitally important phase in the history of the European mind, the phase which borders on, and presages, the so-called scientific revolution of the seventeenth century', as Prospero is 'clearly the magus as scientist, able to operate scientifically within his world view, which includes areas of operation not recognised by science proper.' Even further, there was 'the element of moral reform in Prospero's outlook and aims, the element of Utopia, an essential feature of the scientific outlook of the Rosicrucian period, in which it was seen to be necessary to situate the developing magico-scientific knowledge within a reformed society', and so 'Prospero as scientist is also Prospero the moral reformer, bent on freeing the world of his island from evil influences' (96–7). This terminology, and especially orientation, has vital affinities with the Hermetic movement. Yates outright names his first chapter about Bruno's activities in England in her classic book as 'Giordano Bruno in England: The Hermetic Reform' (1964: 205). Central for this chapter, and Bruno's attempts at a reform, is the 1584 book *Spaccio della bestia trionfante*, where an assembly of the Roman gods is introduced to set up his ideas about 'a universal religious and moral reform' (218), couched in the attempt by the gods to reform the heavens (219). This is a thinly veiled allusion to his aim of launching a genuine and secular 'reform movement', where the pretence of reforming Christianity is cast aside, as the work is rather 'the glorification of the magical religion of the Egyptians' (211). Thus, and abandoning 'the feeble efforts of Ficino' to circumscribe magic and keep it compatible with medieval Christianity, Bruno 'is taking Renaissance magic back to its pagan source' (214). His aim is particularly modern and extremely preoccupying. As explained in his dedication, 'the reform of the heavens is' pretext for 'the reform, or the production, of a personality' (220). With this, not just any limitations about magic are cast into the wind, but also concerning the glorification and divinisation of the human personality: the aim is 'a personality whose powers are being formed into a successful whole' (221); or, 'the divine virtues or powers predominate in the reformed personality' (222). Such aims did not remain mere words, as Bruno tried personality-transforming magic on himself. In 1592, back to Italy, he spent three months in Padua to prepare himself for his mission of convincing the pope, so 'would no doubt have been in a high state of incandescence at this time, working with every kind of magic, both demonic and natural, to heighten the power of his personality with which he hoped to impress Pope Clement VIII in favour of the great reform' (362). While the direct results were hardly satisfactory, as it led him to the stake in 1600, the undertaking had its long-term effects, especially in the field of education, but also in the increasing obsession with overall 'reform'.

This obsession with reform, joint to the obsession with methodology and system-building, had a major impact on the emergence of modern rationalism and the scientific methodology. This can be seen with particular clarity in a movement towards which in his later works Yates developed a particular interest, the Rosicrucians.

In between Renaissance and Enlightenment: The Rosicrucians

In our days hardly anyone heard about the Rosicrucians, even among social theorists; and those who did so are bound to set aside any work which as much as mentions their name. However, as Yates made it clear, her work aimed at liberating the study of certain aspects of European intellectual history from the grip of occult studies, as marginalising and even quarantining such concerns led to the neglect of their otherwise crucial impact on the rise of modernity. Thus, the Rosicrucian movement, far from being an obscure and irrelevant historical episode, not only should be considered as the last flame or spark of the Renaissance, but, as Yates argues in detail, Bacon and Descartes had close connections to it, while it, strikingly, and in several ways, pointed directly towards the Enlightenment.

While Yates' connecting this obscure occult movement to the glorious Enlightenment might be considered as her most outrageous unorthodoxy – not surprisingly, attacks against her work intensified after and against this book – the near identification of Rosicrucianism as an Enlightenment was emphatic by the title of her book and its last chapter. The reasons are given in the last pages, as a prophesising forecast: 'The most striking aspect of the Rosicrucian movement is the one to which the title of this book gives expression, its insistence on a coming Enlightenment' (1975a: 277). The Rosicrucian vision emphasised a new illumination, which would lead, through new discoveries, in science and technology, and especially mathematics, to a new age. This vision emphasised 'the necessity for a reform of society, particularly of education', even a new reformation of religion (277–8) – ideas that were not far from those of many protagonists of the Enlightenment, but even more of figures like Henri de Saint-Simon and Comte. Or, as Yates puts it in her last page, '[t]hough the Enlightenment proper, the *Aufklärung*, seems to introduce a very different atmosphere, yet its rationalism was tinged with illuminism' (278).

Yates' argument can be complemented and reinforced by two closely connected points, one which she mentioned but only to indicate that she will not discuss it, and one which she does not mention though the book is much about it. The first concerns the existence or not of a Rosicrucian secret society. The play with secrecy is certainly central to Rosicrucianism, but there is still no agreement concerning the existence of an actual Rosicrucian secret society. Note that, apart from the much-discussed connection between Rosicrucianism and Freemasonry, the Enlightenment also had a secret society aspect (Koselleck 1989).

The second and even more vital point concerns the way Rosicrucians played with the emerging public sphere. Beyond trying to solve the elusive and evidently impossible problem of whether the Rosicrucians existed as concrete persons forming a secret society, the more interesting issue is the radical novelty that such a problem *could* have emerged. Any form of 'communication' – to use now a very problematic word – implies some human beings formulating some message in order to address some other human beings. However, apart from the evident concreteness of speech, books, or letters, even in their printed and thus multiple versions, always assumed a degree of concreteness, an aim, a purpose, an interest, whether connected to religious belief, entertainment, or the selling of a product. However, in the case of Rosicrucian manifestos, the aim remained vague; they addressed everybody and so nobody in particular; and as the author(s) remained hidden, there was nobody to support, refute, or persecute. Thus the Rosicrucians, probably for the first time in history, played with the anonymity of the public sphere: a play which at the same time involved another play between secrecy and publicness. This play, on the one hand, revealed the full theatricality of the public sphere, at the moment when the modern public sphere was just about to be formed; and on the other hand, it intimated that through and due to this public sphere the very realness of reality becomes compromised. In the empty stage, or void, of the public sphere anybody can perform, or imitate, any act; by the very fact of being performed, and finding an audience, this becomes real; in this way it not just 'became' real, but transformed the very idea of reality, by disturbing or outright destroying the difference between reality and unreality. This is particularly so, and dangerous, if this public act is explicitly about change or transformation, because it then becomes a mixture between a self-fulfilling prophecy and a performative speech act: by saying publicly that it wants to change reality, it actually changed reality, by the 'reality' of this pronunciation, by investing this uttering into the social body. In this the Rosicrucians were pathbreakers, followed, almost immediately, by the English economic pamphlets (see next section), the *Communist Manifesto*, and the Dadaists, to name but a few – theorised, absurdly, as the redemption from the ills of modernity, by Habermas.

Parallel Puritan eschatology

While the Reformation, and especially Puritanism, are considered as opposites to Renaissance Hermeticism, Yates managed to link the two together, through connecting the Golden Age hopes of the Renaissance to the eschatological hopes of Puritanism. The Golden Age of the Elizabethan Renaissance, of which the virgin Queen was guarantor as Astraea, Greek virgin goddess of justice, would at the same time be 'the age of purified religion' (1975b: 61), establishing a continuity between the Renaissance and Puritanism, culminating in Milton's *Paradise Lost*. In the penultimate chapter of her last book, entitled 'The Occult Philosophy and Puritanism: John Milton', Yates programmatically connects the two movements through the epic poem. Already Sidney and Spenser, key figures of Elizabethan Renaissance were members of the circle around the Earl of Leicester, leader of the Puritan party, and their works 'expressed a Renaissance philosophy turned towards Puritan reform and infused with what has been called "Puritan occultism", that is to say a Puritan version of the occult philosophy' (1979: 207). This was rendered possible because – and this is the second great discovery in Yates's later works, after that of the Rosicrucian Enlightenment – a key impulse to the late Renaissance was given by Cabala, from Spain, complementing the Byzantine impulse, and giving rise, first in the works of Pico (whose works were absolved of heresy by the Borgia Pope Alexander VI, on 18 June 1493, quite soon after being elected), to Christian Cabala. It was 'this outlook' that passed 'into Puritanism proper, into the Puritanism of the Revolution and of its great epic poet, Milton' (207). This brought out particularly clearly an aspect of English Puritanism that Max Weber (1976: 163–5) called 'English Hebraism', and that according to him was central for the contribution of the Protestant ethic to the rise of capitalism: 'Milton's vision for England was that of a nation of chosen people, chosen in the Hebraic sense', leading the fight against the Pope, identified with the Antichrist (Yates 1979: 207).[5] According to Yates, while the influence of the Cabala on Milton was long recognised, this should be assigned not directly to Lurian Cabala, but to Christian Cabala, transmitted by Robert Fludd, who was in a line of direct descent from the Renaissance Hermetic tradition, and was also closely associated with the Rosicrucians (208). Thus, 'Fludd was the inheritor of the Elizabethan Cabalism which influenced Spenser', while 'Milton would now come out as the inheritor of Spenser's Hebraic type of patriotism' (209). So, concludes Yates, Milton was 'not a Puritan in the narrow sense, but Renaissance Puritan, like Spenser, preserving within his Puritanism the Renaissance traditions' (211–2). Through him, and related channels, 'the Puritan revolution took over some of the aspects of the projected Rosicrucian revolution' (212). The interlacing of the Enlightenment and Revolution thus should be traced back, from 18th century France to 17th century England, and connected with both Puritanism and the rise of the modern scientific method.

An Epilogue on Pico

Pico's oration *On the Dignity of Man* is often mentioned as a key example of the Renaissance self-assertion of Man.[6] However, as emphasised by Edgar Wind, the closest colleague of Yates in the Warburg school, Pico offers a very strange glorification of man. In Pico's account 'man's glory is derived from his mutability', as he has 'the power to transform himself', and even the exploration of the universe is only derived from 'his adventurous pursuit of self-transformation' (Wind 1967: 191). Elsewhere he argued that 'man was originally of a Janus-nature', or dual-faced (212). Pico's (self-) admiration of man is expressed in a stunning claim: ' "Who would not admire this chameleon?" ' (191). Pico's ideas foreshadow Hegel's dialectic – not surprisingly, as both Hegel and Renaissance Neoplatonists use Plato's *Parmenides*, especially through the commentary of Proclus (192–3). However, *Parmenides* is a significantly corrupted dialogue (Brumbaugh 1982), while Pico furthermore particularly appreciated the ' "Asiatic richness" ' (Wind 1967: 10) of Proclus. Even further, Pico and Hegel also share '[t]he same use, or abuse, of ambiguity' (196).

Wind explores further this mutability in Pico through two Greek mythological figures evoked by him, Pan (Greek deity of 'everything') and Proteus (sea-god of transformation). This is elaborated in 'Pico's parable that Pan is hidden in Proteus. Mutability, in Pico's view, is the secret gate through which the universal invades the particular. Proteus persistently transforms himself because Pan is inherent in him' (196). Pico further claimed that Plato held an androgynous or bisexual vision of man, which Leone Ebreo further extended even to the Bible (213). In his commentary Wind here adds a reference to alchemy, as an illustration of the degradation or debasement of Renaissance Neoplatonism, where 'Hermaphrodite, called *Rebis*, represents the apex of transmutation' (214). It is thus not surprising that John Donne would ridicule Pico as 'the "Judeo-Christian Pythagoras" ', demonstrating Pico's 'coincidence of opposites by an irresistibly felicitous example: he proves "the numbers 66 and 99 to be identical if you hold the leaf upside down" ' (216).[7]

Joyce Appleby: The birth of the modern economy through the flux of goods and the extension of interchangeability

> the general [...] appeared to grow quite faint at the bare thought of reading anything which was neither mercantile nor political, and was not in a newspaper
> Charles Dickens, Martin Chuzzlewit, 268

Appleby starts from the recognition that the emergence of something like the 'modern market economy',[8] was not a simple and natural process of evolution, but a radical *transformation*. Contemporaries were much preoccupied, even stunned, by what was going on; and the new 'science' of political economy emerged both as an effort to understand the nature and character of these changes, and as a normative discourse to promote further these transformations.

The changes appeared in the sixteenth century as a radical disruption or even destruction of the order of things as it was taken for granted. It 'marked the beginning of the end of the old European order', through '[d]isruptions in the most basic relations', which 'made the past an uncertain guide to the future' (1978: 3). Such disruptions were sustained, and were to be located in 'the economy': 'In every aspect of economic life in the 1640s, 1650s, and 1660s, practices violated the expectations framed in an earlier period' (99). For any society or culture undergoing such a challenge the natural response is to resist, to search for ways in which the mode of living that was accepted thus far could be maintained. This was indeed the response offered in the 16th century, in England or elsewhere in Europe. However, '[b]y the beginning of the seventeenth century, English statesmen had ceased to think of turning back to a more contained economy in order to prevent the social disruptions produced by the acceleration of commerce' (19–20). This was because the nature of these changes, as alluded to in a somewhat imprecise manner in the citation above, seemed to be irresistible, inexorable, unalterable – so had to be met by new responses. This was the intellectual challenge, as perceived then, according to Appleby, and we must try to follow her as closely as possible in order to understand the problematisation of the evident crisis, and how the world that emerged as a result, together with the rising scientific rationalism, came to produce the world in which we still are living.

The central issue is to identify the apparently irresistible forces.

For this, we first need to ascertain what exactly new emerged in the 16–17th centuries. Appleby offers two sets of meanings. One is claims about a 'new market economy', even a new society, modern society, of which England was the forerunner. The other is its specification as having at its centre commerce; or, commerce as the new centre of society, even of a coming world society. Thus, she claims that in these decades a 'commercial restructuring of [the] country's economy' (31) was taking place, involving 'economic issues [that] could no more be contained' (33), as the 'commercial realities' (34) of the new 'market economy' implied 'more than a nexus of private profit': it was 'a complicate, new social organization' (34–5). The central issue was that 'it had not been shaped by central authority but rather through informal initiative'; or, the exact novelty was that the 'commercial animation of Englishmen in the second decade of the century had *extended the range* and power of purely economic forces' (35; emph. AS).

The novelty, it is clear, had to do with commerce. Appleby repeatedly states that the novelty was commerce as the centre; or the idea that exchange, that previously an unimportant, even marginal and hardly tolerated human activity, suddenly became *the* centre.

How did this happen? What could have given its force – and right the moment when modern science emerged?

The key term is contained in a 1621 pamphlet by Thomas Mun, which Appleby considers as the single most important text towards establishing political economy; and this is 'flow' or 'flux'. Trade, or commerce, is nothing else but 'the persistent, complementary, and orderly flow of goods and money' (38). This 'flow was better left untampered with, for "by a course of trafficke (which changeth according to the accurrents of time) the particular members do accommodate each other, and all accomplish the whole body of the trade" ' (38–9). From this perspective, what mattered was not wealth but the flow of earnings, wealth being 'a kind of sedimentary deposit from the flow of trade' (39). Thus, '[e]verything followed the flow of trade', including interest rates and prices, and so 'neither prince nor statute could restrain this flow' (39–40). This meant that human life had a new centre: '[t]he market mechanism thus became a regulator of human activity', as it 'turned individuals and their communities outward toward the assessment of the economic demands and productive possibilities of others', implying a 'reordering of social values, placing a premium upon utility and efficiency' (84). In this way 'the vital link between society and economy that justified political direction was cut' (98). The outcome was a new vision of society where – and note that here Appleby is quoting from the Preface to North's 1691 *Discourse on Trade*, many centuries before the current discourse on 'globalisation' – ' "the whole World as to Trade, is but as one Nation of People" ' (173–4). Economic activities, it came to be assumed, 'conformed to a determinable, natural order' (128). In the new world of global trade seemingly disordered, chaotic movements follow a perfect, almost natural rhythm and harmony; and, quite on the contrary, it is the attempt to impose political or human norms and laws that would create artificial barriers, or disorder.

Here we need to stop and take a deep breath concerning what is going on. At one level, we have to do with a radical revaluation of values. Commerce suddenly became the centre of human life; a centre which radiates a natural order that simply cannot be interfered with. The identification of this new centre, furthermore, has the character of a scientific discovery. Commerce existed all the time, the novelty is not commerce in itself but the realisation that it should be – no: it simply IS! – the centre from which suddenly all human activity becomes ordered. Even further: this discovery is fully in line with the main scientific discoveries of the age; advancing some, and following others. The study of fluxes, a central aspect of the new physics of Newton was as if forecast in Mun's treatise on political economy. Similarly, a central feature of modern mathematics, helped by the zero, is the focus on quantification, in contrast with counting and numbers. The point is illustrated by Gregory Bateson (2002: 45) in the difference between counting three tomatoes and measuring three gallons of water; note that his example for quantity is a liquid, or a flow; and even further, that a few pages later he would contrast money as a transitively valued quantity with biological values (50).

However, if the existence of a 'market economy' is supposedly a scientific discovery, with commerce as its irresistible centre, and with various natural science analogies, then there is reason for re-thinking what was going on, starting with the inherent value, or not, of flow/flux, fluidity, and liquidity, from the perspective of human life. Water clearly is the foundation of life, both historically and actually. Nothing can live without water. However, water as inundation, water as mere quantity, water as flooding is the biggest calamity possible, together with an earthquake; two ways to destroy solidity without which meaningful human life is not possible. Human life can only be based, only makes sense, from the perspective of whatever is solid. Pretending the flux as centre is a dangerous and unacceptable piece of sophistry.[9]

Thus, far from accepting the new discourse around the economy as an unsurpassable discovery, the entry point to the good life, we need to identify on *what* exactly this new centre was founded; and what it has to do with the new, 'scientific' vision of the world. The book of Appleby, as it deals with reflections on 'the economy' the moment it was born, contains extremely valuable material for these questions.

The central feature of the economy, everybody knows this, is that it is capable for growth; in fact, in our world, and since many decades, the central not just economic, but political or even social question is economic growth. If 'the economy' is growing, everybody is happy, things go fine; but the moment economic growth stops, as if an unmitigated disaster would be upon us. But what does this mean?

We must try to understand, for a start, what we mean by economic 'growth'. And here we immediately bump into the realisation that the idea is a metaphor; and rather a questionable, if not an outright abusive one.

This is because growth, literally, is an exclusive feature of living beings. Mountains do not grow, rocks do not grow, even rivers do not grow, though under some conditions they might flood; and they certainly contain less water in dry seasons. But they do not grow.

Animals and plants, however, do grow, and do not only grow, but even reproduce themselves, increasing even in this manner. It is this growth that is the model for the idea of an 'economic growth'. The economy is growing if it produces more and more goods for exchange and consumption. But how does it do so?

Extension of markets

The trivial answer would be efficiency, the better use of resources, and of course technological change. However, in Appleby's account, emphasis is elsewhere: *the extension of markets*. This means that 'the economy' can grow also by incorporating products and activities which previously were not subject to buying and selling. In this sense, the growth of economic activities, or of 'the' economy, was a by no means natural or organic process, for which Appleby uses the crucial adjective 'intrusive': the attention of economic writers slowly extended to an ever increasing part of social life; '[i]n the works of these men [and here it should again be observed that these people were *exclusively* men], almost every observable social fact became a dependent variable of an economic cause'; or, '[f]rom fact to fact these writers worked themselves back to the economic starting point as they slowly created a new reality for their society'; and so '[t]he intrusiveness of the market became a subtle and persistence force' (83). Still in other words, the 'growth' of the 'economy' implied incorporating beings and pieces of reality that previously did not belong to 'the economy': the 'propensity to value things by their utility extended to the valuing of people and land. The involvement of people and land in the logic of the market was a critical stage in the transformation of modern society' (84). What all this means is that under the seemingly benevolent terminology of 'growth' a much more problematic and tricky process was going on: the intrusion of the kind of valorisation characteristic of 'the economy' to areas and beings that previously were outside its scope. In a still different terminology, directly evoked by the term 'intrusiveness', a main feature of the trickster, the 'growth' of the economy implies the spreading of a trickster logic to ever greater areas and segments of social life.

Still, what exactly does this mean? It is here that Appleby offers the perhaps single most important term of her entire book: *interchangeability*. It also helps us to understand, finally, what it means to move from commerce to the modern exchange economy.

Interchangeability

Commerce is the exchange of goods and services, mediated by money. This is simple and trivial enough. But it also means that for something to be exchangeable, or to enter the economy, it must be offered for sale. And offering something for sale, or for exchange, is by no means a simple and natural act.

Let me illustrate the point by a linguistic analysis, which has its own method-logical importance, and at several levels. In Hungarian, two words have the meaning of 'selling' something: *árul* and *elad*. The first word has as its root word *ár* 'flood', a word with the most negative possible connotations in Hungarian. Even further, *árul* has two meanings in Hungarian: not only 'selling', but also 'betraying'. The clear implication is that if somebody decides to sell something, to make it into an object of the 'flux' or 'flood' or exchange, it means that inherent connections with that object had to be literally 'betrayed'. This is the same thing that in Roman law a piece of land could only be sold if it was previously legally 'alienated', or again literally 'betrayed' (Fustel de Coulanges). Interestingly, the analysis of the second Hungarian word yields the same result. The root word of *elad* is *ad* 'give', *el* being a prefix for 'up' or 'away', and indeed even in English 'betray' can be expressed as giving up or giving away something. Giving is the opposite of selling: giving is part of gift logic, animating normal social life, while selling implies the opposite, the giving up, the renouncing, the alienation of the object which then becomes an object of mere exchange. This is why Mauss was wrong in coining the oxymoron 'gift exchange', which helped to systematically misunderstand his ideas.

If an object was previously given up, it can then become object of exchange, or can *become interchangeable* with other objects. It can thus become the object of economic analysis. But all this also makes it evident that to claim that everything primarily has an economic value, or that everything belongs first of all to the economy is – to put it mildly – ludicrous nonsense. The *limits* of what belongs to the economy and what doesn't are flexible, and the growth of the economy first of all, not only historically but even in the present, means the extension of those entities, objects, activities, and services that belong to the economy; or that are interchangeable with each other. The physical extension of the market and the intellectual extension of those goods that are interchangeable among each other meant the same thing:

> The extension of the market was absolutely dependent upon the extension of consensus on equivalent values. Regular market dealings in land and labor required that the perception of the uniqueness of persons and things be replaced by the peculiar cognitive processes of market calculations. Thus, evaluation replaced appreciation as a fundamental attitude, and the depersonalization, the calculations, and the uniformities introduced by this change of consciousness helped prepare for the imagining and accepting of the scientific model of economic relations.
>
> *(246)*

Interchangeability means the same thing as substitutability, and implies a system of valorised calculation. It is an intellectual operation that is the condition of possibility of gaining. Economic theory assumes that the central aim of human life is to *gain*, but far from being trivially true this is simply a lie, as the aim of human life is not to 'gain', but the *good life*, whatever this might mean. Today the common claim is that it is not possible to discuss the 'good life', as everybody has a different idea about the good, but actually even this is not true, as Plato did discuss the good, even centrally, and *this* is the foundation of philosophy. However, what is clear, from the perspective of Plato, is that gain cannot be the aim of the good life, as it simply has no substance: it merely implies an infinite game of exchange and substitutability. Gain is the aim of merchants, to be sure, but this was exactly the reason why in all societies merchants were held in rather law esteem, as they lacked a commitment and faithfulness to certain stable things which again everywhere were considered as a precondition to a decent life. Interchangeability simply implies to make 'the buying and selling of goods the basis of everything' (45).

With the rise of the modern economy this mode of thinking was extended from commerce to the entire social world; an idea that was truly revolutionary:

> Innocuous as it may sound, the idea of a commerce in money was loaded with implications subversive to the concept of the world as containing an order of real things. A commerce in money suggested fluidity instead of fixed points and, even more insidiously, gave to common merchants a power that only princes enjoyed: to set the value of coin.
>
> *(44)*

Thus, a society based on interchangeability and substitutability implied to make common, as a model, the way of life and thinking specific to merchants; and even more, to transfer power over to merchants. The end result was a 'new age in which "necessity or gain will ever find some means to violate" legislation inimicable to profitable enterprises' (160–1, with a direct quote from a 1628 pamphlet by Thomas Mun).

But how was this possible? Here we approach the heart of this great mystery, as we now live in a taken for granted manner in this global world trade order, but we still do not understand how this world has come into being, replacing the quite different medieval world order. The economic thinking of the 17th century, as reconstructed by Appleby, seems only to imply a kind of recognition of this development as a fact, advising politicians not to try to legislate against free trade, as it would not be efficient anyway, and whatever happened since seems to confirm these claims, but why? What happened that rendered it possible? What actually conferred power to the merchants, at the end of the Renaissance, when princes evidently still believed that they had all the power? What kind of changes took place that transferred, as if in the background, power to the merchants – at the same time of the victory of the 'scientific world view'?

Here three factors will be shortly mentioned, aspects of the rise of the modern economy, which strangely – or perhaps not so strangely enough – so far received very little attention. The first concerns the role of fairs, in contrast to markets. The modern economy emerged out of fairs, and not markets, so strictly speaking should be called a fairground economy, and not a market economy. This fact is known by economic historians (for e.g. see Braudel), but is systematically ignored by economic theory. This is all the stranger as the stock-market, the real centre of the modern economy, developed out of late Renaissance fairs, even can be considered as a 'permanent fair', though to increase perplexity the rise and the characteristics of the stock-market is also all but ignored in the classical theoretical treatises and even textbooks of economics. The model for such omissions is Ricardo, in whose account the rise of the market follows a gradual, linear evolutionary progress, from simple barter, and who fails so much as to mention fairs or the stock-market, though before he became a political economist he was a successful stock-market broker, so knew well what he was omitting. Thus, one cannot avoid stating that classical political economy, accepted at face value even by Karl Marx, was a camouflage operation since the very beginning. Economic theory is an ideology that helps to absurdly legitimate highly questionable transformative operations as the very nature of things.

The second factor is the joint emergence, in the context of permanent fairs, of modern police and theories of reason of state, exact contemporaries of early economic theories, that in a quite similar manner advised princes about following only their 'real' or 'rational' interests – a study projected but never completed by Foucault (1981a).

The third factor concerns the conditions of possibility of the operations of a permanent fair. A fair, just as any marketplace, was originally an event in a concrete time and place, even though, again just as any market, had its recurrence. Its extension, in time and especially beyond place, required certain intellectual instruments which enabled the conducting of transactions from a distance. These were the famous bills of exchange, which were nothing more than a sheet of paper, and yet whose validity were accepted by long-distance merchants who knew each other. And while princes could regulate the value of coin and prohibit the collection of interest, they had no power over the terms of such bills of exchange – a bit like democratic authorities have no power over what is being discussed in Davos.

With this, the stock-market was born, assuming a power that seems to be irresistible and omnipotent; the second of the most powerful – and most evil – inventions of human history, after the world-conquering – or, in the terminology of Voegelin, ecumenic – empires, that were attempting to incorporate into themselves all lands and people by force. With it, the second, modern 'axis of evil' was formed, the Lyon/Antwerp-Amsterdam-London-New York axis, after the Babylon-Alexandria-Constantinople axis (here, again, the focus is not simply on imperial centres, but on *founded*, so in a way *tabula rasa* centres); similarly intending global world rule, with means that pretend to be less openly violent, but which nevertheless are just as much so, and where the domination over other humans is compounded by the direct destruction of Nature, so the created world.

Conclusion

> Shakespeare is a great satirist of the modern world, which had its true beginnings in the late Renaissance
>
> René Girard, The Theatre of Envy, 149

Appleby only deals with British authors, but the rise of political economy, even the term, can be traced to four French treatises, written by Louis Turquet de Mayerne, Barthélemy de Laffemas, Olivier de Serres, and Antoine de Montchrétien, slightly earlier than the 1620s. As a striking confirmation of Weber's Protestant Ethic thesis, each author was associated with the Huguenots. The two most important of these books were written in 1611 and 1615. To the exact same time can be dated

Shakespeare's *Tempest*, confirming the insight of Girard, and two works identifying the period as an increased and pervasive corruptness, John Donne's 'Anniversary' poems and Traiano Boccalini's stunningly titled *Advertisements from Parnassus*, also considered as a main document of the rising 'reason of state' literature, and which were exact contemporaries (1611–3).

This offers a vital confirmation of Yates's insight concerning the importance of this precise liminal moment:

> History falls inexorably into "periods": for Europe as a whole it divides into the Renaissance and the seventeenth century; for England, it divides into the Elizabethan age and the Stuart age. In this periodisation, the important interstices tend to be overlooked, the times between the periods, times when survivors of an earlier period are still alive and influential, times when an earlier period has not fully ceased, and the new period is not yet fully born. The first fifteen or so years of the seventeenth century were such a time in all Europe.
>
> *(1975: 80)*

This was the moment, and the conditions, out of which modern rationalism and its 'scientific methodology' grew out, championed by Bacon and Descartes, in radical complicity with the two other monsters of the modern world, the modern state, and the modern economy.

Notes

1. The same applies to Kant, who similarly lived in times on the limit, but failed to perceive this, and thus considered the world as being always in chaos, setting up the task to himself, and similarly minded philosophers, to 'construct boundaries'.
2. Significantly, this exact terminology will be taken up by Henri de Saint-Simon.
3. The most important parallels with Yates's project are Voegelin's 'Modern Gnosticism', and the works of Toulmin, Foucault, Bateson, and Serres.
4. This is another allusion to the centrality of theatre; see also Agnew (1986).
5. This was combined with a certain attitude to nature, identified in the Epilogue Henri Frankfort wrote to his classic *Kingship and the Gods*, which is a kind of master key to his entire work: 'In Hebrew religion – and in Hebrew religion alone – the ancient bond between man and nature was destroyed' (Frankfort 1948: 343). This contributed in a crucial way to the world view propagated by modern science.
6. See, programmatically, Blumenberg (1983; on Pico, pp.524–5).
7. The term 'coincidence of opposites' was first used by Cusanus, in his book *On Learned Ignorance*, written after his boat trip back from Constantinople with Bessarion and Gemistos Plethon. He evidently had his 'liminal' initiation into the secrets of Byzantine magi sophistry.
8. The right term would be 'fairground economy'; see Szakolczai (2022, Ch.10).
9. Note that 'solidarity', a concern so much outside modern economics, is derived from 'solidity'.

6
THE IDOLS OF SCIENTIFIC METHODOLOGY

'You are to be in all things regulated and governed,' said the gentleman, 'by fact. We hope to have, before long, a board of fact, composed of commissioners of fact, who will force the people to be a people of fact, and of nothing but fact.'

Charles Dickens, Hard Times, *14*

Most thought-provoking for our thought-provoking times is that we are still not thinking.

Heidegger (1977: 358)

This chapter engages in a formal attack against the very principles of the scientific method, in particular as it was pioneered by Bacon and Descartes, thus taking further the arguments of Chapter 4. The central thrust of the chapter concerns the presumed scientific methodology proposed for the social and the human sciences; it certainly does not engage with what physicists, chemists, and other scientists are actually doing. However, the thrust of the argument applies to science *tout court*, as the chapter, in line with the book, claims that science *as* science requires, and promotes, a frame of mind that is alien from the concerns of everyday human existence, even from life, and thus is mortally dangerous to our lives – to *us*; an argument to be traced to Nietzsche and Foucault; in particular, as recognised by Heidegger, formalised science is simply hostile to thinking. Not just technology but science is our problem; scientific knowledge must be constrained within strict boundaries; a 'knowledge society', in which science is literally adulated as the highest possible value inevitable destroys the possibility of a decent human life – mostly through its applied handmaid, technology, but also directly through its characteristic frame of mind, promoting the lifeless, life-alien way of living that has become our fate. Furthermore, such adulation of science promotes the ridiculous and dogmatic ideology of atheism,[1] a justification of hubris, the arrogant extolling of merely human power, which every single human mythology, spirituality,

DOI: 10.4324/9781003275138-8

and religion reveals as the greatest danger. The clearest example, of course, is the myth of Prometheus, and the championing of Prometheus as hero by the radical Enlightenment, of which Marx's Preface to his own doctoral dissertation, analysed so well by Voegelin (2000a), is an emblematic model, and which absurdly promotes atheism through the *hatred* of gods – a paradox that clearly reveals its own mendacity, in line with the evident original intentions of Aeschylus.

A proper discussion of this issue, of course, would require a book on its own. Within the limitations of this short chapter, a specific and personal perspective is offered as a necessary short-cut, through my own education into the 'scientific method' under Communist Hungary.

The limits of scientific methodology: a personal encounter

> Though was afraid, my ground I held,
> Was born, got mingl'd in and ex-cel'd
>
> *Attila József,* The inventory is ready, *1936*[2]

Studying economics in Hungary, in 1976 – an almost exclusive possibility then there to pursue an interest in something like 'social understanding' – necessarily involved systematic indoctrination, or at least its attempt, into the basic principles of Marxism-Leninism and scientific socialism. Strangely enough, it was combined with the central ideas of neo-Kantianism, which at that time I did not even realise, though found it almost as much intolerable. As my family upbringing rendered me impenetrable by such indoctrination, I searched for possible ways out, to keep my mind sane, and found it in the study of mathematics, mathematical statistics, mathematical economics, and econometrics on the one hand, and languages on the other. However, as my interest in economics, and especially the efficient management of the economy through various mathematical modelling was minimal, I succeeded to move towards sociology, a minor but vocal subject matter within the university, and still during my undergraduate years, based on my skills in mathematical statistics, managed to join the activities of a research group then in formation in the Institute of Sociology of the Hungarian Academy of Sciences, whose aim was to pioneer the application of real, scientific, Western methods in Hungary. This was like a revelation to me, a unique possibility, and so immersed myself in no time into the basic principles of survey research methods and the corresponding statistical and computational techniques. We managed to obtain some computer programmes, running data analysis through the central computer of the Academy, and with my eventual colleague and later close friend László Füstös we wrote programmes, on a small Texas Instrument machine, that complemented the ones we had on the large central computer.

My enthusiasm only lasted for a year or so, as quite soon I noticed that between the extremely interesting and erudite ideas of Elemér Hankiss, leader of the group, the most important intellectual in Hungary at that period – and who was prohibited to teach at the university, thus giving me the incredible opportunity of learning under him, not as my distant professor, but as a close colleague, literally day by day – and the results we managed to produce, with all our efforts, through the statistical programmes, there lay a yawning gap. It started to give me considerable head-ache, as it was difficult enough to live completely outside the dominant modes of thinking of my homeland – when I published my first paper, in a Hungarian journal, one of my colleagues suggested that after all I need to incorporate into my argument the ideas of socialism. Quite taken aback, I could only reply that I cannot deal with nonsense. Still, then, was not what we were doing also non-sensical? In particular, I found that the techniques of Exploratory Data Analysis were somewhat interesting; the enormous data sets we managed to obtain did reveal certain interesting *patterns* (the word is crucial) inside real social life, but I found the obligation to put them into the Procrustean bed of 'hypothesis-testing' and 'causal modelling' genuinely non-sensical. When expressed my doubts, I was told that such a way of proceeding is required for reasons of 'aesthetics'. This did not convince me; my problems concerned truth; and also, I did not find any 'aesthetically rewarding' elements in 'causal modelling' and the like. What we were doing – and I was told, then and later, that *everybody* is doing so – was running a huge number of regression and like analyses, which gave us some results, and at the end we acted as if we always knew in advance what the actual results would be. I thought this pathetic, and was not sure what to do.

However, at that moment I got the opportunity to study for a PhD in economics in Austin, TX – which was problematic enough, given that I have already left economics, and had no interest in returning there – but such an opportunity, then, in Hungary, was impossible to refuse, so I took it up. When I returned to Hungary in 1985, my first question to Elemér Hankiss concerned the fate of the book we had just finished when I left in August 1982. His response was that it was not published: he took it back from the press, as he saw something in my eye when we last met in August 1982. In fact, he had asked me whether his interpretation about the applicability of Weber's Protestant Ethic thesis could be confirmed through our data, and I said something like 'you can say anything'. Still, I was dreadfully mortified, as it was far from my intentions to stop the publication of the book – though probably he did the right thing; he always did the right thing, as he was a parrhesiast.

Still, the problem remains: what exactly is wrong with 'scientific methodology'? Can anything meaningful be said, through statistical data, about social life and human existence? And what does it mean that the precious little that such techniques reveal are hidden and distorted behind a cocked-up organisation of the results, in the name of 'full scientificity'?

The following sections, I know, only scratch the surface, but with the limits of this book this is all I can offer.

On some idols of scientific methodology

Objectivity

A key idol of the scientific method is objectivity. The idea is that social and human scientists must treat the targets of their studies in the same way as the 'natural' scientists are doing, as pieces of an external reality with which the researcher is not involved, thus gaining the same distance, supposedly necessary for a truly scientific 'analysis'. While by today this idea is considered almost as a truism, there are a series of self-evident and extremely serious problems with it. To start with, the 'targets'[3] of the social sciences are not objects but living human beings, with similarly living cultural traditions, and even the 'targets' of the *genuinely* natural sciences are not objects, but living beings: plants and animals, or entities like mountains, rivers and the like, which are 'almost' living, and which indeed should be better treated as if they were living beings, and not as 'objects'. Even dead objects, like animal bones or timber from trees maintain characteristics similar to the living.

Even further, as it will be discussed in detail in Part Three, gaining knowledge in the social and human sciences is helped by incorporating into the study design the fact that the 'subjects' and 'objects' of investigation are not distant and alien to each other, but share many communalities, and participate in a given reality. 'Objectivity' in the social sciences, according to the methodological essays of Max Weber, implies not to proceed as if dealing with distant objects, rather to overcome the preconceptions of the researcher.

In conclusion, the idea of conducting investigations in the social and human sciences as if the aims of these studies were objects is an unwarranted and mechanical imitation of the 'natural' sciences, and strictly speaking it simply does not make sense.

Hypothesis testing

The idea that genuine science means the testing of hypotheses is one of the cornerstones of empiricism or positivism. The idea, to be taken back to the Second Sophistic, is that the researcher is supposed to formulate a clear and distinct statement, called 'hypothesis', which it wants to prove or refute; then sets up a formal, preferably causal model by which the statement is 'operationalised',[4] or put into a testable form; and then should collect empirical evidence by which such a testing can be performed. The end-product is confirmation or refutation of the hypothesis.

Such a way of proceeding is standard, and for many is simply *the* way to conduct any genuinely scientific investigation into human and social affairs. Yet, as I will now try to demonstrate in some detail, this way of proceeding for social and human life is seriously flawed, and the results it produces are practically meaningless.

To start with, the formulation of a hypothesis, as it is understood today, is a fixating interference in the process of thinking, research, and understanding. Research means to gain ideas about a particular theme or topic; the more one familiarises oneself with the theme, the more ideas one is bound to have; the more inspiration one receives to read further, and eventually, after a time, a certain degree of consistency and coherence is found, a saturation point is reached, enabling to resume these ideas in the form of a working paper, an article, or a book. A hypothesis, however, implies the fixing of this process into a single, formalised statement, at which moment thinking comes to a stop, and the process of research is taken over by a rigid, mechanical activity of formalising models, gathering data, running computer programmes, and analysing the results. The moment ideas are fixed into hypotheses thinking stops. This is artificial and plainly wrong, a clear instance of trickster logic (see the 'trickster fixer') as under normal conditions ideas should lead to a *growth* of ideas; thinking is a living, organic process.

But the actual situation with hypothesis testing is even worse, as very often in contemporary empiricist positivism the hypotheses that are tested are not ideas that a researcher developed by one's own research, but are taken from somebody else, and this mode of proceeding, far from considered a shortcoming, is rather suggested as a model, helpful for the glorious accumulation of objective scientific results. But in this manner genuine and important ideas are fixed into meaningless, abstract formulations, which are then mechanically tested, producing results which promote no understanding whatsoever. A particularly clear example is offered by the entire industry set out to 'test' 'scientifically' Max Weber's ideas about the connection between Protestantism and capitalism. Thus, 'data' are collected, from practically any time and place, where the connection (meaning: the empirical correlation) is tested between religious confessionality and economic success, and in the worse cases then researchers pontificate about whether Weber was right or not. However, Weber's original 'thesis' was historical, or rather genealogical, about the condition of possibility for the emergence of modern capitalism in Western Europe, and whether in any other time or place there is or isn't a connection between Protestantism and money-making is completely irrelevant for the significance of Weber's work. Thus, the value of any such 'scientific hypothesis testing' is exactly, and not asymptotically, zero, a modern version of scholasticism – though appointments and even chairs can be gained in the contemporary academic world in this manner. Which is nothing short of a scandal.

A central aspect of hypothesis testing as 'method' is that the sources of ideas are irrelevant; what only matters is whether they can be tested or not. As justification, if any ever, it is occasionally mentioned that the popular ideas of Marx and Freud about the sources of ideas are mistaken. However, while this is certainly true, the source of ideas is an interesting question, and matters much. The first point is that we indeed do *not* know where ideas come from, but do know that people *do* have ideas, and some people much more than others. Having ideas is a question of talent or genius; it is indeed a *gift*; but it simply exists, it is a recurrent fact of life.

Yet, most of the times such ideas do not come out of the blue, but after a long process of research, or familiarisation with the subject matter. We always arrive at the same point, that understanding is produced in the mind or the soul; that this simply happens; but it is conditioned by prior experiences, learning, reading, familiarisation. In the terminology of Aquinas, which hardly can be surpassed here, learning and understanding is a combination of grace and works: one must make efforts; without proper efforts nothing is reached but the actual result cannot be mechanically connected to the amount and kind of efforts taken.

The point is formulated with particular poignancy in Greek mythology. There, ideas are attributed to the Muses: semi-divinities who select some people to don the talent of creativity. This, at a certain level, is purely arbitrary, though one might address the Muses and ask for their favour – this is called invocation, by which many Greek works of art start. However, at another level, the Muses are the daughters of Mnemosyne (Apollodoros 1.3.1.), or the Greek goddess of memory; so in Greek mythology the two threads concerned with the origins of ideas are connected, as memory is gained by experiences and familiarisation so the gifts of the Muses are conditioned by previous experiencing and working.

At this point, even granting what was exposed so far, one could say that still, if properly conducted, based on ideas developed on the basis of one's own work, the testing of hypotheses could have its importance. Yet, I argue that this is not the case: for social and human understanding, or even the explanation of why certain social processes or human behaviour take place, the very idea of hypothesis testing is mistaken and meaningless. This can be shown through a simple example.

Hypothesis testing is routinely used for introducing a new medicine. As a social scientist, I certainly do not have and do not claim competence in biochemistry or related disciplines. However, this fact does not refute my claim about the meaninglessness of hypothesis testing for social understanding, as between research done for introducing a new medicine and any social scientific investigation there is a *radical incommensurability*. This is because we are human beings, and so exist and operate within certain definite limits. We live on Earth and have a certain size, so processes which take place either very far from us, or at an extremely small level, are *incommensurable* with our lives and understanding. We cannot see what happens on Mars or inside the cells of our body; we need instruments like telescopes or microscopes, and also formal models and their testing, as otherwise we have no clue about what goes on at those levels. So we have to give up the possibility of gaining a direct understanding of what is going on and expressing an informed judgment, as we have no way to do so.

This, however, is not the case in *any* aspect of social and human reality, as whatever human beings are doing involves meaning, and the primary aim of *any* research is to understand and explain that meaning. This exposes the radical failure and fallacy of hypothesis testing in the social sciences, as by closing thinking with the formulation of a hypothesis, and then relying solely on quantitative data and computer programmes we gratuitously give up the possibility of understanding, treating human behaviour *as if* it would solely conform to some law of large numbers. But this is wrong, as here no incommensurability is involved: the researcher can directly try to understand what *any* human being in *any* time and place is doing – though for this, of course, one must give up the belief that the meaning of those acts are immediately and directly transparent. Funnily, this is exactly what empirical positivists are doing, who when collecting data simply wash together any response, and any behaviour, on purely external criteria, instead of trying to understand the meaning of those acts in their proper contexts.

Great figures of European culture were well aware of the problem. Goethe, for one, problematised the modern ideas about colour, opting for a Platonic perspective; and also claimed that microscopes and telescopes are truly disturbing (*verwirren eigentlich*) the right human perception (*reine Menschensinn*) (Goethe 2015: 470). And how can the *disturbance* of human perception produce meaningful truth?

Controlled experiment

The single biggest idol of scientific methodology, without the shadow of a doubt, is controlled experiment. 'Experiment' is considered as the measure of scientificity, at least back to Bacon, and the only significant 'advance' in this regard is adding the by no means trivial adjective 'controlled' to it. Yet, by our days, given our 'situation', any human being who thinks that a 'controlled experiment' is the best measure for human truth and meaning certainly has something seriously wrong about him.

Both words are extremely important in the expression, and equally problematic.

Let's start with control, as the problematic character of this word in our present is plainly evident – *clair et distinct*, using the terminology of Descartes. 'Control' fundamentally is a word of power, and indeed lies at the very heart of contemporary effective power. We still tend to associate power primarily with violence as physical force, and command as a certain verbal statement requiring to perform a certain activity, against our will; and while such acts of power are still being exerted, the specifically contemporary and more insidious kind of power has the character of control. 'Insidious' does not necessarily mean 'worse', and concerning the modalities of power it really makes no sense to risk such evaluative judgments, just as it is meaningless to argue whether Nazi Germany or Bolshevik Russia was worse as a political regime. 'Insidious' as a term, however, has two major characteristics that are quite different from violence or command, and this difference must be not just recognised but assessed concerning impact. First, it indicates a certain indirectness: the use of physical force or the issuing of a command is plainly evident for all sides concerned; there is no question of misunderstanding. It hurts, it harms, it forces one to comply or suffer. A control is different: one is not forced to anything, at least directly, only certain people, with asserted or presumed authority, make a posterior examination whether the 'right' kind of behaviour was performed. Second, the insidiousness of control implies a roundabout, stealthy, subtle, tricky, even devious mode of proceeding. Of course, one can second guess even the reasons of violence or command; but it is evident what is going on. This is not always clearly so in the case of control: especially because often – as Foucault analysed paradigmatically through the Panopticon – it is not clear who, when, and how will exert such control. The central issue is that there is a temporal displacement, or even reversal: in the case of violence or command the person in charge, 'possessing' power, carries the initiative; in the case of 'control', the act of power comes *after*, though at the same time having a tight relationship with prevention, thus implying some 'planning' coming *before*.

That 'control' is a kind of power, and an insidious one, this is clear enough; in order to understand what this implies for a 'controlled experiment', let's now review in some detail the second term.

'Experiment' as a word is derivative of 'experience', or a most fundamental, and in a way general, term characterising human existence. 'Experience' is simply the way we live our lives. Anything that happens to us is an experience; anything we do produces in us an experience. An 'experiment' thus is a kind of 'experience' – but exactly what kind?

And here we immediately perceive certainly analogies with 'control', captured in the expression 'controlled experiment', as if there were some 'elective affinities' between the two terms. While in a sense, most evidently, an 'experiment' is a kind of 'experience', the derivation of the word cannot be accidental, a kind of trying and testing, but in another sense, it is the exact opposite of an 'experience', as it lacks the spontaneous character of an event that is the very stuff of life. Instead, an experiment must follow, by its very nature, a series of rigidly prescribed steps, and cannot deviate from it. Thus, far from being spontaneous or organic, it is fundamentally artificial.

Now, in its original meaning, as a trial or testing, an 'experiment' was something that someone did for oneself, often on oneself, in order to try something out,[5] which involved a degree of risk, so the focus was not so much on purposiveness and control than on playfulness: why *not* do this? However, the moment in which an experiment was made *not* on oneself, but on something or especially someone else, immediately fundamental ethical issues emerge: what right can one have to play *on* another being, in this sense – meaning, not to play 'with', but to play *on*? And the answer is immediate and unconditional: none whatsoever.

Part of the point is immediately evident: human beings cannot be made the objects of experiment. Nobody, yet, questions this idea, and it is certainly instructive that only the worse totalitarian regime(s) of the past made such experiments, and only with human beings who were previously deprived of their humanity. For a long time the central ethical dilemma of 'science' concerned experimenting with living animals; and then the central issue of bio-ethic became the manipulation of life.

If I may make a suggestion, at this point: it should be prohibited to experiment with anything *in nature*; as nature, anything living or even simply belonging to a part of Earth *and* commensurable to our existence should not be submitted to decontextualised experimenting.

Causality

Etymology, as always, offers a crucial starting point. A combined perusal of Indo-European (Greek, Latin, and Germanic) and non-Indo-European (Hungarian) languages indicates that the word and concerns have a double, and closely related origin: on the one hand, it indicates mental power (this comes out most clearly in Hungarian, where *okos* 'clever, smart' is simply the adjective version of *ok* 'cause'). On the other, the word is closely connected to legal issues, as it is about identifying the source of a phenomenon, mostly an injury (clearest in Ancient Greek). In this sense, it is close to the word used for a 'thing' – just as, from the other side, even the English word 'thing' has a legal origin.[6] The philosophical and scientific use of the word, then, closely follows this legal origin, just as many other words and aspects of scientific reasoning (inquiry, search, testing, and so on). As a result, scientific analysis, at a time, was all but identified with the search for causes.

Strictly within science, this was challenged by two major developments: system analysis, and cybernetics, with the idea that science, instead of a mechanical search for causes, should be concerned with the study of relations within systems; and by quantum mechanics, which pursued changes that could not be traced to causes.

Yet, and at the same time, the debate around causality gained a never explicitly expressed but clearly perceptible ideological dimension: powerful forces pushed, as if from the background, for the reassertion of strict causality as the foundation of 'real' science. Again, one can only speculate about the reasons for this, but speculate one must, as it is a central issue in the dogmatic and yet very powerful deployment of science; one aspect of our situation in which religious dogmatism was replaced by scientific dogmatism, which is way more dangerous, as it ignores and neglects those inner aspects of human life that are central for any genuine religiosity. Thus, there seem to be two major sources of such dogmatic assertion of the need for causality: first, because it is better compatible with the hubristic atheistic vision according to which 'man' is fully in control of things, including his destiny; and second, a rather sinister modality of this vision, a central trick used by scientists and technologists, in collusion with the holders of power, which is that scientific knowledge about such causality helps them to control, and thus profit, from things, just as from people; or, knowledge of causality is *the* knowledge that is central for manipulation.

Causal modelling

This can be perceived in one of the great tricks of 'scientific methodology' in the social sciences, causal modelling. Here again history, including conceptual history, is a most helpful tool, as 'causal modelling' was developed out of 'path analysis'. That terminology, developed for a certain statistical analysis of data, was correct and truthful, as it merely argued that by statistical analysis it is possible to identify certain patterns, or 'paths', in a data set – just as a path literally develops out of the way many people trod on the same field, thus forming a road. At that time, statisticians had a definite hostility to causality – Pearson, a main founder of modern statistics, introduced the term 'correlation coefficient' specifically to exclude the term causality from statistics. However, for the reasons mentioned above, combined with the eternal search of social scientists to be as 'scientific' as the 'natural' scientists, the use of the term 'causal analysis' became reintroduced. The coincidence of hubris, combined with the luring of power-brokers, offering means to increase their manipulative control was irresistible.

There is an important corollary of these two sections, concerning the tight connection between mere intelligence (smartness, reasoning), and the search for manipulative control. This coincidence identifies the magi-tricksters of all times: those individuals, developing into an occupational sect, the *first* and arche-typal occupational sect, who use the sheer power of their mind, and the knowledge and control this allows over the external world, to gain control over others by manipulating their emotions, while not having any interest or concern with the truthfulness of their own emotions; even downgrading it as mere sentimentality. The opposite point is represented by Pascal and his reasons of the heart.

Empirical evidence

At one level, the need for empirical evidence is a truism. Any research is an attempt to gain knowledge and understanding about reality, so it needs to know what concretely *is*. However, scientific methodology is not satisfied with constraining the working of the mind into fixed, artificially preconceived schemas, but is proposing to do the same with reality. What matters is not a genuine encounter with reality as an experience, but the collection of 'empirical evidence' in a mechanical manner, where furthermore – and this is really serious – the manner of data collection, in line with the ideas of 'hypothesis testing' and 'falsification', all but prescribes the results as well: whether the hypotheses are confirmed or not depends on what the 'data' show (though even this, as we have seen, is significantly manipulated), but any other substantial possibility is excluded *in advance* and *in principle* – according to the very logic of hypothesis testing. Following the precepts of a 'scientific methodology', from the works of Bacon and Descartes up to the most advanced computer programs using statistical techniques is systematic brainwashing: alienating the researcher from his/her most basic life experiences, and replacing a knowledge starting from there with whatever bureaucrats, managers, politicians, disciplinary associations, and various media think important and interesting to be 'scientifically tested'.

As so often, the point can be illuminated through words. Empirical evidence in everyday 'scientific' terminology means data, and it is understood that this is the same as fact. Any empirical-quantitative researcher will tell that he deals with real data and hard facts, not those 'speculations' in which mere 'theorists' (their words of abuse; and indeed a problematic word) are engaged. However, etymology shows that a 'data' and a 'fact' are radically different things. A fact is what is made (*factum*), while 'data' simply exist, are a given (*datum*). The confused identification of what is just there as given, and what was specifically and purposefully fabricated is central for the modern episteme, foundation of the absurdity of a 'social construction of reality'. It is also present in the neo-Kantian idea that transforming the given (*gegeben*) into a task (*Aufgabe*) is an intellectual duty, central in the kind of constructivist indoctrination Marburg neo-Kantians attempted, unsuccessfully, on Ortega; and certainly also attempted on many others, prominently including Heidegger.

Falsification (Popper)

The last term to be discussed in this short and preliminary overview of the idols of scientific methodology is falsification, an artifact of Karl Popper, possibly the greatest ideologue of scientific methodology – as it helps to introduce shortly this figure as well, through some choice words about him by some important Political Anthropologists.

Karl Popper (1902–1994), widely considered as the most important philosopher of science of the 20th century, inventor of 'logical positivism' and direct mentor to a series of influential thinkers and social scientists, starting from Milton Friedman, who modelled his classic article on 'positive economics' on Popper's works, is truly 'representative' example for modern-day methodological scientism. His term 'falsification' had an unparalleled impact on generations of social researchers.

Yet, dissenters to Popper were also numerous and most distinguished, as they prominently include Ludwig Wittgenstein, Eric Voegelin, Michel Foucault, and Norbert Elias. Such dissent concerns no minor matters, as these key thinkers, recognised as milestones figures of philosophy and social theory in the past century, not simply objected to some ideas of Popper, but questioned his entire work, even qualifications and character.

Voegelin's telling remarks are contained in a letter to Leo Strauss, where Strauss's question concerning whether he has encountered the work of Karl Popper produces a passionate response (as in Cooper and Emberley 1993: 66–8), amounting to a genuine philosophical wrath (Voegelin 2000b: 45). Voegelin starts by stating that

> The opportunity to speak a few deeply felt words about Karl Popper to a kindred soul is too golden to endure a long delay. This Popper has been for years, not exactly a stone against which one stumbles, but a troublesome pebble that I must continually nudge from the path, in that he is constantly pushed upon me by people who insist that his work on 'the open society and its enemies' is one of the social science masterpieces of our times.

Far from accepting such characterisation, according to Voegelin

> Popper is philosophically so uncultured, so fully a primitive ideological brawler, that he is not able even approximately to reproduce correctly the contents of one page of Plato. Reading is of no use to him, he is too lacking in knowledge to understand what the author says.
> *(1993: 66).*

Michel Foucault as if takes up where Voegelin was leading. Thus, in his lecture on Plato's 'Seventh Letter' he offers the dismissive aside that 'the rather fantasist [*assez fantaisistes*] interpretations of the good Karl Popper do not take into account, of course' (2010: 235), the rather complex game that is involved in Plato's claims concerning the political role of the philosopher, including him as a supposed king.

Karl Popper was also a choice target of Norbert Elias's essays about the sociology of science (Mennell 1992: 190–1). He gave a talk against Popper already in a staff seminar around 1969 in Leicester, scandalising his colleagues that he dared to attack 'the great Popper' (Elias 1991: 85–6). He later developed his views into full papers, with telling titles, which accused Popper, father of 'logical positivism' as being rather a metaphysician and a 'reality-blind philosopher' (Mennell 1992: 299). Focusing on Popper's *The Logic of Scientific Discovery*, first published in 1935, Elias argued that Popper thought in terms of a 'single eternal logic of science', which furthermore took physics as its model, with explanations approaching a law-like regularity and eventually being formalised through logic; positions that Popper never questioned later (Mennell 1992: 191). The account can be rounded up by the extremely negative views on Popper by Wittgenstein and Stephen Toulmin, a main student of his. The unbridgeable divergence between Wittgenstein and Popper came to the surface in the famous encounter between Wittgenstein and Popper, on 25 October 1946 in Cambridge, when Wittgenstein simply left the room, after Popper repeatedly failed to address his questions.[7]

These accounts can be complemented by two personal experiences. The first is an information that I directly received from a former student of Popper. According to this, Popper's extreme dogmatism and arrogance, just as his lack of concern and care for his students, was common knowledge at the LSE, and so students only referred to his famous book as 'the *Open Society*, written by one of its enemies'. Second, more than once I was told, no doubt by acolytes of the great Sir Karl, that anybody who considers history as important is certainly a Marxist.[8]

In sum, while for most people Popper is one of the greatest philosophers of the 20th century, certainly its most important philosopher of science, for some of the most important and erudite thinkers of the same time he was hardly more than a charlatan.

His views concerning falsification fully support such a disparaging view. The term is widely considered as one of his most important innovations, a genial solution for validating scientific results. However, quite on the contrary, it can be shown to be misleading, dangerous, and plain wrong.

To start with, the idea directs the issue of scientific validation outside any direct concern with truth, proceeding rather on the reverse, placing the emphasis on falsity. Truth for Popper is what cannot be falsified. This, to put it mildly, is putting the cart before the horse: instead of trying to face truth directly up, it rather avoids the issue altogether and, as if taking the back door, proceeds by a path outside truth, literally justifying the claim that the idea misleads. As the story of the Cambridge encounter demonstrates, Popper indeed had difficulties in giving a straightforward, true account: as told by him, Wittgenstein asked him for an example of a moral principle, and stormed out of the room, hearing Popper's answer ' "Not to threaten visiting lecturers with pokers" ', as if defeated by Popper's quip, which Popper even planned to offer as the start of his autobiography. This account, however, does not stand up to truth, according to eyewitnesses (Edmonds and Eidinow 2002: 185, 203–20, esp. 215); even the epilogue-anecdote, according to which at the train journey back to London his book was discussed by fellow travellers was his pure invention (228); or – and here using the word rightly – was nothing but a *falsification*. But Popper's entire attitude, the obsessive focus on polemics, both in this case and as a general aspect of his character is extremely problematic, as argued by both Foucault and Serres. Second, it not simply reverses and goes aside or around, instead of being up front, but it expressly negates, even using the most problematic trick of double negation: truth becomes not simply the true, but what is 'not' 'false'. A double negation, in mathematics, and in 'Aristotelian' logic, might be the same as a positive assertion, but in human life, and in the real world, it isn't. Third, there are a great many things, again in human life and the real world that simply cannot be falsified. Hardly anything can, as life is not a methodological hypothesis, or a scientific experiment, it just happens, and is, and the truth concerning such events, experiences, and existence is all that matters in human, social and political life. Following the method of falsification is thus extremely dangerous, as it disorients all those touched by it. It furthermore even has a clear aura of paranoia; according to Stephen Toulmin, a main student of Wittgenstein, ' "Popper's own philosophy of science had this element of paranoia in it. Because what he used to teach us is that the nearest thing to a true theory is one that hasn't betrayed you yet" ' (as in 229).

Falsification thus offers a completely irrelevant and misleading perspective on life. It is therefore plain wrong.[9]

Political Anthropology cannot follow a 'scientific methodology'. The third and final part of this book will present, from basic – literally the most basic – tools of human knowledge and understanding, words and images, some of the ways and methods used by Political Anthropology.

Notes

1 Here of course one leaves the thinking of Nietzsche. Atheism is ridiculous among others because it pontificates about something it does not understand. See also Szakolczai (2023).
2 'Ha féltem is, a helyemet megálltam/ – születtem, elvegyültem és kiváltam.' (*Kész a leltár*); own translation. The poem was written in November-December 1936, thus just a year before the tragic death of the poet, on 3 December 1937. The translation of the last word follows Michel Serres' practice of hyphenating (see Bandak and Knight 2023), taking into account that Hungarian *kivál*, derivate of the crucial root *vál*, means both excellence and separation.
3 This frequently used synonym of 'object' is particularly interesting, as brings out the militaristic terminology of modern science, emphasised by Serres (1982).
4 In light of Yates's ideas about the 'will to operate', the term has special poignancy.
5 Note that this was the way Kierkegaard uses the word in the subtitle of one of his most famous works, and particularly relevant for Political Anthropology, for all kinds of reasons, *Fear and Trembling*.
6 See also German *Sache* 'cause' and *Ur-sache* (also cause, but here pointing to something deep down in the past). The problem of 'causality' is discussed by Weber extensively in his 'Vocation' lectures. Nietzsche in the *Untimely Meditations* states that anything with history in it will always elude those who always looks for 'causes' (*Ursachendenken*). I thank Harald Wydra for bringing my attention to this.
7 For details, see Edmonds and Eidinow (2002).
8 Popper's ideas on history, exposed in another awful book, *The Poverty of Historicism*, also border on fraudulence, as the book is a frontal attack on the most absurd ideas of Marxist-Leninist, even Stalinist, dialectical materialism, but Popper and Popperians generalise this to an overall dismissal of any reference to history. This is helped by the misleading title, as 'historicism' is a – mostly German – movement in the history of thought, but the book does not deal with this.

9 The nonsensicality of Popper's other famous related idea, the method of trial and error as the best way to advance knowledge, swallowed fully by Bertrand Russell, can also be simply shown. The methods and terminologies of science, from causality through inquiry and testing up to proving, were taken from law. But can one imagine a legal system in which judges make their decisions on trial and error? The closest to this – and the analogy is quite revealing – is the medieval practice of fire and water trial, which closely recalls similar African and Asian techniques of 'justice'. Instead of trial and error, genuine knowledge progresses through carefully weighted experiences, informed judgment, the care for truth (not the possibility of falsification) and the love of wisdom.

PART III
Some Methods of Political Anthropology

7
WORDS

> Words play tricks on us when we describe the past
> *Joyce Appleby, 1978: 129*

> The origin of the word – that is, of human speaking in terms of Saying – its origin which is in the nature of Appropriation [*der ereignisarten Herkunft*], is what constitutes the peculiar character of language
> *Martin Heidegger, 1982: 133*

> 'Is smartness American for forgery?', asked Martin
> *Charles Dickens*, Martin Chuzzlewit, *258*

Bacon's famous critique of idols offers the condensed essence of a Gnostic vision of the world, aiming at dismissing as insufficient all previous forms of knowledge and understanding, and replacing it with the only perfect and saving knowledge, gained and collected in a methodologically advanced and correct scientific way. The idols of the marketplace have some special, as particularly problematic, features even among them, and for a series of reasons. Problems start with the presumed identification of words and language with the marketplace. This creates the mistaken impression that language developed out of interaction between strangers, so is mere communication, the exchange of information. However the exact opposite is true: language is a most intimate, inner aspect of human life,[1] while mere communication is always an intrusion from the outside, an interruption of personal activities in the intimate sphere, weapon of parasites and tricksters, using message-missiles. It also mistakenly intimates that words were coined by a process of bargaining, just like prices, the 'right price' being a model to set up the 'right word', also recalling Popper's mistaken idea about 'trial and error'. This further interconnected the rising economy and sciences, reinforcing them as exclusive reference points of human existence, helping to empty intimacy – as jointly alluded at by Appleby, discussed in Chapter 5, and Heidegger, to be discussed in this Chapter.

All this is bad enough, but the worst is the central idea, the dismissing of existing words, and thus language, as being scarce, imprecision and prejudices heaped upon each other, to be replaced by a proper, scientific terminology, based on unambiguous, one-to-one relations between words and things.

However, this perspective is radically wrong. Far from being a collection of gossips and prejudices, language – all languages, every single language – is rather the repository of timeless wisdom, based on the experiences of countless generations. Instead of dismissing existing words as insufficient, in a mad search for a perfect, scientific terminology, producing libraries of books which are illegible except for those initiated into scholastic duckspeak, knowledge about human and social life should start with and be based upon a thorough understanding of the human languages that exist as *gifts*.

This chapter will explore the method-logical importance of words for social understanding through paradigmatic writings by representative figures of linguistic anthropology, historical linguistics, and linguistic philosophy, Edward Sapir, Mario Alinei, Martin Heidegger and Michel Foucault.

Edward Sapir on language as gift

Sapir's essay, written for the first 1933 edition of the *Encyclopedia of the Social Sciences*, simply entitled 'Language', which was then selected by the editors of the representative, posthumous collection of his essays as the lead-off chapter, starts with a sentence that must be quoted in full and analysed extensively, as in a significant sense it is simply unsurpassable: 'The gift of speech and a well-ordered language are characteristic of every known group of human beings' (Sapir 1949: 1). Thus, in its very first meaningful word, the essay characterises language as not simply a given, but explicitly as a *gift*. The essay thus can be inscribed into the Maussian paradigm, and by implication also into the vision-claim that social life is based on a *charis* logic. If language as such, its words, are gifts, then any knowledge and understanding must start by valorising such a gift, and make it clear, from the start, that anything we do with such gifts, any talk, conversation, writing, discourse, search for knowledge must be based on the genuine appreciation of the gift-like character of the words we use. We need to recognise and practice humbleness and gratitude towards the very possibility that we live in a culture, where language exists, and therefore we can feel at home there, having a meaningful existence. Anything else is arrogant and abusive – a piece of sophistry, starting with Bacon's claims about the idols of the marketplace.

Moving further, it is important to discuss what exactly is identified as a gift by Sapir. It is, to start with, speech – and the article will repeatedly lay the emphasis on *speech* as the most important aspect of language. In a way, of course, *every* aspect of language is equally important, and necessary, and belongs together, but such clear emphasis on speech has its importance, in its contrast to the view according to which *real* civilisation, beyond 'mere' culture (implying 'primitive' culture), starts with writing – a standard bias of 19th German scholarship, but also imported into anthropology – and social theory – by such influential figures as Ernest Gellner and Jack Goody. Language is not simply a system of signs, an aspect of a broader unit like culture and society, but it exists first of all when used by some human beings. It is indeed a practice, which implies two things. First, that speech assumes a *concrete individual* who is speaking – if more people speak at the same time, that is only noise – and 'society' cannot talk, only individuals can. This is *not* 'methodological individualism', that expression is meaningless, a sophistic concoction. This becomes evident in the second thing that is implied *at the same time*: that speech also necessarily assumes that there is at least another human being who listens; otherwise speech has no meaning. Talking to oneself is always and everywhere considered a sign of madness – something Cartesians should reflect on carefully. Thus, the very first and most basic consideration on language, taking Edward Sapir as our indeed best guide, implies not just a Maussian-classical Greek perspective, but also a perspective that takes seriously, in an inseparable unity, concrete individuality and sociability as a twin pair.

Furthermore – and we are still in the very first line of the essay! – apart from speech, what is a gift is not simply language, but a *well-ordered* language. What is well-ordered is also pleasing, whether to the eye or the ear, thus is simply *beautiful*. Thus, in his opening sentence of the essay Sapir alludes not only to grace, but also to beauty, or the gift-grace-beauty unity of the classical Greek vision of the world, but which can be taken back not just to Minoan Crete, but also the Palaeolithic, as evidenced by its cave art. With this, he further emphasises his dissent from the Germanic vision, according to which 'real' civilisation starts with writing. This is simply not true: *all* languages are *equally* well-ordered – which of course does not mean that they are 'equal', in any sense.

This is reinforced by the second main claim of the essay, made in the middle of the first page, and emphatically revisited later several times: that 'language is an essentially perfect means of expression and communication among every known people' (1). Sapir and his main student Whorf are often accused of 'cultural relativism', but that expression is just one of the many labelling-stigmatising exercises used by modern rationalism to get rid of uncomfortable positions. The term is at least twice unapplicable to the crucial point made by Sapir: first, because the claim is not relativist, but – if you want – 'absolute': it is not a meaningless acceptance of 'anything goes' but a positive assertion of the *perfection* of all languages – at least, in their 'origin' or 'essence'. Second, the claim is only about language, and not an acceptance of any practice in any culture.

The claim concerning the perfection of all languages is reasserted, and specified, in several places. Thus, concerning the sound units, or phonemes, he adds that 'there is no known language which has not a perfectly definite phonetic system' (4). Furthermore, concerning the psychological peculiarities of language, he adds that 'language is a perfect symbolism of experience' (11). Finally, Sapir offers a crucial characterisation: 'Speech as behavior is a wonderfully complex blend of two pattern systems, the symbolic and the expressive, neither of which could have developed to its present perfection without the interference of the other' (14).

All this implies a crucial corollary concerning Bacon's 'idols of the marketplace', and the various 'scientific' and 'scientistic' attempts to 'improve' on existing human languages. If something is perfect, it cannot be substantially improved. Of course, the encounter with new realities requires new words; and occasionally great thinkers might need to coin terms which did not exist before, or were not used in that manner before. But these are only exceptions; a general attack against historical languages as mere idols simply won't do.

Sapir's essay contains a series of further gems for the purposes of this book. Thus, while language and speaking of course imply a 'purposeful' and 'conscious' activity of the mind, the way we actually speak, including its most complex aspects, often takes place outside consciousness: 'Language is not merely articulated sound; its significant structure is dependent upon the *unconscious selection* [emph. AS] of a fixed number of "phonetic stations" or sound units' (3). The point is emphatically repeated in the next sentence, and with a crucial added idea: 'the essential point is that through the unconscious selection of sounds as phonemes, definite psychological barriers are erected between various phonetic stations, so that speech ceases to be an expressive flow of sound and becomes a symbolic composition with limited materials or units' (3). This statement contains two important additional points. First, it calls attention to the inherent link between sounds (or vowels) and the flow or flux; but this is done exactly to put the focus *not* on the flow itself, but on certain barriers or limits that stop this flow and in this way render speech, and meaning, possible. The Newtonian focus on fluxions, and the focus of early economic theories on the growing flow of trade, perform the opposite movement, turning attention back to the flow, or actually liquidising-liquidating stable entities by returning them into a flow, and thus have technically, verbatim deculturing effects.

The paradoxical results of a liquidisation produced by the confusion of distinct phonemes can be seen in the contrast between the use of vowels in English and Hungarian. In Hungarian, there are 14 distinct vowels, which enable the formation of a large number of short root syllables, and make diphthongs – sliding or flowing between vowels – unnecessary. In Hungarian, diphthongs only exist in a few dialects, and are considered as lapses in speech. In English, on the other hand, there are only 5 vowels, the same five as in Latin, but due to the way language developed these vowels assumed expressions quite different from the original vowels, and also a large number of diphthongs emerged, leading to current claims that English actually has as many as 21 vowels. However, the pronunciation of these diphthongs became extremely particular, appropriating such nuances later in life being almost impossible, and thus this flowing, hybridised, vibrating uttering of diphthongs became the clearest expression of differences in social class – something which in French is done through grammatical rules, or the complexities of written codes.

Second, the specification of phonemes as limits of the flow is equivalent to the Sanskrit word for syllable, *aksara*, or 'not-flow', as *ksara* means 'flow'. This is more than a simple peculiarity, as *aksara* also means 'indestructible', and apart from the syllable it is also applied to the atman, or the soul. Even further, one of the words used by Plato for the indestructibility of the soul, *adiaphthoros*, is a direct etymological derivate of *aksara*; while the very word syllable, in classical Greek, from which the English term is derived, is an invention of Plato.

This is of crucial importance, as the ideas of Sapir, Plato, and the Vedas here tightly hang together, forming an anti-Baconian – and by implication anti-modernist, anti-scientific methodology – vision of the way language, or the condition of possibility of learning and understanding, necessarily operates. Language is fundamentally speech, or a set of sounds; but these sounds are not random flows, as 'natural' sounds are, but are composed of indestructible units, combining sounds (vocals) with barriers made by the tongue or the larynx (consonants), not by a conscious effort of the mind, rather through the unconscious operations of the other great indestructible, the soul. We humans speak because something inside the core essence our of person which is usually called the 'soul' manages to convey and express our experiences, feelings and thought in the form of an *unconscious* selection of a series of phonemes, or verbal expressions, or speech (units). It is due to this unconscious aspect that language has 'a tremendous intuitive vitality' (11).

Sapir's essay contains a series of further claims that help to understand this process. To start with, language does not 'mediate' experience, in the sense of Hegel, rather forms an inseparable unity with it: language 'does not as a matter of actual behavior stand apart from or run parallel to direct experience but completely interpenetrates with it' (8). Thus, 'it is generally difficult to make a complete divorce between objective reality and our linguistic symbols of reference to it' (9). Instead, '[f]or the normal person every experience, real or potential, is saturated with verbalism' (9). In a connected manner, while every language possesses a formal, structural, 'quasi-mathematical form' (10), or 'quasi-mathematical patterns' (11), it also has an 'almost unique position of intimacy' among forms of symbolism, which is due to its being learned in early childhood, piecemeal, and 'in constant association with the color and the requirements of actual contexts' (10). Here Sapir performs two feats in contrast to modern rationalism: re-valorises the learning experiences of children, in contrast to the exclusive focus of Kantian rationalism on adults ('maturity'); and also re-valorises the positive contribution of everyday experiential *contexts*, downgraded by Bacon into the idols of the marketplace – while at the same time correcting Bacon that such purported 'idols' were not acquired in the semi-public realm of exchange, rather in the intimacy of the *home*.

A final point to be mentioned manages to put Habermas into his place. According to Sapir, 'the purely communicative aspect of language has been exaggerated. It is best to admit that language is primarily a vocal actualization of the tendency to see realities symbolically, that it is precisely this quality which renders it a fit instrument for communication and that it is in the actual give and take of social intercourse that it has been complicated and refined into the form in which it is known today' (15).[2]

Sapir died in 1938, at the age of 55. His legacy was continued by his best student, Benjamin Lee Whorf – though only for a very short while, as Whorf himself died in 1941, aged 44. Thus, as a truly colossal tragedy, the two most important anthropologists of language together did not live for 100 years.

Mario Alinei on the origins of words

Etymology is important for method-logical reasons and not only as it offers, in the sense of *etymos* coined by Plato in *Cratylus*, the original, authentic meaning of a word. It is also important because of the way it helps to *recognise*, rather than build, connections between different words, and in this way promotes understanding, and by helping to feel more at home in the language, recognising that words which until then we simply took as signs of things actually carry much deeper meanings.

Mario Alinei's 2009 book is the culmination of a life-work. Alinei (1926–2018) was a linguist of considerable distinction, Emeritus Professor of Utrecht University, founder of the Italian Society of Linguistics, founder or president of a series of other international linguistics societies, championing an interdisciplinary approach to linguistics in several hundred publications that brought linguistics into dialogue with anthropology, paleo-ethnology, archaeology, genetics, and computational studies (Benozzo 2019). With this book of almost 1000 pages, (his list of publications in the Bibliography runs to over 4 small-print pages), Alinei intended to place etymology on a coherent theoretical basis.

Alinei presents his ideas, highly critical of conventional etymology, by comparing and contrasting them to Saussure's general linguistics. He accepts Saussure's central claim about the arbitrary nature of the sign, but claims that exactly for these reasons it is necessary to pay more attention to the motivation why such presumably arbitrary signs were selected in order to identify certain referents in a language. Etymology should be concerned with explaining motivation, and so it should be preoccupied with the study of meanings, and changes in meanings, rather than with formal changes, as it is now customarily being done, due to an excessive focus on written language (Alinei 2009: 131; 184–5).[3] Etymology is the opposite of arbitrariness, also for Heidegger (1982: 28): 'I would like to start from the etymology of the word; it will show you that my use of the word is not arbitrary'.

The cornerstone of Alinei's approach is his key terminological innovation 'iconymy', or 'image-name' (Alinei 2009: 65–79), introduced as improvement, following Ogden and Richards, of Saussure's signifier-signified dichotomy. As typical Kantianism, Saussure argued that foundational for linguistics is the contrast between the 'signifier', or a set of sounds (say, d-o-g, two consonants and a vowel), and the 'signified' (the concept of a 'dog', representing the animal in a word). Ogden and Richards argued that a further distinction is necessary, as the letter 'l-i-g-h-t' might refer to the opposite of heaviness, or the opposite of darkness, extending the dichotomy into the symbol-thought-referent triangle. Alinei adds a fourth term, 'iconymy' [*iconimo*], capturing the way forming a new word is motivated, by using previous words as 'image-names'. He illustrates the point through the example of 'spectacles', a relatively recent technical innovation which in most European languages is expressed in a quite different – though in a theoretical sense identical – manner: in French *lunettes*, or 'small moons'; in English, due to its material 'glasses'; while the German word *Brille* refers to the crystals (*berillio*) from which in older times glasses were made. Common to all these words is that a new name is not constructed out of the blue, but uses previous names as *images* (67).

Alinei identifies four modalities of iconymy: onomatopoeia, phono-symbolism (a term taken from Roman Jakobson; 68, 905), metonymy, and metaphor, each well-known in themselves, but now taken as modalities by which the formation of new words is motivated. In this way, while accepting the starting point of Saussure about the arbitrary character of the word-sounds, he focuses on the way meaning is assigned by word-formation, shifting attention from semiotics as artificial meaning-construction to the historical way meaning systems were formed in a culture. For Alinei etymology is not a Sophistic play with erudition, but helps us understand how words we use in everyday life are saturated with meaning, and how this meaning-construction was result of poetic work by countless generations. Alinei repeatedly underlines the poetic aspect of language, the coining of words, establishing clear affinities between his thinking and Heidegger's – though also makes it clear that he leaves the pursuit of such hints to others: 'The argument should be further elaborated here, given that the roots of this "poeticity" of language must, obviously, be found at the origins, and thus in our cognitive faculties. We leave the study of this interesting theme to others (80)'.

Before moving further, a few comments are needed about Saussure – as Alinei grants too much in accepting the idea about the 'arbitrary' character of word-sounds. The central issue concerns the exact stance taken up by Saussure as researcher. This can be seen, apart from his ideas concerning arbitrariness, in the presumed 'chaos' surrounding thinking and linguistic signs; the idea that the 'motivation' in the formation of linguistic signs is only necessary 'to avoid the chaos' (59).[4] This makes it evident that Saussure's life-work is based on a hubristic Kantian constructivism: the stance of the single thinker, agent of the transcendental mind, who forces himself, with all his might, to incorporate into his mind as much knowledge as possible, in the future analogy of inputs into a computer, and then uses the powers of his mind to *impose* some order on this recalcitrant chaos, or recidivist sinner, that is the world.

The perceived arbitrariness of language, thus, is a mistake, consequence of a Kantian perspective. From inside a language, *any* language, *all* words can be made sense of, by tracing them to their roots, following the four operations of iconymy (908). These four types can be traced, ultimately, to some sounds, or images. Concerning sounds, the founding relationship is clear; but concerning the ultimate source of images, Alinei only offers, at the very last substantive subsection of the book, a rather cryptic suggestion: 'when etymology reaches the earliest form that can be reconstructed for the given language (for e.g. PIE for Italian), the iconymy will be considered by definition as sound symbolic' (670).

With agglutinating languages, especially those agglutinating languages that use many and long vowels, like Hungarian, etymologies can be traced back to very short and basic roots, many of which can be assigned onomatopoeic or phono-symbolic value. These particularly illuminating meaning-families can be identified between important concepts that in other languages are not etymologically connected. This is the reason why, apart from more standard, Indo-European etymologies, this book also indicates, where appropriate, Hungarian etymologies that could help to bring out such meaningful relations.

Four additional points, in conclusion, with method-logical importance. First, just as Sapir, Alinei emphasises the gift-like character of language: language is a 'gratuitous artifact', freely available for everyone to use (46–7). Second, just like Heidegger, Alinei emphasises that we are at home in the world through language, and etymology is important as promotes participatory experience. Finding an iconymy, uniquely in linguistics, can produce a genuine '*aha-erlebnis* [sic; experience]', an 'intellectual illumination', or an 'illuminating discovery' (288) – which can be taken as Alinei's unique answer to Heidegger's question about facing 'a possibility of undergoing an experience with language' (Heidegger 1982: 90–1). The third point is Alinei's 'theory of continuity', to which he devoted several similarly thick monographs. According to Alinei – and this is a point of enormous significance for social understanding – language produces no intrinsic alteration. A language identifies a community and is transmitted, unchanged in its basic structure, from generations to generations (Alinei 2009: 41–5). It certainly produces new words, according to need, but this does not alter its nature: 'it would last *forever* [...] except for the intervention of external factors that can transform it, or mark its end' (45). Finally, the study of semantic transformations, which for Alinei should be the central concern of etymology, instead of formalistic changes, can be performed through archaeology. Such integration of linguistics and archaeology, and also anthropology and folklore, is probably Alinei's most important idea, and his book offers numerous examples, focusing in two long chapters, on 'etymological archaeology' (438–547).

Martin Heidegger on the way to language

A central guiding principle of Political Anthropology is that the methods and ideas of cultural anthropology closely correspond to those of philosophical anthropology, especially the ideas of Plato, and the modern approaches closest to his works, taking inspiration from them, philosophical hermeneutics. Most important for this chapter are Heidegger's late reflections on language, singled out for attention by Michel Foucault (1994, IV: 703) as having had a central impact on his work.

German as language is patently appropriate to express the gift character of language and existence, as there the phrase 'there is' is expressed by the words *es gibt* 'it gives'. Heidegger's thinking is centrally preoccupied both with existence (the question of Being), and words (the nature or essence of language) as gifts.[5] This is the reason why – apart from the problematic character of German philosophical thinking, a legacy of Kant and Hegel – his thinking is so difficult to follow, as it tries to penetrate the heart of Being, but this can be only done through language, which necessarily misses aspects of true Being; while the study of language again requires the use of language, or itself, inevitably risking circularity or even tautology. Heidegger was well aware of this problem, going back to the start of his philosophising. It was a main reason why for a long time he didn't publish his ideas:

> I know only one thing: because reflection on language, and on Being, has determined my path of thinking from early on, therefore their discussion has

stayed as far as possible in the background. [...] it was all of twenty years after my doctoral dissertation that I dared discuss in a class the question of language.
(1982: 7–8)

Heidegger's most important related reflections are contained in a series of lectures and a conversation published in the volume *On the Way to Language*. The English edition lacks the first chapter, published elsewhere,[6] and the chronological order of the original publication was inexplicably altered.

The lectures address, again and again, the same issues, stubbornly returning to the impossible task of penetrating the heart of language by language, often using the same poetic or philosophical sources, though behind the evident repetitions there is always a different movement of thinking. The paradoxical progress of Heidegger's thinking is marked by the strange, counterintuitive sequence of titles, as the chronologically first lecture is entitled 'Language', the second series 'The Essence (*Wesen*) of Language', while the third 'On the Way to Language'. A crucial moment is reached at the end of the first lecture of the series 'The Essence of Language', where he first modifies the title, to 'The Essence? – of Language?' (70–1), and then offers a 'guide word [*Leitwort*]', with the expression 'the essence of language: the language of essence', discussed in detail in the third lecture and in a non-conclusive but concluding way in the lecture 'On the Way to Language'.

In the second lecture-chapter, a series of three lectures, Heidegger presents his way to the way to language, through a question, repeated at the start of each lecture in an identical manner, concerning the 'possibility of undergoing an experience with language' (57, 73, 90–1). The German word used here for experience, *Erfahrung* – Heidegger significantly fails to use the Goethe-Dilthey term *Erlebnis* – is derivate of the verb *fahren*, which captures travel in its different modalities, thus is concerned directly with the way. Also significantly, these terms are absent from the first lecture-chapter.

Erfahrung is the term Kant used for his empiricist-rationalistic-constructivist reading of experience, this is why Goethe and Dilthey introduced *Erlebnis* 'lived experience'. Heidegger makes it clear at the start of the first lecture of the second lecture-chapter that he is not using the term in the Kantian sense: for him, 'experience' does not assume a prior, conscious subject, rather it is something that 'befalls us, strikes us, comes over us, overwhelms and transforms us' (57).[7] He needed this word, and not *Erlebnis*, as his focus is on the links between 'experience' and the 'way'. In this sense the lectures contain key 'anti-methodological' reflections on method, and in prominent places: at the start of the second lecture (74), where – using Nietzsche – Heidegger contrasts his way of proceeding with purported scientific methods; and at the start of the third lecture (91–2), where he reflects on various terms used for the 'way'.[8]

The question of how language can be experienced in the way Heidegger specified experience is not a trivial manner, as one either knows a language, and then an encounter with something familiar cannot produce a shaking up, or does not know it, in which case it can hardly produce an experience. An in-between situation, the way of learning a language, is also evidently irrelevant here. The issue can be formulated in the terminology of Pizzorno: it is not the cognitive but recognitive aspect of an encounter with language *as* language.

The first, in a way preliminary lecture of the second chapter offers philosophical reflections on poems, especially Stefan George's 1919 poem 'The Word', to approach the question, concluding in the guide-word. A philosopher using poems to reflect on the nature of language is certainly another calculated provocation, but Heidegger as if takes this to the second level by focusing not on their written character, on poems as texts, rather on the oral character, on what they say, singling out for attention the capitalisation of the word 'Saga' by Stefan George (89; see also the importance of poems as songs, 88). We'll soon see in detail that Heidegger, as if following Sapir, focuses on language as Saying and not as writing (96). But just as important is, in the second lecture, the introduction of a series of concrete, spatial metaphors, capturing the ways of language. Experiencing language, in line with the *Erfahrung – fahren* link, is a paradoxical road, as it has to reach, or attain, itself, or what is already granted. Thinking – especially thinking about language – does not require a rigorous method, as it rather implies a *region* where one is supposed to freely *walk* – another crucial material metaphor (74–5). This spatial terminology helps to capture the relationship between poetry and philosophy: while they certainly are not identical, they are not separated, as if by a cut, but are near, even share a neighbourhood, and due to this nearness even their differences in terms of their Saying are helpful for understanding the possibility of an experience with language: '[t]his divergence is their real face-to-face encounter' (90). The way in which they together can help to understand how language can be experienced will be central theme of the third section of the second lecture-chapter.

The guide-word of Heidegger, an entire phrase, identifies the essence of language as the language of essence, or a linguistic expression that captures something fundamental, a kind of original experience – this is why the recognition of such an original experience can offer a genuine experience. Such linguistic essence-experience captures the heart of speaking as Saying, and Saying as Showing: designating something, calling attention to something vocally, or characterising this event-experience by the uttering of a word: an 'ancient primary word' (92; *Urwort*, 1985: 187; the example given is particularly important, as it is *Weg* 'way'). Uttering such a word, especially for the first time, capturing a feeling, an experience, a vision in a word, is a poetic activity in the original Greek sense of *poiesis*,[9] but is also central for the activity of poets. At the same time, it is here that poetry and philosophy, in their divergence, also come near, become neighbours, recuperating, identifying, recognising such originary, basic, essential experiences, by driving words to their primordial meaning – evoking etymology. This is where not only poetry and philosophy become near, but also Heidegger the philosopher and Alinei the linguist, concerning the only such experience available in linguistics: discovering the iconymy (Alinei 2009: 288; see above). Thus, if the essence of language is Saying as Showing, or to let something appear (Heidegger 1982: 93, 126), then the heart of language is the word, the experience of coining a word, and the reflective experience of recognising such original creation, not grammar; and so the real concern with method in a research, or of finding one's way, necessarily leads to a central concern with words: of getting at the bottom of the meaning of the key terms which we use, through etymological analysis and semantic history;[10] and of being able to create, poetically, a word which does not exist but is needed, not through the artificial concocting of a life-hostile 'scientific' terminology. This is the reason why Heidegger repeatedly returns to Stefan George's 1919 poem 'The Word', eventually devoting to it an entire lecture. This ends by stating that it is by pondering on poetry, as word, as the coining of the word, that 'poetry and thinking belong together'; that together they help us return to our origins, where 'we come face to face with what is primevally worthy of thought' (155). This evokes nothing less than the rule of the word as – his ultimate interpretation of the last line of George's poem – it is the word that 'makes the thing be a thing', as it shines 'as the gathering which first brings what presences to its presence'. Here he evokes the 'oldest word' used for such 'rule of the word', *Logos*, a term standing not only for Saying but also Being, or 'for the presencing of things. Saying and Being, word and thing, belong to each other'.

The rest of the third lecture explores further this originary experience with words, and the meaning of its renewal. A crucial phrase, whose translation is particularly problematic, states that 'what concerns us as language receives its attuning [*Bestimmung*; certainly not "definition"] from Saying as that which moves all things' (95; 1985: 191); in particular, it moves the soul. Heidegger, however, turns here not to the soul, but to hinting, or beckoning, a concern explored in depth in his conversation with Professor Tesuka (1982: 24–6), here applied to the operation of the guide-word, which leads to 'the neighbourhood of the two kinds of saying, poetry and thinking: in nearness as Saying' (96).

The last part of the third lecture is devoted to exploring, through the neighbourhood of poetry and philosophy, the meaning of their nearness, or nighness (101–2). Such nearness is not a matter for the calculating mind, as it cannot be exactly measured, but implies an intimate belongingness, a face-to-face relationship that only became breached with the rise of modernity (103–5). The pursuit of face-to-face encounter leads very far to the 'world's fourfold' (104) of earth and sky, god and man – the original encounter out of which the gift of language emerged; also expressed as language is 'the House of Being' (used first in the 1947 'Letter on humanism'), or that it is 'the foundation of human Being' (112). The focus is 'on the movement paving the way for the face-to-face of the regions of the world's fourfold' (104; see also Heidegger 1977: 328).[11] It is this nearness, the possibility of experiencing again original experience-encounters that the modern technological world threatens to encroach and eliminate, by 'the thoroughgoing calculative conversion of all connections among all things into the calculable absence of distance. This is making a desert of the encounter of the world's fourfold – it is the refusal of nearness' (1982: 105).[12]

Heidegger returns to his central question, the essence of language, on the penultimate page of the chapter. The possibility of experiencing language is traced to nearness, the presence of nearness, which 'manifests itself as the motion in which the world's regions face each other', or their 'face-to-face encounter' (107). In this sense language as Saying, the uttering of meaningful vocal sound, becomes the liminal moving force of the world, no doubt the reason why in so many languages spirit and soul are connected not simply to the air that we breath, but also the air that transmits, as waves, the voices of language, or Saying. The face-to-face intimacy of the spoken word is thus just as important a feature of our reality as the face itself; reducing direct words to electronically transmitted texts is the equivalent of hiding faces behind obligatory masks. Experiencing language means experiencing words, as they were coined; the thinker who through etymology and conceptual history retrieves the original, poetic meaning of language is like the audience to a theatrical performance, or the beholder to an image: the encounter where the two, creative and recognitive experiences meet.

The last lecture on language

The third and last lecture was delivered in January 1959, when Heidegger was approaching 70. It starts by resuming basic method-logical guiding principles, and offers a new formula. Concerning the former, it will only offer what can be considered as 'a chain of unverified and scientifically unverifiable [or unfalsifiable] propositions', but which rather focuses on how 'we experience the way to language in the light of what happens with the way itself as we go' (111); or, instead of imposing an external model or theoretical framework on language, its 'point is to approach more closely language's own peculiar character', leaving it to language to show itself 'as our way of speaking' (120). Concerning the latter, the formula 'speak about speech *qua* speech', containing the same word three times, serves as a way to lead into the significance of the essentially spoken, vocal, sounding character of language, as Saying-Showing. The focus is on the original face-to-face encounter of the fourfold, where language is given as a gift, through inspired poetic creations, and which can be retraced through thinking.[13]

It offers two crucial new characterisations of this encounter, at the start of the last, third section of the chapter. First, retracing such originary instances offers us a 'plain, sudden, unforgettable and hence forever new look into something which we – even though it is familiar to us – do not even try to know, let alone understand in a fitting manner': an 'unknown-familiar something'; and second, characterises this experience as a recognition of being-at-home or belongingness as owning: '*The moving force of Showing as Saying is Owning*' (127). This owning he furthermore calls Appropriation, characterised as experiencing 'the abiding gift yielded by Saying' (127). Appropriation is translation of German *Ereignis* 'event', but Heidegger is reading *Ereignis* as *Er-eignis*, or 'becoming own [*Eigen*]', which is etymologically not supported, but certainly sounds plausible. The central issue is that through Heidegger's reading the single word *Ereignis* captures both the sudden, illuminative character of the originary experience and the participatory sense of being-at-home or 'ownership' produced by it – a crucial link, and which again rhymes perfectly with the ideas of both Sapir and Alinei; an event that however is not a simple incident or something that merely occurred, but can be experienced only as a gift – the 'abiding gift yielded by Saying'. Thus, when we recognise language as our own, but our own only because of its nature as a gift and not the result of our activity, we reach the end of our search for the nature of language – but this end is nothing else but the way itself: the way that there is, or 'is given' (*es gibt*). This is also why language is more than mere communication: rather 'language alone brings beings as beings into the open for the first time. [...] Language, by naming beings for the first time, first brings beings to word and to appearance. Only this naming nominates beings *to* their Being *from out of* their Being. Such saying is a projecting of lighting' (Heidegger 1977: 185).[14]

What we reach here, by experiencing the owning of language as Saying-Showing, is the experiencing of language as at once natural and historical-cultural. It is natural, to be traced back to *physis*, as it involves the materiality of concrete sounds or voices that can never be fully formalised (1982: 132). But this language is also historical, as language is inseparable from design and destiny. Thus we are taken back to the origin of language, of the word, which is at once a natural occurrence, the utterance of some sounds, and an historical event; not a matter of chance but the experiencing of a gift: 'The origin of the word – that is, of human speaking in terms of Saying – its origin which is in the nature of Appropriation, is what constitutes the peculiar character of language' (133). Language, in this sense, cannot be destroyed, not even by the 'destructiveness of information-language', so is indestructible.[15] Appropriation can remove everything from its present 'subjection to a commandeering order and bring it back to its own' (133). This is true for any language, as all language is perfect, in the sense emphasised by Sapir: 'All human language is appropriated in Saying and as such is in the strict sense of the word true language – though its nearness to Appropriation may vary by various standards' (133). This line of thinking was continued by Whorf, resumed in the Foreword written by Stuart Chase to his collected writings in two claims: 'all higher levels of thinking are dependent on language'; and 'the structure of the language one habitually uses influences the manner in which one habitually understands the environment. The picture of the universe shifts from tongue to tongue' (Chase 1956: vi).[16]

We are humans because we speak, because we are already inside language: 'In order to be who we are, we human beings remain committed to and within the being of language' (Heidegger 1982: 134). It means that we are both at home in language, in the sense that language is ' "the house of Being" ', and at the same time have a 'relation to language', and a quite special one, as 'appropriating, holding, self-retaining is the relation of all relations', and so '*our* saying – always an answering – remains forever relational' (135). Yet, exactly because we can never step outside language, such relation becomes always partly inaccessible, we always need to look at it with a new eye, we can always only be on the way and never reach the end, and so always need to change our relationship to it. Before concluding with the example of von Humboldt, evoked at the start of the lecture, Heidegger offers a final word about the experience that can awaken us for the change needed in our attitude towards language: 'All reflective thinking is poetic, and all poetry in turn is a kind of thinking' (136). It does not offer a 'methodology' in the conventional sense, but all the better; it rather helps to appreciate (*not* criticise) the words we all necessarily use to advance research and thinking.

Michel Foucault on words and things

The argument of this chapter is concluded through Michel Foucault's classic *Order of Things*, originally 'Words and things', certainly a take on Heidegger's concerns with language and being; a book mis-classified as structuralist, but that rather is a prime example for the fruitful combination of anthropology/ ethnology and philosophical hermeneutics. It investigates the issue as if from the reverse angle: reconstructing the manner in which, in two steps, the significance of words and language were ignored by 'scientific methodology'.

Foucault places the first break, a rupture between words and things, in between the Renaissance and the 'classical age' – an important neologism, bringing together the period of early scientific discoveries and rationalism with the Enlightenment – at the first half of the 17th century. Up to the Renaissance, words and things shared the same universe, a world created by God. Creation implies similitudes or likenesses present in things; even man was created to the likeness of God. The marks through which things demonstrated their likenesses were themselves signs:

> [t]here is no difference between the visible marks that God has stamped upon the surface of the earth, so that we may know its inner secrets, and the legible words that the Scriptures, or the sages of Antiquity, have set down in the books preserved for us by tradition.
>
> *(Foucault 2002: 37)*

Gaining knowledge implied recognising likenesses through the way things resembled each other, considering the universe as a vast text: 'Knowledge therefore consisted in relating one form of language to another form of language; in restoring the great, unbroken plain of words and things; in making everything speak' (44).

Such a vision of knowledge assigned a special place to the subject gaining knowledge, and the way knowledge was to be gained. The searcher for knowledge participated in everyday life, was not separate from it. The central terms characterising this knowledge were erudition, implying the ability to 'read nature and books alike as parts of a single text' (53), and wisdom, the accumulation of life experiences by which resemblances in the world of nature can be recognised and identified.[17]

It is in contrast to this continuity that a gap emerged with the classical age, breaking the seamless link between words and things in the first half of the 17th century (51–2).[18] Foucault presents this through an analysis of *Don Quixote*, a choice particularly significant for two reasons: first, because the novel was published in the first decade of the 17th century, thus an exact contemporary of the changes discussed in Chapters 4–5; and second, because the novel is a prime document of the thorough, ongoing theatricalisation of social life, promoted jointly by the re-emergence of the theatre and the romances mass-produced by the printing press and spread in particular through the fairs (see Chapter 10). The immediate transparency of words was lost; what was uttered no longer had a direct contact with reality; words had to be examined and verified, as

> to know is to speak correctly [...] The sciences are well-made languages, just as languages are sciences lying fallow. All languages must therefore be renewed; in other words, explained and judged according to that analytic order which none of them now follows exactly; and readjusted if necessary so that the chain of knowledge may be made visible in all its clarity.
> *(2002: 96)*

This new situation went together with the idea that words are to play a purely instrumental role in the new project of universal science: words are supposed to unambiguously represent things, helping to collect knowledge in encyclopaedic tables. The break with the world of the Renaissance was not yet complete: the 'insistent murmur of resemblance' (76) was still there, in the background, out of which scientists selected the things to be represented in the Table; and God was still assumed as creator, assuring that the universe is well-ordered, making possible to reconstruct this order by science (83). The central tool of this ordering, the sign system, however, was now supposed to be arbitrary, product of convention and no longer based on marks left by God, or natural signs: '[f]rom the seventeenth century, the values allotted to nature and convention in this field are inverted: if natural, a sign is no more than an element selected from the world of things and constituted as a sign by our knowledge.' Thus, '[n]atural signs are merely rudimentary sketches for these conventional signs, the vague and distant design that can be realized only by the establishment of arbitrariness.' (68–70). The growth of knowledge, just as the growth of state power, in the parallel project of 'reason of state' (Foucault 1981a), cannot be stopped in its search for perfection, and will continue into infinity. Language – scientific or scienticised language only, to be sure – has a key role to play in this, as

> language is a spontaneous science, obscure to itself and unpractised, this also means, in return, that it will be brought nearer to perfection by knowledge, which cannot lodge itself in the words it needs without leaving its imprint in them [...] Languages, though imperfect knowledge themselves, are the faithful memory of the progress of knowledge towards perfection.
> *(Foucault 2002: 96).*

The 'reciprocal kinship between knowledge and language' would continue, though in a changed form, in the modern episteme, where 'intermediary languages – descendants of, or outcasts from, both knowledge and language – were to proliferate to infinity' (98).

The rule of representation broke down around 1800 (176–7). Now both the murmur of resemblances and the creator God were left out of the search for knowledge, leaving the man searching for knowledge free but also alone to construct an order out of chaos in an alien world, embodied in the object-subject dualism of Kant:[19] the new rule of empiricist positivism and formalist structuralism on one hand, and the philosophy of consciousness, or transcendental phenomenology on the other (see also Foucault 1969: 21–2). This stance was not that different from that of Bacon and Descartes, or the Gnostics and Sophists of all times, only became radicalised with the onset of the new project of 'secular politicised humanism' (Szakolczai 2017a: 234–5), which by our times became so extremely radicalised that, in the form of artificial intelligence, transhumanism, posthumanism and the like not only God, but also Man became cancelled out of the view, as impediment of 'Progress'. This stance is nihilism itself:

> [t]he whole pose of 'man *against* the world,' of man as a 'world-negating' principle, of man as the measure of the value of things, as judge of the world who in the end places existence itself upon his scales and finds it wanting the monstrous insipidity of the pose has finally come home to us, and we are sick of it. We laugh as soon as we encounter the juxtaposition of 'man *and* world,' separated by the sublime presumption of the little word 'and'
>
> *(Nietzsche, Gay Science, 346)*

and it is on this stance that 'the final delusion' of the 'project' is based: the illusion that 'man everywhere and always encounters only himself' (Heidegger 1977: 308).

Significantly, the vacuity of the modern episteme was exposed at the very moment when it became fully established, by the first sustained critique of Kant and great adversary of Hegel, Schleiermacher, who at the same time offered the foundation of a possibility to return to Plato, with his critical edition; reasserted the links between philosophy and theology; and, by promoting hermeneutics, not only contributed to a better, contextualised thus properly historicised approach to sacred texts (which would be immediately side-tracked by the Kant-Hegel inspired Biblical criticism), but also returned philosophy, away from constructivism and dialectic, to studying the 'murmur of resemblances', or recognising language, and being, as it is there, as opposed to as 'we' would like to construct and wish them, through our activist utopian dream-nightmares (Voegelin 1990).

Notes

1. This will be taken further in Chapter 11.
2. Whorf had similar ideas; a key essay, which remained in MS and was published posthumously, contains the following marginalia: 'Conclusion – error supposing function of language to be only the COMMUNICATION [*sic*] of thought.' (Whorf 1956: 85).
3. Alinei's emphasis is shared by Whorf: '[t]he very essence of linguistics is the question for meaning' (1956: 79), also critical of the focus on formal and structural characteristics, emphasised by traditional linguistics (74).

4 See the July 1915 Preface by Charles Bally and Albert Sechehaye to the first edition: 'Throughout his life-time, he stubbornly continued to search out the laws that would give direction to his thought among the chaos' (in Saussure 2011: liii). See also p.112, trsl changed, where Saussure claims, in a typical Kantian-Durkheimian-alchemical manner, that language not simply 'helps' or 'renders possible' thinking, rather literally 'polices' it: 'The characteristic role of language with respect to thought is not to create a material phonic means for expressing ideas but to serve as an intermediary between thought and sound, under conditions that of necessity bring about the reciprocal delimitations of units. Thought, chaotic by nature, is forced to make itself precise by decomposing itself.'
5 See the following passage from his 'Letter on humanism': 'To embrace a "thing" or a "person" in its essence means to love it, to favor it. Thought in a more original way such favoring means to bestow essence as a gift' (Heidegger 1977: 196). Note that 'favour' is identical to *charis*.
6 This is his most famous writing on language, but the later ones are much more important.
7 Michel Foucault's concern in his last writings about experience preceding the subject starts directly from here.
8 Note that the translator has cut out the passages in which Heidegger supports his argument through Bavarian dialect, even though method-logically – certainly not methodologically – these are of considerable importance.
9 On *poiesis* as bringing-forth, presencing or bringing into appearance, see Heidegger (1977: 293).
10 About this, see Koselleck, whose work cannot be covered here, due to lack of space.
11 This captures liminality, similarly to Florensky. See also how this liminality is elaborated in the 'Building Dwelling Thinking' article (Heidegger 1977: 336), through the example of the bridge.
12 It is astonishing how prophetic Heidegger's words sound today, with electronic communication and mask-wearing truly threatening to wipe out the last remains of face-to-face encounter and speech.
13 Such return to basic sources was central to Heidegger, and is central for his relevance, according to Gadamer (1985: 53).
14 See also the discussion of lightning in the key late Heraclitus seminar (Heidegger and Fink 1992).
15 See Sanskrit *aksara*, meaning both syllable and indestructible; literally, the limit set to flow (*ksara*).
16 Whorf's vision can be illustrated by the following, astonishing quote: ' "Does the Hopi language show here a higher plane of thinking, a more rational analysis of situations than our vaunted English? Of course it does. In this field and in various others, English compared to Hopi is like a bludgeon compared to a rapier" ' (Whorf 1956: 85).
17 Such world vision was not a creation of Christianity, but deeply rooted in Antiquity: '[t]he idea of the universe (world) which reigned in the West up to the seventeenth century was determined by Platonic and Aristotelian philosophy' (Heidegger 1977: 257).
18 Such discontinuities are central for archaeology; see Foucault (1969: 31–7). These can be considered as liminal moments.
19 It is based on the inversion of the meaning of object and subject by Descartes (Heidegger 1977: 280).

8
IMAGES

> That which is primally early shows itself only ultimately to men.
> *Heidegger (1977: 303)*

Two of the central tenets of contemporary discursive rationalism, which could be even considered as part of its basic 'methodological' principles, concern words and images. They could be expressed in two short phrases: words don't matter; and images don't matter. While these tenets are not formulated in this exact way, the short formulations capture the 'essence' of what is stipulated.

Concerning words, and following on Bacon's 'idols of the marketplace', it is asserted that what matters are concepts, and not words. One can use any term if it is properly defined, and it is even better if for one's central concepts one does not use a word that has been as if 'soiled' by everyday use (note that Kant, in the footsteps of Bacon, talks about *pure* reason). Therefore, any concern with etymology and semantic history is irrelevant; at the limit, it can be dismissed as pure sophistry.

Concerning images – in spite of the contemporary obsession with images, ranging from cinema and the advertising industry to the excesses of 'photoshopping' in creating fake realities in the media, and including the obsession with selfies – in mainstream rationalism, and even in social theory, images simply are not discussed, almost as if they did not exist. This closely follows the previous argument. Images, to be sure, cannot be defined; and if something cannot be properly and 'rigorously' defined, it is useless for 'rational science'. This presumed principle is certainly followed by modern rationalist approaches, as one hardly can find an image, or even the discussion of an image, in a book by Immanuel Kant or Jürgen Habermas.

Yet, words and images do matter, in their concreteness, as crucial aspects of human reality and social life. They render understanding possible, in the way they exist, as they are perceived and used since timeless times. Even further, their first, original formulation, whether coining or depiction is fundamental in so far as it

DOI: 10.4324/9781003275138-11

then becomes assumed and taken for granted for successive expressions or formulations, as captured by Heidegger in the motto, thus can indeed be considered as not simply a 'given' but a *gift* which is out there for everybody else to use. Thus, using a common word in a sense different from everyday use is a very questionable undertaking, as it is bound to start a disturbing play between the original and the 'scientifically defined term', inevitably generating all kinds of misunderstanding; while the coining of a new word must have a very good reason, as otherwise it only renders the ideas difficult to follow and understand, again disseminating confusion – or, it becomes just a Sophist trick.

The rationalist ignoring of images gives a good indication how far modern rationalism deviated from the original thinking and ideas of Plato, as the very word 'idea', today considered as merely a simpler or even 'rougher' form of a 'concept', is derived from Plato's use of the term *eidos*, but *eidos* originally meant not something spoken but a form or shape that is *seen* – etymological source, among others, of the term 'video'. We think largely in images, our memory preserves our experiences in images, thus an image, once depicted or formed, can have the same arche-typal effect as a word.

Enrico Castelli on the demonic in art

A particularly good example for the role images offer in promoting understanding is the 1952 book by Enrico Castelli, *The Demonic in Art*.

Castelli (1900–1977), a Jesuit theologian, was one of the most important Italian thinkers of the past century. However, as his thinking incorporated currents in 'existentialism' and phenomenology, it became hardly tolerated in official catholic circles, while being a Jesuit he was anathema on the left, it failed to gain the recognition it deserved.

The genesis of the work has its method-logical importance. As captured in the title of Corrado Bologna's Introduction to the 2007 edition, Castelli fell 'slowly in love with a category'; 'the demonic became his family demon, his *genius* [sic]' (xiv; see also xix). The work was done in the years immediately following WWII (x), in parallel with the Warburg school, inaccessible for Castelli, while at the time he was writing 'neither philosophers nor theologians were occupied with the hermeneutics of art' (xxix). His work also has close affinities with Kafka's philosophico-theological *Zürau Aphorisms*, again not yet available (xviii-ix, xxviii).

Castelli was by no means alone in recognising the importance of those images. The 'Temptation of Saint Anthony', an incision made by Martin Schongauer (c.1445–1491) around 1470 was *the* most influential early incision. Michelangelo copied it in 1487–8, at the age of 12, and is his first known painting. It later became an obsession for Flaubert, who wrote different versions throughout his life. Flaubert's preoccupation became theme for a famous 1967 essay by Michel Foucault, 'Fantasia of the Library'.

It has its own interest that the motive is from the Far East, according to a classic study by the Lithuanian Jurgis Baltrušaitis (1981: 237–238), the first representations appeared in Japan, mid-14th century, as part of a Buddhist dream imagery.

Castelli focuses on images depicted at a particular time and place: Flanders, the late 15th and early-mid 16th centuries, the Golden Age of Flanders, time of the great fairs, culminating in Antwerp, city of Pieter Brueghel the Elder (c.1525-30 – 1569), in the emergence of the first stock market, in the 1530s. As Castelli's analysis reveals, this is more than just a coincidence, as the central themes and motives correspond one by one to aspects of the fairs, and the joint emergence of the modern economy and the techno-scientific and public spectacle interests that grew out of them. The images capture the endless fracases, the limitless fluxes and flows produced by the ongoings of the fairs; the inventions that pretend to discover the secrets of nature, but only produce monsters which denature it; the manner in which the cheap fairground spectacles, ruthless and cunning tricks, still manage to incite the interest of practically everyone; and finally, the way in which the perversely and seductively incited interest in the secret and monstruous, by inviting to discover what is hidden, through charlatans and alchemists, direct heirs of Renaissance magi and their Hermetic philosophy, contributed to the rise of the modern scientific world vision.

Castelli's vision about the connection between thinking and painting is contained in his subtitle: 'The philosophical significance of the demonic in art'. It is qualified in the first sentence of his Preface, but only to identify 'demonic temptation' as the central concern; a theme that evidently requires the ample use of images not just to illustrate the argument, but to carry its substance. A further precision, in line with Castelli's status as philosopher *and* theologian, is added in the Foreword by his son, Enrico Castelli Gattinara jr, claiming that the book also implies that in a large extent 'some artists were true and proper theologians' (in Castelli 2007: x). However, and inevitably given the theme, Castelli was also aware of the paradox of studying temptation through images, as images depicting temptation were themselves tempting, while 'showing something so that it won't be seen' is outright 'a Satanic formula' (22). The paradox is expressed through a citation from Jan Ruysbroeck (1293 – 1381), the great Flemish mystic to whom Castelli devoted a chapter (50–7), given his impact on the images studied: ' "We can only defeat the temptations if we manage to get rid of all images" ' – which at the time when the temptations were depicted in Flanders, the Reformation attempted to accomplish in Switzerland and Germany.

Many of the central images discussed by Castelli have a single theme: a saint is not so much tempted but attacked and tormented by a swarming of demons. These demons manifest frenetic movement and action, and the same movement is characteristic of a mass of people in other images by Bosch or Brueghel. The images thus capture infinity, flux, and flow, by the sheer number of actors, the vehemence and violence of their acts, and also by the lack of any inherent connection between them. The polar opposite word of the character of acts and events depicted is *harmony* – the images utterly lack any harmony. But harmony is the same as proportionality or ratio – so the images are literally irrational, though at the same time every demon attacking the saint, but also every human being or cadaver depicted in the images perform an evidently purposeful act: trying to kill, hurt, beat, steal, seduce. Taken together, these 'rational' acts produce the greatest possible confusion, fracas – a genuine pandemonium; in the case of saints being attacked by demons, in the most literal sense.

Still, the central issue is not winning, by defeating someone or gaining something; the images, according to Castelli, are primarily about *temptation*. This is clear for the saint-and-demons images, but by implication for Castelli this holds also for the other images, the scenes about disordered and decomposed humans. The connection between the two types is given by two sets of etymologically connected words, with further links to the argument, so method-logically fundamental. The first captures the character of beings depicted in most images: animals, demons or objects that are equally out of place, disproportional, decaying or decomposed, in one word *monsters*; while the second the character of the impact exerted by the images, which is terrifying, terrible, horrible, dreadful, tremendous, which are just other terms capturing a *monstrous* feeling or experience. These terms can all be related to each other in one way or other, as 'terror', 'terrible', and 'tremendous' all derive from 'tremor', but 'horror' is derived from 'bristle with fear, shudder', which is the same thing, just as Kierkegaard's *Fear and Trembling* is about 'dread', while 'dreadful' and 'monstrous' again mean the same thing. Concerning the second set, for Castelli these figures are fantastic, products of the imagination; while on the other hand – and perhaps *this* is his most important word – they are denatured (*snaturato*). Fantastic figures are technically monsters; they depict beings that do not exist in the real world, and are thus 'unnatural'; and finally, the circle is closed by evoking that the etymology of 'monster' is 'to show', still visible in English 'demonstrate' and Italian *mostrare*. So the images that show monsters are monstruous images, but it is almost a pleonasm as showing itself is – etymologically, at least in Latin – is 'monstruous'. So we are led back again to the warning of Ruysbroeck.

The warning Castelli perceives, in making sense of the images which try to use Asian imagery by following medieval Christian mystics – the meaning of this combination merits a book-length treatment on its own[1] – is that temptations cannot be actively resisted and fought, but must be encountered by passive staticity. They follow a most perplexing Biblical advice: do not resist evil (Mt 5:39), not evoked by Castelli – probably because this short book, in which practically every word says something new and worthwhile to ponder upon, did not want to waste time evoking the self-evident. This is what all the saints are doing, when encountering the pullulating flow of demons: they do nothing. They don't fight, they don't resist, they don't react; they don't even try to escape. This is because active resistance, even flight is impossible: 'the monsters are invincible if we try to measure up with them. The temptation of monstrosity cannot be overcome if one wants to challenge it' (30). The only way out is to pray, or to call for grace (see also 33).

However, there is more here, as enormous, monstrous challenges that cannot be defeated, no matter how ferocious they are, are at the same time irrelevant, as there is no substance behind them. Demons are not-beings; they are the *nulla* itself; with them 'it is the *nulla* [sic, italics in original] that attempts to hit, and the *nulla* cannot do anything [*il* nulla *nulla può*]' (33). This is why im/passivity is the central theme of these images, since their first great representations by Martin Schongauer (32–3). Their source and paradox, and the temptations they capture, is that they share the same root: in imagination and fantasy. This shows the insubstantiality and at the same time the danger of the challenges by sophists of all times and places, whether they use images or words, as they merely play with the imagination, evoking our fancy, yet the fantastic beings they conjure up gain reality solely by virtue of being evoked. This is why this tradition of mystic thinking rejects imagination (xliii; for a modern offshoot of this perspective, see Rilke); considers fantasy and fantastication as the antithesis of the divine (10), and the fantastic as a form of deceit (35). Chapter 1 is entitled 'The fantastic', and starts by describing it as an 'unreal' that seems comic but in actual fact is tragic (9); it is an attack (*assalto*) that never stops, becomes unfinished as unfinishable, leading to a scuffle and soon becoming a deformation and a defiguration, which becomes tragically oppressive and that has affinities with the mask, a play with hiding and showing (10–11). Castelli immediately at the start evokes Bosch as perfect illustration for the point: in his images 'the fantastic masks the mask, because the monstrous personages of his Hell cannot be masks, that is symbols, because there is no image there, and if the symbol is impossible, then nothing there can give peace. Everything is demonic' (11).

However, there is still more here, as Castelli takes great pains to show that these unnatural, monstrous images, these images of monsters, these terrifying images denaturing our eyes and minds by the unnatural creatures they demonstrate are not mere plays of fancy, conjured up by any imagination, but are products of a specific type of knowledge; a knowledge that is almost science; but that at the same time is very much magic. Many of the monstrous objects and beings are not products of the imagination, but alchemical symbols. This might lead one to suspect the artists as themselves members of Gnostic or heretic sects, and indeed some of them were tempted by magic and alchemy – but in these images they are not presented programmatically, but rather document the source and mode of denaturation. In some images even the magus, or the alchemist, is depicted, and not in a favourable light – rather as part of an effort to lay bare the mechanisms by which they operate. In order to be efficient, they need assistants, and these are also depicted in some images – mountebanks, actors, fools (Montagni 2019). However, in his book, Castelli places the emphasis not on these actors, but on the mode of operation by which attention is lured and seduced towards the denatured – the hint or sign (*cenno*), and the character of the knowledge behind the evident, visible, manifest, and natural: that it is concealed and hidden (*celato*). Castelli takes great care in guiding us how the images show the generation of an expectation, by cunning indications, that there is something beyond the evident, disguised, of great value, which can only be gained by secret knowledge: this is the great temptation; but what is there – and this is the great deceit – is only the non-existent, the *nulla*, or – and this is the greatest temptation – the denatured, the monstrous which, *once* one is lured there by the promise of great, secret pleasure and knowledge captivates one fully and without leaving a way back, as the road by which one arrived there broke the unity of the self.

If the invitation (*cenno*) to discover what was hidden (*celato*) is successful, and one is entrapped into the contemplation of and even desire for the denatured, overcome with the *tremendum* of the horrible, then not only there is no resistance possible, but no way out, no return. All this can be illustrated through a single basic Hungarian root – though with an important twist.[2]

The greatest threat is the horrible, continues Castelli, as the seduction of the desirable, the beautiful, the sins of gluttony and lust can be resisted, and even if one yields, there is a way back, but if one yields to the perverse attractiveness of the horrible, there is no way back, as such seduction separates, splits, breaks, it destroys the unity of the being, the self, so the parts become deprived of any connections, and one's feelings become identified with what was felt (Castelli 2007: 28–9). At this point 'the object of the feeling will no longer be distinguished from the sentient [the self-aware being], because this being lost the unity of its being' (29), and so can no longer distinguish itself from the objects of its feelings. Relying on reason is illusory, as 'the ways of pure reason only lead to mere reason, which has no reason to find anything else but itself' (29) – implying the already split being. The only way out, for Castelli, is grace – but for this man must call for (*chiama*) this grace (30). The arguments can be strengthened further by Hungarian etymology. In Hungarian 'to call' is *hív*, but the same word as adjective means 'faithful, sincere, trusting, true', the word for 'faith' being its derivative (*hit*).[3]

The idea that the heart of the demonic is a luring into denaturing, and that behind it one can suspect the emerging scientific world vision, with its promise to uncover the hidden secrets of nature – an uncovering that is bound to entail apocalyptic consequences – is the great discovery of Castelli, and the entire book comes together if we identify behind the terrible, vertiginous flux the daily reality of the increasingly permanentized fairground. Many of the most famous images of Brueghel depict carnivalesque, fairground scenes, as this is also behind the claim, in itself misleading, that the images of Bosch are also carnivalesque. This is because no merry carnivalesque fun is depicted by these artists, as they rather captured, on the spot, the tragedy, even the horror, behind the apparently cheerful festivities: the kidnapping of an entire culture. Though Castelli calls no attention to this point, not just Brueghel but a great many of the artists discussed by him were from Antwerp, while Bosch's native city, 's-Hertogenbosch was the second biggest town of Flanders in his life-time. The main agents of a theatricalised society lured into infinite substitutability by the unveiling of secret knowledge are all there: the magician-scientist, the charlatan, the alchemist. In the spirit of Frances Yates, Castelli evokes a direct complicity of knowledge and science in these theatrical fairground games of alchemist charlatans, luring their public by evoking an appetite for the pleasures of the hidden. In one image Bosch captures 'the illusionist (*giocatore di prestigio*) who uses our distraction to rob us'; while another is the 'sour parody of those who are so fool to believe that they can be cured of madness by the help of science (the charlatans of knowledge)' (59). Geometry and logic, central for ancient and modern sophists, are main instruments of entrapment: 'one of the modes to hide existence is to geometrise. The devil geometrises' (24, fn.3); while 'logical incontrovertibility is, in a sense, the rational aspect of damnation', adding that it was a common idea in the Middle Ages that logic is an *ars diaboli* (24, fn.4). In both cases Castelli continues the point with the same argument about geometry and logic building up a water-tight prison: geometry attempts to 'close accounts without any residuals [...] not leaving any possibility of evasion', while from logic similarly 'it is not possible to escape'; an argument evoking Michel Serres' *écart* (gap). The importance of the point does not concern geometry or logic *per se*, but the attempt to extend their validity, without any limit, into our life. It is *this* project that is modern; it is technically evil (the etymology of evil is limitlessness); and according to Castelli, it is also theologically diabolical.

The dark, hidden, secret knowledge, for which fairs evoke the desire, and which science then will try to pursue, is the knowledge of death,[4] a prelude to death: 'in the Flemish art of the 15th and 16th centuries it is particularly interesting to note the transformation of the Edenic tree of knowledge into the tree of death'; while 'the great key next to a monstrous exploded egg' in Bosch's 'Garden of Delights' is 'a clear allusion to that key of knowledge paraded by the Pharisees of all times', offering in this way 'a symbolic-tragical representation of the failure of human science' (57). This amounts to a betrayal by the external world (25), where simply 'Everything is betrayal' (59). With the fairs as the background, one cannot avoid looking again back to Hungarian, where 'selling' (*árul*) and 'betraying' (*elárul*, or literally 'selling off') are the same words. Works, within this treacherous world, are in themselves unhelpful, as 'the devil also acts, sneakily, through works', and under confusing circumstances distinction becomes difficult (47); the devil even can build an entire artificial paradise with its 'attractive artifices' (59). This culminates in the 'Triumph of Death', the great painting of Brueghel, now in the Prado, where 'mankind itself advances towards an enormous trap, an open pitfall, pushed by skeletons' (64). The complicity of the magic-alchemy nexus, advancing towards modern technologised science, is evident for Brueghel: another image, representing anger, shows a figure with the vase of Hermes in hand, 'perhaps to indicate that the science of opposites brings destruction', being – like anger – the 'fruit of the temptation to separate what in nature is harmonious', and – just like alchemy – intent to 'join what in nature is divided' (67–8).

With this denatured world, produced by the systematic rape of nature by techno-science, no compromise is possible (59); any compromise would imply death: 'who concedes surrenders [*chi concede cede*]' (62). The *nulla*, and the destruction unleashed by the *nulla* cannot be acknowledged and recognised: in one the most beautiful of the many striking formulations Castelli states that 'salvation depends on the refusal to consider a world in dissolution as existence' (30). Castelli evokes another way out, beyond the impassivity of the saint: the force of simplicity, as 'only those who are simple possess the secret of existence' (58). This is because the demons eventually cannot help but construct a work that will fool even them: 'the deceiver will be deceived by its own deceit', the monster will be divided in two halves, and so 'innocence wins' (7). At that moment 'it will be restored to nature what the will against nature took away, creating the magic world of horror' (66).

It is this same image-metaphor of nature that is hidden but that should be forcefully taken out of its hide by scientific knowledge that returns to animate the book of Pierre Hadot – though the idea of the *cenno* is specific to Castelli.

Pierre Hadot on nature hiding

> He is indifferent to everything but his calling. His calling is the acquisition of secrets and the holding possession of such power as they give him, with no sharer or opponent in it.
>
> *Charles Dickens,* Bleak House, *437*

Pierre Hadot (1922–2010) was one of the most important French philosophers of the past century, Professor of Collège de France, following the modes of thinking of Kierkegaard and Nietzsche, being deeply dismissive of modern rationalism and the kind of philosophy ruling contemporary universities, and introducing the perspective 'philosophy as a way of life' which had such a huge impact, among others, on the last period of Foucault's work. He not only studied theology, like Castelli, but for a time was ordained priest. In this book, published when he was 82, on a theme he pursued almost through his lifetime, Hadot not only takes up a central theme in Castelli's book, but also the method-logical focus on iconography – the reason why it is discussed in this chapter. However, the book demonstrates a unique combination of three methods, for its three central themes: a philological exegesis of Heraclitus' fragment (B123), the starting point of the investigation; a conceptual history of the idea that Nature has 'secrets'; and the iconography of this theme, through images of Isis.

Hadot starts his book not simply with Heraclitus, but with his city, Ephesus (2004: 19), as he is said to have deposited his book – lost – in the temple of Artemis, or Isis, and the virgin goddess indeed has much to do with the 25-century-long reception history of the famous aphorism. The city, which also was a harbour, has even more to do with the set of themes touched upon in the book, as St John lived his last years there, composing his Gospel which starts with the *logos* that had so much affinities with the *logos* of Heraclitus, while the *Book of Revelation* attributed to him is associated with the island of Patmos, not far from the city.

The first main theme of the book is an exegesis of the three words of the aphorism. Hadot starts by demonstrating that the original meaning of *physis* was not simply 'nature' in the sense this word gained later, but the phenomenon of growth, fertility, or the dynamic principle of life. The association of *philia*, or love, with this nature immediately recalls the connection in John between *logos*, the created world and love. While in his exegesis Hadot places the emphasis on the meaning of *phulein* as implying a natural tendency, a spontaneous emergence, appearance or habit (25, 35–6), this only underlines the *charis* world vision of classical Greece, where love, in the context of nature as growth, is considered as normal and natural.

This joining of *physis* and *philia*, on the one hand, rhymes with the evocation of Goethe and his scientific work on 'originary plants' (13–4), and on the other again has an affinity, of method-logical importance, with Hungarian roots. Concerning the first, the growth of plants was a life-long interest of Goethe, about which he published a book – a work that had such an impact, in its time, that when Alexander von Humboldt, brother of the founder of Berlin University, published in 1807 his book on the 'Geography of Plants', he dedicated it to Goethe, and the page of dedication contained an image of Apollo unveiling the status of Artemis-Isis, by Bertel Thorvaldsen (13–4). Concerning the second, in Hungarian *nő* as a verb means 'grow', corresponding to the original, first meaning of *physis*, while as a noun it means 'woman', corresponding to the representation of nature as a woman.

It is with the third word that the exegetic exercise of Hadot yields the greatest novelty, as he reads *kruptein*, in the context of the displacement made with the first two words, as implying the opposite end of human life, passing away or death, as the second main meaning of the word is 'cover in the earth, bury'. The central idea is not to offer a single and novel reading of the complex aphorism, rather to evoke the full range of meanings of the fragment, and so Hadot ends his first part by offering five different readings of the fragment (27).

Conceptual history and the related iconography, of course, cannot be fully separated, and Hadot's book also contains many passages between the two threads. Their joint and method-logical importance is stressed at the end of the Preface and the start of the Conclusion, as 'formulas, representations, images invented in ancient Greece' were shown to have an 'extraordinary longevity' (315). Their evolution throughout the ages helps to identify 'spiritual attitudes and world visions' which are still with us. The fragment gained its standard interpretation, 'nature loves to hide', already in classical antiquity: the main difference in interpretations, over time, concerned whether this hiding implies a kind of *pudeur*, considered everywhere as central for proper femininity, and so acceptable, or whether it implied a more active and less respectable hiding away of something. The standard meaning throughout the centuries became assimilated with the representation of nature as a deity, first with Artemis of Ephesus, goddess of the wilderness and wild animals, thus of 'Nature', which then became identified not just with Roman Diana, but also with Egyptian Isis – all virgin goddesses.

To this meaning, associated with female reserve and modesty, two quite different though connected modalities of meaning came to be associated. One is secrecy – the nature that hides itself *has* something to hide that we humans by all means should discover; and that nature therefore should be treated as an enemy to be forced to reveal this secret, to our benefit. Hadot claims that the idea of the 'secrets of nature' only emerged in the first century BC, with classical Latin thinkers like Cicero or Seneca (48–51, 106), but this cannot be fully accepted, as Plato claims that the Sophists held a secret knowledge, that in nature everything is in flux – a thinking amazingly close to Newton's.

The second, connected idea of hostility to nature as an enemy is traced by Hadot – implicitly – to almost the same period, as the text he evokes, the pseudo-Aristotelian *Problemata mechanica*, was recently assigned to Archytas (435/410–360/350 BC), a student of the Pythagorean Philolaus, and contemporary of Plato. According to Hadot (2004: 116–7), the Introduction to this text contains four crucial points: that mechanics can be situated inside a fight of man against nature; that the aim of this struggle is to support the practical interests of humankind; that mechanics fundamentally implies the use of craftiness, tricks, cunning (*ruse*), and the construction of machines for such purposes;

and finally, that mechanics is intimately connected to mathematics. Much of the most interesting ideas of Hadot's book, whether concerning ancient mechanics or modern science, are connected to these points.

These include, to start with, reflection on the meaning of a fight against nature in the context of a representation of nature as a virgin goddess. Any fight implies violence; in the cause of the 'secrets' of nature, being associated with a veiled goddess, the unveiling of a goddess is itself violence; but in the case of the secrets of nature, with the frequent metaphor of 'penetrating such secrets', alludes to rape – as discussed repeatedly by Hadot (2004: 107, 131). Concerning the alleviation of the sufferings of mankind as a justification of a cruel fight against nature that knows no limits, the point is raised by enlighteners and sophists of all times, and ultimately goes back to the myth of Prometheus – another central theme in Hadot's book. Concerning the affinities between mechanics and cunning, Hadot again turns to philology and etymology, as in classical Greek *mekhané* simply means cunning trick; while the word *mekhaniota* is applied to Hermes as trickster in the eponymous Homeric Hymn.

Hadot identifies, and discusses in detail, three main modalities of violence against nature, back to Antiquity: experiments, mechanics, and magic. Central to each is to force on nature something that is deeply unnatural: 'as mechanics, magic also aims to produce in nature movements that do not seem natural' (109). It is these three techniques that 'become integrated and also profoundly transform themselves in order to give rise to modern experimental science' (115).

The bringing in of the name Prometheus in a way is evident, given the connection frequently made with modern science, technology and the Enlightenment, but offers a problem, as the time horizon of the myth certainly moves beyond Heraclitus, the starting point of Hadot's book – and so Hadot does not pursue this point. However, *Prometheus Bound* by Aeschylus actually contains a reference to unveiling what is hidden in nature, and this is where Prometheus identified himself as the inventor of mining and metallurgy (see lines 498–504).

We need to resume the classic heritage concerning the violent unveiling of the secrets of nature, before we turn to the modern usage. The key point is that while Heraclitus, Artemis, and the representation of nature as a virgin Goddess who has reserve and modesty belongs to the heart of classical Greco-Roman culture, the idea of a forced unveiling of the secrets of nature does not. This is a theme associated with hubris; with a kind of ruse that is unbecoming to a decent man and can only be applied under extraordinary circumstances (note that the ruse of Ulysses is used in the Trojan War, or in his efforts to gain home); or with the base activities of mining and metallurgy. We only need to add here that the knowledge gained by Hermes the trickster gave rise to Hermeticism; that the theoretisation of metallurgy gave birth to alchemy; and that the fight against nature which is our enemy is a typical Gnostic idea, to realise that the particular direction which the metaphor of Heraclitus gained at the periphery rather than centre of Greco-Roman thinking gave birth to and spread inside the undercurrent, occult traditions that surfaced eventually in Europe after the arrival of the Byzantine *dotti*, misdirecting the Renaissance, as unearthed by Frances Yates. In sum, Hadot (109–10) is quite right in placing the *violent* and cunning uncovering of the secrets of nature 'under the patronage of Prometheus'.

Finally, in the context of the stripping away, by ruse and violence, the hidden secrets of nature, by unveiling – or undressing – and violating her, under the imagery of a Virgin Goddess, one can intuit the ages-old impact of Magi misogyny. Here one should add that Heraclitus not only identified, in an important and much-quoted fragment, the 'mysteries of men as unholy mysteries' (Fragment B14), but also connected with them the magi (*magoi*), in the same fragment ('those wandering at night: magi, Bacchants, Bacchantes, initiates'), which actually, is the first occurrence of the term 'magi' in ancient Greek.

We can now return to Hadot's exploration of the modern history of the metaphor. The imagery of the secrets of nature, together with attempts at unveiling them, and even some use of magic, persisted in the Middle Ages, but only as a hardly tolerated undercurrent. According to the medieval Christian world vision Nature was God's creation, so a hostility to it was unthinkable – not surprisingly Gnosticism was considered as a most dangerous heresy. A hostile, legalistic attitude towards nature, that should be as if subjected to a full-scale legal investigation, by processing it, even torturing it as an accused, would only become part of the mainstream with and after Bacon and his experimental method. An experiment, Hadot argues, is not simply a neutral or even possibly uplifting trial, but a full-scale and threatening legal process. Even when Bacon seems to suggest humbleness, claiming that man is only a servant of nature, Hadot agrees with Eugenio Garin that it rather evokes the 'cunning servant' of Plautus, who only fakes servitude to better abuse his master (108–9). The main trick is to use the laws or 'reasons' (*logoi*) of nature, but 'only to obtain results that seem contrary to the course of nature' (117). And while legal metaphors for experiment were in use in Antiquity, in modern times they were aggravated by a brand new idea: that of the *conquest* of nature.

It is in the context of such a conquest, an exact contemporary of the conquest and colonialisation of the Americas, that experimental techniques and legal metaphors were intensified, but so also was the joint use of mathematics and geometry, as pioneered by Descartes. While all these elements can be traced back to Antiquity (119–20), their systematic joining and intensification was something new: part of a new project, the 'mechanisation of the world' (119). Apart from Bacon and Descartes, Hadot places emphasis on the figure of father Mersenne, for whom the fantastic developments in knowledge outright indicate the closeness of the end of the world (135), as if advancing the transhumanist apocalypticism, and about whom Adrien Baillet, the first biographer of Descartes, said the following: "'no other mortal ever was so curious as him to penetrate all the secrets of Nature, to bring all the sciences and arts to their perfection'" (140–1).

As from here the story is well-known, only one, method-logically relevant point will be mentioned. It concerns an iconographic idea, the popularity of the representation of the unveiling of Isis as an illustration of the progress of science throughout the 17–18th centuries (265–6). This iconography, underlies Hadot, did not take into consideration the warning contained in the main Hellenistic texts on Isis, by Plutarch and Proclus, who emphasised that no mortal did, and so should, lift this veil (269). Here a great change took place at the end of the 18th century, with the French Revolution, when Isis became the very embodiment and representation of the deification of nature in the revolutionary cult of the Supreme Being; a part of the contemporary cult of Egypt, culminating in the Napoleonic invasion of Egypt. The source of this development, argues Hadot, is the masonic emphasis on Isis and Egypt, particularly characteristic of the Viennese lodge, according to Assmann, and which implies an assimilation of Isis-Nature to Yahweh, under the influence of Spinoza (269–71).

Pavel Florensky on royal doors

Florensky (1882–1937), Russian theologian, philosopher, and mathematician, was born Azerbaijan from an Armenian mother, lived most of his early years in Tbilisi, Georgia, and was executed under Stalinism. He was the most highly regarded thinker of his time and place, mentor of Mikhail Bakhtin. An orthodox theologian attempting to build into his thinking ideas from Western philosophy, he was also mathematician, incorporating the ideas of George Cantor on integers, while in some essays anticipated the work of Norbert Wiener (in Florensky 1976: 13). His philosophy returns to Plato and the theory of forms, arguing that modern science, especially mathematics, took up the same road.

The book, originally entitled *Iconostasis*, meaning the area separating the nave and the sanctuary in an Orthodox church, place of the main icons, was intended as central part of a larger work, 'Philosophy of the cult', to be devoted to exploring the ' "intermediate world" ' (14), technically liminality, starts in the most classical way for a theologian, the first verses of the *Book of Genesis*, focusing on the act of creation as separating earth and sky, or the division of the world into two parts, visible and invisible things. The significance of the in-between or liminal zone is thus apparent, as it is this borderline that both separates and connects the two worlds. Florensky situates the image here, as a crucial threshold or door between them.

Florensky's characterisation of our world is as little abstract as possible, as it is the concreteness of the world as Nature, as authentical, as created and edified by God (125–6), in its givenness as a gift, and claims that its refusal, the failure to accept the fullness of life in the world is Protestant-Kantian arrogance (139). It is this concrete, given life we live that continuously pushes us to the confines of the visible world, giving us unmistakable glimpses at the other world. A first step is the dream, a contact point between the two worlds which opens up 'inside us' (19–20), offering us images and visions, so much like our memories, similarly preserved in two-dimensional images. The most visionary part of our dreams is itself a borderline, as it happens not in deep sleep, but on the limit between sleeping and waking up (20).

Our dreams, just as our memories, produce images. Images thus play a crucial role in this intermediate realm, between the visible and invisible worlds; or, as the Italian title of the book says, in the analogy of a 'royal way', they are 'royal doors'.

But certainly not every image is such a 'royal door' – and so we have arrived at the question of grasping what images are; or what kinds of images there are.

Images as 'royal doors'

An image is certainly not simply an imitation of the world, something that would make no sense, only implying an immanent circular loop, inside the world, failing to take seriously the image as a liminal phenomenon, a door – just as Freud's dream-interpretation theory encloses the dream in an immanent circle of self-consciousness, or the isolated mind. Considering an image as 'representation of reality' offers smug neutrality, while helping to overlook that images *matter*. Far from 'imitating' reality, they *are* part of reality, once they were made; and even more importantly, they have the power to *shape* reality. So they must be taken *very* seriously.

While Florensky is an orthodox theologian, his ideas about images have relevance way beyond the scope of theology, orthodox or not, entering the heart of what images are, and what is in their power.

Before going further, we need to evoke some of the most astonishing and powerful images ever made, not accessible to Florensky, the cave art of Lascaux and Chauvet; images that were made on cave walls, so in a most liminal setting. Even further, we know it from anthropologists that people who are – or until recently were – making contemporary rock art, in South-Africa, North-America or Australia, consider paintings on rock walls as *doors* to the other world.

So images can be doors, to another world, or to a different perception, but certainly not all images are such. Still, what is true for all images is that all have a *relation* to reality (this is what Gell (1998) calls the 'agency of art'), they are at the limit, border or confine of reality: not fully real, yet at the same time super-real. Staying with Florensky's example, but having relevance for all images, Florensky argues that 'the dream is just a dream, a nothing, a *nihil visibile* [sic in original]' (32; 1993: 16). An image is on the limit of reality, or is liminal, perhaps most evidently in its two-dimensional character – reality is always three-dimensional, but its image, or limit, is two-dimensional.

All liminal situations open new possibilities, but also dangers, so images are similar to all other passages between spheres of life (1976: 34). But the dangers associated with them are particular. Florensky expresses this in the terminology of vulnerability, temptation and deceit: 'at the limit and at the threshold of this world we accede to a condition of life which, even if unceasingly new, is radically different from the normal conditions of everyday life. In this is the greatest spiritual pitfall for whoever approaches *the threshold of this world*' and who is vulnerable or impotent, in the sense of 'not being mature enough for the transit', as 'the danger (*opasnost'*) lies in the deceits (*obman*) and self-deceits that at the edge of the world surround the wayfarer' (36, 1993: 20; note that Florensky, the mathematician adds that here he is using a geometrical-physical mode of speaking).[5] Each liminal passage is full of temptations and seductions; but 'half-way between time-space reality and the angelic world, at the threshold of this world, deceit and seduction is at its maximum' (1976: 37). The warning is repeated later: images which are deprived of concreteness, which 'depict nobody in particular' easily represent 'the maximal spiritual deceit, provoking confusion' (83).

This is why one must identify the particular character of the image at stake. The fundamental difference, according to Florensky, is a question of directionality, related to the different modality of transits: whether the images represent elevation from below to above, or descent from above to below. The first type of imagery is characteristic of mystic painters who capture their experiences of elevation in powerful symbolic images. However – and here Florensky enters the heart of his diagnosis of modernity – at this point also emerges the temptation of mistaking 'the reveries that surround, confuse and seduce the soul at the moment when the road opens for him towards the other world' as 'spiritual images' (36). Faced with such temptations Florensky offers, based on Tasso's 'Enchanted Forest', an interpretation that closely rhymes with the ideas of Castelli. The liminal passage is full of spectres and demons that are only shadows of reality. They are insignificant for those who 'possess spiritual firmness' and will not be frightened by them and yield to them. However, from the weak, lacking faith, being 'victims of their own passions and predilections' the spectres 'receive an influx of reality, become strong, attach themselves to these souls, and take on human form the more the soul weakens itself by attracting them' (38).

Florensky offers a striking description of such confusion and loss, focusing on self-deceit. The central point is – and here again Florensky rhymes with Castelli – that the great danger of the images is not simply the standard temptation by earthly passions, rather the *self*-deceit of believing that salvation is gained just when one becomes completely lost – a danger that threatens especially if such self-deceit is animated by arrogant pride (39). This results in the soul being closed upon itself, which he also describes as a 'smug self-satisfied [*samodovol'stvo*] Pharisaic self-consciousness',[6] or a 'Pharisaic ascent' (40, 1993: 24; Florensky here evokes Mt 12: 43–5 and Lk 11: 24–6). The reason for confusion is mixing the images of ascent and descent (1976: 40): someone believing oneself to be able to transform oneself by one's own force actually becomes entrapped in the basest drives. The result is an ordered but meaningless emptiness, where the masks are mistaken for reality.

The opposite of mask is vision, and its close companion, the regard (*lik*). This is because – and here again it is necessary to quote at length – a 'vision appearing at the confines of the visible and invisible worlds might be due to an *absence* of the real world', in which the soul can be emptied of any objectivity and – in the absence of guidance from above – 'in the open and ordered room' of the soul will become 'populated by the masks of reality' (40). At the same time this 'vision can be due to the *presence* of a reality, the superior reality of the spiritual world' (40); what Castelli calls grace. Such vision cannot be attained by our own forces – this belief, again, is the greatest sin of arrogance and smug self-satisfaction; but requires a certain prior 'orientation of the interior life',[7] implying a call or a prayer, and 'not by trying to use our own forces to overcome the status given to us in order to overstep thresholds that are not accessible to us' (41). Under such conditions 'the vision can manifest itself', or there may appear an 'image from above', sign of an 'invisible gift' that can stay with us and penetrate our daily existence (41–2). Such a vision is 'more objective of earthly objectivities, more substantial and real than them, is the solid point of support for worldly works, the crystal around which and following its law of crystallisation, as a model, the worldly experiences will be crystallised' (42).[8] As example for such visions, Florensky evokes Raphael (75–6), which is particularly significant, given that otherwise he considers the Renaissance as the definite fall from grace of European civilisation.

The ontological contrast between these two visions can be best characterised – and here we reach the method-logical core of Florensky's ideas, and also their relevance for our actuality – by the contrast between *mask* and *regard*. He starts with the second, through entering a linguistic excursion. In Russian 'regard' *lik* and 'face' *litso* are etymologically connected words.[9] 'Face' is the term we use in daily life, and it applies not only to humans but to other beings, and is even used metaphorically. It can be said as synonymous of 'manifestation', as it indeed manifests everyday consciousness. However, 'the boundary between subjectivity and objectivity in a face is not clear' (42), and while reality is present in it, it is only a rough basis for proper understanding and recognition. The artistic elaboration of the face is a portrait, but it still stays at the level of decoration, where the key role is played by the 'cognitive organisation' of the artist, and it does not give an ontological account of the person the artist depicted (42–3). The regard (*lik*), on the other hand, is an ontological manifestation. It is what animates the face; what brings out the soul (*anima*) behind a face. The human face captured in an icon is never just the depiction of a concrete face: 'it is the expression of inner life and of everything that is not a face, meaning the conditions and manifestations human life, the whole world in so far as created for man' (153). Here Florensky enters the core of an at once theological and philosophical discussion, using jointly the Bible and Plato: man was created not just as an image of God, but in its likeness, and in the regard, or in this likeness everything exterior to the essence of one's being was discarded: 'the face became a regard. The regard is the likeness of God made present on the face' (44). At this point Florensky turns to Plato and his term *eidos*, usually translated as idea, but originally means regard, or 'revealed spiritual existence' (44; note that the etymology of *eidos* is Proto-Indo-European ★*wéydos* 'seeing, image'). The Conclusion Florensky draws cannot be weightier: through Plato, and its translation as 'idea' the term became the foundation of philosophy; but 'by reversing the direction of the walk, from the idea to the regard, we can render the significance of this term fully transparent' (44–5).

The opposite of regard is the mask (*litsina*, another derivate of *lik*). If the regard shows the likeness of God, the mask is a mere likeness of the face, but 'inside it is empty, in both a material, physical, and also metaphysical sense' (45). Even worse, a mask outright deceives, 'indicating, by guile, non-existent things'. Florensky warns that he is not talking about the antique, sacred sense of masks, as these were similar to the icons; rather once the sacrality of the mask is forgotten the modern sense of the mask is born as pure deceit, even having a taste of *terribility*.

Worse, the loss of genuine sacrality implies not simply secularisation, but sorcery. Florensky evokes the word *larva*, used by the Romans for masks, but also designating something like the astral body, the 'insubstantial imprint left by the dead'. Capturing the mask and the astral body in a single word is most significant, as they both share emptiness and pseudo-reality, having 'an apparent reality that lacks force and being' (47).[10] Similarly, a focus on the external aspects of a person, common to positivism and Kantianism, ignores the deeper, Platonic sense, which is the apparition or revelation of reality, still preserved in the everyday term 'phenomenon' in the sense of being 'phenomenal' (48). The way a face can be separated from the inner person and lose its life can be illustrated by Stavrogin, anti-hero of *Demons*, who according to Dostoevsky wore a mask – and a stone mask – on his skull, instead of a face (49). Disconnected from the sacred the mask lost its role, but 'in its cadaver continue to live alien, non-participatory religious powers. Contact with the mask became contaminating' (185).

After such introduction Florensky turns to his central theme, icons, in particular 'iconostasis', the threshold between the two worlds. Their central aspect is the regard of saints captured in them, 'these penetrating and memorable gazes', in the act of contemplation, the royal doors or windows between the two worlds, which 'render almost public the inaccessible visions' (63–4; see also 69). This is why icons possess an almost insupportable force; they *overpower* (emphasis in original), they are 'like a blazing vision, overflowing with light', and are capable to produce an 'acute, penetrating sensation in the soul' for those who encounter these works for the first time – offering an 'encounter with the reality of the spiritual world' (69–70).

It is through this idea that Florensky approaches the difference between Western Renaissance art and Eastern icons, justifying his radical critique of the former. An icon is not a portrait of the Virgin Mary, rather through it one 'can see the Mother of God as if through a window' (65). The painter was not really the creator of this image; he only received an inspiration for it, the reason why the main, canonical (or 'iconic') depictions of the Virgin are attributed to the apostle St Luke.[11] Icons are spiritual symbols; they capture archetypes and not a piece of reality. Instead of a 'representation', one should rather talk about 'a propagating wave' of reality itself, or 'emanations', just as all the other vital energies that animate our souls (66).[12] These last pages were written as an explicit advice given to icon painters, leading Florensky to discuss another central term, much at the centre of the iconoclasm debates of all ages: *evocation* (67–9).

Icon painting reached perfection in the 14–15th centuries, especially in the works of Andrei Rublev,[13] his 'Trinity' representing the height of heights (64), a work that 'has no equivalent in the history of art' (88–9). Such perfection is present in the materiality of icon painting, which expresses a 'metaphysics of surface' (112), theme of his other key book, as real painting can only be made on a hard surface, like a wall or a wooden table, not on canvas (110–6). This perfection can only be compared to Greek sculpture – which 'similarly managed to actuate spiritual images and encountered the same kind of rationalistic and sensualistic decline after the splendid elevation' (90);[14] and to Egyptian art, especially funeral masks, the internal decoration of sarcophagi, painted using gold on wood, which thus can be considered 'as the first primordial icon paintings' (186).

This is why religious painting in the West, since the Renaissance, was engaged in a 'radical artistic falsity' (63), the more it pretended to be 'realistic'. In contrast to icon painters, Western artists since the – later – Renaissance, with some exceptions, are devoted neither to the spiritual world, nor to the objectivity of material reality, but became self-centred, of which the 'fatal manifestation' is perspectivism (114). This is visible in incisions even better than in oil painting – an art, not surprisingly, developed in areas that would become centres of Protestantism (115–6). Incisions are 'based on rationality', and have nothing in common with the objects; are 'images constructed on the basis of the mere laws of logic; identity, contradiction, third excluded and in this sense have a deep link with German philosophy: in both cases the aim is to draw or rather deduce schemes [...] from affirmations or negations deprived of reality', or 'to create out of nothing' (115–6).[15] With German idealism, especially Kantianism, space disappears from thinking. The ideology is freedom of consciousness for the artists and focus on pure, formal constructive activity, but this is only deceit, revealed in the confusion between calling such images 'incisions', when the actual work is done on the reverse, and what we actually see is only its stamped version (118–20). Incision is a profoundly technical and not artistic undertaking, rendering possible the mechanical reproduction for mass use of a product of which the original, except for the printer, nobody ever sees (120–1). There is a profound link between Protestantism and incision: in the name of arbitrary freedom (paradoxically produced by Luther's *denial* of free will) artists work in an exclusively rationalistic manner, as if anticipating 'pure reason', while ignoring the structure of reality, whether natural or spiritual: 'to any chosen material it applies a schema that has nothing in common with it, and manifesting his own freedom as self-determination such reason enslaves the freedom of all that are external to it, and by such self-determination it tramples on the self-determination of the world' (122–3). This is why icon painting is always a collaborative work, never conceived of as a solitary undertaking (152).[16] Protestant individualism leaves its mechanical stamp on everything, and even its freedom of choice is illusory, as it is rather a violent proliferation of uniformity. Its main instrument, reason as ratiocinating, is only a cloak of genuine reason, as it rather unleashes the imagination (123–4). Even further, Protestant thinking, in imitation of its choice art, incision, 'does not start from the light of true reality, but from the absence of reality, from darkness, from nothingness' (141). Its main representatives, like Böhme or Husserl, 'far from having a spiritual equilibrium', rather 'create their fantastications [*vozdusnie zamki*; 1993: 106; literally 'castles built out of air'; note the recurrent metaphor 'thin air' in Bulgakov's *Master and Margarita*] out of nothingness' (1976: 124). The summary is pithy: 'Protestant thought is drunkenness for oneself, while it ferociously preaches sobriety' (124). Returning to the Renaissance, Florensky recognises that Renaissance culture is 'eclectic and contradictory in its profound essence'; it is only kept alive by its roots in the Middle Ages, and once this connection was severed, 'it would fall into simple self-destruction' (168).

In contrast to this, icon painting is 'a metaphysics of being' – but in a concrete, not abstract sense. It 'perceives what it depicts as sensible manifestation of a metaphysical essence' (125). Icons are 'visions of beauty', that reach directly the archetype, and thus are 'instruments of supernatural knowledge' (62). The regard of icons even help to overcome the separation between man and nature, evoking 'primordial, Paradisiac harmony' (153–4). As the essence of world-nature is unspeakable beauty, icons are also so beautiful that they almost hurt; they produce an enchantment that provokes tears of joy.

Icon painting even has method-logical relevance for thinking. Regard cannot be depicted by hesitations, corrections and returns, but most follow a single vital creative act: 'one should not interrupt the process of thinking, in which there can be no breaks' (127). Every living organism is a concrete totality, containing vital energies, and anything casual is alien from it – just as from an icon.

Florensky's ideas have evident, striking relevance for both Political Anthropology and the Present Age. By emphasising the liminal nature of images, Florensky captures their at once unreal and super-real character. They are not real, as an image is not a thing of reality, only a human making, and has no usefulness in everyday life; yet, at the same time it is super-real, as it evokes an existence outside this world, which can have a main impact on the world itself. This helps to understand the damage inflicted on all of us by the imposition of mask-wearing, forcing us to see only masks around us and not real faces with their animating gazes and glances; and especially making the irreparable damage of forcing generations of children and young people being brought up in this way, depriving them of the unsubstitutable experience of seeing and experiencing human faces. This is the spiritual equivalent of not talking to infants in their early years, until they lose the capacity of learning to speak.

Aby Warburg: 'Forms of expression' and the 'serpent ritual'

Aby Warburg (1866–1929) is widely recognised as a founding figure of art history. Yet, due to the quite extraordinary nature of his character, life history, ideas, and the history of the publication and reception of his writings, his influence and legacy remains subdued, and is also controversial.

Warburg is best introduced through a series of anecdotes. Born as first son in one of the wealthiest Jewish banking families of Germany, he was destined to lead the firm. However, at the age of seven, when ill with high typhoid fever, he had an extraordinary dream experience, with grotesque and satanic figures of immense dimensions (Gombrich 1983: 25), which could be considered – in the analogy of Ted Hughes's (1992) interpretation of Shakespeare's life – as a shamanistic initiatory dream. As a result, he not only gave up his primogeniture, trading the bank to buying as many books as he ever wanted, but even the career of becoming a rabbi. He decided to study art history, attended the first lectures of Henri Thode, who with his 1885 book was destined to revolutionise the study of the Renaissance, tracing it back, in Tuscan art, to Giotto and the Franciscans. Warburg became enchanted by Thode, but did not become his student, and while he indeed revolutionised the study of the Renaissance, he did it in ways quite different from Thode's. This was a pity, as it led to Warburg's ignoring the 13th century and not simply the Franciscans, but the way in which a highly emotional style of Byzantine icon painting, rooted in the apocalyptic experience of the Fourth Crusade and the sacking of Constantinople, brought into Europe through Pisa, had a vital impact on the Tuscan Renaissance.

Based on such a unique experiential background and learning, incorporating among others mythology, psychology, linguistics, and philosophy, Warburg started to develop original ideas, but these were not met with approval in the Prussian university system, obsessed with formal rationalism and increasingly strict disciplinary separations. His Professor, Justi, failed to appreciate his thesis, and so Warburg never managed to enter the university system. While the library he collected over the years and whose aim he defined as 'a collection of documents that refer to the psychology of human expressivity' (Gombrich 1983: 222; see also Agamben 2005: 127) gained fame, and while he also increasingly acquired a quasi-cultic status, he lacked official academic recognition, this leading to a failure to write and publish works that could have secured broader recognition: most of his works were short occasional pieces, at most articles published in some specialised reviews, never a book. During WWI he had such a deterioration of his mental health that he spent most of six years (1918–24) in the Kreuzlingen sanatorium, under Ludwig Binswanger whose uncle, Otto Binswanger treated Nietzsche there. The situation strikingly recalls that of his exact contemporary, Max Weber (1864–1920), who also suffered the rule of the neo-Kantian mandarins (Ringer 1969), going through a similarly 6-year long depression (1897–1903), giving up his chair and not writing anything during this period, and only publishing working papers, not a single book, up to the last year of his life, when he died just when the first volume of his collected essays on the Sociology of Religions was in press.

Given his precarious academic and health situation, Warburg was much concerned with finding a proper heir, keen in securing the support of Ernst Cassirer, then a rising star of German philosophy. He personally guided Cassirer through his library, showing every treasure and their meaning, so was confident in success. The response of Cassirer, however, was unequivocal: he would never enter again this maze, as that would force him to give up the knowledge he gained that far.[17]

Warburg died of a heart attack in October 1929 in Hamburg. The most astonishing story about his life is connected to his death: soon after he died the dead apple tree of his garden, which he refused to have cut, started to blossom. As if this were not enough, among the notes he made in his last weeks the following text was found: 'who will sing me the paean, the song of grace-giving, the lode of the apple-tree which flowers so late' (Bing 1980: xvii; Spinelli and Venuti 1998: 9).

While by now Warburg has become an iconic figure, a founder of art history and in a way one of the most influential intellectual figures of the 20th century, problems of reception keep troubling the proper recognition of his work and its significance, just as it is the case with Max Weber. Most persons cultivating his legacy were either neo-Kantian philosophers like Cassirer or Erwin Panofsky, specialists lacking the breadth of his vision, or – like Ernst Gombrich, for long head of the London Institute – followers of Karl Popper, and obsessed with imitating the natural sciences. The true spirit of Warburg's research ideas were only continued by a few, like Frances Yates and Jean Seznec, who did not even know him, or Edgar Wind (1900–71), who unfortunately followed Warburg even in having difficulties in finishing his work as – though he gained the first chair of Art History in Oxford and gave lectures to full and enthusiastic audiences – he only published one proper research monograph, never finishing his planned book on Leonardo, with his collected papers only appearing after his death.

Tensions around the legacy of Warburg were brought into the open by the – anonymous – publication of Wind's very negative review of Gombrich's biography of Warburg, which created quite a stir. Since then, bemoaning this fact is a standard feature of the literature around Warburg, but leading to no change in academic power hierarchies.

While Warburg is widely recognised as a founder of art history as a discipline, he was quite a paradoxical founder, as his approach was highly interdisciplinary (Calabrese 1998: 11). In particular – and this was a great novelty inside history at that time – he brought in the social sciences, including anthropology (Frazer), and also sociology (Durkheim, Mauss, and Lévy-Bruhl), which served as a bridge towards the present (Warnke 1998: 21; see also Johnson 2012: 71). According to Agamben (2005: 142–3), at the close of his original essay, 'there is no doubt that the viewpoint from which Warburg looked at human affairs coincides with that of anthropology', so perhaps the best way to characterise his 'nameless science' is as a future 'anthropology of Western culture', and where the first steps were made, among others, by Mauss, Sapir, Kerényi, and Dumézil – though in his 1983 'Postscript' he seems to take back this suggestion (144). Perhaps this is what 'Political Anthropology', as practiced around the journal *International Political Anthropology*, would like to bring closer to realisation. The need for such a separate field, inside history, was based on a fundamental method-logical recognition: the need to study images in their own right, and not just as illustrations of historical movements and trends, rooted in politics, economics or even social forces. It is for this reason that Warburg championed the term 'iconology', even 'critical iconology' (Warnke 1998: 23), with his 1912 conference in Rome considered as the baptism ritual of the new 'discipline' (Warnke 1998: 14–5). Even here, however, his approach was not just broad but paradoxical, as his interest in images went together with a concern with words. Warburg not only had a tendency for an 'inveterate conflation of *Wort* [word] and *Bild* [image]' (Johnson 2012: 122), but 'attempt[ed] to forge a synthesis of "Wort und Bild" ' (134).

Words

Warburg used for these purposes a central figure of German linguistics, Hermann Osthoff, key representative of the 'neogrammatical' school, inventor of the term 'suppletion'. Osthoff perceived, and analysed with success, the way language handles heightened emotional states: in the use of certain superlatives, or terms for close relatives, it becomes irregular. Thus, while the superlatives of standard adjectives are formed in a regular manner: fast, faster, green, greener, those expressing strong emotions become irregular: good, better, bad, worse. Similarly, while gender differences are usually indicated by different noun endings, terms denoting father and mother, or brother and sister, are unrelated in most languages. Warburg explicitly discussed Osthoff's ideas in two programmatic writings: the 1905 article on Dürer's 1494 drawing 'Death of Orpheus', and the 1929 Introduction to the Mnemosyne exhibition. In the former, which introduces Warburg's key term *Pathosformeln* (translated as 'pathos formulas' by Johnson (2012: x, 12), and also Wood (2014: 14), but perhaps better as 'forms of expression'),[18] Warburg connects this term 'to the linguistic, stylistic process of intensification' (Johnson 2012: 137). In an unpublished and similarly programmatic essay dated to the same period, entitled *Festwesen* (the essence of festival culture), Warburg argues that ' "there exists in the field of the visual arts a phenomenon, which is the same as the one Osthoff has observed in linguistics – a switch and a supplementation of the roots used in the superlative" ' (as in Guillemin 2008: 616–7); or, according to Johnson (2012: 138) Warburg again 'conflates' Osthoff's suppletion with the *Pathosformeln*. In 1929, alluding back to the 1905 article, Warburg re-states that, just as 'the entry of a foreign root produces an intensification of the original meaning of the word', a similar effect is produced in art when the dancing Salomé appears as a Greek maenad, or when a servant girl in Ghirlandaio imitates a gesture from a Roman triumphal arc (Warburg 2016, B2–3, pp.3–4). The effect is even more striking with the gesture of a Roman emperor, as 'through an energetic inversion of meaning, the imperial gesture [is transformed into] Christian piety' (B8, p.5).

Such tight links between words and images culminate in the idea, advanced by Gombrich (1970: 244), that Warburg aimed at offering a fundamental lexicon of human passions, close to Goethe's *Urworte*; or these ' "originary words of a pathos-laden dynamic" ' that 'fuel Warburg's pioneering efforts in iconology' (Johnson 2012: 62).

Goethe's originary words are five Greek terms that capture the ultimate driving forces of human life.[19] *Daimon* is untranslatable, with its Christian transliteration as demonic creating thorough confusion, among others around Plato. Here it means the specific 'guiding spirit' of a concrete human being, different from Goethe's 'daemonic', which is identified with the unique guiding spirit of very special individuals. Still, Goethe's interest in the *daimon*, but also the other forces of one's fortune and fate, has close connections with his interest in his own horoscope. The first Book of *Poetry and Truth* starts by telling, in as much detail as possible, the situation of the planets at the moment of his birth, indicating a particularly auspicious constellation (Hadot 2008: 182). *Tyché* can be best approached as Latin *Fortuna*, meaning the external forces guiding individual fate, different from mere 'fortune', and close to the sense of Machiavelli. *Eros* is again untranslatable, again due to its Christian transliteration as 'love', in Greek meaning a *daimon*; again a kind of guiding spirit but coming more from the outside, or rather the 'in-between'. *Ananké* captures external fate or inevitable necessity. The final term *elpis* 'hope', the central word for Goethe, though Greek, is outside the classical Greek spirit, having clear Christian roots, yet Goethe's meaning is not a simple reassertion of Christian hope, as its focus is on human activity.

The wings of hope for Goethe do not mean a 'waiting for Godot', the delivery of a final, saving solution; rather, argues Hadot (236),

> the Hope of the *Urworte* is a power which, while pulling us upwards, allows us to reinterpret the destiny that has been imposed on us and to act with confidence by situating our activity in the perspective of Everything and the will of God-Nature. Hope is inherent to life and activity. Hoping is being alive, being active

– ending the argument with an allusion to the last moment of Faust's life, at the ending of *Faust II*, a poem on which Goethe was working for about six decades, and which he only allowed to be published after his death.

The originary words have manifold links to the central concerns of Warburg's lifework. The struggle between the demonic forces and the attempt of our reason to subdue them is perhaps the central concern of his entire work. Similarly central is love, in all its modes and ambiguities, and especially the way in which it is, or can be, depicted in images. The meaning of the lasting importance of astrology was again one of the central themes of his entire work. Hope, of course, is central for every person, but few went the distance that Warburg covered, after 1918, as the apocalyptic events of WWI, at its ending, produced mental disturbances lasting for six years. His reaction to his troubles was strictly in line with Goethe's message, as intuited by Hadot, and as formulated in the Conclusion of the main argument in a crucial and much related work, 'Pagan-Antique Prophecy in Words and Images in the Age of Luther', published not as a finished work but rather as a fragment at the heart of this period, in January 1920: 'Athens has constantly to be won back [*züruckerobern*] from Alexandria' (Warburg 1999: 650; also selected by Gertrud Bing (in Warburg 1980: xxxi) to conclude his Introduction to the Italian edition of the collected writings);[20] and also in his lecture on the serpent ritual by which he, as if a Samson, pulled himself up by his own hair, in April 1923. However, the most evident and direct connection is that the subtitle-word of Goethe's poem is 'Orphic', while Warburg introduced his central term 'forms of expression' in his 1905 analysis of Dürer's 'Death of Orpheus'. According to Hadot (2008: 180–1), Goethe's subtitle-word could not have referred to the figure of Orpheus as – except for *Eros* – the originary words did not have an Orphic character, rather belonged to the part of classical mythology that had an astrological orientation – which should only have made them more intriguing for Warburg – and for this reason Goethe's poem was a kind of theological poetry. In this sense, Warburg's 'forms of expression' can also be considered as a quasi-sacred 'originary word'.

Images or forms of expression

For all his interest in words, especially *Urworte*, Warburg was primarily interested in images; the question of 'what is involved in our encounter with pre-existing images transmitted by memory' (Wind 1983: 26). It is a bit strange that he made no significant use of the term *Urbild*, the probable reason being that his interest was not Antiquity per se, rather its re-emergence in the Renaissance and after. His question was how certain experiences, and especially emotions produced by these experiences, were expressed in images; and the uses to which such images, once created as a model, can be put later. Such forms of expression, once created, though produced in a particular context and for a particular reason, came to acquire an existence on their own and could be used for a different purpose, while preserving a certain emotional energy which could be not only used if reanimated, but also *intensified*. For this reason neo-Kantian methods, built on strict, dualistic separations, like between form and content, are useless, as artistic expressions do not simply give a form to a specific content, but in their very form capture something substantial, an emotional charge, which however can be used to represent quite different contents; or, in the words of Agamben (2005: 125), there is 'an indissoluble link between emotive charge and iconographic formula'. Warburg's central interest lay not simply in mere differences in purpose, but in the ways in which the possibility of intensification was actualised.

The emotion-experiences dominating medieval European imagery were beauty, grace (in its manifold modalities), and love – mostly a form of divine love, alternating with images of suffering. The ways in which these were expressed were themselves legacies of Antiquity, partly transmitted, in various ways, in a modified form, by the Byzantine world. This was the context into which, at a specific moment, roughly around the middle of the 15th century, not simply the discovery of ancient works of art but their forms of expressions took place. The distinction is important, as Warburg emphasises – and the key works of Seznec (1972) and Wind (1967) confirm – that antique themes and concerns did not disappear in the Middle Ages; what was missing, and was rediscovered from around the mid-15th century, was their original, highly emotional forms of expression, which only emerged in the Medici Renaissance, and then – most paradoxically – became dominant, without any restraint, in the Baroque, partly due to the Jesuit championing of allegorisation (Seznec 1972: 274–5).

Allegorisation played a central role in the survival of pagan mythology during the Middle Ages, where it became a moralising subcurrent, discussed extensively by Jean Seznec (1972; see esp. 109, 224). It became revitalised, and with a particular force, in Medici Florence, the most eminent allegoriser being Poliziano (96, 112), central source for the painting of Botticelli. The outcome in art was trite banalities and commonplaces, where the esoteric and the didactic aims were conflated, resulting in a pseudo-scientific pseudo-Platonic merging of Christianity and pagan mythology (101–3; see also Wind 1967), culminating in the baroque, which paradoxically returned to the same allegorical method with a vengeance (Seznec 1972: 320–1).

It is most significant that the artist most closely associated with this reorientation, Sandro Botticelli, at the same time is the main representative of the Ficino circle that combined Neoplatonism with Hermetic philosophy and mythological themes, especially after Leonardo left Verrocchio's workshop, from around 1476 up to about 1485. Botticelli's works, especially the *Primavera* and the *Birth of Venus* illustrate best that 'decorative pathos', the almost childish focus on the graceful movement of ropes of hair and clothing, without following any purpose or will-power, characteristic of festive occasions – which, however, as later developments confirmed, were pregnant with 'explosive potential', as they implicitly attacked the norms of tranquil serenity and stability (Warnke 1998: 22). Here we immediately enter the heart of the central, quite Platonic concerns of Warburg and his closest followers, as such playful images are not just innocent games (Wind 1963: 3). Rather, we must take Plato's problematisation of images quite seriously, as Plato was by no means motivated by the censor's worry concerning conformity to formal rules, rather by a genuine 'sacred fear' of the power of images, as miming is a perilous activity, and especially so is the imitation of evil (2).

The Neoplatonic inspiration behind the revival of Pagan Antiquity, characteristic of Medici Florence, was particularly problematic as – Neoplatonism being itself a phenomenon of late Antiquity – most of the imagery that was revived in that period was the product of late Hellenism, thus decadent Antiquity. Returning to Botticelli, a central, indeed guiding role was played in his most famous images by Hermes/ Mercury, the trickster deity, discussed extensively by Wind (1967), also associated with Hermes Trismegistus whose writings, supposedly containing the most ancient truths of mankind but actually being Hellenistic forgeries, were translated even before Plato, and avidly read.

Forms of expression always emerged in a particular context, which was most important for Warburg as – keen follower of Nietzsche even here – such forms captured, and transmitted, the specific content of the experiential context by their form (Saxl 1998: 33). In this perspective, special attention deserves to be paid to the fact that, as a kind of cunning of history (Wind 1967: 152), most of the art objects that were discovered and made an impact in the 15th century were made not in Classical Antiquity, but again in later Hellenistic and Roman periods. They transmitted the decadence under the sign of which they were created and thus inevitably produced and spread decadence on their own (Gombrich 1983: 32; Seznec 1972: 196ff), contributing to the impure soil of Renaissance masterworks (Wind 1967: 15) – just as the 'neo-barbaric fashion' of Medici Neoplatonism was inspired by ' "Asiatic richness" ' (10), helped by the excessive emphasis of Ficino on Hellenistic commentaries even of the classics, contributing to the 'hybridisation' of classical and Hellenistic, Pagan and Christian, a prelude to the much later secularisation (24). The violent gestures and excesses of emotions, of which the Laocoon group was a prime example, are not acceptable in the visual arts; they are signs of weakness, even of moral decadence (Gombrich 1983: 29).

It is only in the context of the experiential background that the creative process behind capturing a form of expression can be understood. In his classic essay on Warburg's 'methodology' Wind (1983: 29) significantly evokes Schleiermacher, who himself only evokes some ancient principles: that ' "all art springs from inspiration [or] the lively awakening of the innermost emotional and intellectual faculties"', and that ' "all art must bear witness to the process of its creation" '. In this process, Warburg places the emphasis on the intermediate level, central for the formation and the recalling of the images: the 'expressively charged muscular movement' of gestures, and 'the expressive use of an implement' (32).

For the Renaissance, however, the central issue was not so much the creation but the re-creation of these images. This required, beyond their actual rediscovery and imitative copying, the ability to re-live such experiences, or empathy (see especially the Prefatory Note to the 1893 Botticelli essay; see also Wood 2014: 19). Empathy is a term connected to the philosophy of Dilthey, and was again thoroughly expurgated from the history of thinking by neo-Kantians, neo-Hegelians, and neo-Marxists alike.[21]

This explains Warburg's interest in psychology, his attempt to characterise his work as a kind of historical psychology (Bing 1980: xxx; Carchia 1984: 94–5; Wind 1983: 33) – another anathema for neo-Kantians.[22] However, this also establishes a common ground with the works of Borkenau and Elias, who also considered sociology as a close ally with historical psychology, and who were also (especially Borkenau) much influenced by Dilthey – though also, and way too much, by Freud. Warburg considered the sudden discovery of a long forgotten form of expression as a particularly strong surprise-experience, close to a mystical experience or an epiphany (Johnson 2012: 60; this is close to way Alinei or Heidegger describe the discovery of an etymological root; see Chapter 7). Wood (2014: 24) agrees: 'Warburg's symbol is so strong that it is almost a portent of epiphany'.

Intensification

The impact of forms of expression became magnified through a process Warburg called intensification. The term, as we have seen, was taken over from linguistics. In its use by Warburg, we can distinguish between two different modalities. One concerns the taking up of a form in a context different from its original provenience. Thus, the frenetic movement of Dionysian maenads themselves originate in the orgiastic divinity cults of Asia Minor, presented in the last, posthumous play of Euripides, and was not part of the classical heritage. When such images were taken up in the Renaissance, at first only the movements of the hairs and the cloths were depicted (Warburg 1999: 15, 174), not the frenetic movement, not to mention the violent nudity, as the commissioners, like Sassetti, while merchants and thus in fight with the words, were still observing Christian obedience and medieval modesty (1980: 22). It was only later that, in consecutive steps, where an important role was played by Pollaioulo's depiction of the labours of Hercules, presenting Hercules 'as an idealized symbol of the unfettered superman' (1999: 556), the medieval constraints to expressions were removed (1999: 558). The second modality, closely following the first, is the intensification of the emotions evoked, helped by the contrast between the original emotional charge of the expressive form and the impact its evocation produced in the new context. Such intensification was helped by images that depicted the most extreme human emotions, like grief or anger (Johnson 2012: 21), which at first were only occasionally depicted by artists, but then, under certain circumstances, and for certain reasons, were used increasingly, gradually drumming up the emotions that can be produced through certain forms of expression. Here a crucial role was played by the publication and reading of the Hellenistic text ascribed to Pseudo-Longinus, *On the Sublime*, of obscure (but most probably Alexandrian) origins, that was not analysed specifically by Warburg, but which had a crucial impact, in a series of successive steps, on the intensification of the depictions of violence and sexuality, and which eventually culminated, on the one hand, in Kant's replacing of beauty with the sublime at the core of aesthetics, and on the other in the central concerns of the contemporary movie industry, whether inside or outside Hollywood.

The Mnemosyne atlas

A paradigmatic illustration of forms of expression, and their significance, was the *Mnemosyne atlas* exhibition, collected in between 1926 and 1929, having a major impact on Benjamin's *Passages*, though remaining incomplete and unpublished – just as Benjamin's *Passages*; and also recalling the 'memory theatre' of Giulio Camillo (Agamben 2005: 134; see Horvath and Szakolczai 2018a: 43–6; Yates 1992). The atlas is 'Warburg's nearly wordless account of how and why symbolic images of great pathos persist in Western cultural memory from antiquity to the early twentieth century' (Johnson 2012: ix). It arranged, on 63 wooden panels, about a thousand images, attempting to express and understand the emergence, persistence, and effects of Renaissance art, 'map[ping] the dynamics of historical memory'. Mnemosyne being the mother of the muses, the exhibition was tapping into the very sources of art, while at the same time for Warburg art was the mother of the human sciences (Calabrese 1998: 11). The atlas was intended to be much more than a mere illustration of the history of art, rather it followed well-defined method-logical purposes: it placed art and artists in context, always a central concern for Warburg; and it emphasised the forces against which the rebirth of antique forms of expression had to fight, in particular Nordic realism, which focused on the beauty of bodies covered with layers of clothing (Saxl 1998: 33–4). Works of art were expressions of social memory, depositories of experiences which, to be authentic, had to be passionate, but also having a social dimension (Warnke 1998: 20). Such social memory was carried by a 'chain of pathos-formulas', like a 'living charge', or by 'the recursive sequence of pathos-formulas' (Wood 2014: 19). This gave the importance to the Medici Renaissance, which was a 'concrete evidence for the operation of "social memory" ' (Wind 1983: 26). The basic method-logical principle of the Mnemosyne atlas was openness and not theoretical closure: '[b]y pinning them to panels, Warburg declined to submit the images to the hierarchies of grammar or argument, but rather allowed them to pulse in all directions at once, connecting laterally with one another' (Wood 2014: 20). Or, as Warburg offers an authoritative argument in his 1929 Introduction,

> memory, whether collective or individual, comes to the help of the artist who oscillates between a religious or mathematical vision of the world, not only by creating a space for thinking, but also by intensifying the tendency between

tranquil contemplation or orgiastic abandon on the limit-poles of psychic attitudes [*wohl aber an den Grenzpolen des psychischen Verhaltens die Tendenz zur ruhigen Schau oder orgiastischen Hingabe verstärkend*].

(Warburg 2016, A2).

This leads the argument directly on to liminality.

Warburg and liminality

Periods of transition or in-between spaces already played a significant role in this section, and not accidentally, as Warburg – though he evidently could not know about the term – can be considered a major thinker, *avant la lettre*, of liminality. Johnson argues, including references to various notes, that Warburg work amounts to an iconology of in-between areas (Johnson 2012: xii, 56, 84, 139, 190), used as an almost technical expression, as 'Pathos formulas […] mediate between the desire for the absolute and the pure contingency of sensuous experience' (Johnson 2012: 63; see also Weigel 2020: 398)

Terms evoking liminality are particularly present in Warburg's most important writings. They start with his 1893 dissertation on Botticelli, where a quote from Cartari alludes to the gates of Heaven, where ' "the Horae stand guard with Janus" ' (Warburg 1980: 102–3), joining the divinities of temporal and spatial liminality. A privileged liminal moment is the transition between dreaming and waking up, and this is exactly what the paintings of Botticelli capture:

> One is tempted to say, of many of Botticelli's women and boys, that they have just woken from a dream to become aware of the world around them; however active they may be in that world, still their minds are filled with images seen in dreams
>
> *(1980: 141)*.

At the other end of Warburg's career, concern with liminality dominates a last word, the 1929 Introduction to the Mnemosyne exhibition. Warburg starts by arguing, evoking the start of the *Book of Genesis* as well as the gates of Heaven, that 'the conscious creation of a distance between the self and the external world may well be called the foundational act of human civilization' (Warburg 2016, A1). The next phase terms this distance as *Zwischenraum*, translated by Johnson (2012: 190) outright as a 'liminal space', identified as the soil of artistic creativity, which, as 'an instrument of spiritual orientation', through its adequacy or failure can have a decisive impact on the very destiny of human civilisation (Warburg 2016, B1). Furthermore, as artistic creation 'oscillates between an imagination tendentially identifying with the objects and a rationality that rather tries to distance itself from them', it has an inherent duplicity in that it is caught in between an anti-chaotic function, the 'de-demonisation of inherited phobias', and at the same time 'the pretence to make the spectator accept the cult of idols which is presented to his sight' (Warburg 2016, A3–4). Most importantly, and in striking agreement with

Florensky, a symbol-image is itself an 'in-between space (*Zwischenraum*), a sort of no man's land at the centre of the human' (Agamben 2005: 133).

Perhaps most importantly, Wind's renowned essay on Warburg's 'methodology' makes a dominant use of Warburg's concerns with in-betweenness. Throughout history, the actual impact of images is not constant, as

> their pre-existing expressive values undergo a polarization which corresponds to the extent of the psychological oscillation of the transforming creative power. It is by this theory of polarity that the role of an image within a culture as a whole is to be determined.
>
> (Wind 1983: 26)

Following Vischer, he identifies three types of connections between image and meaning, the 'magical-linking', the 'logical-dissociative', and a third, in-between type, between a mere, lifeless concept and a ritual act, 'where the symbol is understood as a sign and yet remains a living image', and this is where Warburg situates the image as a product of artistic creation (28–9). Thus, both artistic creation and its contemplation or reception, draw 'on the darkest energies of human life', reaching some kind of harmonious equilibrium is never guaranteed, and is always threatened (29). Such ambiguities characterise even Greek culture, as recognised by Burckhardt and Nietzsche, moving beyond the jejune idealisation of their supposed 'noble simplicity and serene grandeur' by Winckelmann, using terms like 'transitory' and 'pregnant moment' in order to intimate 'that crisis in which the tensions embodied in a work of art irrupt and threaten to destroy the actual artistic achievement' (29). Thus, the central problem of art, as Plato and Nietzsche both understood so well, is 'the polarity of the psychic reaction' (33),[23] necessary to understand the periodicity of art, a question that purely formal approaches fail to solve. For understanding a proper periodisation Warburg 'always chose to study those intermediate fields in precisely the historical periods he considered to be themselves times of transition and conflict', while 'within those periods he always tended to apply himself to the study of men who, whether through their profession or their fortune, occupy ambiguous position', or combining liminality and marginality (33–4).[24] Such focus on marginal liminality, or liminal marginality, is characteristic also for the Warburg library, a central aspect of its rationale, and the concluding theme of Wind's article. Compared with specialist libraries, it appears haphazard and fragmentary, as it covers way more areas, while within specific areas it is not complete. Still, 'its strength lies precisely in the areas that are marginal', but this is not a liability but an asset, as 'these are the areas that play a crucial role in the progress of any discipline' (34; obviously meaning marginal in the sense of liminality, and not idiosyncrasy and irrelevance).

In between the demonic and the rational: the serpent ritual

A central area of Warburg's interest in liminal phenomena, in art, but also extending to the core of his personality and life, was the persistent struggle to

144 Some Methods of Political Anthropology

overcome and pacify demonic forces. Beyond academic classicism, he realised, following Nietzsche, that Antiquity carried a deeply ambivalent heritage: the Olympic, but also demonic conception of the world (Bing 1980: xxx). This is why he had a strong interest in astrology, despite personally disliking it, as it was the return to Antiquity that caused the descent of Europe, in the midst of the Renaissance, into blind superstition (Bartozzi 1985: 20). Thus, and in the best tradition of Plato, reason for Warburg was not an anthropological constant, reducible to a concern with facts, forms and logic, but was an active force that one *needed* to use in order to counter the strong and seductive, demonic forces of the darker regions of the soul and the spirit. Warburg also emphasised that such interest in astrology was alien to the Greek spirit, was its travesty and a phenomenon of late Antiquity, having oriental sources, especially in so far as the 'astral demons' were concerned (Saxl 1998: 35; Seznec 1972: 158–9). This concern was continued by the works of the best heirs of the spirit of his work, Wind, Seznec, and Yates.

The tragic drama between the forces of magic and reason, which he traced over time, was also, not surprisingly, 'in an almost magical way a question about himself' (Wind 1983: 26). This is perhaps best shown in his famous account of the serpent ritual, and his interest in it. The lecture was based on the experiences and notes taken on his visit among the Pueblo Hopi Indians in 1896, during his visit in America that was made for family reasons, thus almost three decades before.

The Hopi ritual – which Warburg evidently did not fully witness – offered him the possibility of observing, in an enclave that survived in the midst of a most modern technical culture, the presence of belief in the efficiency of magical rituals, among people whose daily life otherwise was dominated by utilitarian rationalism (Warburg 1998: 12). The culmination of the ritual was a dance with live serpents, animals associated throughout the planet with dark, demonic, chthonic forces, only underlined by the serpents being rattlesnakes, a most dangerous venomous snake. Yet, while the struggle to subdue such demonic forces in historical religions often led to cruel sacrificial cults – including the nearby Aztecs – among the Hopi the snakes were not sacrificed or harmed, rather literally charmed. This occasioned a series of dense reflections, for Warburg, comparing various anthropological and historical cultures, extending to the very fate of modern civilisation.

The central point of Warburg is that the history of the religious sublimation or rational control of such forces cannot be arranged on an evolutionary straight line. Religious monotheism or the rationalism of classical Greek culture is usually considered as limiting the cruelty of sacrifices, magic and idolatry, and yet the victory of Moses in the desert was helped by the bronze serpent, while the dancing maenads of the Dionysus cult ended their act by the cruel killing of the animal. It is in contrast with such rituals that, within Greek culture, the cult of Asclepius represented a different pacification of the forces associated with the serpent; and yet, the Laocoon group, in its manifold history, shows in itself that the process was not irreversible (Raulff 1998: 98).[25]

Warburg was particularly fascinated by the way in which and the reasons why the Hopi managed to reach a certain non-violent equilibrium. He pointed out two reasons. First, as the Hopi lived in close proximity with the various forces of nature, especially the animals, they knew them intimately, feared but also respected them, 'considering the animal a superior being, because the integrity of its wild nature makes it a creature possessing forces way above the human weaknesses' (Warburg 1998: 29–30). Here Warburg's position was very close to those of Hubert and Mauss about the specificities of a magic way of thinking, continued, improved and amplified by Lévy-Bruhl in the direction of a sense of participation, mystical or not, and concerning the Hopi in particular, by Whorf (96–7, 103). The second point concerns the way in which the tension between the enigmatic, demonic forces and human reason can be captured by symbols. This again helps to realise how Warburg's views on symbols were different from the trite neo-Kantianism of Cassirer, interested in the formulation of a formal, universalistic theory of culture. The Hopi, for Warburg, found this equilibrium half-way between magic and *logos*, and 'the instrument with which they orient themselves is the symbol' (28). One such symbol is the dance itself, while other drawings in which snake-like symbols, characteristic of prehistoric art and rituals, kept being designed by modern-day Indians, even in schools, as indications of the world in which they felt at home (14, 47, 94).

The reversal of such an equilibrium and harmony is always tragic, sign of an increasing pessimism of the times, and for Warburg, just as it happened with the uses of the Laocoon-group in the past, it is happening to us, right here, right now, as 'modern civilisation forces itself to refine, eliminate, and substitute with something else' that 'primordial condition' (65).

However, argues Warburg at the end of his lecture, what modern civilisation replaces them with is rather problematic, namely, by conceiving the forces of nature as merely

> infinite waves that obey with docility to human command. In this way the civilisation of machines destroys what natural science, born of myth, achieved with much effort: the space for prayer, then transformed into a space for thinking. The modern Prometheus and the modern Icarus, Franklin and the Wright brothers, inventors of the airplane: they are the sinister destroyers of the sense of distance that threatens to push the world back into chaos. The telegraph and the telephone destroy the cosmos. Mythic and symbolic thought, with its attempt to spiritualise the link between man and the surrounding world, create the space for prayer or for thought that instant electronic contact kills.
>
> (62)[26]

The thinker as seismograph

In an important passage, part of a 1927 lecture, Warburg characterised his main predecessors and sources, Burckhardt and Nietzsche, as 'highly sensitive seismographs' (Warburg 1999: 27). Johnson (2012: 144) argues that the metaphor was deployed 'to reconceive the Dionysian-Apollonian split'. However, the reference, of course, was again partly autobiographical, and he indeed applied it to himself, and in important contexts: in the same year, in the context of a planned return to America (Steinberg 1995: 107); and in 1923, in Kreuzlingen (Weigel 2020: 398). This last is worth quoting at length, among others because it was written only shortly before the delivery of the serpent ritual lecture:

> now, in March 1923, in Kreuzlingen, in a sealed institution, where I find myself a seismograph made of pieces of wood stemming from a growth transplanted from the Orient into the nourishing north-German plain while carrying a branch inoculated in Italy, I allow the signals that I have received to be released from me, because in this epoch of a chaotic defeat even the weakest one is beholden to strengthen the will to cosmic order.
>
> (as in Steinberg 1995: 74)

The seismograph metaphor poses all kinds of method-logical questions: what does it mean that somebody is not just a thinker, a researcher, but a seismograph? What does it mean to *be* a seismograph? How to recognise a seismograph? How to read a seismograph? These are questions that conventional methodology not only fails to ask, but fails to recognise as legitimate. And yet, such questions must be raised – and, to some extent, in so far as possible, even answered.

Notes

1 See Huxley (1982) for a good starting point, extending the connection to 'reason of state'.
2 Many of the related English words (terror, terrible, but also horror, horrible) are traced back, through Latin, to roots meaning to tremble, shiver, or bristle, and which are supposed to have an onomatopoeic origin. This is also true for Hungarian, with 'tremble' *remeg, reng* being much the same words, with the same onomatopoeic origin; and even *retten* 'being terrified' is connected, as its reverse, to 'terror', similarly to the way English 'pat' in Hungarian is *tap*. In Hungarian even 'monstrous' *rémes* is part of the same figuration. However, and further, in Hungarian 'multitude' *rengeteg* or the flow is connected to the same root, implying the frenetic movement or shaking of the earth, produced by a multitude (strangely evoking here that earth in Latin is *terra*). Still further, in Hungarian 'hide' is *rejt*, which thus starts with the same basic root *re* as *remeg* or *reng* 'tremble, shake, rock'. Finally, while Castelli claims that once the attractiveness of the denatured got hold of one, there is no longer any hope, which is certainly true, in Hungarian trembling, the experience of being tempted *while* it is not yet fully successful, is etymologically connected to hope, as in Hungarian 'hope' is *remény*, traced to the same root *remeg* (tremble). The very state of being subject to a temptation, or trembling, is the source of hope – as it is evoked in the much-quoted lines of Hölderlin: where danger is great, the saving power is also near.
3 Heidegger also 'plays' with the verb call (1977: 362).
4 See also Foucault, *Birth of the Clinic*.
5 The Russian word used has particular significance, as derived from *manit'* 'to become, lure', cognate with Sanskrit *májá*, the presumed illusionality of the world (Wade 1996: 116), identified by Castelli in the Flemish paintings.
6 Note that the root word is *dovod* 'proof, reason/ érv', or *dovod'it'* 'lead,'; in both cases implies somebody who leads oneself, or relies on oneself as one's proof, or captures the smugness of modern scientific rationalism.

7 Orientation is also a key word for Warburg.
8 In his pathbreaking book reading together Foucault and Eastern Christianity Sergey Horujy (2015: 4) compares Foucault and Florensky in the following way: 'Both thinkers summon one to incorporate into philosophy itself the experience that grounds it'.
9 *Litso* 'face' is derivative of *lik* 'representation of a face on an icon' (Wade 1996: 110).
10 The parallels are tight with Horvath's (2021) 'living dead' and 'replicator'.
11 The most famous of such image, *Hodegetria*, traditionally attributed to St Luke, literally means 'Our Lady of the Way'.
12 Similarly for Ingold (2010a: 16), images are not so much 'representations' of things, rather help us to find them, implying 'recognisability'.
13 See Tarkovsky's film, an unparalleled masterpiece.
14 Icon painting started to decline in the 16th century, through the diffusion of allegorism and its schismogenic double, theological rationalism (88).
15 Florensky claims that this theological argument is characteristic of Western rationalism, alien to the thinking of Eastern Christianity (157).
16 The collaboration between Verrocchio and Leonardo was culmination and swansong of this practice in the Western Renaissance. Raphael would already be 'educated' by the first entrepreneur-trickster-artist, Perugino.
17 For a closely related story, in many regards, see the anecdote about Herbert Simon, Nobel prize laurate in economics and founding figure in AI, in Dupuy (2009: 27–8), at the start of the chapter 'The Fascination with Models'. In his 1991 autobiography Simon claimed that he learned nothing from his varied travels abroad that he could not have acquired sitting at his desk in his office, or in good libraries, formulated in a ' "Travel Theorem" '. Thus, 'the first time Simon and his wife visited Europe, in 1965, already fully convinced of the truth of this theorem, they arranged their itinerary so that they would see nothing that they did not already know through books or pictures'. Thus, though visiting the exact spots where Cézanne painted his famous pictures, ' "within three feet exactly" ', they claimed that ' "We learned nothing new; we had already seen the paintings" ' (28). For them, nature was imitating art, and history was a copy of literature. These are the people who brought you first neo-Kantianism and neoclassical economics, then rational choice theory as a justification of boundless egoism and hedonism, and now artificial intelligence and transhumanism: not inquiring spirits exploring the world, driven by genuine curiosity, but people of an infinite dogmatism, closed into the nooks of their own mind, and who now, through tricks by which communication through electronic means is imposed on us as an actual or virtual obligation, enclose us in *our* own rooms. This is also identical to what Calasso (2019) calls as 'Rabbinic modernity'; even recalls the last Zürau aphorism of Kafka.
18 Already in late Antiquity the Latin adjective *patheticus* 'pathetic', derived from Greek *pathos* 'experience', turned into a mode of expressing, not experiencing, and a rather specific one – closely reflecting the kind of decadence due to intensification depicted by Warburg.
19 I will rely on the penultimate chapter of Pierre Hadot's last book, devoted to Goethe and entitled 'Don't forget to live', published when he was 86. Hadot's entire lifework exudes the conviction, mirroring that of Hermann Broch, that modern academic philosophy is simply a fraud, and a civilisational disaster.
20 This aside is of fundamental importance, as Alexandria belongs to the key tradition of founded imperial centres, the Babylon-Alexandria-Constantinople series, locations from which Magi control spread in the world. While it also infiltrated Rome, the central lineage by which it took over European culture is Venice-Antwerp-Amsterdam-London-New York, as can be best followed through the intertwined developments of theatres and stock-markets.
21 Not surprisingly, according to Wind (1983: 108–9) Gombrich, as good neo-Kantian, was particularly exasperated by Warburg's such attempts.
22 At the same time when rejecting 'life-philosophies' and the concern with empathy, the neo-Kantian mandarins also attacked the 'psychologising' tendencies in philosophy. The encounter between Husserl and Dilthey is particularly relevant in this regard.

23 Warburg repeatedly evokes such polarities, with close affinities to Bateson's schismogenesis. See in particular the claim, in a note written in preparation for the Kreuzlingen conference, that ' "the whole of mankind is eternally schizophrenic" ' (as in Agamben 2005: 134).
24 Such focus on transitions closely parallels the interests of Borkenau and Elias (see Szakolczai 2000b); on marginality and liminality, see Szakolczai (2000a).
25 The caduceus was also associated with Hermes, and thus the figure of Asclepius – whose cult was closely connected to that of Hermes (see Kerényi) – at the same time played a role in the Greek pacification of the demonic trickster deity, in the figure of Hermes (see Hadot 2008: 188, 215–20). Warburg (1998: 57) emphatically recalls that in a North-German Protestant church in Lüdingworth he saw a depiction of Laocoon, due to the association between the caduceus, in the hand of Laocoon, and the bronze serpent in the hand of Moses.
26 Here Warburg's diagnosis of machine technology, with its destruction of distancing, becomes particularly close to Heidegger's concerns with technology. Note that Ludwig Binswanger, who followed Warburg very closely, became a Heideggerian psychiatrist, and his work in this sense was theme for the first published writing of Foucault (in Foucault 1994). Heidegger, however, became an anathema in Warburg circles after his heated Spring 1929 debate with Cassirer in the second Davos conference – an event of particular actuality.

9
UNDERSTANDING THROUGH AUTHORS

> It would almost seem as though our better thoughts and sympathies were charms, in virtue of which the soul is enabled to hold some vague and mysterious intercourse with the spirits of those whom we dearly loved in life.
>
> *Charles Dickens,* Nicholas Nickleby, *2000: 525*

> It has gradually become clear to me what every great philosophy up till now has consisted of — namely, the confession of its originator, and a species of involuntary and unconscious auto-biography; and moreover that the moral (or immoral) purpose in every philosophy has constituted the true vital germ out of which the entire plant has always grown.
>
> *Friedrich Nietzsche,* Beyond Good and Evil, *6*

Modern thinking, in line with its standard schismatic tendencies, is torn between two, equally unsatisfactory and untenable positions on the role of authors, or the personal component in social research and thinking. On one side, the role of the individual is exaggerated out of all proportion, in line with the hubristic egoism that is the norm of modernity. Everybody is supposed to build his own theoretical framework, then theory, trademark and sell every idea, considering oneself as the legal subject behind his every statement uttered. It is in contrast to this position, and in this sense quite rightly, that Barthes and Foucault developed their famous positions problematising the presumptions of authorship, arguing that most discourses in social thinking are situated in a taken for granted epistemic field, and so are by no means original products of a sovereign subject.

On the other side, however, and as an evident paradox, when building their theoretical framework researchers are encouraged not to treat the authors of their readings as concrete persons. They are supposed to use only certain ideas, as concepts or hypotheses, preferably only one from every other thinker read, using another buzzword of the present, depersonalisation, and build these anonymous, lifeless,

DOI: 10.4324/9781003275138-12

decontextualised terms into their *own* theoretical framework, to be 'trademarked'. Any effort to understand a thinker on its own terms, as an author, as a complex person engaged in his own quest for understanding, is discouraged as a kind of dogmatism, close to a personality cult, characteristic of Marxist, Freudian, and similar intellectual dogmatisms.

This, however, is simply wrong, as in this way the ideas encountered would only be fitted into a preconceived conceptual framework, concocted by the researcher, acquired from his professors, and increasingly from the trite commonplaces circulated by medias. Understanding the social and human world lies through understanding authors who offer understanding: certainly not a single author as a unique master thinker, comparable to a Gnostic paraclete, but several authors *as* authors; reading many if not all their works, and trying to understanding the character of their quest; of as many authors as possible – certainly at least 2–3, for a thesis; and keep collecting such authors as one's career progresses, reading in depth always new and new authors as sources of inspiration. Otherwise, one becomes a boring mouthpiece of one's professors, and especially of the commonplaces recycled by medias or professional disciplinary associations.

Following Weber and Heidegger, we must re-think the nature of understanding.

Understanding

Understanding is the primary and central aim of the social and human 'sciences' and also of philosophy. It is way more than the mere accumulation of knowledge, gathering information, predicting events, or the ability to produce transformations in objects. It implies, as words in different languages (English under-standing, German *Ver-stehen*, Hungarian *ért*, French *com-prendre*, or Greek *epi-steme*) indicate, a form of knowledge that has depth, and can only be *reached* through *maturation* (in Hungarian, both terms are expressed by the root-word *ér*, source of *ért* 'understand').

The at once archetypal and ideal-typical form of understanding is an intimate relationship between two persons; in fact, understanding is exclusively human, or 'inter'-human (following the etymology of understanding, where the prefix 'under' originally had the sense of 'inter'). Machines can perform incommensurable computations and register a similarly incommensurable amount of data, but can never understand – the idea of 'artificial intelligence' is non-sensical, as it is based on a confusion between the genuine and the fake, constitutional for modernity, through its technologised science. Even animals cannot understand. On the other hand, we can only understand other humans – in the memorable expression of Zygmunt Bauman (1978: 33), 'one cannot understand a tree'.

Intimacy implies close acquaintance, or familiarity – in fact, both terms are synonyms of knowledge. But intimacy is much more than cognitive knowledge, even more than recognition, as it almost inevitably implies an emotional attachment. The highest degree of intimacy is love, and we can indeed hardly love someone whom we do not know intimately or understand; the idea of love at first sight, as shown by René Girard, is pure mimetism, a 'romantic' illusion. However, love by no means is identical with sexual attraction – in many languages filial and parental 'love', and conjugal or romantic 'love' are expressed by different words. Knowing someone intimately might also lead to the opposite emotion, dislike, even hatred.

The central issue is that understanding, or intimate knowledge, inevitably implies a degree of intermingling of cognitive and emotive elements – using the terminology of Dilthey, pioneer of psychology. If we come to understand somebody and it involves a positive appreciation – and social life is based on humans living together having a positive appreciation of each other, otherwise life is unbearable – then this appreciation does not necessarily involve 'love', but certainly a degree of respect, esteem, or approval; a positive judgment which nevertheless has an emotional component. Or, and again, we enter this crucial realm where the intellect and emotions cannot be separated; where being guided by reason necessarily implies a reliance on the heart as well. The central issue is the overall appreciation or adjudication of a person *as a person*.

This has fundamental relevance for the way to gain of knowledge, thus the method-logic of Political Anthropology. Every human being gains knowledge through intimate relations, in one's family – source of the more general term 'familiarity'. This continues, through schooling, from the elementary level up to the university, ideally without any rupture of continuity – the manner in which so many lecturers in our days consider as their duty to 'enlighten' students; tearing them away from the knowledge they gained that far in their families is only a proof for the radical existential corruptness they inculcate – of course, mostly unbeknownst to them. This is revealed in some key terminology of education in German, like *Maturität* and *Doktorvater* – German education having some of the best and the worst aspects – one is tempted to say, *only* best and worst. Or, education means that children are personally guided towards understanding and maturity by people they love and respect – emphasis gradually shifting from the former to the latter, but the key emotional component remaining.

Such direct and personal modality, however, is also increasingly complemented by appropriating more impersonal modes of learning, through books, and other written (or 'mediated') material. This is most evident for a PhD education: a candidate who would only use what his supervisor and professors lectured about would certainly fail in any normal educational institution. A good supervisor only acts as a *guide*, giving into the hands of his students those books and articles, those *authors* the student would need to know.

The central question concerns the meaning of 'guidance'; and the personal component that necessarily must lie here. Such guidance does *not* mean to familiarise the student with the mainstream readings of an academic discipline. This has nothing personal in it, and indeed is rather a way to depersonalisation, one of the main evils of modernity, according to Max Weber; a means to follow the 'best practice' ideas of HR Departments, according to which all students in a given field must be given ideally the same Bibliography, containing the 'main' books and articles by the 'main' figures of the field – in a worse-case scenario accompanied by the video-registered lectures of the 'star performers' in the field, from Harvard or

Oxford. This is not an ideal not yet reached, but the *worst* possible nightmare, that hopefully will not be realised – though it is already being prepared, evidently, in the background. This worse-case scenario, apart from many other problems, to be discussed shortly, promotes not excellence, but a reduction to the smallest common denominator helped by the increased mediatisation of intellectual life and the degradation it necessarily promotes.

However, and beyond the evils of compartmentalised professionalisation and mediatisation, such a road is problematic simply because it ignores the *personal* component that is at the heart of any learning process – necessary because only such a personal touch keeps the cognitive and emotive aspects together. Students should not be force-fed an obligatory and extensive reading list, but must be allowed to consult books and articles, and first of all *thinkers*, with whose approaches they feel some kind of affinity. Such affinities might be misdirected to some extent, results of various accidents of life history, and yet this does not justify education as a generalised brainwashing. A proper education, the guidance of a young soul, requires extreme delicacy, as Hölderlin realised it so well (see *Hyperion*). The vital aspect in any learning process is a good teacher – and consulting the biography of any major thinker one can easily identify a teacher, whether in the high school or in university, who managed to *enchant*, in the best sense of the word,[1] his/her students.

Still, every teacher has limits in his knowledge; education implies to learn from those one does not know personally, reading their works. Here comes the central idea of this chapter, a crucial aspect of Political Anthropology as method: we can truly learn from books if we try to treat their authors *as if* they were our concrete, personal teachers; we should not treat their works as dead words, fixated forever, mere ideas or theories, but as much as possible 'intuit' the person who has a quest for understanding – and therefore can help our own quest for understanding.[2] Thus, a main guidance a supervisor or a professor could give is not simply by suggesting some readings, even if these are tailor-made to the *genuine* interests and needs of a student, but by guiding them to authors as authors; and, even further, by turning these authors themselves into guides.

This leads to the three remaining sections of this short chapter: how to understand authors *as* authors? How to gain understanding *through* authors, by using authors as guides? And finally, how to *become* an author, how to write important works, that both depart from personal experiences and concerns, thus interesting and relevant for the scholar writing them, and *due to this* also reach concerns of general interest and relevance, and not merely carry forward the narrow, compartmentalised agenda of a scientific discipline, on the way to hyper-specialised professional fragmentation?

Understanding authors

The theme was discussed extensively in my previous books,[3] so only a short overview will be given here. The suggestion is that a good way towards understanding authors is offered by combining Dilthey's hermeneutics with liminality analysis – an approach all the more relevant as Turner recognised the close affinities between his central concerns and Dilthey's work.[4] This implies two issues. First, the central underlying method-logical idea is not to focus on the ideas of a thinker, as they were published in well-known works, but try to restore to the works the character of a living quest: not so much as a conscious 'project', which has its 'ends' and 'means', again part of the standard neo-Kantian terminology, rather as a 'going concern': a re-search,[5] a *zetesis*, a quest for understanding. So, in so far as possible, the entire life-work of the thinker should be consulted, and the dynamics of his life-work reconstructed. Second, this is enabled by a focus on formative liminal experiences, and on similarly liminal moments of crisis, helping to give a structure to the dynamics of these life-works – not an imposed structure but, following both Dilthey and Turner, by following the effective structuring impact of liminal experiences.

The general relevance of such an approach can be illustrated by the World War generations. The central idea, based on liminality analysis, is that situations that are liminal in more ways than one might produce particularly strong effects. A particularly relevant example is the coincidence of social and individual liminality. If an individual goes through a significant 'rite of passage' during major socio-political events, especially a world war, then one might expect particularly significant lasting effects. The two world wars precisely define two generations, those born between 1895 and 1900, and those born between 1920 and 1927, or those who went through their 'maturity' school examination and entered university during a world war. The WWI generation includes most of the reflexive historical sociologists, those thinkers who carried forward the insights of a Nietzsche-Weberian genealogy, like Norbert Elias (born in 1897), his friend Franz Borkenau (1900), Lewis Mumford, the great American historian of cities and technology (1895), and Eric Voegelin (born on 3 January 1901). The list can be extended with Karl Löwith (born in 1897), Georges Dumézil (1898), Frances Yates (1899), Hans-Georg Gadamer (1900), Henri Frankfort (1897), Edgar Wind (1900), Enrico Castelli (1900), Károly Kerényi (1897), and Béla Hamvas (1897). Members of the WWII generation include both 'reflexive historical sociologists', like Michel Foucault (born in 1926) and Reinhart Koselleck (1923), and political anthropologists: Victor Turner (1920), Mary Douglas (1921), René Girard (1923), and Colin Turnbull (1924); and also Erving Goffman (1922), Alessandro Pizzorno (1924), Shmuel Eisenstadt (1923), Zygmunt Bauman (1925), Wilhelm Hennis (1923), Michel Henry (1922), or Pierre Hadot (1921). Specific to the work of each is the relentless pursuit of an at once erudite and personal research agenda, irrespective of disciplinary and mediatic interests.

Understanding through authors

This way of proceeding not only helps a better understanding of key thinkers – certainly much better than following, as a start, standard textbooks, which only regurgitate the most egregious commonplaces, when not getting the main ideas completely wrong (this latter is the case, almost everywhere, with Max Weber) – but turns such exercises into catalysts for one's own research. Taking up only isolated ideas as 'concepts' from various books results in a work combining, at the level of a 'theoretical framework', three sources, themselves interconnected with each other: one's own fixed ideas; the standard approaches of the mainstream disciplinary sub-field; and mediatic commonplaces about freedom, equality, democracy, modernity, development, well-being, etc., combined with the seemingly opposite but in fact schismogenically complementary commonplaces about inequalities, oppression, repression, domination, suffering, etc. However, entering the 'mind' of several key and interesting, unusual, maverick thinkers at the same time provokes a literally explosive effect on one's own thinking, helping to gestate and explore new ideas. In other words, by this exercise authors becomes genuine, almost personal guides in one's own research.

This is because this exercise cannot be done once and for all, but must be renewed with every new work. Thus, I found that having read extensively Nietzsche, Weber, and Foucault was not sufficient: for every new book I needed to consult in depth new and new thinkers, instead of just applying the perspectives gained from Nietzsche, Weber, and Foucault to a new field; it is only by finding new sources of inspiration that I could meaningfully progress with my own work. And these authors, I found, had to be not simply read, but written about, in a reconstructive manner: it is only by entering *their* works, on *their* own terms, that I felt that I could write something meaningful, without simply repeating myself – which would not have been worth the ink and paper used.

Reconstruction means not writing from memory once the works were read, but the preparation of extensive notes, and then an effort to reconstruct the central argument, or even the underlying quest, of the thinker. This does not mean writing a book review, as such review, in a necessarily imitative manner, follows the argument of a concrete book on its own terms. The idea, rather is to penetrate the very core of the work, which nevertheless and inevitably will be sifted through one's own concerns and interests, but not by simply 'reading into' somebody else's work one's own ideas, rather generating something new, a productive synthesis between the central ideas of another thinker and one's own concerns; it is such a reading that, while being faithful as much as possible to the spirit of the author, quoting extensively his works, would also be helpful in launching one's own research by producing the new ideas by and through such reconstructive reading. It will not be a 'reading into' one's own ideas, as quite the contrary, it is such a reading experience and the exercise of writing about it, that literally *produces* new ideas. The attempt to revitalise someone else's project literally propels forward one's own.

Far from being a radical novelty, the idea leans back to the most classical advice always – though, sadly, no longer – given to young academics: to immerse oneself in a library, and read as much as possible, *without* considering the immediate usefulness of books, even for one's concrete research. If one is serious about understanding, such reading is never meaningless, as it relies on trusting one's own intellectual drive. It builds up reading experiences, thus a kind of erudition, eventually wisdom, beyond the narrow limits of 'useful knowledge'. And in the 'long run', and for real human concerns, *this* knowledge will be genuinely useful, and not the search for immediate 'practical' significance.

Understanding and becoming an author

Even if the aim of the social and human 'sciences' is understanding, the purpose and outcome of a research quest is to produce works that reveal and further promote understanding, or primarily to write books – books that matter; that are relevant; that do not simply take up space on a library shelf, but will be read, and not just due to a temporary fashion. For this, and just to repeat, for the last time, it is not sufficient to follow 'scientific methodology' in a 'most rigorous manner'; quite the contrary, as that would secure the complete meaninglessness and irrelevance of the work. Instead of following the advice of Bacon and Descartes, one should do the opposite: not doubting oneself, and human mental powers in general, but rely rather on the powers of one's own mind or soul (following Plato and St Bonaventure, for whom these are the same); and those of one's heart (following Pascal, and the 'reasons of the heart', but also the Old and New Testaments – see Chapter 11). Instead of trying to set up experiments or gather quantitative data through survey research or other means, one should rely on life experiences – one's own again, first of all, to start with, and of course also those of many others. The central issue is not to repress, regulate, and constrain one's mind, to force it into following pre-set rules and ways, but to keep it alive instead, to let it resonate with one's life experiences and those of the others – not of 'the other', a meaningless device of modern philosophy, but with concrete, living beings, and their everyday lives.

For this, it is fundamental not to follow the sirenic voices of the media, the disciplinary mainstream consensus, and the agenda dictated by the managerial bureaucratic quasi-elites – three non-substances that are closely interwoven, spiralling in the void of the 'public sphere'; but at the same time cultivate one's perceptivity and build up a personal erudition – close to the classical, mostly Platonic concerns of the 'care of the self/soul', rediscovered by Hadot, Patočka, and Foucault (also close to Voegelin), though not in the direction of techniques of askesis, that are too close to Descartes.

Weber's methodological essays, especially on 'Objectivity' (his own quotation marks), are of special use here, as these do not support a mindless positivism, but argue instead for the importance of escaping the flights of fancy – not just one's own, but especially those spun by various 'media'; central also for the last words of Socrates, in the reading of Dumézil, commented by Foucault in one of his last lectures. For this, one should keep one's own personality intact, implying no rupture in one's experiences, keeping the unity of one's self, as again centrally and recurrently argued by Foucault in his 1980s Collège de France lectures, but which was formulated most clearly by Augustine, also based on Plato, as it will be again argued in more detail in Chapter 11.

Trusting one's mind does not involve hubris, but the continuous building up and amplifying of one's own personality, and especially sense of judgment. Adjudicating what is real and what is not, what is genuine and what is fake, what is relevant and of lasting importance and what is a passing fad is fundamental, and in making such judgments one cannot rely on *anybody*, but on one's own good sense which must of course be continuously developed, and which can only be done by trusting in the opinion and judgment of some other persons whom one can trust. This cannot be modified by fashions, campaigns spun by the media, or by statistical data and the views of experts concocted by official bureaucracies in collusion with the media. The most tragic aspect of current COVID-based policies is that a concrete health emergency was not simply magnified out of all proportion, but is systematically used to undermine personal trust, in oneself and others, in the name of following ever stricter, purely statistics-based, and evidently highly problematic if not completely irrelevant measures which furthermore are continuously modified. For somebody who lived through Communism and heard many further detailed personal stories, this mode of acting frighteningly recalls the Communist policies, where it was required to follow by the letter the party line all the time, though this line was continuously shifting: confusing the sense of judgment was primary state policy there, to secure 'robotic obedience' (Agnes Horvath). With COVID, it became state policy even in Western liberal democracies, and the consequences of this development are unforeseeable. Most importantly, in both regimes this mode of acting strictly follows the logic of 'scientific methodology'.

Relying on one's own experiences and sense of judgment and building up a personal erudition does not mean arrogant hubris or a renewed cult of the genius. Quite on the contrary; the focus is on cultivating an ever increasing set of guides, not self-enclosing into one's own theoretical system, 'objective' or 'subjective', in the manner of Kant, Fichte, Hegel, or their numerous followers. The idea is different: if somebody has the strength to enter the current academic world, attempting to pursue a significant personal project, it means, almost certainly, that that person does have sufficient talent to bring forth meaningful results.

Notes

1 See Curry (2023).
2 This is central for Dilthey's historically oriented philosophy.
3 See especially Szakolczai (2003), Chapter 2.
4 For details, see Szakolczai (2004).
5 Note that in current language the meanings of 'search' and 'research' got inverted: 'research' designates boring standard activities, chasing funding, while 'search' has the open-endedness that should characterise a re-search, in the analogy of the difference between cognition and re-cognition.

10
UNDERSTANDING THROUGH NOVELS

> the whole pattern [...] is always before the eyes of the story-weaver at his loom
>
> Charles Dickens, Our Mutual Friend, 776

> The magic reel, which, rolling on before, has led the chronicler thus far, now slackens in its pace, and stops.
>
> Charles Dickens, The Old Curiosity Shop, 538

> 'The power of this woman is astonishing. She has been acting a part the whole time.' But he can act a part too—his one unchanging character
>
> Charles Dickens, Bleak House, 559

As the previous chapter emphasised the importance of the personal component in understanding, it is not surprising that works of art play a significant role for Political Anthropology. This was already rendered evident in Chapter 8, concerning images, but the same holds true for texts. A study of works of art as a source for understanding is incompatible with scientific methodology, but this has no relevance for Political Anthropology, as this field is not interested in imitating science, but in understanding reality, searching for meaning; and art, in the memorable expression of WB Yeats, is but 'a vision of reality' (*Ego Dominus Tuus*).

While all kinds of art can have relevance for social understanding, novels, arguably, take up a special place, and for a variety of reasons.[1] Some of this is evident – novels are the most 'realistic' form of art, with protagonists speaking in prose and impersonating the most varied characters of social life. Novels also tell stories, thus are close to both history and biography, central modes of hermeneutic philosophy, according to Dilthey, key reference point of Weber's method-logical reflections. But the most important reason why novels offer a royal road to understanding modern life is the excessive theatricality of the modern world. Novels can not only be interpreted as

DOI: 10.4324/9781003275138-13

describing the world 'like' the theatre, but they capture and present a world, modernity, that has become thoroughly transformed into a global theatre. The theatre effectively transformed the world, and novels effectively present and even analyse this 'theatricalised' world – much better than the main instruments supposedly destined to study reality, philosophy and sociology, in the throes of neo-Kantianism and neopositivism.

Sociology came into being for the single purpose of analysing the modern world. It explicitly rejected all previous forms of knowledge, arguing that the analysis of this new reality requires fundamentally new methods, especially the systematic, meticulous collecting of facts, making full use of the tools offered by modern 'natural' science and technology. Yet, if the idea concerning theatricalisation is correct, this project is thoroughly misdirected, a blind alley, as the accumulation of mere facts prevents recognising and analysing the falsification of the real. Mainstream and critical sociology alike, with their fact-mongering and number-crunching, but also interviewing, discourse-analysis and social constructivism, and above all with their obsession with 'critiquing' the 'given', is a not only sophisticated but technically Sophist enterprise, hiding the most important, genuine problems of a theatricalised world and – with its reification of the apparently real – legitimating the fake.[2]

Novels offer unique guidance in a theatricalised world because they present a storyline (note the close connection between 'history' and 'story'; in some languages, like Italian, even the word used in the same – *storia*), which reveal the full character of the protagonists, just as it happens in real histories,[3] whether biographical or world political, thus manage to render evident the fine distinction between the real and the fake: genuine human acts and passions, and their theatricalised imitations. Theoretical accounts, in themselves, cannot perform this feat, as they merely *argue* about reality and genuineness, and any such argument can be repeated, imitated, and faked. This is the ultimate reason for the insufficiency of any purely discursive, ratiocinating description.

Needless to add, not all novels perform such feat; most of them, just as most films, and other forms of art, simply proliferate theatricality to infinity. It is against such theatricality, realistic or not, that time and again the fad of 'new novels' or 'new films' comes up, pretending to break with narrative, but in this way only end up in static, frozen, lifeless *l'art pour l'art* irrelevance. The key modern or hypermodern novelists recognised the need to keep narrative intact, and thus the tight connections with history, but instead of simply imitating (theatrical) life they managed to bring out, through the presentation of various personalities in act, the distinction between the genuine and the fake. This is why, here again, classical education and classical culture was right, in contrast to current, hyper-modern reformist and revisionist fads: understanding requires familiarity with the most important classics, ancients and moderns, as knowing in depth the plays of Shakespeare and the novels of Dickens does not mean belonging to a snob cultural elite who 'knows' who Macbeth or David Copperfield was, but these and other characters, in their complexity, helps us to talk about human passions and acts which otherwise are impossible to capture in a purely discursive manner. The modern world, up to the minutest details, can be understood, and this understanding can be *shared* and *discussed*, through the literally hundreds of characters conjured up by the astonishing imagination of Dickens – unique gift of the Muses, sources of inspiration for the Greeks; characters that nevertheless are way more *real* than the 'rational' accounts and 'positivistic' descriptions concocted up by sociologists or philosophers. In an 'ideal' world, all social scientists would read *all* of Dickens' novels, just as have a good introductory course on the main discoveries of archaeology and their meaning and significance, and so by mentioning personalities like Pecksniff, Mrs Gamp, Barnaby, Paul and Florence Dombey, Mr and Mrs Micawber, Bradley Headstone, Lady and Sir Leicester Deadlock, Little Dorrit, Mr Merdle, or Twemlow, to mention only a few, just as the number of trickster figures present there, Puritans and not so, one could immediately convey ideas that are way beyond the remit of 'scientific' terminology.

Understanding through novels requires the use of particularly good guides. There are, fortunately, a series of contemporary master thinkers who placed the study of novels at the centre of their work. The list can be started with René Girard, whose work took an anthropological turn, and which started by a pioneering analysis of the novels of the 19th century, helping him to unearth the mimetics of desire, beyond the Romantic celebration of liberating autonomous desire. It includes Mikhail Bakhtin, the most important Russian thinker of the past century (with Florensky), aiming at founding a philosophical anthropology along the lines of Dilthey's philosophy, and moving explicitly beyond his neo-Kantian teachers. Bakhtin's work has many parallels with the arguably most important Hungarian thinker of the past century, Béla Hamvas, who also worked on a foundational anthropology and considered modern novels as vital in that undertaking. Bakhtin and Hamvas were exact contemporaries, though ignoring each other, and developing strikingly similar ideas, like their re-classification of major figures of philosophical anthropology like Plato, Kierkegaard, and Nietzsche as novelists; Hamvas even argued that *Hamlet* is rather a novel. For the two most important Spanish philosophers of the 20th century, Ortega y Gasset and Miguel de Unamuno, who similarly tried to escape neo-Kantianism through Dilthey, Kierkegaard, and Nietzsche, developing ideas in parallel with Huizinga or Heidegger, reflecting on *Don Quixote* was central for their philosophy. Such guides prominently include two Italian scholars, Pietro Citati, and Roberto Calasso, each of them having produced a unique oeuvre and recognised as iconic figures of Italian culture. The list can be closed with two of the most important historically oriented social theorists or genealogists, Michel Foucault and Eric Voegelin, in whose works novels have a certain prominence.

Understanding through novels is helped by some main modern novelists themselves having a background in philosophy or other modes of knowledge. Albert Camus had a university degree in philosophy; Hermann Broch also studied philosophy, until he recognized that philosophy in the Vienna manner was irrelevant for understanding reality; J.R.R. Tolkien was an Oxford Professor of Language and Literature; Mikhail Bulgakov came from a family of theologians, while Aldous Huxley – just as Gregory

Bateson – from a family of scientists. In some cases, the distinction between novelists and theorists breaks down: Hamvas wrote novels, Camus or Broch not just essays, but works which belong to philosophy or the social sciences, while Kafka's notes and diaries are recognized to have philosophical, even theological depth (see Calasso and Citati on Kafka).

Referring to works of art, in particular characters from novels, is not an 'embellishment' of the argument,[4] but belongs to its substance, promoting understanding in a way that otherwise would remain inaccessible.

Notes

1 For details about the role of novels in understanding, see Szakolczai (2015, 2016 and 2017).
2 On using novels for Political Anthropological study, see Boland (2008, 2018), Boyle (2018), Ferguson (2010), McMylor (2018), O'Connor (2022), Stenner & Greco (2018).
3 This is why anecdotes, at the intersection point between 'story' and 'history', have such method-logical importance, ignored or denigrated by rationalistic sociology or philosophy, at their peril.
4 One of the worst recent changes concerning copyright legislation is the claim that mottos only 'embellish' the text, and so require special permissions. Utilitarianism on the rampage.

11
HISTORICAL METHODS

So little knows
Any, but God alone, to value right
The good before him, but perverts best things
To worst abuse, or to their meanest use.

John Milton, Paradise Lost, *IV.202–5*

... this world's general sickness doth not lie
In any humour, or one certain part;
But as thou sawest it rotten at the heart,
Thou seest a hectic fever hath got hold
Of the whole substance, not to be controlled,
And that thou hast but one way, not to admit
The world's infection, to be none of it.

John Donne, An Anatomy of the World *(1611)*

Both understood her instantly, with a much more delicate subtlety than much better educated people, whose perception came less directly from the heart, could have brought to bear upon the case

Charles Dickens, Our Mutual Friend, *612*

The modern world, and in particular modern thought, has a puzzling, paradoxical relationship to history. In our contemporary (un)reality, dominated by science and technology, any concern with history is deemed as all but irrelevant. What matters is useful knowledge that works; how this was gained is at best a night-time story, with no genuine relevance. Yet, and at the same time, one of the most distinctive identifying features of our civilisation is the utmost importance it attributes to history. Simply no other civilisation is interested in the careful and cumulative

DOI: 10.4324/9781003275138-14

registration of historical events, literally anything that happened; and, strikingly, this exact same concern is extended and trivialised by the means of contemporary technology.

The third point, partly illuminating, partly problematising the previous two, is that not just Western civilisation and its various parts place a particular emphasis on history, but the self-legitimation of the modern world is also based on a particular historical narrative, the idea of progress: that we, moderns, are not only enlightened, democratic, and free, but that we are part of an irreversible historical march forward, the Great March captured in Kundera's *Unbearable Lightness of Being*, using science, technology, the markets, and so one, to improve ourselves, all the time.

Political Anthropology, this field which is constituted by a dissent from such dominant modernist narrative, evidently questions, term by term, such a perspective on history – though not completely, and not without its own ambivalence. That Political Anthropology is itself a method is best visible through the tight connections between political anthropology and what came to be called, after Nietzsche and Foucault, the genealogical method, or genealogy, closely affine to comparative historical sociology. Political Anthropology does not simply use historical evidence, but is constitutionally historical; it is a type of knowledge that takes not science but history as its background reference point. The pervasiveness of history is expressed strikingly well by Aldous Huxley (1982: 20): 'Any given event in any part of the universe has as its determining conditions all previous and contemporary events in all parts of the universe'. The central aim of this chapter is to clarify what exactly this means and implies.

Genealogy as method

Genealogy is not offering technical advice about using historical evidence in order to support one's theoretical points, rather is primarily a vision of history; more precisely, it offers a vision of human existence as being fundamentally historical. In doing so, it is based on two points, one negative, the other positive, which are not exactly 'dogmas' in the sense that they cannot be debated, but yet which nevertheless make certain basic distinctions between approaches to historical analysis that are simply erroneous, and conditions which must be met if a historically based approach wants to reach valid results.

Negatively, this implies that any attempt to impose a linear, evolutionary, progressive storyline on the course of human history must be dismissed from the start as unacceptable. All the main figures associated with genealogy started by questioning the progressive vision into which they were brought up in a taken for granted manner, while realising at the same time that the critical or alternative approaches, especially those connected with Marx, share the exact same problem, thus do not offer in any sense a way out. As it is only too well known, in the *Communist Manifesto*, Marx (and Engels) argued that the 'bourgeois revolutions' were a necessary step in the right direction, but in themselves not sufficient, so further steps are needed. For a genealogist, this line of reasoning makes no sense, it is just a presentist self-justification; human action cannot be guided by guessing the direction to which progress must necessarily lead. History cannot be instrumentalised as a technique to discover the road to the future.

But this does not mean that history is irrelevant; quite the contrary. Genealogists were convinced about the fundamental importance of historical studies. In spite of any difference, they all agreed concerning the specific way in which history mattered: not for the future, as in various progressist readings; not simply for the sake of the past; but specifically for the *present*, as a history of the present. This means that their interpretation of history, or genealogy as a method, was a way to understand how our current reality, including the social, cultural, and institutional framework, the modes of conduct characteristic of our times, and even the way human beings perceive and shape their own selves or identities is historically specific, the result of a specific and concrete course of history. Conceiving the present, *us* as we are, as the culmination of a historical development, implying us as enlightened, free, democratic, progressive, reaching unprecedented levels of knowledge, science, wealth, and well-being, is not simply not true, but is preposterous, the height of arrogance, *cannot* be true. History, to be sure, is part of our identity, but this applies to any human group or culture. The *study* of history, as the heart of social understanding, in contrast to a simple maintaining of tradition, is important in so far as it can help us understand how we got to the point where we are, *in so far as it is problematic*. And, to be sure, it *is* problematic, and in many ways. So the kind of history we need is not the one offering smug self-satisfaction, but in-depth understanding.

Genealogy, as it is now understood inside social theory, is an approach for the study of formative historical events, pioneered by Friedrich Nietzsche and developed further by Michel Foucault. There are also important links between genealogy and the comparative historical sociology developed by Max Weber and his most important followers.

The main source of genealogy is the work of Friedrich Nietzsche, in particular his *Genealogy of Morals* and *Birth of Tragedy*. The central idea is that contingent historical events play a decisive role in the formation of institutions or subjectivity structures which then are taken for granted, even considered as 'natural' or 'rational'.

Nietzschean genealogy implies two claims about studying a concrete phenomenon, be it morality, modernity, or a political system. The first, indicated by the word 'birth', is that the conditions under which a particular entity comes into being matter, and in a lasting manner. Political institutions or social practices coming into being at a certain moment are concrete and specific responses that gather their 'justification' over time. The second is concerned with lasting effects: even once a particular institution ceased to function, its ways of acting and thinking might be carried over for a considerable time.

Still, in contrast to Derridean deconstruction, this does not mean that for Nietzsche genealogy was a purely negative undertaking. The ability to persist had a value for Nietzsche, just as he was interested in the re-birth of what lay dormant (see the Renaissance). This animated his interest in the cultivation of human qualities, visible in his concerns like 'what is noble', and who is a 'good European'.

Genealogy for Nietzsche also had a self-reflexive component: it is an attempt at a self-understanding.

Michel Foucault explicitly returned to Nietzsche's genealogy, using 'birth' in titles or subtitles, and being credited with developing a 'genealogical method'. He defined the middle part of his work as 'genealogy of power', acknowledging the second essay of the *Genealogy* as inspiration behind *Discipline and Punish*. The period is marked, at both ends, by major method-logical statements: the 1971 essay 'Nietzsche, Genealogy, History' (Foucault 1984), a meticulous study of Nietzsche's writings; and a 1978 roundtable discussion focusing on the importance of events for historical understanding (Foucault 1981b). His final statement about genealogy as method is in the Introduction to *The Use of Pleasures*.

Max Weber's comparative historical sociology also followed a genealogical design (Szakolczai 1998). This is visible in *The Protestant Ethic and the Spirit of Capitalism*, which claims that the moving spirit of capitalism is rooted in the inner-worldly turn of medieval monastic asceticism (the third essay of the *Genealogy* was on the 'ascetic ideal'); the first page of the section on religion in *Economy and Society*, focusing on the conditions and effects of social actions; and the importance attributed to 'stamping experiences' in the Introduction to the 'Economic Ethic of World Religions'. Nietzschean inspiration also characterises those who followed the spirit of Weber's work: Norbert Elias, with his sociogenesis and psychogenesis; Eric Voegelin, who argued that the spirit of the modern nation state, characterised as 'intramundane eschatology', grew out of the apocalyptic expectations of medieval sects, and introduced the term 'historiogenesis'; or Reinhart Koselleck and the 'pathogenesis' of modernity.

It is important to clearly mark the distinction between genealogy and critique; all the more so as in his last years Foucault was evidently cajoled into recognising the Frankfurt School as being among his predecessors. The main difference is that while critical theory in its various modalities attempts an absurd, wholesale critique of European civilisation in the name of an ever more radicalised 'post'-modernity and hyper-democratisation, in Political Anthropology the emphasis remains on the problematisation of modernity, without simply falling back to a plain affirmation of pre-modern Europe.

This book argues that a particularly helpful way to wedge this gap between classical genealogy and doing Political Anthropology historically is by taking up the dissent of genealogy against modernism and its linear vision of history as progress, but beyond its standard presentation, by focusing on and taking seriously its source.

The linear vision of history

Concerning the linear vision of history as progress two points are generally known. First, the idea can be traced to the Enlightenment; in fact, this is one of the most important distinguishing feature of Enlightenment thinking. The second point is that, however and paradoxically, the source of the idea is specifically Christian. The ancients had no idea about historical linearity; their vision of history, no doubt following the rhythms of nature, was cyclical. The idea that history follows a linear course was formulated canonically by St Augustine. So the Enlightenment idea of historical progress is a secularisation of the Augustinian theological philosophy of history.[1]

While these two points are certainly valid, they can only serve as the start and not the end of the related investigation, as practically every element in them leads to a set of further, ever more mysterious questions: in what way the Enlightenment vision of progress carries forward, or is entrapped in, the Augustinian philosophy of history? What were the precedents, and sources, of Augustine's vision? In what way these precedents, whether Manichean or Gnostic, Ancient Judaic or Iranian, conditioned Augustine's perception and perspective, and thus, by implication, the Christian and *even* the Enlightenment vision of history?

Such questions present a huge challenge for this book, as they certainly cannot be dealt with, in any depth, within the limits of this chapter, and yet they cannot be ignored either, as in that way the very 'foundations' of the historical 'methods' of political anthropology would remain shaky. Thus, and as a way out with its own method-logical relevance, the question will be followed through a series of guides. Following Eric Voegelin's efforts to re-think the foundations of a philosophy of history, which amounted to a life-long struggle to literally 'exorcise' the linear vision of history from his own mind, and John Pocock's similarly epic struggle to reconstruct the way Gibbon created modern historiography out of his attempts to go beyond the Enlightenment vision of history, discussed in my previous works (Szakolczai 2003, 2015), it will now use as guide Charles Cochrane's magisterial effort at understanding Augustine's theological anthropology and philosophy of history. Cochrane's work is historical and not theological, and was considered by Harald Innis as the ' "the first major Canadian contribution to the intellectual history of the West" ' (Beer 2020), highly appreciated among others by WH Auden.

Cochrane's reconstruction of Augustine

While Augustine's name is duly mentioned in any histories of philosophy or political thought, he is rarely discussed in any length in more recent works, no doubt as being considered as merely a Christian apologist, with no importance outside Christian theology. Yet, there is a major issue here, as one can hardly mention any other thinker in the history of the world who produced a similar real effect – strange as it may seem, the only comparable case is Marx. This is because Augustine did not simply offer an interpretation of the world, or of the Bible, but his work and ideas helped to bring into being medieval Christian civilisation, single-handedly consolidating the work of Constantine – which, by the way, was similarly based upon a genuine conversion experience, as it has been recently confirmed by Paul Veyne.

This leads to the second starting question, and the heart of Cochrane's work: Augustine evidently solved, with his vision about the course of history, a problem posed by the Constantinian shift that until his work remained unanswered, and that rendered the very existence of a Christian civilisation precarious. What was the character of this problem? And what does it mean that the establishment of Christianity as a civilisation, becoming the guiding spirit of the Roman empire, *the* Empire, required an intellectual contribution?

Here parallels are particularly strong with St Paul, and the perplexities concerning Paul's conversion. Paul was the 13th of the 12 apostles, one who was not chosen by Christ during his earthly career, who only replaced Judas, but who evidently, with untiring efforts, made the greatest contribution to the historical organisation of the early Christian communities. One cannot help avoiding the impression that his conversion, the conversion of a Pharisee, represents a kind of re-thinking concerning the entire history mission of Christ: the 12 originally selected apostles were simple people, mostly fishermen, with no specific intellectual qualities – except for John, but he evidently had interpretive rather than organisational intellect; and so, after all, a Pharisee had to join their rank, as otherwise the apostolic mission would have lacked intellectual power. And so the question returns, and with a vengeance: what does it mean that the proper establishment of Christianity so desperately needed a specific *intellectual* force, when after all it was so markedly hostile to any mere intellectual efforts? And this is joined with a meta-question, also of fundamental importance for Political Anthropology as method: what does it mean that the three persons most important for the rise of Christianity as a civilisation, certainly among those who did not know personally Christ, all gained their own mission through a conversion experience? Thus, what *is* a conversion? And how effective is it, after all? And here again, among these three, the figure of Augustine in a way stands out, as Constantine was not a thinker, only a political figure, while Paul, though certainly both a great community organiser and theologian, was emphatically not a philosopher. Augustine, however, was primarily a philosopher, or at least was educated in philosophy, and on this basis, after his conversion, he not simply became a theologian but came up with philosophico-theological formulations that laid the groundwork for an entire civilisation – our civilisation; and, in particular, our question is how this was done *primarily* through his novel vision of history.

Augustine's work departs from and is based upon a heightened awareness about the times in which he was living; a ' "rotting and disintegrating world" ' (Cochrane 2003: 236, 560). In this, as it is emphasised by Voegelin, he shares the fate of all the great political thinkers of mankind, and this is almost bound to be so, as only such extreme conditions would both stimulate and render possible such milestone works. Yet, at the same time, as a kind of cruel joke of history, the same works are also bound to be damaged by such conditions, partly as the confusing times inevitably disturb the solidity of judgment, and partly because the intellectual traditions into which one was born are again inevitably themselves corrupted and damaged, so their education had to be highly defective, and consequently their reading of their own traditions would be influenced by the sad, corrupted character of these very traditions which they cannot help reading back into their very essence. Thus, in the case of Augustine, he not only had to overcome the various Manichean, Gnostic, and Neoplatonic ideas which influenced him during his youth, seeping into the very substance of his mind and exerting an impact on the frame of his thinking even after his conversion, but having been only acquainted with the late and decadent versions of Plato's and Aristotle's ideas, aggravated by the fact of having few if any Greek, he took these readings for the original. This was because the history of philosophy in Antiquity was not simply a fight between the followers of Plato and Aristotle with the Sophists, but that the winners in this struggle, and in several steps, were the Sophists, managing also to insinuate themselves as the 'true' defenders of Plato and Aristotle. To give only one example, Hegel's *History of Philosophy*, source of mainstream academic reading until our very days, is a direct proliferation of such Sophist interpretations, which goes unnoticed because basically anybody anywhere studying philosophy is indoctrinated in his education by this sophistry. And if this is the case now, one can imagine how much this was the case in the time of Augustine.

A further problem was caused by the existence of the Empire, by then Christian. Empires are simply absurd, just as the contemporary global economy is, products of concupiscential expansion and conquest (Voegelin 1974), and are bound to explode, leading to an almost hopeless situation afterword, but at the time of Augustine this was the actual reality, and so in his vision of philosophy he asserted the existence of empire as evidence.

Thus, when following Cochrane, we try to reconstruct the intellectual solution offered by Augustine, which was so powerful that it survived for over a millennia, thus was arguably the ever most powerful work of the human mind, we must start by recognising its inevitable shortcomings – a consequence of the limitations of the human mind, which he emphasised centrally in his own work, so any such 'critical' remark is formulated strictly in his spirit.

Augustine's linear vision of history

The linear view of history certainly derives from Augustine. Cochrane (2003) discusses this extensively. The issue at stake, however, is not to demonstrate this point, as a piece of antiquarian interest, but to investigate the question whether the secularisation of this view makes sense at all. The suspicion is that Voltaire, instead of – so to speak – putting Augustine 'on its foot' performed an operation that rendered the entire idea meaningless, a mere piece of ideology. The reason why Augustine's vision of history has to be now reconstructed is to investigate this suspicion.

But there are two further issues to be explored in this context. The first concerns the sources of Augustine's ideas, and whether already *his* vision was impaired by those sources; or, whether he managed to overcome the problems he identified with such Gnostic-Manichean sources. The second concerns the broader significance of Augustine's views on history. Augustine did not offer, especially did not 'construct', a (theological) philosophy of history. His views on the course of human history were central for his theological-philosophical thinking which became foundational for the Church and thus a history-forming force, an aspect of 'effective history'. The question concerns, first, the basis of the *force* from which this historical vision was derived; at a second level, whether such a vision of history, a *pure* vision of history, could have had such force if it wasn't, at least to a very significant level, true; and on a third and ultimate level, whether its secularisation in the Enlightenment did not *by force* imply a fatal abandonment of this truth component, thus turning it (meaning: the 'pure' linear vision of history as a 'rational' construct) into a mere ideology – in the analogy of Kant's 'pure' reason, that in fact is nothing else than *mere* discursive ratiocination: the construction of verbal sand-castles from the absurd perspective of a 'transcendental mind', supposedly existing in the void, instead of trying to understand our real world by recognising what it is, from our perspective.

Why does history have a linear course, according to Augustine?

We must start by recalling the obvious, Augustine's own historical situation, especially when writing the *City of God*. Augustine was living in a period recognised, especially by himself, as a major civilisational breakdown, confirmed by the Sack of Rome by the Goths in 410. Arguing at that moment about linear historical progress would seem the height of ideological folly – but then, how could this have been so extremely powerful as to become the guiding force of a new civilisation, *ours*?

So, we need to pay very close attention to the details, in taking Cochrane as our guide – all the more so as Cochrane's account was also written, and especially appeared, at a very particular liminal moment of history.

The direct precedent, and source, of Augustine's linear vision of history is the Christian apocalyptic literature, and also the various Gnostic, Manichean, and similar dualist visions of history (266). This immediately opens up an enormous, all but intractable viper's nest type set of problems, which cannot be discussed here, except for mentioning two issues. First, Augustine, as we'll see, definitely went beyond this literature, so his philosophy of history cannot be dismissed as another dualist apocalypse. Second, however, the moment in which one abandons the strict position of Augustine, as it would happen with the Enlightenment-modern idea of linear progress, the possibility of a regression to such Gnostic/ Manichean positions must be revisited, as it is quite likely that those ideas, carried as if latently within Augustinianism, would be reactivated – just as a virus can become alive again inside a body where for a time it lay dormant.

The Augustinian linear vision of history rests on two tightly interwoven pillars – in fact, the nature of their connection will be a most delicate issue to specify. One is the idea of original sin, itself one of the most fundamental ideas of Augustine, but which also 'constitutes one of the supreme problems of Christian thought' (264). Obviously by-passing the theological aspects, what matters here, concerning Augustine's view of the course of history, is that a singular event, or set of events, happened in history by which humans, we all eventually became entrapped into deteriorated living conditions. This idea, in the form of the Golden Age and its loss, is not unique to Christianity, but considered everywhere a myth and not an historical event, which poses another intractable question, the extent to which people believed in their myths (Veyne 1983). Through and in Augustine's view of history this became a *historical* event by another historical event, the incarnation of

Christ as Redeemer from the original sin. The two events are strictly connected and do not make sense one without the other: we wouldn't know about the Fall as an historical event without the coming of the Redeemer; and the coming of a Redeemer would not make sense without the Fall from which mankind needs be redeemed. But these two events would not make sense without now *assuming* a third, the Second Coming of Christ. The linear vision of history is based on the historicity of these events, and in the following way: the First Coming of Christ, as a decisive step towards Redemption, necessarily projects towards the past the Fall, and into the future the Second Coming, to complete the work of Redemption. It is in this sense that our age, or *saeculum*, necessarily implies linearity.

However, here we must add the second pillar, already implied in the first, and which is the working of the Holy Spirit inside history. The linearity of the Augustinian vision is not just a mere fact, the mechanical drawing of a line between two events, but assumes, on strict scriptural basis, that in between these two events, the First and Second Coming, mankind receives direct guidance from the Spirit, transforming the time elapsing between them from a merely passive waiting into an active, joint work. The term 'joint' is to be intended in a complex sense, as it means both that the historical events are not simply produced by the random collision of various forces but are guided by the Spirit; but also that the main actors of that history, human beings, are also guided by the Spirit from the inside, from the heart of their personality – in so far as they 'listen' to this guidance. Linear progress, in *this* sense, would imply an increasing reliance on the inside, on the guidance of the spirit – though this certainly cannot, and should not, be taken for granted in a mechanical way.

The vision of history as a process of linear progress in Augustine is therefore a very specific idea. It does not say anything about the course of history before the Fall, or even between the Fall and the coming of Christ;[2] and works under specific assumptions even in the *saeculum*. To claim that all history inherently and objectively progresses by the mechanics of its 'immanent' forces is radically different from the Augustinian idea; in fact, it is not simply its untenable misinterpretation, but a dangerous abuse – an extremely dangerous one, as it can be used to justify basically *anything* that happens, any simple and mechanical extension of power, knowledge, or wealth, as sign and proof of this progress. One cannot stop even here, and must draw the conclusion that a purely secular idea of linear progress, the idea that we all as mankind must follow the road of progress by further promoting such growth of power, knowledge and wealth is simply the *worst* possible idea that can be imagined, as it not only implies an entrapment in certain machinations, but involves the *acceptance* of such entrapment as an inevitability. So the Enlightenment vision of progress, far from being a liberation from the ideas of Augustine, setting us up on the road of genuine liberty, is actually the worst possible historical entrapment.

If this is so, then Augustine's philosophy of history confirms one of the most banal yet fundamental truths of human life: the most important and valuable things in life are also the most dangerous.

So, we need to investigate his ideas, as related to history in more detail. This is all the more necessary as Augustine's views on history are intimately tied to his anthropology of the personality, which is furthermore closely tied to his Trinitarian theology, about the three divine persons, itself the foundation of his views on history.

Augustine's vision of history, and his mature thinking, is based on a singular recognition, inspired by his concrete conversion experience: recognising the fundamental significance of the historical Christ. That in itself, one might still say, is just a personal matter, expanded into a theology; but through Augustine's way of proceeding it became much more. The statement above implies two positions that are not personal or theological, necessarily implying a limited sense, but are epistemological, thus having the widest possible validity and generality: that knowledge and understanding is fundamentally an issue of *recognition* and not cognition; and so real understanding, as wisdom, is not based on the quantitative accumulation of pieces of information but on the recognition of their significance; and furthermore, that meaningful knowledge is *historical* and not natural – or that, in fact, even the knowledge offered by nature is an historical knowledge.

Concerning the first, anthropological – and narrowly epistemological – point, it implies that the gaining of knowledge has a necessarily personal component, in so far as acts of recognition are concrete and unique, and both the acquisition *and* the further promotion of understanding only proceed through such singular acts, and not by the mechanical accumulation of pieces of information. The latter, to be sure, is a basic precondition, but only gains meaning through the former. Personal and concrete components are not idiosyncrasies, but necessary and fundamental aspects of understanding. The second, historical point is connected more to the substantive aspect of knowledge (though the two points, again, are inseparable): any knowledge about anything that actually exists has a fundamentally historical character. Thus, concerning understanding human existence, any house, any book, any language is not the outcome of an interaction between elementary particles in a void, but the outcome of long and concrete historical processes, whose origin is necessarily lost in the mist of time. The same applies to any 'natural' object, whether animal or plant, mountain or river, but even stone or mineral, that again is the outcome of history, except that there 'history' goes by the name of natural history, evolution, or geology. A presumed necessity of returning them, or 'breaking them down' to their elementary particles is partly meaningless – what does it mean to list the elementary molecules of which a dog is composed?; and partly implies a perspective of utilitarianism or even more sinister perspectives of exploitation, manipulation, and control.

This epistemological perspective is of extreme importance, as it immediately reveals the radical shortcomings and problematic character of post-Newtonian science, in that the untenable and dangerous character of a non-historical, universalistic starting point becomes evident. Newton's ideas about quantities and fluxions in the void might be true – though, and *not* funnily, recent advances in the 'sciences' call even that into question – but certainly have a very limited validity for *our* world, where what really matters is a concrete, historically based understanding, and where our current plight (climate, environment, you name it) is produced by unwise and unnatural universalisms. If we start from valorising our concrete world, then the epistemological untenability of controlled experiments, the heart of the 'scientific world view' becomes evident – as any such experiment necessarily intrudes and destroys, and so any 'benefit' to be gained from it becomes deeply suspicious and problematic. Augustine's starting point, against even classical atomism and naturalism, is thus rock-solid and genuinely realistic. Newton's is not realistic: it is utopian, transformationist and activist, in line with his basic background position, which was anti-Trinitarian and alchemist.

Here we come to a third point, a theological corollary, drawn by Augustine: the source of his recognitive and historical epistemology was his conversion experience, or was due to an external – evidently, divine – intervention. *He* could not ignore this, as this was a fact of his life, and a definite fact – and we can again only ignore it to our peril, as this is what made Augustine what he became – and, subsequently, we became what we are, in this particular civilisation, much due to the work of Augustine's mind, and so we must understand his ideas properly.

For this, we need to tie more tightly together the historical and theological aspects, as the 'divine' evidently is brought into 'knowledge' by way of historical concreteness.

The historicity of the divine, or the primacy of experiences, events, records

The trouble with presocratic philosophy, from an Augustinian perspective, was its obsession with reducing everything to elements and first causes – a feature no doubt due to the alchemic inspiration of *physiologia*. This was overcome by a focus on the history of every natural object and being, but a focus on history implies more, a similar – and even more – importance attributed to human events and experiences, posing the question of historical records.

Such records about the enormous history of mankind – as even then it was evident that such history goes back to many thousand years, an enormous time for human measure – were scarce. What mattered primarily, not just for Augustine but for the entire perspective he established, is the manner he came to the realisation of the significance of concrete history: first, an absolute certainty in his own experiences, in particular the event of his conversion;[3] and then, in part as an implication, the certainty of the historical existence of Christ *as* the incarnated word. This implied an extremely tight, inseparable connection between an anthropological theory of (conscious) personality (of which the various modern philosophies of consciousness are weak, bastardised and secularised, as exclusively cognitive copies); a philosophy of history, or a history that requires a primarily philosophical interpretation and a philosophy that is fundamentally historically based (of which Hegel's philosophy of history and history of philosophy are dim, bastardised and secularised copies); and a theology of the Trinity, a kind of theology integrating the divine and the human in a way that has no parallels in world history, and which is based on the Scriptures, especially the New Testament, which is not a set of laws or normative regulations, but is considered, and can only be considered, except for reclassifying one's own deepest experiences as the ravings of a madmen, as document, and in part interpretation, of historical events produced by an unprecedented encounter between the otherwise externally incommensurable human and the divine spheres.

It is again necessary to go into detail step by step, knowing that none of the three fields can be discussed within mentioning the other.

Personality

Augustine is widely considered as having discovered the depths of the human personality, and while this might be an exaggeration, his reliance on Plato makes his ideas philosophically sound. His ideas were only attacked, at their core, by Freud, and thus between Augustine and Freud a Kierkegaardian either/or imposes itself: taking Augustine seriously necessarily implies ignoring Freud, which is the position this book will follow, except for claiming that this choice is not a free decision, but a necessity: opting for Freud against Augustine is an act of mad ignorance not just of our culture and traditions, but the heart of our own selves.

Augustine's anthropology of the personality is fundamental and even foundational, and yet it only follows, and is based upon, his 'linear' philosophy of history and Trinitarian theology. It also has a philosophical centre, as it was part of an attempt, in the footsteps of the similar efforts by Athanasius, the Cappadocian trinitarians and Ambrose, of 'a synthesis of human experience for which there had been no parallel since the time of Plato' (Cochrane 2003: 398). The success, however, source of his 'extraordinary influence', was his own, as 'far from neutralising Christianity with Platonism, Augustine appropriated such elements of this and other existing philosophies as suited his purpose, in order to build them into the system which bears his name' (417). The centre of this was that he managed to offer, 'in the spirit of Plato but from a fresh standpoint [...] a synthesis of experience' (424).

To start with, we exist, concretely, as distinct, individual, unique persons, and to doubt this, our own existence, is a meaningless and dangerous, destructive intellectual pastime. We don't just exist, but *know* about our own existence, which is almost the same thing; at least the two things, our existence and our knowledge about it are inescapable, but this is not a cognitive kind of knowledge, but a *recognition*. Our knowledge about our existence does not construct anything – we only *recognise* the *fact* (or rather *givenness*) that we *exist*.

Every word in the sentence has its special importance, illuminating the others. Knowledge, the work of our consciousness is primarily an act of recognition: we become aware about something that we in a way knew before, but through such awareness our existence reaches, or ascends to, a different level. Such recognition, as the connotations of the French term *reconnaissance* indicate, and in contrast to mere 'knowledge' or 'cognition', imply gratitude: this is because such recognition implies the realisation that whatever we have, include our existence, is primarily a *gift*, or part of a *charis* logic. This leads to the second main term, givenness, where due to our in-depth existential corruption by Cartesianism we are bound to say 'fact' to what simply exists, and wrongly, as a fact is what is made (*factum*), but what simply exists is a given (*datum*) – though that word is also used badly, thus abused, in our sadly taken-for-granted Cartesianism. Which then leads to existence, not as the end-result of a rather absurd speculative train of thought, but as the realisation of something that was primary, as our train of thinking is not constitutive of existence – as that would be, again wrongly, codified by Kantianism – rather recognises, eventually, what was already there. Which leads us back to the start in this circle of recognition, giftedness, gratitude, and reality, in contrast to constructed existence. Or, going alongside the same circle in different words, self-consciousness, or the knowledge of oneself, is what distinguishes man 'from other beings whether animate or inanimate', but only to the extent in which it is recognised as a gift; and furthermore 'it was by virtue of this gift of self-consciousness that man was enabled to recognize his powers and limitations' (263). Thus, knowledge as self-consciousness is not foundational, but on the contrary, leads to the recognition of the gift-like character of our world and our very existence, and so implies not our own Promethean, hubristic autonomy, rather that we are, 'as a creature in nature', and so just like those other creatures, 'completely dependent upon "the will of God" ' (263). Thus, the uniqueness of our self-consciousness does not assign us complete independence, rather singles us out for *recognising* our dependence, and thus feel a kind of gratitude and love that otherwise would be impossible. So, '[p]aradoxical as this may sound, it nevertheless underlay the whole of Christian teaching with regard to the constitution and history of mankind' (263).

Yet, this same recognition of dependence on gifts, on giftedness and grace at the same time did not imply complete dependence, as extremes of Puritanism would have it, misreading Augustine, rather also implied, as another unique specificity of man, a degree of deliberate choice. This idea was already central for Athanasius, and the term used (*proairesis*) tightly connects Christian theology back to classical philosophy, here the ideas of Aristotle. Furthermore, and as it has only been elaborated by Augustine, such free will is central for the idea of the Fall, as man could only commit the original sin, this turning point of world history, through a free act.

The centrality of the idea, and the connection it establishes between the New and the Old Testaments, can be best seen through the semantic links established through the crucial Hungarian root *vál*, interpreted through Calasso's recent book on the Old Testament (see Szakolczai 2021).

The Hungarian root establishes intimate connections between a series of central terms for social understanding, like choice, election, selection, excellence, separation, crisis, divorce, secretion, and becoming. The central meaning of the root, still used in ordinary Hungarian, is 'becoming': it captures the process of development by which something, from its origins, turns into a full, mature being: a child becomes an adult, a seed becomes a plant, and so on. Note that such development follows a strictly linear path: a lion cub becomes a lion and not a lioness or a mouse; an acorn produces an oak tree and not a poplar, and so on. However, the outcome does not follow an iron logic of necessity: every development, while continuous and cumulative, has its own liminal moments, or points of crisis (*válság*), where the concrete being, whether human, animal or plant, must show its qualities or excellence (*kiválóság*) – otherwise would not become what it could have been, but would die, or suffer other kind of decays and lapses. The process of becoming thus turns to a kind of historical interaction between the being and its environment, as a result of which the entity – *every* entity that exists, in so far as it really exists, as it brings out its own essence, as it was promised at the moment when its original 'seed' came into being – comes to exist as a *concrete* and *historical* being, and not just an automatism that mechanically runs its programme to the end – and neither as an entity that 'freely chose' its mode of existence, the two extreme visions of modernity, schismogenic doubles of the same civilisational madness and paralysis.

A *concrete* being, however, as its etymology shows, is not an isolated unit, but can comprehend several entities that 'grew together' (*con-crescere*), after an act of selection or choice (*választás*), in another but different kind of existential liminal moment, and so became 'one', whether as a married couple or a community – until their existence undergoes another liminal crisis, analogous to the one any single organism can undergo on its own, for e.g. as an illness, and which can lead to a painful separation (*elválás*) or an even more painful divorce (*válás*). Thus, any process of becoming, any road by which an entity, whether an organism, an object, or a collective unit comes to existence, implies a series of actions and reactions of which conscious choice is a specific feature of humans, connected to self-consciousness and recognition-gratitude, as it was discussed before, but only a part of this extremely complex existential process, and so cannot be trivialised. A choice (*választás*) is not a trivial matter, because the results of a choice become reality (*valósággá válik*), *we* become what we now are as a result, and a piece of reality cannot be unmade, or separated (*szétválaszt*) into its elements without destroying it. So freedom or free choice, in the sense of Jean-Paul Sartre or Milton Friedman, is pure non-sense. Free choice, just as self-consciousness, is a phenomenon of liminality, when things become liquid or pliable, in a liminal void situation, but whatever choice or decision we make then becomes binding: the liminal moment passes, history becomes effective, and things, beings, and relations follow their trajectory until the next liminal moment. Thus, the dynamics of free choice and necessity can only be understood through liminality – the incorporation of a Political Anthropological framework is necessary even for properly understanding Augustine.

Such ideas on becoming also illuminate Augustine's vision of experience.

Augustine on experience

Augustine's ideas about experience is at the very heart of his thinking, and also where he managed to forge a unity between Christianity and Platonism, the very source of his ' "greatness" ' and 'extraordinary influence' (Cochrane 2003: 417). Based on his own conversion experience he came to be 'in a position to resume, in the spirit of Plato but from a fresh standpoint and with fresh resources, the long-neglected attempt at a synthesis of experience' (424); thus, from the complementary perspective of Foucault, to overcome the breach of this experience inserted into Christian thinking by Tertullian (see the section on Foucault in this chapter). Central for this new vision of experience, as it is exposed in the *Confessions*, is 'a discovery of fundamental importance, viz. that experience is both continuous and cumulative' (428). It means that 'from the most primitive indications of consciousness to its highest and fullest manifestations, it involves a progressive unfolding [...] without *saltus* or break' (428–9). While this might seem to contradict his own conversion experience, this is not so, as such conversion did not imply a radical rejection of one's former self, a presumably completely new personality, rather a reorganisation of one's consciousness based on a *recognition* that was due to the presence and action of a different, superior, and benign power. This experience is radically different from the kind of extraordinary, heroic struggle for excellence that has become a central virtue of philosophical life, based on the influence of Eastern spirituality, a kind of ascetic heroism, different also from the type of heroism exalted by Nietzsche. It is such continuous and cumulative experiences that form one's personality, including the more sudden, illuminative acts of recognitive consciousness, which however only amplifies or deepens, does not radically alter the person. The Augustinian understanding of personality has two fundamental, at once radically new but also classical, even archaic aspects: its ideal, instead of the ascetic hero, is 'naïve simplicity; they betray not the most remote suggestion of pretension or priggishness' (427). This ideal will shine through on some of the most striking and lively heroines of Shakespeare and Dickens, from Cordelia in *King Lear* to Agnes of *David Copperfield*.[4] The second, closely connected feature of the Augustinian vision of personality is that 'with Augustine each individual human being is envisaged as a center of radiant energy' (429). This ideal most closely recalls the Graces, especially Aglaia, the radiant one, the irresistible though also vulnerable power of graceful beauty, and thus closely complements the point made in the previous section about the crucial feminine component at the very heart of Augustinian Platonic Christianity – the 'eternal feminine' of Goethe that lures to perfection, evoking the Virgin at the ending of *Faust Two* that already Goethe did not dare to publish in his lifetime.

The corollary of such simplicity and radiance, combined with the power of recognitive and grateful self-consciousness, instead of hubristic arrogance and exclusive belief in one's own powers, is a new 'ideal of wisdom [...] the wisdom of Christian insight' (558). It is based on a unity of reason and emotion, instead of a pure reason separated from feelings and thus 'operating *in vacuo*', in its classical as in its Kantian versions (559), to which we can add Habermas's 'public sphere'. The ideal to separate reason and emotion is 'humanly speaking impossible and absurd', as 'there can be no knowledge without feeling and no feeling without knowledge' (559). Such unity of reason and emotion, furthermore and again, has a radiating force, combining a substantial as opposed to formal truth and morality: '[a]s truth it may be described as reason irradiated by love; as morality, love irradiated by reason' (558). Such unified experience offers both a 'divine truth' and 'the law of love', and it alone can offer a way out of ' "a rotting and disintegrating world" ' (559–60).

Such unity of experience is the foundation of a unified and not broken, schizoid personality; a personality which furthermore is triune – an almost self-evident extension of the previous overcoming of the reason-emotion dualism. Here Augustine, having refuted *ante letteram* Kant, does the same with Descartes. Starting from doubting, scientific objectivity as a foundation, and 'teaching nothing except what was clear and evident to reason' are illusions: reason simply cannot be accepted as a starting point, as Augustine challenges 'that reason itself present the credentials by virtue of which it presumes to operate' (445). So the proper question, instead of pulling reason up by itself, like a rational Samson, or attempting to doubt ourselves out of existence, is the following: 'What must I accept as the fundamental elements of consciousness, the recognition of which is imposed upon me as an inescapable necessity of my existence as a rational animal'?

The answer is offered by the triune character of personality, involving in an indissoluble unity existence, knowledge, and will: the Trinity is, knows, and wills (445–6, 453–4). Cochrane offers here long quotes from the three most important works of Augustine, the *Confessions*, the *City of God*, and the *Trinity*. Thus, Augustine argues in the *Confessions* (xiii.xi.12) that

> I am and know and will; I am knowing and willing; I know myself to be and to will, I will to be and to know. In these three, then, let him discern who can how inseparable a life there is, one life, one mind, and one essence; how inseparable a distinction and yet a distinction.
>
> *(445–6)*

The same argument is presented in the *City of God* (xi.26): ' "We both exist, and know that we exist, and rejoice in this existence and this knowledge […] It is beyond question that I exist, and that I know and love that existence" ' (Cochrane 2003: 446). Another passage in the *City of God* (viii.5) anticipates verbatim Descartes, but yield a better result:

> 'But who is there to doubt that he is alive, remembers, understands, wishes, thinks, knows, and judges? Since even if he has such doubt, he lives; if he doubts, he thinks. Whatever doubts he has, therefore, regarding other things, he ought not to have doubts regarding all these; for if he did not exist, he could not have doubt regarding anything'.
>
> *(Cochrane 2003: 448).*

But a perhaps conclusive formulation, and not surprisingly, as bringing out best the triune character of the personality, can be found in the *Trinity* (ix.5.8):

> 'In these three, when the mind knows and loves itself, there may be seen a trinity, mind, love, knowledge; nor to be confounded by any intermixture, although each exists in itself, and mutually in all, or each in the other two, or the other two in each'.
>
> *(446)*

Such knowledge is certain, ' "as the truth of which I am speaking is not perceived through the eye of the flesh. It is by virtue of an inner knowledge that we know we are alive" ' (xv.12.21.; Cochrane 2003: 447). Thus, the personality or the self is a substance and cannot be reduced to mere relations:

> 'These three, therefore, memory (i.e. the sense of being or personal identity), intelligence and will, since they are not three lives but one life, nor three minds but one mind, must accordingly constitute not three substances but one substance. [...] these three are one, embracing one life, one mind and one essence'
>
> *(Cochrane 2003: 449)*

This vision of personality is illuminated by the Trinitarian theology, which it itself illuminates, just as Trinitarianism offers a vision of history, and is illuminated by this historical vision.

Which leads us to the Trinity, facing a discussion that cannot be avoided.

Augustine on the Trinity

Everybody today knows, or thinks to know, what the Trinity is, but considered as a mere piece of Christian theology it is then safely dismissed as irrelevant for social and political understanding. That point, however, won't do, as, first, the Trinity is a very specific idea that does not exist in any other culture or historical tradition, and thus requires some attention in a work dealing with historical and anthropological methods of understanding; and second, it has been an extraordinary history-forming factor, as it has been argued in great detail and convincing power by John Pocock, in his magisterial series devoted to Edward Gibbon, who simply *was* the founder of modern historiography. Pocock demonstrates that Gibbon started with a standard Enlightenment narrative, having no intention to be occupied centrally with Trinitarian controversies, and originally had only dismissive ideas about Byzantium. Yet, it was the force of the material, and of the dynamics of historical change he wanted to reconstruct that imposed on him, step by step, the preoccupations with the Trinity, and eventually the realisation of its history-forming force.

So – what is the Trinity?

First of all, we must use a central, perhaps *the* central, methodological principle of Political Anthropology, taken jointly from philosophical hermeneutics, Nietzschean genealogy, and 'liminality theory', and start from the middle; the middle figure of the Trinity, Christ as a historical figure. So, who was Christ *as* a historical figure? Prophets exist in many traditions, visions of deities are common, there are even gods who take up a body and mingle among men, but the idea that not just a god but the only living God has a son which *becomes* a man is unique. The method-logical significance of this idea is truly Earth-shattering, as it places an unprecedented value on concrete history as it happened. In all other traditions of mankind history as a sequence of events happening has limited importance – restricted to those with whom something is happening sometimes somewhere. There is no 'History', as the gods, deities, spirits, and demons are immortal, exist eternally, so for them history does not matter, their activities are accounted by myths. A myth does not have the character of a history; the question whether it is true cannot even be posed, it does not even have a sense. History, similarly, does not matter for nature, as nature follows its eternal cycles, irrespective of human events, while its geological cycles are incommensurable to human existence.

The Trinity, however, is different, as with it religion becomes fundamentally an epistemological matter, in terms of the historicity of truth. Christianity is not based on a set of rules, laws or customs that the gods revealed or bequeathed in some ways, and that must be maintained, but on recognising and transmitting the truthful memory of certain historical events. What matters is not the solemn words of a deity, no matter how faithfully transmitted by the special, selected hearers, but the words that were pronounced, and the deeds that were done, by a concrete human being who also claimed himself, and was personally recognised by many, as the Son of God. Christianity was not a moral revolution, even Nietzsche is wrong, but was first of all an *epistemological* revolution; but this epistemological revolution was not concerned with the revelation or possession of some secret, new, powerful knowledge, but a historical truth, the concrete materialisation of a super-real existence, the embodiment of God. What mattered was to believe in the concrete reality of some historical events; or, from the other side, the perspective of those who witnessed such events, the questions were how to transmit an historical truth; how to convince others about the truth of these experiences and memories.

Authenticating historical truth

Authenticating or validating the truth of historical events poses three different epistemological problems. The first concerns the truth content of accounts by witnesses, which in the case of liminal conditions and religious experiences presents almost intractable problems, with Roman and especially Greek law offering an historical background. Historiography of course has its own methods and techniques, but here we enter a circle, as much of these techniques are applicable and developed for European history, taking for granted ways of registering historical events that developed as a consequence of the Christian interest in history. What we call today methods of science have limited relevance for any historical question, as historical events, any event in human life cannot be submitted to controlled experiment, just like most natural processes, and judging an event from the material objects that were left by it is as meaningful as trying to assess the meaning of a wedding from the amount and character of garbage disposal it produced. It tells *something*, depending on what one is interested about; but not that much.

So we have to fall back on the problem of truth-telling, the manifold problems posed by the question of how we can tell whether someone is telling the truth; how anybody at all *can* tell the truth – what it implies in terms of memory, capacity of speech and judgment, and so on; how can somebody convince others that one is telling the truth – a question quite different from rhetorical victory in a debate, or convincing others of an idea or a theory. The problem of truth-telling was rarely formulated in this way by modern philosophers, certainly not by those rationalists who tried to imitate the 'natural' sciences, as there this entire issue does not even come up. It is posed in this way by Nietzsche in the Fifth Book of his *Gay Science*, and this became the source of inspiration for Foucault's interest in parrhesia, or the practice of courageous truth-telling in his last lecture courses at the Collège de France. These are of exceptional importance, and not only because they end up being the last research work of Foucault, but also because they represent the culmination of his life-long interest concerning the connection between the 'subject' or the human being and truth; and because they are closely connected to his attempt at tracing the emergence of the modern form of subjectivity, also central for Max Weber and Norbert Elias, among others, and its links to Christianity.

So the problem is the following: what does it mean to tell the truth? How can somebody be certain that one is telling the truth – including oneself? What is at stake in telling the truth? How can somebody convince somebody else that one is telling the truth concerning an event that is strikingly out of the ordinary? Put it in an even more challenging way, under what condition does truth require a neutral validation, and what kind of truth, or even judgment, may or even must require a deep familiarity with the person, to accept it? Truth is an extremely delicate question; it is at the same time beyond language – truth is about what is, what happened really, and not just about a verbal statement; and is *just* language, nothing else but language, as truth is a linguistic statement about what is an aspect of existence or an event – or, at least, it must be a sign given to an explicit verbal uttering. Truth is both what is *not* just language, and yet that can only be assessed by linguistic means. The 'scientific' perspective about true knowledge hardly scratches the surface of the problem truth represents for human existence – and a puzzle that must be continuously posed, even if this is not a problem to be solved, following again Wittgenstein and not Popper.

The second epistemological problem concerns the status of truth beyond the level of living eyewitnesses; or when the liminality and liquidity of the events passed, and all that can be known about them is contained in fixed, written accounts. In the case of Christianity, this concerns the Scriptures: what written documents can be accepted as true, and what not; and, especially, what exactly is the truth that is contained in these documents, beyond the concrete factual truths they describe: what is the truth they reveal? It is here that we move, from the middle of the Trinity, so to speak, from the historical existence of Christ *as* the Son of God to the Father, the *arkhé*, the creator and the first person of the Trinity – 'formerly' considered as 'simply' God; and then, as another interpretive effort, and strictly based on the reading and interpretation of the Scriptures, as there remained no other way, adding the third person of the Trinity, the Holy Spirit; as an effort to interpret the course of history, starting from the middle, the historical figure of Christ, but extending it back, to the origins of times, or at least as far as possible, and through the promised and – at least for some – evident working of the Holy

Spirit, into the present, and *due to this* offering now a linear reading of history as genuine progress.

This is because the Holy Spirit can be ignored, but this does not make it non-existent. Regeneration is always possible – and this idea is at the heart of a Political Anthropological reading of history – but only through 'the gift of divine grace'; such gifts arrive through the heart: '[a]ll that is beautiful – virtue and wisdom – has its residence in the heart'; so 'values' ultimately come not from experience, but are gifts (498, 500–1). In this sense '*bona voluntas*, a "good will" is [...] the greatest gift of God to man'. This is the heart of Augustine's 'doctrine of grace', which is also a psychology, disclosing the guiding principle of human life: 'the greater love is ultimately irresistible' (501). The ultimate meaning of 'justification by faith', or Trinitarian Christianity, is thus not institutional or dogmatic, but 'serves to overcome weakness and to provide a release of creative energy (*l'élan vers le bien*) by the disclosure of a goal which is at once intelligible and, in the highest degree, worth while' (502). This goal is the integration of the personality, which incorporates the classical ideals of freedom, detachment, and peace, 'by revealing a vision of personality which is not truncated at any point and in which self-consciousness has at last ceased to be the blight of life' (502, last sentence of Chapter 11, leading to the first sentence of Chapter 12, which continues to move along the same, comprehensive and not empty circle, between Trinity, personality and history, by stating that '[t]he discovery of personality was, at the same time, the discovery of history' (503).).

The third epistemological problem is the question to which Foucault's parrhesia leads the way, but it could hardly pose, and not discuss properly, and which is whether and how truth can authenticate itself; or, under what conditions can somebody authenticate his own truth. This question was posed, and answered, in the last, magisterial work of Michel Henry, which at the same time revisits central issues of the early chapters of this Part Three, the Word and the Image.

After Augustine

We can now return, after this necessary and extended digression on the real sense of Augustine's linear vision of history, to the question of the meaning and the relevance of its secularisation. Concerning the first part of the question, the answer is simple: such an idea has no sense whatsoever. Augustine's work was based on a very specific and concrete recognition, certainly not originated by him, but given a new intellectual foundation: the unique significance of the concrete events that took place in Palestine, in the times of Augustus and Tiberius: the reported incarnation of the Son of God. Outside this recognition as a *concrete* event Augustine's historical-theoretical constructs have no sense; so secularising Augustine is meaningless. Even worse, such secularisation only regressed to the historiogenetic constructions, characteristic of Near Eastern empires (Voegelin 1974).

The significance of this nonsensical idea, however, was tremendous, as the modern world, and in particular its self-understanding as the embodiment of progress, was based on it, and so this modern world, *in a way*, is a thoroughly illegitimate deviation of European civilisation. I say 'in a way' because not just the secular idea of progress, but the entire institutional framework and practices of modernity are still closely based upon not just Augustine's work, but the sacred *and* civilisational history which developed around it. This is one of the reasons for the inevitable ambivalence of the work of genealogists, as while their main aim is to show the contingent and problematic character of those modern developments that are attuned to the secularised idea of progress, they do not really want to question and dismantle, wholesale, the entire civilisation that has grown around it. The central idea driving them is to diagnose the illnesses of modernity, by liberating us from the mistaken belief that all this is inevitable, part of the price we all must pay for 'progress'. But if progress does not exist, such prices are meaningless; mere parts of the 'pyramids of sacrifice' (Berger 1976) that litter the path of modernity and modernisation.

In the standard modernist perspective, Augustine's historical work was superseded by the Enlightenment idea of progress, then radicalised by Marx's vision of history; his ideas on the person cancelled by Freud, and the general 'disappearance of interiority' (Lyons 1986); while any reflection on the Trinity is assumed to be a merely theological concern. Yet, two of the most important French philosophers of the post-WWII period, Michel Foucault, and Michel Henry (the third being Michel Serres), beyond problematising the modern idea of progress, reached the central issues raised by the Augustinian perspective in their very last sustained words: Foucault in his last Collège de France course, delivered between 1 February and 28 March 1984 (he died 25 June 1984); and Henry in his last book, published in July 2002 (he died 3 July 2002).

Michel Foucault: truth-telling and its authentication by life

> now he heard the voice of his accomplice stating to his face, with every circumstance of time and place and incident; and openly proclaiming, with no reserve, suppression, passion, or concealment; all the truth. The truth, which nothing would keep down; which blood would not smother, and earth would not hide; the truth, whose terrible inspiration seemed to change dotards into strong men
>
> *Charles Dickens,* Martin Chuzzlewit*, 751*

The work of Michel Foucault has a special relevance for the concerns of this chapter, as it problematises, since the start, scientific epistemology, with a focus on history. His famous expression power/ knowledge captures the long-standing complicity between modern science and state power. His approach, as he eventually recognised, had manifold parallels with those of Weber, also in that their focus was never merely on the state and its institutions, or one various fields of knowledge, rather on their impact on the human subject. It is in the third and last part of Foucault's work that such focus on the subject has become explicit; yet, with a difference. Such shift is visible in his terminology: while around 1980 he frequently characterises his then current work as being concerned with the genealogy of the subject (in the West), in the later and decisive self-characterisations he came to describe the central problem of his work as being concerned with the relations between the subject and truth. Such links could not be reduced to genealogy; the specifically genealogical angle was rather concerned with a problematisation of the modern secularisation and governmentalisation of those relations.

Foucault's work was interrupted by his untimely death, and it is meaningless to speculate what could have become its eventual outcome. Yet, one can risk the statement that even in this last period the work could not escape the limitation of the road by which he arrived there. This implied a certain apprehension to touch anything that might involve the charge of dealing with 'metaphysics'; thus, the use of terms like the 'soul', the 'heart', or even the 'person' – significantly, the term 'person' does not even appear in the comprehensive and excellent index to *Dits et écrits*. Also, the project which led Foucault to this concern was a history of sexuality, or a genealogy of the techniques of power/ knowledge that led to the construction of sexuality, and while most of his Collège de France courses in the 1980s did not deal with sexuality, he was in a way tied in his written, especially book publications to stay with the broad theme and – for various reasons – could not fully overcome the shadow-casting umbrella of the history of sexuality project. This can be seen particularly clearly in his extremely limited treatment of Augustine, never going beyond the genealogical perspective – excepting the recently published volume 4.

The most important aspect of his last period of research was the question of truth-telling, or parrhesia, to which he was led by his discovery of the centrality of the care of the self in classical philosophy, thus radically altering the merely genealogical perspective of his project. He was helped here by a series of important encounters, especially in California, by Paul Rabinow (an anthropologist who would write a major study about the rise of biotechnology) and Hubert Dreyfus (a philosopher and foremost Heidegger scholar in the US), who would produce one of the first and – due to the active collaboration of Foucault – in a way unsurpassable book on Foucault, but also by Peter Brown (one of the most important historians of late Antiquity who also wrote a classic biography of St Augustine). Among others, these encounters helped him to revisit his most important reading experiences, Heidegger's essays of language and Nietzsche, having a particularly strong impact on his interest in truth-telling, through the classical concern with parrhesia, to which he was directed by Peter Brown.

The subject and truth

In the 1980s, the last years of his life, Foucault repeatedly characterised his work as being always concerned with the relations between the subject and truth, confirmed in the closing parts of his last Collège de France lecture, which he did not have time to pronounce (Foucault 2011: 338–9). Or, as it was formulated in the first lecture of the 1981 Collège de France course, 'what experience may the subject have of himself when faced with the possibility or obligation of acknowledging something that passes for true regarding himself?' (Foucault 2017: 10). In other words, 'What relationship does the subject have to himself when this relationship can or must pass through the promised or imposed discovery of the truth about himself?' (10–1). This preoccupation is at once a historical question and a question of fact. The existence of such a discourse about the truth of the self is a historical fact; but it is also a question of effective history, or genealogy, as the existence of such a discourse has an impact on the formation of the self. Foucault's historico-philosophical question is concerned with the effects this true discourse about the self has on the way personal identity came to be conceived of in European civilisation.

Such statements could be considered as mere self-justifications, or the retro-jecting of his later interests to the earlier work. However, on the one hand, these were part of a sustained effort by Foucault to put behind his crisis years (1976–79), restoring the proper focus of his work; and on the other, they correspond quite well with the actual trajectory of his work. Thus, his very first published work, the 'Introduction' to Ludwig Binswanger's *Dream and Existence*, states that his interest was concerned with the background assumption for any concrete knowledge in the human sciences in the being of men, thus having a genuine anthropological orientation, in the broadest sense of the term, a concern also evident in his minor thesis on Kant's lectures on philosophical anthropology; and at the same time also identifies his concern in the formative character of experiences, which would return in the series of formulations, offered in the 1980s, about such experiences forming the subject, instead of the subject, transcendental or not, being the condition of possibility of experiences.

It is inside this broadly conceived philosophical-anthropological framework that Foucault's investigation about truth, knowledge, and true discourse can be fitted. Starting in a way in the middle, the question concerned the nature and significance of the idea of having a 'true discourse' about human beings. To be sure, doctors, teachers, and many others needed to know something about us humans in order to help us; but Foucault always felt, and quite rightly, that there is something problematic about such 'will to knowledge'; and so he posed the following question: what is the kind of power that can be, and actually *is*, exerted over us, in the name of 'helping' us, through a presumably true knowledge of our real nature?

In the second part of his work, corresponding almost perfectly with the 1970s, Foucault thought to have found the definite answer to this preoccupation, through developing the term power/ knowledge, and by connecting such will to knowledge to the emergence of the disciplinary networks of the modern state, eventually leading to the idea of biopolitics. It is out of this framework that he came up with the project of a history of sexuality, that was supposed to play a major role in the rise of the modern biopolitics, planned for six volumes, and which originally had, as a historical background chapter, a study of the emergence of Christian confessional. However, when starting to finalise the project, he realised that the connections between the subject, disciplining, and true discourse was much more complex and interesting that he originally thought. The crisis led to a series of conceptual innovations, as it is often the case with liminal moments, of which the most important were governmentality, which resumes in a captivating term the kind of rationality characterising the modern state, and pastoral power, through which Foucault's work on the rise of modern power can definitely be assigned to the secularisation 'thesis', all the more so as by that time, through Alessandro Pizzorno (as conveyed by Pasquale Pasquino and Giovanna Procacci), and Paul Rabinow he became familiar with the work of Max Weber (Foucault's 'truth-teller' or *parrhesiast* is remarkably close to Weber's *charismata*).

However, and still, he felt that something was missing here, as his studies about the origins of Christian practices increasingly convinced him that the relations between the subject and truth cannot be contained within the limits of a genealogical work; they embody a philosophical and even human value from which we cannot simply distance ourselves. Such ideas crystallised, in two steps, in two key concepts: the care of the self, theme of the 1982 Collège de France lectures; and parrhesia, or the practice of courageous truth-telling, theme of the 1983 and 1984 Collège de France lectures. The care of the self, and related terms like the practices, techniques, and technologies of the self, implied that the ways by which the modern state came to shape and discipline individuals did not originate with Christianity, and a presumably sinister effort to increase power over men, rather can be traced to certain philosophical concerns and schools of Antiquity, and their main aim was not to control, rather to empower individuals for a free life. It was only eventually that such techniques became incorporated in systems of power, first with the Church, and then with the modern state – themselves quite different entities. The question here concerns what exactly in these techniques made such use or abuse possible – a question that Foucault did not have the time to resolve or even tackle, which is visible in the ambivalence of his related terminology (the terms 'techniques' and 'technologies of self' were used interchangeably).

Foucault on truth-telling

This leads to the last and most important issue of Foucault's work, the question of truth-telling, to which practices of the self were subordinated – not just in Foucault's work, but evidently, according to him, in Western civilisation itself. This concern he also traced to Antiquity, first to antique politics (1983), and then to philosophy (1984), focusing on Plato, and the figure of Socrates, especially through the *Apology*. However – and here we enter the greatest paradox of Foucault's last period, and perhaps his entire work – he then devoted the core of the 1984 course, lectures 5–9, out of nine, to the practice of truth-telling characteristic of the Cynics. Here not just paradox but ambivalence reaches its zenith, as it is not fully clear whether he performs here a genealogy of critique, showing up in the unkempt and repulsive cynics the distant spiritual fathers of the modern critical tradition – a tradition Foucault never felt as his own, as otherwise he would have become just another critical theorist, which he wasn't (even from Kant, he never made use of his 'critical' books); or whether he considered the cynics as the models of his own perspective.

The central issue is that, in spite of the evidently rough and problematic characters of their ideas and entire approach, the ancient Cynics offered a new connection between truth and the 'subject' that for Foucault was for some reason particularly attractive – so much so that he said that the course of the next year would be devoted to the theme of the 'true life'. Here an idea of Frédéric Gros (2011: 355) is particularly helpful: according to him, for Foucault Christianity amounted to a combination of Plato's thinking and Cynic practice.

The second half of Foucault's last lecture was indeed devoted to a very cursory study of parrhesia in Christianity, including Judeo-Hellenistic, New Testament, patristic and monastic texts. The presentation, necessarily, was extremely sketchy, ending with presenting as the two key noyau of Christian experience mysticism and asceticism, closely recalling Max Weber's related works. Time was so limited that Foucault did not even manage to present his reflections on the general framework of the course, with which he evidently intended to say his farewell – as within less than three months he was dead.

It is again meaningless to speculate what if anything Foucault could have said about Christianity in a would-be course about the true life. However, in his excellent book about Foucault and Christianity Philippe Chevallier (2011) offers an insight that sets a definite limit to the possibilities: in all his work on Christianity Foucault failed to enter the great theological works, in particular St Augustine, limiting himself to books on Christian practice – except, in a way, in volume 4.

Such limitation, however, is unacceptable, as a matter of principle, concerning the theme whose importance Foucault recognised and set to study: the constitutive link between the truth and the human person, in particular the telling of the truth, as related to the very authenticity of the human being. The issue is not to enter theological discussions in their own terms, but the impossibility of excluding such works from the question of the search for the truth – in so far as it is connected to the core of our own civilisation. Or, as Foucault came to formulate his problem at the start of the third lecture of his 1980 course, the question is to identify the moment in Western history when 'the telling of truth can authenticate itself', or when 'the person who speaks can say that this is me who detains the truth'.

Fortunately, it is exactly this point that was raised, and conclusively discussed, by one of the most important French philosophers of the 20th century, Michel Henry, in a similarly conclusive book – a book he managed to proof-read on his deathbed, but which was only published shortly after he died.

Michel Henry on truth-telling: the words of Christ

Two preliminary comments, to start with. First, through the genealogical investigation, and especially through Foucault, we came to the same point as already established by St Augustine: the extreme importance of the truth, the truth of concreteness, the truth of history, the truth of the concrete person, for our own civilisation. This does not mean that other cultures and civilisations do not care about the truth, but that such concern does not become so preoccupying anywhere else – preoccupying also in the sense of a genuine obsession, which then can become deprived of any value and turned into its opposite, just as the 'will to truth' has become, through a 'will to knowledge', with modern technologised science, where any piece of 'true' knowledge becomes its own justification, even though evidently the increasing uses of such pieces of knowledge end with our own destruction. So, while we cannot dismiss truth, and the search for truth, we must try to set certain limits to it – and for this we must understand the real sources and moving forces of this will.

Second, Michel Henry, through whom this undertaking, this book claims, gained a genuine resting point is indeed a very particular figure of the intellectual landscape. Born in 1922, thus part of the great WWII generation, but of all places in Vietnam, thus in Asia and a French colony, and losing his father when he was not yet three weeks old, he returned to France at the age of seven. The eventual outcome of such life experiences was a passion for philosophy combined with a rare independence of spirit, including active participation in the Resistance, which led him to give up any career opportunities other than the search for truth inside philosophy. Even there, he shunned the 'world', in spite of showing extreme promises: not yet 21, he wrote a thesis on Spinoza that his supervisor wanted to publish with Gallimard, only the wartime conditions preventing this to happen. For a series of reasons, much due to his independence and perfectionism, he only finished his thesis in 1963, with an all-star jury including Jean Hyppolite, Jean Wahl, Paul Ricoeur, and Henri Gouhier being particularly and univocally impressed by his work. Hyppolite already in 1960 wanted him at the Sorbonne, and after his defence such offers were renewed practically yearly, yet Henry decided to accept an invitation at the University of Montpellier and stayed there until his retirement in 1982.

The theme of Henry's 2002 book is the veracity of a very particular kind of – indeed unique – discourse: the speech (or words, same in French: *paroles*) of Christ when he talks as the Son of God. Note that Henry emphatically asserts, in the first sentence of the book (2002: 7), that he is writing as a philosopher, not as a Christian or a theologian. Note also that there is nothing wrong in writing as a theologian – several key thinkers discussed in this book either started to study theology (Heidegger, Hadot), or were theologians *as well as* philosophers (Florensky, Castelli). This is even a main asset in our intellectual climate, dominated by secular intellectuals who were either mendaciously corrupt (Sartre and Lukacs), or engaged in skilful academic politics, helping them to gain the renown enjoyed, in spite of the heartless coldness and trite banalities of their ideas, often combined with plotting (Durkheim, Horkheimer, Lévi-Strauss, Habermas or Bourdieu).

The theme, of course, is bewilderingly complex and disarmingly daring, but indeed cannot be avoided, as on the one hand it touches the very foundations of our civilisation, and on the other, it indeed is not just a theological argument, but a historical and philosophical one, as it is primarily concerned with *truth*. The historical question, at a first level, is the following: did a person called Jesus Christ exist, and did he say the things that was attributed to him in the Gospels? Of course, not only there is no scientific method to ascertain this, but hardly any other historical evidence *outside* the Scriptures; thus the question poses a complex puzzle concerning trust in the claims about what happened, important on its own, a preoccupation of biblical scholars since many centuries. But the question of Henry is different and philosophical: given the texts as they are, and not forgetting about the effects these texts produced, can a philosopher *as* a philosopher say something about the way they can be validated? Can the meaning of their truthfulness be philosophically investigated?

The foundational claim of Christianity concerns the double nature of Christ – both human and divine. Henry starts from here as, say, a philosophical hypothesis, claiming that this would also imply that the words of Christ have a double nature: human and divine. Henry's interest is limited to the second and pursues three paths of inquiry about them: what is their actual content; how can they be understood by us humans; and how if at all can their character as truly divine words be ascertained.

Concerning the first line, Henry distinguishes between two types, corresponding to the same double nature of Christ: words that concern the world, or us, *our* world, and words that reveal, or assert, the divine nature of Christ. The direct words of Christ about our world are shocking, exploding natural relations, producing separation and division and not unity, thus not simply dislocating but outright ruining social organisation (32). They require us to renounce all we hold dear, in some passages even 'with a violence where paradox reaches its limit point' (61, citing Lk 9:24, Mk 8:35, Mt 16:25), genuine eruptions that were never heard before and are perhaps even inaudible (88), making immediately manifest that they could not simply come from the world. Most importantly, they reject outright and in a most violent way reciprocity (36–9, 43–5, 48–9), the most basic ties keeping together any human community. This extends to all kinds of family ties and kinship obligation, including filial respect, the duty for the dead – sentences so well known by everyone in the Christian world that it is pointless to cite them, except that we cannot now fathom the radical novelty they must have meant in their own times and place – a method-logical point recalling Weber's *Protestant Ethic* and the historical novelty of eventual commonplaces like time is money.

These statements were accompanied by another set of statements, even more shocking, about his own nature, which together constitute '*a discourse of Christ on himself* [sic]', which is 'the most important part of his teaching, of which all the rest derives', and which are 'declarations without equivalent in the history of human thought' (11). In these Christ asserted that he could make such statements as he was sent by God the Father; he is his only Son, and the embodiment of the Divine Word. Using a particularly important and expressly liminal metaphor Henry claims that Christ is not just the one who opens the door but *is* the Door (57–8).

Such a combination of unprecedented and shocking claims tests the limits of any audience, posing the question of how they are, and could be, understood. The reactions of the listeners were indeed divided – though in a quite striking manner. Simple, common people, in spite of the enormity of the claims, in ever greater numbers came to listen to him – with the significant exception of those who knew him since childhood, thus could not handle the contrast; while the 'learned' elite, the scribes, high priests, and especially the Pharisees, with few exceptions, were scandalised by his messages and vehemently opposed them. What this immediately makes evident is that understanding the words of Christ did not require an intellectual effort, rather a different capacity that concerned not the brain but the heart.

Here we reach the extremely important and radically non-modern centre of Henry's philosophical reading of Christ's words. Reason is not only not the anthropological distinguishing feature of us humans, but not even the most important organ of our understanding, as it only has relevance for the world, and can make us blind to reality, even animate a hatred of real truth (122–6). Even our judgments are based on the heart (34).

But how and why? And, to start with, why the heart?

At one level, heart is just a word. However, as Chapter 7 already argued, and this chapter makes the point even more strongly, words have their own importance – and the heart is a particularly important word, as it captures the inner centre of our existence. This word, as it is used in the Gospels – and is used there quite frequently – designs the essence of the human condition: 'human reality, our reality, *our life*' (19). It also indicates that our reality is 'essentially affective, it is such, in truth [*ce qu'elle est en vérité*]' (19). It is in and through the heart that life speaks – 'in its immediate pathos-full self-revelation [*auto-révélation pathétique*]', and so 'the "heart" is the only adequate definition of man' (134).

Yet, adds Henry immediately – and this is where the point gains its true depth – at the same time evil also only exists in man, the world *as nature* is free of evil: 'every material process, everything that science studies, everything that does not feel [*sent*] and does not experience [*éprouve*] anything, everything that is external to man, is innocent' (18); so the seat if evil is also the heart: nothing external can make a man impure – only what comes out of the mouth, the perverse thoughts render him impure (18, quoting Mt 15: 11–20 and Mk 7: 14–23). The list of evils that come out of the heart in Mark and Matthew include some of the greatest presumed human values, so the heart of also the centre of subversion: the evil rooted in our heart can 'grow without any limit [*s'accroître démesurément*]' (122–3; see also 131). The search for a pure reason, therefore, back to the core of Greek philosophy, is meaningless, as such reason only deals with the external features of the world, and so is powerless to deal with the evil that is inside the heart (19).

This leads to a fundamental dilemma: if the heart is the seat of both good and evil, if we as human beings must rely on the judgments of our heart, in the ultimate instance, and yet the heart can also be the very seat of evil, how can we make a proper distinction; how can we find the true way, how can we tell the truth, and live in truth? This dilemma, by the way, was already recognised in debates about parrhesia in classical philosophy, central for Foucault's discussion of the Stoics in his 1983 course, who argued that an individual by his own forces cannot escape a degraded condition; for this, he needs the help of an 'other'.

Such a concern with the other, a *mere* other, being necessary for truth-telling, became a central preoccupation of Foucault, literally until the last minute: in his discussion of the Cynics, and especially at the end of his unpronounced 'last words' of his last lecture. There, he centrally poses the contrast between an 'other life' (*vie autre*) and 'other world' (sometimes expressed as '*monde autre*', sometimes as '*autre monde*'), or the contrast between the Cynics on the one hand, and Plato and Christianity on the other;[5] a dilemma that he posed, without even trying to resolve.

It is right here that Henry offers a solution; or, rather, he claims that the solution offered by Christ lies. The central issue is that we as humans indeed cannot offer a solution to this dilemma: faced with it, we must recognise our radical powerlessness (120). The other, as just another other, offers no way out,[6] as that other can only reinforce the same and certainly widely shared erring in which one is entrapped. Foucault by the way says as much in another crucial part of his most important 1984 course, his commentary on the then recently published book of Dumézil on the last words of Socrates. There, using the full arsenal of his philological erudition, Dumézil demonstrates that the famous call of Socrates to offer a cock to Asclepius was not due to his overcoming the sickness of life, as even Nietzsche assumed, rather to overcome the sickness of common opinions, or the opinions of the *others*.[7]

The solution, the real solution offered by Christ, as conveyed by the Gospels, is as simple as stunning at the same time: we must indeed listen to the heart, in so far as our reasoning power does not offer a solution, but recognising that it is not 'our heart' that offers the solution, in its autonomy, but only in its dependence on a force greater than us: a force that reveals itself in our heart.

With this statement, however, one might argue, Henry left philosophy, or thinking, entering a theological argument. It seems almost inevitable, as he already claimed that mere reasoning power, having to do only with external things, cannot be relied upon for internal matters, or matters of the heart. Yet, Henry insists that his book, and argument, is philosophical; that following a purely philosophical argument it is possible to ascertain the not just truth-telling but self-revealing and self-authenticating character of Christ's words.[8]

How so?!

Henry proceeds by first exploring the contrast between external and internal. The answers to the dilemmas posed at the start of this section are in this internal life, of which the main repository is the heart, as symbol and concrete reality, and where the human and the divine worlds touch each other. It is in and through this that the divine words of Christ can be heard and understood, and this same internal life authenticates them as truly divine words; in them, words and things coincide in their essence. Furthermore, it is through the words of Christ, and *only* through the words of Christ, that the existence and character of such a divine reality, otherwise inaccessible for us humans, reveals itself, unmistakeably, in our world – so clearly and evidently that it is beyond any reasonable doubt for those who are ready to see and experience it, and are not blinded by a false analogy – the mistaken idea that human understanding can proceed only externally, through the kind of evidence that characterises the external world – as if in order to become fully convinced of the love of one's wife or husband one must hire a private eye and ascertain that the other does not cheat on us.

Henry demonstrates the inexorable character of these inferences through a minute, step-by-step phenomenological-philosophical analysis. He starts at the exact same point as Heidegger or Foucault, by problematising the modern philosophy of language, but proceeds differently. According to Henry, the problem is that this approach identifies human words with the 'language of the world'; or that we can only talk about what appears to us outside, what shows or manifests itself for us. However, this approach is imprisoned in the '*referential character of language*' (92), or that language cannot create: 'the incapacity of the word to produce the reality which it designates is the most general character' of this kind of language (92). But this is not the only possible language: 'these theories are dupes of the naïve belief according to which the visible universe constitutes the domain of the only true reality and in consequence the only object of knowledge and language'. The outcome is an immense void inside our culture: 'an other word, more originary and essential than that of the world, became totally occulted' (92).

Henry proceeds to explore this 'other word', and 'other world'. He starts by asserting the reality of our own feelings and the insurmountable truth of those words that directly express them, without the possibility of doubt or duplicity (96–7): when we are overcome by joy, or suffering, the words expressed capture and convey this condition. Here the connection between life and word is direct, not theoretical or speculative; the words by which we express our inner feelings constitute an 'irrecusable experience' (94). Suffering, joy, love, hatred are real experiences, and the words by which we express them capture this reality; on the other hand such experiences only exist, can only be real because we can name them: in such cases as well, and not just in the case of 'performative speech acts', words *do* produce reality. In such words life itself reveals itself; these words are the 'self-revelations of life' (97). The words of Christ, that touch our hearts, have the same character; except for the additional element that in such cases not simply life but *absolute life* reveals itself (98).

Here we reach the culmination of Henry's stunning book, the solution of Foucault's dilemma about the self-authentication of truth: humans cannot authenticate the truth of their own claims without external help, but Christ could and did authenticate his words; furthermore, it is his words that can help us sort out our own hearts, finding inside our hearts, and *only* inside our hearts, the true way, and even to say it.

Henry proceeds in three steps. First, just as the words of life, the words of our most basic life experiences directly touching our hearts are issued from there, similarly the words of Absolute Life, the words of God, whether conveyed by the prophets, in the old times, and especially as conveyed by Christ, who talks not as a prophet but the only Son of God, directly touch our heart – through the written Scriptures, our only possibility of listening to them, written by those who not just heard but were also deeply touched by them, so registering both the words of Christ and the reactions of the audience.

The next step concerns the content of these statements, having a direct impact on hearts comparable to the most elementary life experiences; a content that concerns not just our concrete life, but Absolute Life itself; the claim that these words, the words of God, are at the same time the words of Life, though 'the word of Life is the great omission of contemporary reflection, just as of traditional philosophical thinking' (102). The characterisation of the words of God as the words of Life, or of Word and Life, is central both for the Old and the New Testaments, with the important difference that in the New Testament these are pronounced not by humans (the prophets), but are 'professed by someone who declares himself the Word of God himself, and thus God himself' (103). The most important such declaration is contained in the Prologue of John, at the limit-place of the two Testaments (*à la frontière des deux Testaments*; 103), a text Henry outright calls initiatory, and which is not an isolated instance, but is repeated in the very last chapter of John, immediately after the events of the Passion, thus the other liminal place of the same Gospel, in the very last words of Christ reported by John.

These liminal declarations of John (*déclarations johanniques liminaire*; 104) are not concerned with the existence of God, or similar speculative questions of philosophy and theology; such issues are simply 'placed out of game [*mise hors jeu*]' (104). The question is not existence, but Life. And this has two major consequences: first, any debate about the existence of God is meaningless, as simply 'we know what is God': not through processes of reflection and thinking, which in this case only mislead, but *'we know it because we are living and no living is alive without bringing in oneself Life not as one's own unknown secret but in which one experiences oneself* [*s'éprouve*] *as one's proper essence and even one's reality'* (sic; 104).[9] Quoting here Master Eckhardt, Henry asserts that our most basic knowledge, the knowledge that we live, at the same time implies the knowledge of God.

This statement is so important that it requires two immediate comments. First, if knowledge is fundamentally the knowledge of life, as knowledge only proceeds through words, and words are primarily the words of life (experiences), and which is identical to the knowledge of God, then this sheds light on the prohibition concerning the 'tree of knowledge': all knowledge that comes from outside and does not primarily proceed from the inside is problematic, as it can result in leading away from our essence, and thus subvert our existence. External knowledge, knowledge of the world, knowledge that *starts* from the world, is indeed *the* problem. Second, if knowledge fundamentally is knowledge of life, the knowledge of *our* life, the knowledge that we live, then this also implies the recognition that this life comes from outside us, it is a gift, and that we are dependent on the power that granted us this gift. Denying such dependency is hubris, implying egoism and the worst evil.

The second puzzle of Henry, based on this knowledge of life (and its source), is: how can we exist? How can our limited life be derived from infinite absolute life? *'How can something which in itself is deprived of the power to life live anyway'* (sic; 105)? How can an unlimited life give a limited life? The answer, even to these questions, if offered by the Prologue of John, in the self-generation of life, the distinction between creation and generation. It is such generation, and not creation, that is accomplished by the Word (106–7); such self-generation of Absolute Life, by the Word, is radically immanent. Thus, situated at the limit point (*césure*) of the two

Testaments, the Prologue of John illuminates both – even corrects, retro-actively, the *Book of Genesis*, or rather its usual reading. The first chapters of the Old Testament do not offer a naïve account on the creation of the world; they have nothing to the with the 'science' of the 'world'; rather, they offer *'the first true and rigorous analysis of the human condition'* (sic; 108). This reading is illuminated and extended by the Prologue of John, at the same time advancing and interpreting the words of Christ as Words of God; as the living Word (*logos*) of God. The manifold declarations of Christ, reported in the Gospel of John, according to which his words are the words of God and also the words of Life, or the 'discourse of Christ on himself' amount to the same: *'the definition by Christ of himself as the One who is'* (sic; 110).

Thus, we reach the third and final level of Henry's analysis, the solution to Foucault's dilemma of how truth can authenticate itself: the words of Christ authenticate themselves as they reveal themselves as the Words of Life, at the same time revealing himself as the Son of God, and we recognise the truth of this, in our heart, just as we recognise there, *beyond the shadow of any doubt*, the truth of our own innermost experiences. The truth of the words Christ says about our world are authenticated by the movements in our heart as not mere emotions but the deepest truths of our real life; and thus the words about himself must by force also be accepted – so these words reveal, manifest, and authenticate themselves: there is no need for further – impossible – external witnesses.

The concluding words, for John, just as for Henry, concern the words about, and the experiences of, the Resurrection – just as it applies, among others, for the greatest modern novelists, Dickens, Dostoevsky, and Tolstoy (see Szakolczai 2016).

Conclusion

Henry's book leads to a corollary, from John (14: 6), whose importance for a book on Political Anthropology as Method cannot be exaggerated: the identity of the way, truth, and life. This is the endpoint reached, in this chapter, of the historical methods of Political Anthropology, starting from Nietzsche-Weber-Foucaldian genealogy; concerning the ways of truth, approached not from the exteriority of the sciences of the 'universe', but from the interiority of the truth of our own history. These same method-logical considerations can also be reached from the perspective of the central anthropologically based tools of Political Anthropology.

Notes

1 See Voegelin (1998: 38–45). The centrality of St Augustine for Voegelin, and the puzzling lack of a sustained discussion of Augustine in Voegelin, is discussed in important recent contributions by Scotti Muth (2022) and Parotto (2016).
2 Here, of course, it is vital to complement Augustine's view with recently discovered historical and especially archaeological evidence. However, instead of dismissing it for not knowing what he could not have known, it should be, precisely, *complemented*.
3 Abandoning this path is the great historical error of Descartes. The theme will be discussed in detail in the last section of this chapter, on Michel Henry.

4 A method-logically crucial related issue is the simplicity connected to the main modern Marian visionaries, a theme discussed, among Political Anthropologists, by Victor Turner and Michel Serres, but which for reasons of space cannot be discussed here.
5 See in particular the Postface by Frédéric Gros to Foucault (2011).
6 It is quite curious that here Foucault moves close to advocating the 'philosophy of the other', central and most problematic point in modern philosophy from Hegel through Husserl to Sartre and Levinas and beyond, which he otherwise is far from supporting. The problem is that this philosophy undermines concreteness in the same way as the parallel tradition of Kantianism and analytical philosophy.
7 The other part of the book is devoted to Nostradamus, offering a method-logically just as intriguing discussion, as there Dumézil, the great philologist, half-seriously, deploying the full arsenal of his erudition, demonstrates that two famous quatrains of the prophecies indeed with amazing accuracy envision two episodes about the unsuccessful flight of Louis XVI in 1792, posing the puzzle of what this possibly can mean.
8 His argument is also closely built upon Pascal and Maine de Biran, two philosophers also lurking behind the work of Foucault, without him ever discussing them explicitly, but all this again cannot be explored here, for reasons of space.
9 Note the enormous importance of the same term *'s'éprouve'* for Foucault's discussions of parrhesia (see again Gros 2011).

12
ANTHROPOLOGICAL METHODS

> But it was home. And though home is a name, a word, it is a strong one; stronger than magician ever spoke, or spirit answered to, in strongest conjuration.
>
> Charles Dickens, Martin Chuzzlewit, 529

> Happy the man, and happy he alone,
> He who can call today his own:
> He who, secure within, can say,
> Tomorrow do thy worst, for I have lived today.
> Be fair or foul or rain or shine
> The joys I have possessed, in spite of fate, are mine.
> Not Heaven itself upon the past has power,
> But what has been, has been, and I have had my hour.
>
> John Dryden, Happy the Man

The best-known, trademark method of anthropology is ethnographic fieldwork and participatory observation. However, apart from the fact that there are problems with the obsession of the discipline with such 'ethnographic method',[1] Political Anthropology is not a subfield of the discipline of anthropology, rather a liminal field connecting various discourses and disciplines.

Here, in this last chapter of the book, three sets of method-logical considerations, taken from anthropology, will be considered. The first is the way in which genealogy, presented in the previous chapter, can be complemented and vastly improved through some of the main concepts used in Political Anthropology. The second concerns participation, a term explored inside anthropology by Lucien Lévy-Bruhl, himself a trained philosopher, and developed further by Colin Turnbull, through the term liminality, towards the idea of 'total participation', a major method-logical advance over 'participatory

DOI: 10.4324/9781003275138-15

observation'. The third, following on this, says a few words about the links between philosophy, especially classical philosophy, and Political Anthropology.

Genealogy through Political Anthropology

Four of the most important concepts of Political Anthropology are particularly helpful in strengthening genealogy as a method: liminality, trickster, imitation, and schismogenesis. In the following, for each term a concise specification will be offered, as the term was developed in anthropology, followed by an application to the present, an extension to the past, including the presentation of analogous terms, and finally it will be shown how the terms can be used in a genealogical analysis.

Liminality

The term, originally developed by Arnold van Gennep in his 1909 classic book, based on his comparative study of rites of passage, was rendered popular by Victor Turner only about 60 years later, as van Gennep and his work was literally ostracised by Durkheim and then his school (a mistreatment reinforced by Lévi-Strauss and Bourdieu), and by now it has become a master concept not only in anthropology but in all areas of the social sciences. Still, even in our days, its use is strongly discouraged by establishment neo-Kantian and neo-Hegelian, Durkheimian, and Marxist circles, for reasons that are rather obscure, as they are rarely presented up front, but used effectively behind the curtains. The central idea is that the crucial transition points of human and social lives, and rites and rituals associated with them, are fundamental in helping individuals and communities in passing successfully through such otherwise most trying moments, forming their very character and identities. Thus, through the study of liminality, one can capture the formative and even transformative moments of human life, without ignoring the fact that the outcome of such moments is largely prescribed by the course of nature (thus, a child must become an adult, and not vice versa; a sick person should become healthy again, otherwise risks dying, etc., etc.).

While developed inside anthropology, the concept can be vitally used for the present as well, though for the same kind of obscure reasons Victor Turner's attempt at such application was strongly resisted by the same kind of obscure forces within anthropology – as if the term were a kind of 'monopoly' of anthropologists. But liminal moments and experiences, like birth and death, baptism and marriage, growing up and falling ill, love and friendship are central features of human life everywhere, so applicable to modernity as well. School examinations, especially something like a maturity examination and a PhD defence, job interviews, or weddings are just as much rites of passage as the tribal ceremonies described abundantly by Arnold van Gennep or Victor Turner, and their followers.

But the term can also be extended in a historical analysis, not simply in the sense of analysing such rites of passage as performed in the past, but the turning points of history, in any culture or civilisation, and at any moment of time, can be conceived of as liminal moments. The added value of such an application is huge, as in this way the empirically based term liminality can be used to capture the actual, formative, and transformative character of such historical moments, beyond considering them as mere transitions within a broad process of history whose outcome is as if given in advance, in the sense of 'evolution' or 'progress'. Quite on the contrary, if a concrete human community or culture is faced with a liminal crisis, whether natural, environmental, or caused by other human cultures, a non-successful response might involve complete disappearance – according to Toynbee, the past course of history is littered with the collapses of not simply cultures but civilisations; but also a kind of entrapment in a low-level situation, a regress rather than a progress.

Thus, using the term liminality for a genealogical study of effective history, history becomes not a linear history of evolution and progress, marked by steady increases of knowledge and technology – an extremely limited and biased vision – rather the effective outcome of a series of liminal crises. Applied to our own present, the rise of the modern world does not represent progress in any absolute sense – such an idea is simply preposterous – rather is the outcome of the specific answers given to a series of liminal crises that included the collapses of the Roman Empire (Western and Eastern), the schism of the Western and Eastern Churches, the Thirty Years War, the great Revolutions (English, French, Russian), the World Wars, only to mention some of the most important such liminal events.

Trickster

The term was originally developed inside North-American anthropology, in the 19th century, taken up by Paul Radin. Even here, and for similarly obscure reasons, both the career of Radin and the term suffered much resistance and neglect by the forces of the establishment, whether mainstream or Marxist-critical – no doubt because the term can be used in a very revealing manner against such establishment(s). Still, the term eventually became used by anthropologists for all kinds of cultures, in practically all parts of the world, but especially in Africa and Oceania.

The term captures a very particular character of folktales, and myths, thus even religion: an outsider to the community, to any community, but also to the basic norms of human life, who ignores the most basic human values and feelings, who cannot maintain any limit and restraint, who is held in low esteem by everyone, but who nevertheless can infiltrate any community through some standard tricks, like the telling of tales, the cracking of jokes or the miming of animals, gain a degree of influence, and eventually – by using one or other liminal crisis moments – can even gain ascendency, in exceptional cases an almost total power over the entire community.

Just as liminality, the term has evident contemporary relevance. The central point is not to label concrete individuals as tricksters – though such a usage historically actually anticipates the use of the term in anthropology, as the term 'confidence trickster', an important variation of the character, was used among others by Dickens and Melville – but to show how certain important, and extremely problematic, if not outright evil, characters of modern history closely recall, in their character traits, the figure of the trickster. Even more importantly, beyond concrete figures, it is possible to coin the term trickster logic (Horvath 2013; see also Szakolczai 2022) in order to identify the very specific modality of action used by trickster figures; a mode of action which they then disseminate and propagate inside the social body, knowing that this is the only way in which not only their concrete activities become tolerated, but a game is inaugurated that renders their power persistent.

Even this term, from its anthropological usage, can be extended historically. This was pioneered by some key mythologists (Georges Dumézil and Károly Kerényi). However, and most importantly, trickster and trickster logic can be extended to concrete historical events and persons, and modes of action, even projected back to the Palaeolithic, while also and centrally applied to the present (Horvath 2013, 2021; Horvath and Szakolczai 2020, Horvath, Szakolczai and Marangudakis 2020, Szakolczai 2022).

The historical application of the term can be combined with liminality, offering a very powerful and novel reading of the course of history, helping to understand how and why in liminal crisis moments certain cultures could – and did – take a turn for the worst, and not the better. A central feature of liminal moments – situations in which the normal order of everyday life is suspended – is widespread confusion, uncertainty, and anxiety. This is why in any culture a rite of passage is a very preoccupying moment, where leadership is entrusted to reliable masters of ceremonies who can lead the community through such a trying period – or, at least, it is believed that they are capable of doing so. If such a liminal void is not foreseen, but emerges out of the blue, the confusion is certainly even greater. Max Weber developed his concept of charismatic leadership exactly to offer an analytical way for dealing with such moments. However, it is not at all sure that a charismatic leader would necessarily emerge to lead the community into safe waters again; rather, such disturbing moments offer an opportunity for trickster figures to present themselves as brave heroes to solve the situation, but actually only plunge the community ever more into the depths of the crisis, eventually making it permanent – creating an entrapment from which there seems to be no way out, as soon even the memory of normality would disappear.

The understanding of such a situation can be helped by a third master term of Political Anthropology, imitation.

Imitation

Imitation is another maverick term, developed outside modern rationalism, first inside sociology by Gabriel Tarde, one of the unacknowledged classics of the discipline, another key figure discredited by Durkheim, and then by René Girard, first in a comparative study of novels, and then extended by a comparative study of mythological and anthropological material. The term is ignored, and its use is actively discouraged by modern rationalism, according to which humans are rational beings; only children and primitive people imitate. However, the untenability of such a position can be demonstrated through the term liminality. Imitation is a feature of liminality; humans imitate when and in so far as they are in a liminal situation. Childhood as such is a liminal situation – and adolescence represents a particular intensification of liminality – but practically any adult starts to imitate the moment one enters liminality. A perfect illustration is any moment of panic: using a famous example, if one shouts 'fire' in a crowded cinema, everybody starts to run in the direction everybody else is running, assuming that 'they' must know the best way. The same logic applies to the stock-market, or to fashion, and many other types of crowd or mass behaviour – or, in general, to the 'public sphere'; especially when the void of such a 'public sphere' is extended to infinity by telecommunication technology.

Imitation has a tight connection not only with liminality, but also with the trickster. One of the most important features of the trickster is imitativity; this is why the trickster is often characterised as a mime, and why trickster figures are particularly present in, and disseminated by theatre or the visual arts in general. People usually imitate people they respect, starting with children who imitate their parents, relatives, or teachers. However, in liminal moments, all standards are suddenly lost, everyone is forced to rely on one's own powers – which are precious little, as such moments reveal – and so the 'masters' of imitation, tricksters, suddenly become the rulers of liminality.

The central importance of imitation lies in a contrast between its two most important and opposed uses. On the one hand, imitation is central for learning; any learning process necessarily involves following and thus imitating others. The ability to do something on one's own, without imitating one's model or master, is only the eventual result of a long process. On the other, awareness about the predominance of imitation, especially as a symptom of liminality, is important to identify faking, arguably *the* key problem of our times, dominated by media – and 'media' by its name indicates an in-between, thus liminal situation.

Schismogenesis

The term was developed by Gregory Bateson, and the history of the term, and of Bateson's career, complements that of the previous terms, and their proposers, in a striking, and most frightening, manner. Bateson was one of the first anthropology PhD-s at Cambridge University, his Professors including Radcliffe-Brown and Malinowski, so was supposed to have red carpet for his life. Instead, due to his deviation from the path laid down by his supervisor and professors, and for making this explicit in his work, Bateson never had an appointment in anthropology. Thus, while van Gennep, Radin, and Bateson were destined to become founding fathers of the discipline of anthropology, becoming professors of and founding departments in major universities, practically none of them were employed as anthropologists in their lives – except for van Gennep teaching in Switzerland for a few years, and Radin being appointed when he was already past 70.

Bateson developed the term during his fieldwork, in Papua New Guinea, together with 'ethos' and 'eidos', each evidently using more of his studies of Plato in

Cambridge then the teachings of his anthropology professors. It was introduced to capture the way in which the unity of an entity is broken into two fragments, and how the new entities develop their identity, both with respect to the previous unity, and in contrast to the other fragment.

While Bateson developed the word for a retrospective analysis of small-scale tribal societies, it is also eminently applicable for a genealogy. If social order breaks down, imitative processes escalate and guidance is hijacked by trickster figures, normality is not restored and the unity of the community could be irretrievably lost, torn apart by 'schismogenic' processes. Schisms are fundamental features of medieval and Renaissance history, starting with the Great Schism between Eastern and Western Christianity, continuing with the schisms of the Papacy, and ending with the Reformation. With the rise of secular modernity, schismogenesis became omnipresent (rich-poor, elite-mass, left-right, mainstream-critical, etc.), and through Kantian and Hegelian rationalism became codified as *the* main feature of the human condition.

Total participation

Participation was already discussed at the start of this book, using Pizzorno's sociology and philosophical hermeneutics, as the foundation of method-logics, a precondition of any possibility of understanding, even the idea of rationality. Here, at the end, I'll return to participation, in the form of a *total* participation, as a method of anthropology, developed by one of the key mavericks of anthropology, Colin Turnbull, by reflecting on his own life-work through another key concept of Political Anthropology, liminality.

The idea contrasts standard terms of mainstream anthropological method, 'fieldwork' and 'participant observation'. Participant observation was developed in anthropology to give time for researchers to familiarise themselves with otherwise unknown areas and practices. However, Turnbull argues that this is not sufficient; it still preserves the basic separation between the anthropologist as someone external to the practices in which the natives are engaged and is thus bound to miss on their real meaning. Instead, proper anthropological understanding requires '*total involvement* of our whole being'; we must 'truly and fully participate' (Turnbull 1990: 51, 76, 79; see especially the section 'The merits of total participation', 74–5). 'Participant observation' is just an oxymoron, as one either participates, so is inside, or merely observes, staying on the outside. Total participation is not 'fieldwork', rather 'field experience': one lives not just 'with' the natives, but for a time 'as' a native, gaining – in so far as possible – the same experiences, precondition of real understanding.

This does not mean 'going native'; it is only a potential risk, to be taken. It is close to Husserlian 'bracketing', except here it is not a hypothetical philosophical position, rather an existential experience-experiment, a suspension of one's own cultural and social 'self', in order to enter a different lifeworld.

Turnbull's 'total participation' is a direct generalisation of his own experiences. When he first encountered the Mbuti Pygmies, his eventual 'objects' of study, he was not yet a trained anthropologist. He could live with them without preconceived conceptual schemes. His central, and quite genial, idea is that this life accident *should* be extended into a point of method. Significant anthropological or sociological research can be done *not* by selecting an area one ignored previously, armed with rigorous scientific methodology, rather selecting one already familiar, through whatever accidents of life, and *return* to this same field, now seeing and experiencing the same reality with the help of in-depth familiarisation of the most interesting and illuminating relevant approaches offered inside *academia*.

Furthermore, such prior field-experience of total participation not only enables understanding, a genuine vision of reality, otherwise inaccessible, but 'provides a wealth of data that could never be acquired by any other means' (Turnbull 1990: 51), offering 'insights that would have been impossible to come by [through mere] intellectual curiosity' (52), and which one 'might well have missed with such an objective, academic approach' (53). It even 'provid[es] "hard data" that might well not be otherwise readily accessible' (76), and compared to which information gained through formal training – while not irrelevant in itself – 'is secondary in importance' (66). Even further, far from being incompatible with rational thinking and analysis, such 'hard data' gained through participatory experience 'led, later, to the most valuable speculations' (73), as these are exactly the 'moments of abandon' that can serve as a 'basis for the most fruitful subsequent investigation' (75). In the context of a liminal experience 'subjectivity and emotional involvement are no longer incompatible with objectivity and reason' (76), as such an experience, including its transformative elements, 'is a mode of perception', being 'not at all unlike [the] use of the rational process by which we recognise without any discomfort that things are seldom, if ever, what they seem to be' (79). While any purely 'objective' study stays on the surface level, remaining 'entirely intellectual and, all too often, spectacularly acrobatic but ultimately meaningless' (79), rendering anthropology 'empty and barren' (81), total participation helps us move beyond the limited horizon of problem-solving (70–71), towards understanding practices that are concerned with curing or make feeling good (57, 66): two terms that for the Mbuti Pygmies are identical, as 'in their own words, whatever *is*, when that moment is reached, is good, otherwise it would not, could not, *be*' (72), thus 'transforming an emotional state of some anguish into contentment' (52). Here again, through his experiences, Turnbull reaches a timeless wisdom inside the Pygmy vision of the world – impossible for any academic merely 'doing' fieldwork and 'participant observation'.

This directly moves to the last theme to be discussed, within the assigned limits of this book, which concerns the links between philosophy, especially classical philosophy, and political anthropology.

From anthropology to (classical) philosophy

The theme has two sides: one proceeds from philosophy towards contemporary anthropology, while the other from anthropology towards philosophy.

For the first, the best example is Plato. The series of anthropological concepts listed above has striking affinities with some key concepts in the thinking of Plato. This starts with liminality, which has two close equivalents in Plato's thinking: *apeiron* and *metaxy*. *Apeiron*, meaning the limitless or unlimited, is the Greek equivalent of 'liminal', derived from Latin *limes, peirar* signifying the 'limited', thus *a-peiras* the limitless. The word is present not only in Plato, but already central for the first aphorism of Anaximander, thus represents the 'first word' of Greek philosophy (Patočka), as the source and origin of all things. It also played a major role in Pythagorean thinking, while in Plato it is central in one of the last, most difficult, and little studied but crucial dialogues, *Philebus*; the dialogue that, arguably, around the two conceptual pairs 'one–many', and 'limit–unlimited', offers the core 'method-logical' ideas of Plato. *Metaxy* is a term specific to Plato, and is not often considered as a philosophical term, but was singled out for attention in his late work by Eric Voegelin, in *Anamnesis* and *Ecumenic Age*, discovered together with his other methodological key word 'historiogenesis', central to identify the constructs created to fix the course of history into preconceived schemes which is so similar to Pocock's interpretation of the 'Enlightened narrative', interestingly both developed in studies concerned with the rise and fall of empires. According to Voegelin *metaxy* thematises the way in which Plato opens up philosophy towards the realm of the divine.

The other central anthropological concepts introduced above also have close affinities with Plato's thinking. This goes without saying for imitation, central for Plato's diagnosis of the influence of Sophists on the agora; applies to the trickster, as the Sophists, as characterised in the various works of Plato, offer a quite comprehensive presentation of the main features of the trickster; while the categories of Bateson were developed explicitly on the basis of his familiarity with Plato's ideas.

Among contemporary philosophers, the perhaps most important examples with definite anthropological affinities are Michel Serres and Giorgio Agamben. Agamben's work continues Foucault's biopolitics, so by definition it belongs to Political Anthropology. Of special interest are his works on words and on images (in particular through Aby Warburg, as it was discussed in Chapter 8; but see Agamben (2005) in general); just as his writings about Economic Theology that were taken up with particular success by the emerging 'Copenhagen School' (see Dean 2019, Schwarzkopf 2020, and also Boland and Griffin 2021, esp. Ch.2.).

Michel Serres used specifically the work of Marcel Mauss, but several of his most important books, and terms, can be brought into direct parallel with Political Anthropology. These include various modalities of liminality, and terms that capture aspects and activities of the trickster, like the joker, the 'included third', and especially the parasite. The connections between Serres's ideas and anthropology are subject of a recent book (Bandak and Knight 2023).[2]

The opposite road, from anthropology to philosophy, was taken prominently by Gregory Bateson, who came to consider his work as a new epistemology,[3] and Tim Ingold. The connections between the themes of Ingold's work and Political Anthropology are manifold, and would merit a sustained discussion on its own. They include the constitutive focus on hunter-gatherers (theme of his PhD work), his related and sustained interest in walking, just as his method-logical focus on concrete activities and making, culminating in his book about the 'four A-s' (anthropology, archaeology, art, and architecture; see Ingold 2013).

Ingold started university studying natural science, but left it, for reasons quite similar to Yates's motives for studying the history of science:

> my initial enthusiasm soon gave way to disillusionment. Like so many of my contemporaries I was appalled by the extent to which science has reneged both on its sense of democratic responsibility and on its original commitment to enlarge the scope of human knowledge, and had allowed itself to become subservient to the demands of the military-industrial complex.
>
> *(2000: 1)*

His work became a relentless problematisation of modern rationalism, its 'scientific methodology', and the world vision assumed and promoted by modern science.

Positively, his work is grounded on an insight-experience that he traces to April 1988: the sudden illumination that beyond the dichotomies of person vs. organism, or society vs. nature, 'it suddenly dawned on me that the organism and the person could be one and the same' (3). Since then, he has been a relentless dissenter from the dichotomising and so life-alien approaches of the main figures of Western rationalism, like Bacon, Descartes, Lévi-Strauss, but also Darwin and Marx. This lead him even to problematise the main 'methodological' approach of anthropology, ethnography, best evidenced in an Epilogue title 'Anthropology is *not* ethnography' (2011: 229). Instead, among others, he came to follow the 'notorious maverick of anthropology, Gregory Bateson' (2000: 3; see the subtitle of the first chapter, 'steps to an ecology of life'; also 2013: 1–2), James Gibson's ecological psychology, and also a series of philosophers like Heidegger, Merleau-Ponty, and Deleuze. The central point connecting an organism and a person is life and living, a concern evident in his chapter and book titles, like the title of the first chapter of *Being Alive*: 'Anthropology comes to life' (2011: 3). It implies that, following the traditional anthropological recognition that 'the road to understanding lies in practical participation' (2011: 20), to which he adds the term 'presence': as participation implies 'the work and presence of others' (2000: 4); so 'knowing' must be 'from the inside' (2013: 1, again a chapter title), and both learning, and making, has the primary characteristic of a journey (2013: 45), or 'I have argued that wayfaring is our most fundamental mode of being in the world' (152), the word 'wayfarer' being recurrently used for the searcher for understanding. Anthropology should not deal with '*the materiality of objects*' (sic, 2011: 20), a term of 'academic perversion', part of the 'language of grotesque impenetrability', product of the 'abstract ruminations of philosophers and theorists', together with 'a host of other, similarly unfathomable qualities including agency, intentionality, functionality, spatiality, semiosis, spirituality, and embodiment' (20). It should rather deal with '*materials*' (sic, 2011: 20), or 'The materials of life' (2013: 17, another chapter title), touching and feeling them, as again it happens in life. The central concern of life is growth, a word again recurrent in Ingold's books,[4] with a focus on 'growing together' (88), which – as mentioned repeatedly in this book – is the etymology of 'concrete'; and implies the recognition that organisms are not made or produced, but '*generated* in the course of development' (2000: 4). While generations of theorists in anthropology 'throughout the history of the discipline, have been at pains to expunge life from their accounts', his aim was 'to reverse this emphasis', rather focusing on the 'recognition of life's capacity continually to overtake the destinations that are thrown up in its course' (2011: 3–4). This mainstream attitude is also nonsensical, as knowledge is not the outcome of testing cold theories, rather 'knowledge is grown along the myriad paths we take as we make our ways through the world in the course of everyday activities, rather than assembled from information obtained from numerous fixed locations' (2010b: S121); and, most emphatically, knowledge is 'not a construction, governed by cognitive mechanisms' (S122). Knowledge, growth, and education are also joined together in another gem of a title: 'Making things, growing plants, raising animals and bringing up children' (2000: 77), with its focus on 'processes of *growth*', in contrast to Marx-Engelsian 'production'. This also led him to problematise both making as production and design as a purely mental activity, evoking that the etymology of design, according to Vilém Flusser, reveals that the word, 'along with a range of other words with which it is associated such as "machine", "technique" and "artifice" […] is fundamentally about trickery and deception' (2013: 62). In contrast walking, material or mental, 'give[s] shape to the inner generative impulse that is life itself' (2010a: 17).

The participatory aspect of understanding, and the focus on life and living also means that knowledge must be personal (2011: xi) – and Ingold's books are also deeply personal, in the best sense, documenting the same, continuous, unending quest for understanding. It is hostile to any abstract, impersonal generalisation, thus is 'Against space' (2011: 145, title of Chapter 12); similarly hostile to straight lines, following Bergson, Whitehead, and Deleuze (2011: 6–8, 83–4; see also 2007), as 'wisdom runs not in straight lines but along the ways of the donkey' (2013: 141, last page of the book, after a commentary on T.S. Eliot, but equally following the spirit of Cervantes in *Don Quixote*); and of course an unreserved hostility to economic thinking: 'evolutionary ecology is the precise inverse of microeconomics, just as natural selection is the mirror-image of rational choice' (2000: 27). It also implies the extensive use of works of art, indispensable tools of understanding, in contrast to 'data' produced by 'scientific methodology'. Art is not imitating life, rather reveals the fullness of being, the pulsation of the senses, that also inhabit things (2010a: 21). It is in that sense that WB Yeats stated that 'Art is but a vision of reality'.

Art is a kind of knowledge that forces us to revalorise the meaning of 'not knowing' (Ingold 2022). This is because in our world,

> [i]n this world of life, of souls rather than selves, not-knowing is not a form of ignorance but a form of wisdom: the wisdom that lies in turning towards the world rather than turning our backs on it, in opening to replenishment beyond fulfilment, undergoing beyond doing, astonishment beyond surprise, […] truth beyond the facts.
> *(2022, just before evoking Rilke in the last lines of the article)*

Notes

1 I owe this insight to Bjørn Thomassen, according to whom 'It is quite interesting even as a psychological mechanism that a whole discipline comes to understand itself as being the owner of a method. Anthropologists are extremely defensive on this point, even aggressive' (personal communication). See also Ingold (2011: 229).
2 My chapter there makes explicit such connections with Political Anthropology.
3 Bateson was mentioned shortly above; his ideas would merit a chapter on its own, but there is no space here. For further details, see Szakolczai and Thomassen (2019, Ch6); and Szakolczai (2023).
4 The parallels are tight here with Lewis Hyde (see Szakolczai 2022, Ch2).

CONCLUSION

'The truth is—'
'Don't say, the truth,' interposed Tigg, with another grin. 'It's so like humbug.'
Greatly charmed by this, Jonas began again.
'The long and the short of it is—'
'Better,' muttered Tigg. 'Much better!'
Charles Dickens, Martin Chuzzlewit, 429

To the modern mind, whose ideas about everything are punched out in the die presses of technical-scientific calculation, the object of knowledge is part of the method. And method follows what is in fact the utmost corruption and degeneration of the way.
Heidegger (1982: 12)

The heart has its reasons, of which reason knows nothing.
Pascal, Pensées, No.277

The evident 'methodological' consensus of our times is that the social and human sciences must follow the 'natural' sciences in developing, to their image, as rigorous methods as possible, using preferably the statistical analysis of quantitative data. This book, in contrast, argues that this is not only not possible but not even desirable; an example of the current corruption and failure of thinking, evoked in the motto from Heidegger, as the idea of 'imitating' the sciences for a better understanding of our own condition is simply absurd.

This can be demonstrated through the term 'incommensurability', applied by Agnes Horvath for characterising the liminal void – the strange condition of being 'on the limit', thus paradoxically experiencing limitlessness. We as humans can directly experience, and understand, what is commensurable to us in its character and dimensions. Thus, to start with, we can best experience and understand other human beings; and then other living beings, like animals, especially those closest to us, again in character and dimensions: not too small, and not too huge. It is much more difficult to gain knowledge about non-living and especially non-organic objects, but this can be gained, and *was* gained, in most cultures, in so far as this was necessary for living inside that culture. Thus, the idea that we can best understand ourselves, or other societies, by comparing them to inanimate objects is simply preposterous, and nobody before the modern world had such an idea – and for very good reasons.

Phenomena that escaped our understanding, events of prodigious effects, beyond our reach, were attributed to external, incommensurable, invisible powers, divine or demonic. Due to the incommensurability of such forces and powers, knowledge about them had no stable and common reference points, everything depending on the manifold combinations of the human powers of experience, memory and imagination.

It is here that science, modern science especially, but also its direct predecessors, came up with something radically new: a presumed exact knowledge of the incommensurable; or, a knowledge to be gained by means compensating our limitations. Examples include the microscope and the telescope, tools that allow us to see things way smaller or way more distant than are visible by our mere eyes. But a just as clear, and historically even more important, example is metallurgy: by heating them, stones, symbols of stability, can be melted, and the ore gained produces metal objects of great utility. The outcome is a second kind of incommensurability: the incommensurability of science, not the divine or religion.

Both the world of the divine and the world of science are incommensurable for us, in a quasi-identical manner. They are not part of our concrete world; they do not exist in our reality. We cannot see or touch an angel or a spirit, just as we cannot see or touch a microbe or a distant star of the Galaxy. The combination of the two incommensurabilities immediately rendered systematic abuse possible, through magic, the limit case of *both*. It is not accidental that the systematic transformative use of magic can be connected to metallurgy and its theoretisation, alchemy; or that in many cultures smiths became ritual specialists, carrying special powers, in particular the control of rituals of human sacrifice – which in other cultures was a specialty of 'experts' of the sky, helping to predict the cycles of nature, central for agriculture, the two concerns eventually joined in the first great agricultural-metallurgic bureaucratic states of Mesopotamia – a joining of which the word 'siderurgy', with its controversial etymology, is a good indication.

Still, both science and religion have a degree of commensurability with us, otherwise they would escape our life and experience. In the case of universal science, the contact point is Nature, or the world directly outside us. The undertaking of universalistic science started from Nature, this is why it is mistakenly called a 'natural science', and the truths of its propositions show manifold connections with Nature – even if ultimately, as the driving force of applied technology, it only produces products incommensurable with Nature – matter out of place, produced and sold for money, the supposed common measure of everything – and for the same reason without any genuine meaning, as having no inherent distinctness. The contact of incommensurable science with us is purely external, even if this contact has an internal component, as we recognise the beauty of Nature as a most important aspects of our lives.

Religion, or the divine, also has a commensurable aspect on us, and this is internal, the impact on the heart. A central common feature of the three main 'religions of the Book' is not 'monotheism' – as Christianity is Trinitarian – rather that each of them, at their core, consider that God fundamentally has an effect on the heart; and this is also shared, to some extent, by other religions, at least in so far these religions are distant from magic and its major corollary, rituals of sacrifice. We perceive the deepest truths of religion, real and genuine religion, not through some external mediation, and not through the indirect powers of our reason, but directly inside our heart, as an unconfoundable and unsubstitutable experience.

The choice concerning the importance of these two modes of incommensurable is for us to make; but there can be no question what the right choice is.

The twin term of commensurability is substitutability; a term whose most important discussion was offered by Roberto Calasso. The resolution of the problem of incommensurability through the inside has a fundamental implication concerning the nature of the proper measure. In our world, it is increasingly taken for granted, even prescribed, that the unique common measure of everything is money. It is through money that every activity can be translated into everything else, and thus the performance of all activities can be optimised. However, money is not simply a merely external measure, which evidently cannot take into account the value of anything internal, thus the most important things, but even further, can only evaluate things that are substitutable. Anything declared unsubstitutable is outside its horizon, and so money as measure has evident and tight limits.

The scope, and power, of money as measure can be increased by extending its scope of applicability – and indeed this is the way this is being done in our days, where more and more matters are defined as belonging to the economy, or subject to be bought and sold by money. However, the idea has a broader historical applicability, leading to the question of a historical analysis of the main fields working by the principle of substitutability.

This poses a difficult dilemma, as everything in human life, and even Nature, is rather based on the principle of unsubstitutability. This does not mean infinite permanence, as everything that is alive must also die. But anything that dies, or is lost in any way, is not 'substituted' in any meaningful sense, rather a concrete *event*, a death or a loss, is compensated by an *act*: the replacement, if possible, by something similar. Thus, to give a trivial example, if a tree dies, it is not 'substituted' by another tree, rather a different tree will be planted that eventually might become similar to the one that perished.

Substitution is a purely mental act, but of a very specific kind – one is tempted to say, it is a par excellence *perverted* act, as the idea of substituting any object, not to say a living being, God forbid a *human* being, with another one definitely goes against nature, and the indelible concreteness of every existing being. Substitution is an offence to the character and integrity of the being that is substituted – as this means that it is discarded, no longer considered as adequate in its concrete place and function; and is also an offence to the character and integrity of the being that is the substitute, as that being again no longer counts in its very nature, is *just* a substitute for something else.

Historically speaking, and following the hints of Roberto Calasso, there are three main modalities of substitution: sacrifice, exchange, and experimenting. In the case of a ritual of sacrifice, the sacrificial victim, whether human or animal, is perfectly substitutable, as it makes no difference who is sacrificed, though in all other rituals the concreteness of every single actor or performer matters. The situation is the same with exchange, as any object that is exchanged, whether for money or another object, can similarly be substituted with any other similar object – in fact, the very act of exchanging implies substitution.

Rituals of sacrifice and practices of exchange are characteristic of most, though not all human cultures. They were identified by two of the most emblematic, but also most problematic, discourses of modernity, Durkheimian collectivist-socialistic sociology and British liberal individualist political economy, respectively, as the origin of culture and main identifying feature of mankind. Two further practices using substitution, developed much later in history, however, in a similarly mistaken manner were identified with the origins of civilisation. They were best analysed, and named, by Lewis Mumford, as two modalities of the megamachine: the war machine and the labour machine, based on the mechanisation of human activities, where he also traced the origins of technology, based on his intriguing idea according to which technologies dealing with inanimate matter were developed on the basis of technologies that were used to subordinate, mechanise, standardise, and overall enslave human beings. Mumford traced these to Egypt and the Pyramid Age, and then to the rise of the major world Empires – the period which Voegelin calls, in his highly compatible approach, the Ecumenic Age. Weber and Foucault, the two most influential genealogists, also focused on the intensification of such mechanisation in the modern age – Foucault in *Discipline and Punish*, when discussing the emergence of the modern army, based on the mechanisation of the movement of soldiers; and Weber in *The Protestant Ethic*, focusing on the mechanical regulation of work. These developments culminated in the world wars and totalitarian regimes of the 20th century, foreseen only by Nietzsche, and to some extent Kierkegaard, which both revitalised, in various modalities, the sacrificial mechanism (Girard), and instrumentalised the utter mechanisation of exchange, both of goods and words, through the stock market, communication technology, and the public sphere.

The third modality of substitution, scientific experimenting, is complementary to the modern versions combining the previous two. Here again, and in contrast to the reality of Nature, concreteness does not matter: every single object used in a scientific experiment can – and indeed *should* – be exchangeable, or substitutable, with any other 'thing' of the same kind.

With this, however, not simply the difference but radical incompatibility of 'scientific' knowledge and the wisdom gained by human experience becomes evident. In human life, knowledge means the ability and capacity to understand and deal with concrete beings and concrete situations. Here substitutability makes no sense. Modern science, just as the modern economy, two parallel developments, are therefore just that: simply nonsensical.

This implies a clear answer to Bateson's paradigmatic, challenging and not rhetorical question: 'can a scientist be wise'? The answer is a resounding no: *as* a modern scientist, one cannot be wise; modern science is based on the absurd absolutisation of merely external knowledge, a knowledge to be derived not simply from Nature but from the world *as* 'universe', or as something not just outside the concrete person, but outside every concrete link; simply outside life as it is lived on Earth. About our lives, it offers nothing but empty generalities; it contributes to our lives only by substituting single parts with something similar, which occasionally can give us considerable benefits – thus, at the limit, it can substitute a failing liver by a functioning one, though even here having the not negligible ethical problem of where and how to take such a liver –; but it cannot address any significant issue that arises in our concrete lives.

Modern science is incompatible with wisdom, as it excludes, from the start, not only anything that is concrete, thus unsubstitutable, starting rather from the dissolution of everything concrete, the incommensurable liminal void, but even more radically excludes any consideration that concerns the inside of our lives, the moving force of our existence, our heart. That the heart is the centre of human life, experience, and existence, is not a Sunday class sermon. It is the deepest possible and at the same time most effective living truth.

BIBLIOGRAPHY

Agamben, Giorgio (1998) *Homo Sacer*, Stanford: Stanford University Press.
Agamben, Giorgio (2005) 'Aby Warburg e la scienza senza nome', in *La potenza del pensiero*, Milan: Neri Pozza.
Agnew, Jean-Christophe (1986) *Worlds Apart: The market and the theater in Anglo-American thought, 1550–1750*, Cambridge: Cambridge University Press.
Alinei, Mario (2009) *L'origine delle parole*, Rome: Aracne.
Appleby, Joyce (1978) *Economic Thought and Ideology in Seventeenth-Century England*, Princeton, NJ: Princeton University Press.
Argyrou, Vassos (2013) *The Gift of European Thought and the Cost of Living*, Oxford: Berghahn.
Baltrušaitis, Jurgis (1981) *Le Moyen Âge fantastique: antiquités et exotismes dans l'art gothique*, Paris: Flammarion. [1955]
Bandak, Andreas and Daniel M. Knight (2023) *Porous Becomings: Anthropological engagements with Michel Serres*, Durham NC: Duke University Press, forthcoming.
Bartozzi, Marco (1985) *La tirannia degli astri: Aby Warburg e l'astrologia di Palazzo Schifanoia*, Bologna: Cappelli.
Bateson, Gregory (1991) *A Sacred Unity: Further steps to an ecology of the mind*, ed. R.E. Donaldson, New York: HarperCollins.
Bateson, Gregory (2000) *Steps to an Ecology of Mind*, New York: Ballantine. [1972]
Bateson, Gregory (2002) *Mind and Nature: A necessary unity*, Cresshill, NJ: Hampton Press. [1979]
Bateson, Gregory and Mary Catherine Bateson (1988) *Angels Fear: Towards an epistemology of the sacred*, London: Bantam.
Bateson, Mary Catherine (1978) 'Daddy, can a scientist be wise?', in J. Brockman (ed.) *About Bateson*, London: Wildwood House.
Bauman, Zygmunt (1978) *Hermeneutics and Social Science: Approaches to understanding*, London: Hutchinson.
Beer, David (2020) 'Reading Charles Norris Cochrane as a Political Theorist: Canada's neglected contribution', *VoegelinView*, 7 February.

Benozzo, Francesco (2019) 'In memoriam Mario Alinei (1926–2018)', *Dialectologia et Geolinguistica*, https://doi.org/10.1515/dialect-2019-0001.
Berger, Peter L. (1976) *Pyramids of Sacrifice*, New York: Anchor.
Bing, Gertrud (1980) 'Introduzione', to A. Warburg, *La rinascita del paganesimo antico*, Florence: Nuova Italia.
Blumenberg, Hans (1983) *The Legitimacy of Modernity*, Cambridge, MA: MIT Press.
Boland, Tom (2008) 'Critique as imitative rivalry: George Orwell as political anthropologist', *International Political Anthropology* 1, 1: 77–91.
Boland, Tom (2019) 'Permanent liminality in novels: Subversion, theatricality and crisis', *International Political Anthropology* 11, 1: 29–41.
Boland, Tom (2019) *The Spectacle of Critique: From philosophy to cacophony*, London: Routledge.
Boland, Tom and Ray Griffin (2021) *The Reformation of Welfare: The new faith of the labour market*, Bristol: Bristol University Press.
Boyle, Evan (2018) '*It Can't Happen Here*: An investigation of the unreal reality of contemporary American society through the novel form', *International Political Anthropology* 11, 2: 33–45.
Brumbaugh, Robert S. (1982) 'The history and interpretation of the text of Plato's Parmenides', *Philosophy Research Archives* 8, Issue Supplement, 1–56.
Calabrese, Omar (1998) 'Aby Warburg, una mostra che insegna la storia dell'arte', in I. Spinelli and R. Venuti (eds.) *L'Atlante della memoria di Aby Warburg*, Rome: Artemide.
Calasso, Roberto (2019) *Il libro di tutti i libri*, Milan: Adelphi.
Carchia, Gianni (1984) 'Aby Warburg: simbolo e tragedia', *Aut-Aut*, 199–200: 92–108.
Castelli, Enrico (2007) *Il demoniaco nell'arte*, Turin: Bollati Boringhieri.
Chase, Stuart (1956) 'Foreword', in B.L. Whorf (1956) *Language, Thought, and Reality: Selected writings*, ed. by J.B.Carroll, New York: Wiley.
Chevallier, Philippe (2011) *Michel Foucault et le christianisme*, Lyon: ENS Éditions.
Cochrane, Charles N. (2003) *Christianity and Classical Culture*, Indianapolis: Liberty Fund. [1940]
Cooper, Barry and Peter Emberley (1993) *Faith and Political Philosophy: The correspondence between Leo Strauss and Eric Voegelin, 1934–1964*, University Park, PA: Pennsylvania State University Press.
Curry, Patrick (2023) *Art and Enchantment: How wonder works*, London: Routledge.
Dean, Mitchell (2019) 'What Is Economic Theology? A new governmental-political paradigm?', *Theory, Culture & Society* 36, 3: 3–26.
Dupuy, Jean-Pierre (2009) *On the Origins of Cognitive Science: The mechanization of the mind*, Cambridge, MA: MIT Press.
Edmonds, David and John Eidinow (2002) *Wittgenstein's Poker*, London: Faber and Faber.
Elias, Norbert (1978) *What is Sociology?*, London: Hutchinson.
Elias, Norbert (1991) *Norbert Elias par lui-même*, Paris: Fayard.
Ferguson, Harvie (2010) 'Comparing (Sick)-notes: Intercultural reflections on modernity and disease in the writings of Thomas Mann and Jun'ichiro Tanizaki', *International Political Anthropology* 3, 1: 29–53.
Florensky, Pavel (1976) *Le porte regali*, Milan: Adelphi.
Florensky, Pavel (1993) *Ikonostas*, St. Petersburg: Mifril.
Foucault, Michel (1969) *L'archéologie du savoir*, Paris: Gallimard.
Foucault, Michel (1975) *The Birth of the Clinic*. New York: Vintage.
Foucault, Michel (1981a) 'Omnes et Singulatim: Towards a criticism of "political reason" ', in S.M. McMurrin (ed.), *The Tanner Lectures on Human Values*, Salt Lake City: The University of Utah Press.
Foucault, Michel (1981b) 'Questions of Method', *I&C*, 8: 3–14.

Foucault, Michel (1984) 'Nietzsche, Genealogy, History', in P. Rabinow (ed.) *The Foucault Reader*, New York: Pantheon.
Foucault, Michel (1994) *Dits et écrits 1954–1988*, 4 vol-s, Paris: Gallimard.
Foucault, Michel (2002) *The Order of Things*, London: Routledge.
Foucault, Michel (2010) *The Government of Self and Others*, Lectures at the Collège de France, 1982–1983, London: Palgrave.
Foucault, Michel (2011) *The Courage of the Truth*, Lectures at the Collège de France, 1983–1984, London: Palgrave.
Foucault, Michel (2014) *On the Government of the Living*, Lectures at the Collège de France, 1979–1980, London: Palgrave.
Foucault, Michel (2017) *Subjectivity and Truth*, Lectures at the Collège de France, 1980–1981, London: Palgrave.
Frankfort, Henri (1948) *Kingship and the Gods*, Chicago: University of Chicago Press.
Gadamer, Hans-Georg (1985) *Philosophical Apprenticeship*, Cambridge, MA: MIT Press.
Gell, Alfred (1998) *Art and Agency: An anthropological theory*, Oxford: Clarendon Press.
Girard, René (2004) *The Theatre of Envy*, South Bend, IN: St Augustine's Press.
Girard, René(2010) *Battling to the End*, East Lansing: Michigan State University Press.
Goethe, Johann Wolfgang (2015) *Aus meinem Leben: Dichtung und Wahrheit*, accessed at http://web568.rs013.glowfish.de/Joomla/images/ebook/Buch00151-Goethe-auf-www.zenisis.de.pdf.
Gombrich, Ernst H. (1970) *Aby Warburg: An intellectual biography*, London: Warburg Institute.
Gombrich, Ernst H. (1983) *Aby Warburg: Una biografia intellettuale*, Milan: Feltrinelli.
Gros, Frédéric (2011) 'Course Context', in Foucault (2011).
Gros, Frédéric (2014) *A Philosophy of Walking*, London: Verso.
Guillemin, Anna (2008) 'The Style of Linguistics: Aby Warburg, Karl Vossler, and Herman Osthoff', *Journal of the History of Ideas* 69, 4: 605–626.
Hadot, Pierre (2004) *Le voile d'Isis: Essai sur l'histoire de l'idée de nature*, Paris: Gallimard.
Hadot, Pierre (2008) *N'oublie pas de vivre: Goethe et la tradition des exercices spirituels*, Paris: Albin Michel.
Heidegger, Martin (1977) *Basic Writings*, New York: Harper & Row.
Heidegger, Martin (1982) *On the Way to Language*, New York: Harper & Row.
Heidegger, Martin (1985) *Unterwegs zur Sprache*, Frankfurt: Klostermann.
Heidegger, Martin (2017) *Ponderings XII–XV: Black notebooks, 1939–1941*, Bloomington, IN: Indiana University Press.
Heidegger, Martin and Eugen Fink (1992) *Dialogo intorno a Eraclito*, Milan: Coliseum.
Hennis, Wilhelm (1988) *Max Weber: Essays in reconstruction*, London: Allen & Unwin.
Henry, Michel (2001) *La barbarie*, Paris: PUF.
Henry, Michel (2002) *Paroles du Christ*, Paris: Seuil.
Hoppen, Franziska (2021) *Liminality and the Philosophy of Presence: A new direction in political theory*, London: Routledge.
Horujy, Sergey S. (2015) *Practices of the Self and Spiritual Practices: Michel Foucault and the Eastern Christian discourse*, Grand Rapids, MI: Eerdmans.
Horvath, Agnes (2013) *Modernism and Charisma*, London: Palgrave.
Horvath, Agnes(2021) *Political Alchemy: Technology unbounded*, London: Routledge.
Horvath, Agnes, Marius Benţa and Joan Davison (eds.) (2019) *Walling, Boundaries and Liminality: A political anthropology of transformations*, London: Routledge.
Horvath, Agnes and Arpad Szakolczai (2018a) *Walking into the Void: A historical sociology and political anthropology of walking*, London: Routledge.

Horvath, Agnes and Arpad Szakolczai (2018b) 'Political Anthropology', in S. Turner and W. Outhwaite (eds.) *The SAGE Handbook of Political Sociology*, London: SAGE.

Horvath, Agnes and Arpad Szakolczai (2020) *The Political Sociology and Anthropology of Evil: Tricksterology*, London: Routledge.

Horvath, Agnes, Arpad Szakolczai and Manussos Marangudakis (eds.) (2020) *Modern Leaders: In between charisma and trickery*, London: Routledge.

Horvath, Agnes and Bjørn Thomassen (2008) 'Mimetic Errors in Liminal Schismogenesis: On the Political Anthropology of the Trickster', *International Political Anthropology* 1, 1: 3–24.

Horvath, Agnes, Bjørn Thomassen and Harald Wydra (eds.) (2015) *Breaking Boundaries: Varieties of liminality*, Oxford: Berghahn.

Hughes, Ted (1992) *Shakespeare and the Goddess of Complete Being*, London: Faber.

Huxley, Aldous (1971) *The Devils of Loudun*, London: Penguin. [1952]

Huxley, Aldous (1982) *Grey Eminence: A study in religion and politics*, Reading: Triad/Granada. [1944]

Huxley, Aldous (2005) *Ape and Essence*, London: Vintage. [1948]

Ingold, Tim (2000) *The Perception of the Environment: Essays on livelihood, dwelling and skill*, London: Routledge.

Ingold, Tim (2004) 'Culture on the ground: The world perceived through the feet', *Journal of Material Culture* 9, 315–340.

Ingold, Tim (2007) *Lines: A brief history*, London: Routledge.

Ingold, Tim (2010a) 'Footprints through the weather-world: walking, breathing, knowing'. *JRAI* 16, S121–139.

Ingold, Tim (2010b) 'Ways of mind-walking: reading, writing, painting'. *Visual Studies* 25, 15–23.

Ingold, Tim (2011) *Being Alive: Essays on movement, knowledge and description*, London: Routledge.

Ingold, Tim (2013) *Making: Anthropology, archaeology, art and architecture*, London: Routledge.

Ingold, Tim (2017) *Anthropology and/as Education*, London: Routledge.

Ingold, Tim (2022) 'On not knowing and paying attention: How to walk in a possible world', *Irish Journal of Sociology* 30, OnlineFirst.

Johnson, Christopher D. (2012) *Memory, Metaphor, and Aby Warburg's Atlas of Images*, Ithaca, NY: Cornell University Press.

Koselleck, Reinhart (1985) ' "Space of Experience" and "Horizon of Expectation": Two historical categories', in *Futures Past: On the semantics of historical time*, Cambridge, MA: MIT Press.

Koselleck, Reinhart (1988) *Critique and Crisis: Enlightenment and the pathogenesis of modern society*, Oxford: Berg.

Linden, Stanton J. (1974) 'Francis Bacon and alchemy: The reformation of Vulcan', *Journal of the History of Ideas* 35, 4: 547–560.

Lyons, William (1986) *The Disappearance of Introspection*, Cambridge, MA: MIT Press.

Makkreel, Rudolf A. (1975) *Dilthey: Philosopher of the human studies*, Princeton, NJ: Princeton University Press.

Mauss, Marcel (2002) *The Gift*, London: Routledge. [1924]

McMylor, Peter (2018) 'Chesterton and Dickens: The theatricalised "drama" of modernity explored', *International Political Anthropology* 11, 2: 23–32.

Nietzsche, Friedrich (1967) *On the Genealogy of Morals*, New York: Vintage.

O'Connor, Paul (2018) *Home: The foundations of belonging*, London: Routledge.

O'Connor, Paul (2022) 'The Terror of Home: The haunted house formula in contemporary culture', *International Political Anthropology* 15, 1: 35–50.

Mennell, Stephen (1992) *Norbert Elias: An introduction*, Oxford: Blackwell.

Bibliography

Montagni, Federica (2019) 'The Fool's Subversion: Technique of estrangement in Bruegel's work', in A. Horvath, C.F. Roman and G. Germain (eds.) (2019) *Divinization and Technology: The political anthropology of subversion*, London: Routledge.

Parotto, Giuliana (2016) *Il corpo del leader: Corpo e politica nella società post-secolare*, Genoa: Il Melangolo.

Pizzorno, Alessandro (1986) 'Some Other Kinds of Otherness: A critique of "rational choice" theories', in A. Foxley, M.S. McPherson and G. O'Donnell (eds.) *Development, Democracy and the Art of Trespassing: Essays in honor of Albert O. Hirschman*, Notre Dame: University of Notre Dame Press.

Pizzorno, Alessandro (1987) 'Politics unbound', in C.S. Maier (ed.) *Changing Boundaries of the Political*, Cambridge: Cambridge University Press.

Pizzorno, Alessandro (1991) 'On the individualistic theory of social order', in P. Bourdieu and J.S. Coleman (eds.) *Social Theory for a Changing Society*, Boulder: Westview Press.

Pizzorno, Alessandro (1994) 'Note sull'uso della nozione di sé nell'indagine sociale', manuscript paper.

Pizzorno, Alessandro (2000) 'Risposte e proposte', in D. Della Porta, M. Greco and A. Szakolczai (eds.) *Identità, riconoscimento e scambio: Saggi in onore di Alessandro Pizzorno*, Bari: Laterza.

Pizzorno, Alessandro (2007a) *Il velo della diversità: Studi su razionalità e riconoscimento*, Milan: Feltrinelli.

Pizzorno, Alessandro (2007b) 'Rational choice', in S.P. Turner and M.W. Risjord (eds.) *Handbook of the Philosophy of Science: Philosophy of anthropology and sociology*, N.Y.: Elsevier.

Pizzorno, Alessandro (2008) 'Rationality and recognition', in D. della Porta and M. Keating (eds.) *Approaches and Methodologies in the Social Sciences: A pluralist perspective*, Cambridge: Cambridge University Press.

Pizzorno, Alessandro (2010) 'The Mask: An essay', *International Political Anthropology* 3, 1: 5–28. [1960]

Raulff, Ulrich (1998) 'Postfazione' to Aby Warburg, *Il rituale del serpente*, Milan: Adelphi.

Rickman, Hans Peter (ed.) (1976) *Dilthey: Selected writings*, Cambridge: Cambridge Ward Method Centre.

Ringer, Fritz (1969) *The Decline of the German Mandarins*, Cambridge, MA: Harvard University Press.

Rossi, Paolo (2009) *Francis Bacon: From magic to science*, London: Routledge. [1968]

Sapir, Edward (1949) 'Language', in *Culture, Language and Personality: Selected essays*, ed. by D.G. Mandelbaum, Berkeley: University of California Press.

Saussure, Ferdinand de (2011) *Course in General Linguistics*, New York: Columbia University Press.

Saxl, Fritz (1998) '*L'Atlante Mnemosine di* Warburg', in I. Spinelli and R. Venuti (eds.) *L'Atlante della memoria di Aby Warburg*, Rome: Artemide.

Schleiermacher, Friedrich (2007) *Hermeneutics and Criticism: And Other Writings*, Cambridge: Cambridge University Press.

Schwarzkopf, Stefan (2020) 'An Introduction to Economic Theology', in S. Schwarzkopf (ed.), *Routledge Handbook of Economic Theology*, London: Routledge.

Scotti Muth, Nicoletta (2022) 'Eric Voegelin's Reading of Saint Augustine: Exploring the symbolism of history and politics', in B. Torres Morales and J. Monserrat (eds.) *Eric Voegelin's Political Readings*, London: Routledge.

Serres, Michel (1982) *Hermes: Science, literature, philosophy*, Baltimore: John Hopkins University Press.

Serres, Michel (1992) *Le contrat naturel*, Paris: Flammarion.

Serres, Michel (2014) *Le parasite*, Paris: Fayard. [1980]

Seznec, Jean (1972) *The Survival of the Pagan Gods: The mythological tradition and its place in Renaissance humanism and art*, Princeton: Princeton University Press.
Spinelli, Italo and Roberto Venuti (eds.) (1998) *L'Atlante della memoria di Aby Warburg*, Rome: Artemide.
Steinberg, Michael P. (1995) 'Aby Warburg's Kreuzlingen Lecture: A reading', in A. Warburg, *Images from the Region of the Pueblo Indians of North America*, Ithaca, NY: Cornell University Press.
Stenner, Paul and Monica Greco (2018) 'On *The Magic Mountain*: The novel as liminal affective technology', *International Political Anthropology* 11, 1: 43–60.
Szakolczai, Arpad (1990) *A fejlődés megkérdőjelezése* (Questioning development), Budapest: Akadémiai.
Szakolczai, Arpad (1998) *Max Weber and Michel Foucault: Parallel life-works*, London: Routledge.
Szakolczai, Arpad (2000a) *Reflexive Historical Sociology*, London: Routledge.
Szakolczai, Arpad (2000b) 'Norbert Elias and Franz Borkenau: Intertwined life-works', *Theory, Culture and Society* 17(2): 45–69.
Szakolczai, Arpad (2003) *The Genesis of Modernity*, London: Routledge.
Szakolczai, Arpad (2004) 'Experiential Sociology', *Theoria* 51, 59–87.
Szakolczai, Arpad (2013) 'Genealogy', entry in B. Kaldis (ed.) *Encyclopedia of Philosophy and the Social Sciences*, London: SAGE.
Szakolczai, Arpad (2015) 'The Theatricalisation of the Social: Problematising the public sphere', *Cultural Sociology* 9, 2: 220–239.
Szakolczai, Arpad (2016) *Novels and the Sociology of the Contemporary*, London: Routledge.
Szakolczai, Arpad (2017) *Permanent Liminality and Modernity: Analysing the sacrificial carnival through novels*, London: Routledge.
Szakolczai, Arpad (2021) 'Roberto Calasso, Il libro di tutti i libri, a review essay', *International Political Anthropology* 13, 2: 177–197.
Szakolczai, Arpad (2022) *Post Truth Society: A political anthropology of trickster logic*, London: Routledge.
Szakolczai, Arpad (2023) 'Michel Serres and Gregory Bateson: Implicit dialogue about a recognitive epistemology of Nature', in A. Bandak and D.M. Knight, *Porous Becomings: Anthropological engagements with Michel Serres*, Durham, NC: Duke University Press, forthcoming.
Szakolczai, Arpad and Bjørn Thomassen (2019) *From Anthropology to Social Theory: Rethinking the social sciences*, Cambridge: Cambridge University Press.
Thomassen, Bjørn (2014) *Liminality and the Modern: Living through the in-between*. Farnham Surrey: Ashgate.
Turnbull, Colin (1990) 'Liminality: A synthesis of subjective and objective experience', in R. Schechner and W. Appel (eds.) *By Means of Performance: Intercultural studies of theatre and ritual*, Cambridge: Cambridge University Press.
Turner, Victor (1985) 'Experience and Performance: Towards a new processual anthropology', in E. Turner (ed.) *On the Edge of the Bush*, Tucson, Arizona: University of Arizona Press.
Turner, Victor (1992) *Blazing the Trail: Waymarks in the exploration of symbols*, Tucson, Arizona: University of Arizona Press.
Veyne, Paul (1983) *Les Grecs ont-ils cru à leurs myths?*, Paris: Seuil.
Voegelin, Eric (1952) *The New Science of Politics*, Chicago: University of Chicago Press.
Voegelin, Eric (1974) *The Ecumenic Age*, vol.4 of Order and History, Baton Rouge: Louisiana State University Press.
Voegelin, Eric (1990) 'Wisdom and the Magic of the Extreme: A meditation', in E. Sandoz (ed.) *Published Essays, 1966–1985*, Baton Rouge: Louisiana State University Press.

Voegelin, Eric (1998) *The History of Political Ideas*, Vol. 6, Columbia, MO: University of Missouri Press.
Voegelin, Eric (2000a) *Modernity Without Restraint*, Colombia, MO: University of Missouri Press.
Voegelin, Eric (2000b) *Published Essays, 1953–1965*, Colombia, MO: University of Missouri Press.
Wade, Terence (1996) *Russian Etymological Dictionary*, London: Bristol Classical Press.
Warburg, Aby (1980) *La rinascita del paganesimo antico*, Florence: Nuova Italia.
Warburg, Aby (1998) *Il rituale del serpente*, Milan: Adelphi.
Warburg, Aby (1999) *The Renewal of Pagan Antiquity*, Los Angeles: Getty Research Institute.
Warburg, Aby (2016) 'Mnemosyne: Einleitung. Introduzione al Bilderatlas (1929)', *Engramma* No.138, online, http://www.engramma.it/eOS/index.php?id_articolo=2991, consulted 7 March 2022.
Warnke, Martin (1998) 'Aby Warburg (1866–1929)', in I. Spinelli and R. Venuti (eds) *L'Atlante della memoria di Aby Warburg*, Rome: Artemide.
Weber, Max (1976) *The Protestant Ethic and the Spirit of Capitalism*, London: Allen & Unwin.
Weigel, Sigrid (2020) 'The Epistemic Advantage of Self-Analysis for Cultural-Historical Insights: The variants of Warburg's manuscripts on his Indian Journey', *Modos* 4, 3: 387–404.
Whorf, Benjamin L. (1956) *Language, Thought, and Reality: Selected writings*, ed. by J.B. Carroll, New York: Wiley.
Wind, Edgar (1963) *Art and Anarchy*, London: Faber.
Wind, Edgar (1967) *Pagan Mysteries in the Renaissance*, Harmondsworth: Penguin.
Wind, Edgar (1983) *The Eloquence of Symbols: Studies in humanist art*, ed. by J. Anderson, Oxford: Oxford University Press.
Wood, Christopher S. (2014) 'Aby Warburg, Homo victor', *Journal of Art Historiography*, 11: 1–24.
Wydra, Harald (2015) *Politics and the Sacred*, Cambridge: Cambridge University Press.
Wydra, Harald and Bjørn Thomassen (eds.) (2018) *Handbook of Political Anthropology*, Cheltenham: Edward Elgar.
Yates, Frances (1964) *Giordano Bruno and the Hermetic Tradition*, Chicago: University of Chicago Press.
Yates, Frances (1969) *Theatre of the World*, Chicago: University of Chicago Press.
Yates, Frances (1975a) *The Rosicrucian Enlightenment*, London: Paladine Books. [1972]
Yates, Frances (1975b) *Astraea: The imperial theme in the Sixteenth Century*, London: Routledge.
Yates, Frances (1975c) *Shakespeare's Last Plays*, London: Routledge.
Yates, Frances (1979) *The Occult Philosophy in the Elizabethan Age*, London: Routledge.
Yates, Frances (1992) *The Art of Memory*, London: Routledge. [1966]

NAME INDEX

Aeschylus 84, 125
Agamben, Giorgio 134, 135, 138, 141, 143, 148, 201
Agnew, Jean-Christophe 61, 82
Alexander VI (Pope) 73
Alinei, Mario 100, 104–6, 108, 110, 114, 140
Ambrose, St 172
Anaximander 201, 203
Apollodoros 88
Appleby, Joyce 61, 75–81, 99, 100
Aquinas, St Thomas 87
Archytas 124
Argyropoulos, John 64
Argyrou, Vassos 33, 58
Aristotle xii, 32, 42, 46, 54, 63, 64, 65, 66, 95, 115, 167, 173
Assmann, Jan 127
Athanasius, St 172
Auden, W.H. 48, 165
Augustine, St 69, 155, 165–81, 182, 185, 192
Augustus 180

Bacon, Francis 29, 30, 38–51, 55, 56, 58–9, 60, 66, 67, 72, 82, 83, 89, 92, 99, 100, 102, 103, 114, 116, 126, 155, 202
Baillet, Adrien 126
Bakhtin, Mikhail 50, 127, 159
Baltrušaitis, Jurgis 117
Barthes, Roland 149
Bateson, Gregory 32, 59, 77, 82, 148, 160, 198–9, 201, 202, 204, 209

Bauman, Zygmunt 150, 153
Benjamin, Walter 141
Bennett, Jonathan 53, 54, 58, 59
Bergson, Henri 203
Bessarion 82
Bing, Gertrud 134, 137, 140, 144
Binswanger, Ludwig 134, 148, 183
Binswanger, Otto 134
Boccalini, Traiano 82
Böhme, Jakob 132
Boland, Tom 58, 160, 201
Bologna, Corrado 117
Bonaventure, St 47, 62, 155
Borgia family 73
Borkenau, Franz xii, 140, 148, 153
Bosch, Hieronymus 118, 120, 121, 122
Botticelli, Sandro 138, 139, 140, 142
Bourdieu, Pierre 7, 19, 186, 195
Braudel, Fernand 80
Broch, Hermann 147, 159, 160
Brown, Peter 189
Brueghel, Pieter the Elder 118, 121, 122
Bruno, Giordano 63, 66, 67, 68, 71
Bulgakov, Mikhail 132, 159
Burckhardt, Jacob 143, 145

Caesar, Julius 55
Calasso, Roberto 147, 159, 160, 173, 207, 208
Callot, Jacques 61
Camillo, Giulio 42, 43, 53, 64, 65, 66, 141
Camus, Albert 159, 160
Cantor, George 127

218   Name Index

Cassirer, Ernst 134, 145, 148
Castelli, Enrico 117–23, 129, 146, 153, 186
Cervantes, Miguel de 203
Cézanne, Paul 147
Charlemagne 69
Chase, Stuart 111
Chevallier, Philippe 185
Citati, Pietro 159, 160
Clement VIII (Pope) 71
Cochrane, Charles N. 165–80
Comte, Auguste xiii, 52, 72
Constantine the Great 69, 70, 165, 166
Cusanus 82

Darwin, Charles 202
Dee, John 67–70 *passim*
Deleuze, Gilles 202, 203
Descartes, René 29, 51–8, 59, 66–8, 82–3, 114–15, 126, 155, 176
Dickens, Charles xi, 3, 8, 17, 27, 31, 37, 39, 60, 75, 83, 99, 123, 149, 157, 158, 159, 161, 175, 181, 192, 194, 196, 205
Dilthey, Wilhelm 29, 107, 140, 147, 151, 152–3, 156, 157, 159
Donne, John 75, 82, 161
Dostoevsky, Fyodor 131, 192
Douglas, Mary 153
Dreyfus, Hubert 182
Dryden, John 194
Dumézil, Georges 135, 153, 155, 189, 197
Dupuy, Jean-Pierre 37, 38, 147
Dürer, Alfred 136–7
Durkheim, Émile xiii, 11, 18–9, 20, 58, 115, 135, 186, 195, 197, 208

Earl of Leicester 73
Eckhart, Meister 191
Eisenstadt, Shmuel 153
Elias, Norbert xii, 26, 32, 56, 59, 93, 140, 148, 153, 179
Eliot, T.S. 203
Elizabeth I 69, 70, 73, 74, 82
Engels, Friedrich 162
Erasmus, Desiderius 42
Euclid 67
Euripides 140
Evans, Arthur 49

Fichte, Johann Gottlieb 156
Ficino, Marsilio 64, 71, 138, 139
Flaubert, Gustave 117
Florensky, Pavel 115, 127–33, 143, 147, 159, 186
Fludd, Robert 64, 74

Foucault, Michel 7, 33, 38, 43, 56, 61, 81, 82, 83, 93, 94, 100, 106, 112–4, 115, 1178, 123, 146, 147, 148, 149, 153, 154, 155, 159, 162–4, 175, 179, 180, 181–5, 188, 189, 190, 192, 193, 201, 208
Foxe, John 70
Frankfort, Henri 82, 153
Franklin, Benjamin 54
Frazer, James George 135
Freud, Sigmund 87, 128, 140, 150, 172, 181
Friedman, Milton 93, 174
Fustel de Coulanges, Numa Denis 79
Füstös, László 84

Gadamer, Hans-Georg 153
Garin, Eugenio 126
Gell, Alfred 128
Gennep, Arnold van 19, 28, 195, 198
George, Stefan 108, 109
Ghirlandaio, Domenico 136
Gibbon, Edward 165, 177
Gibson, James 202
Giotto 133
Girard, René 37, 38, 81, 82, 150, 153, 159, 197, 208
Goethe, Johann W. 30, 88, 89, 107, 123, 136–7, 147, 175
Goffman, Erving 153
Gombrich, Ernst 134, 135, 147
Gouhier, Henri 186
Gros, Frédéric 16, 185, 193

Habermas, Jürgen 7, 73, 103, 116, 175, 186
Hadot, Pierre 122–7, 136, 137, 147, 148, 153, 155, 186
Hamvas, Béla 153, 159, 160
Hankiss, Elemér 84, 85
Hegel, Georg W.F. xiii, 18, 19, 20, 24, 39, 42, 74, 103, 106, 114, 156, 167, 171, 193, 199
Heidegger, Martin 10, 12, 29, 38, 42, 43, 83, 92, 99, 100, 104, 105, 106–12, 114, 115, 116, 117, 140, 146, 148, 150, 159, 182, 186, 190, 205
Hennis, Wilhelm 16, 153
Henry, Michel 153, 180–1, 185–92
Heraclitus 115, 123, 125–6
Hermogenes 64, 66
Hobbes, Thomas 24, 26
Hölderlin, Friedrich 18, 146, 152
Horujy, Sergey 147
Horváth, Ágnes xii, xiv, 16, 43, 45, 56, 61, 65, 141, 147, 156, 197, 205
Hubert, Henri 19, 145, 182
Huizinga, Johan 159

Name Index

Humboldt, Alexander von 123
Humboldt, Wilhelm von 111
Husserl, Edmund 132, 147, 193, 199
Huxley, Aldous 17, 58–9, 146, 159, 162
Hyde, Lewis 204
Hyppolite, Jean 186

Ingold, Tim 15, 16, 59, 147, 201–4
Innis, Harald 165

Jakobson, Roman 105
Jesus Christ 11, 33, 44, 169, 170, 171, 177, 179, 185–92
John, St 11, 123, 166, 191–2
József, Attila 8, 15, 84, 95

Kafka, Franz 117, 147, 160
Kant, Immanuel 7, 13, 18, 25, 29, 33, 43, 59, 82, 106, 107, 114, 116, 156, 176, 184,
Kerényi, Károly 135, 148, 153, 197
Kierkegaard, Søren xiii, 95, 119, 123, 159, 172, 208
Koselleck, Reinhart xii, 21, 66, 68, 72, 115, 153, 164
Kuhn, Thomas 54
Kundera, Milan 162

Laffemas, Barthélemy de 81
Leibniz, Gottfried Wilhelm von 66, 68
Leonardo da Vinci 64, 135, 138, 147
Leone Ebreo 74
Lévi-Strauss, Claude 19, 186, 195, 202
Lévy-Bruhl, Lucien 19, 32, 135, 145, 194
Lipsius, Justus 55
Locke, John 29, 33
Lőrincz, József xii
Louis XVI 193
Löwith, Karl 153
Lukacs, Georg 186
Luke, St. 131, 147
Lull, Ramon 65–8 *passim*
Luther, Martin 42, 132, 137

Machiavelli, Niccolò 136
Maine de Biran 193
Malinowski, Bronisław 198
Mao Zedong 55
Mark, St 188
Marlowe, Christopher 68
Marx, Karl xiii, 81, 84, 87, 94, 95, 150, 162, 165, 181, 195, 196, 202, 203
Matthew, St 188
Mauss, Marcel 12, 19, 21, 79, 100, 101, 135, 145, 201

Medici, Cosimo 64
Melanchton, Philip 66
Melville, Herman 196
Merleau-Ponty, Maurice 202
Mersenne, Marin 66, 67, 126
Michelangelo, Buonarotti 117
Milton, John xi, 3, 73, 74, 161
Montchrétien, Antoine de 81
Mun, Thomas 76, 77, 80

Napoleon, Bonaparte xiii, 127
Newton, Isaac 29, 61, 62, 77, 102, 124, 170, 171
Nietzsche, Friedrich xii, 3, 26, 32, 38, 41, 61, 83, 95, 107, 114, 123, 134, 139, 143, 144, 145, 149, 154, 159, 162–4, 175, 177, 178, 179, 182, 189, 208
Nostradamus 193

O'Connor, Paul 26, 160
Ogden, Charles K. 104
Ong, Walter 66
Ortega y Gasset, José 92, 159
Orwell, George 49
Osthoff, Hermann 135–6

Panofsky, Erwin 134
Parmenides 11
Pascal, Blaise 31, 92, 155, 193, 205
Pasquino, Pasquale 184
Patočka, Jan 155, 201
Paul, St 166
Pearson, Karl 91
Perugino, Pietro 147
Petrarch 64
Philolaus 124
Pico della Mirandola, Giovanni 73, 74–5, 82
Pizzorno, Alessandro 20–5, 26, 30, 108, 153, 184, 199
Plato 4, 23, 32, 42, 51, 54, 56, 64–5, 74, 79, 88, 93, 102–3, 104, 106, 114, 115, 117, 124, 127, 130, 136, 139, 143, 144, 155, 159, 167, 172, 174, 184, 185, 189, 198, 201
Plautus 126
Plethon, Gemistos 64, 70, 82
Plutarch 127
Pocock, John 165, 177, 201
Poliziano, Angelo 138
Pollaiuolo brothers 140
Popper, Karl 92–6, 99, 134, 179
Procacci, Giovanna 184
Proclus 127

Rabinow, Paul 182, 184
Radcliffe-Brown, Alfred 198

Radin, Paul 196, 198
Ramus, Petrus 66, 67
Raphael 130, 147
Ricardo, David 80
Richards, Ivor A. 104
Ricoeur, Paul 186
Rilke, Rainer Maria 120, 203
Rossi, Paolo 58, 66
Rousseau, Jean-Jacques 24, 25, 41
Rublev, Andrei 131
Russell, Bertrand 96
Ruysbroeck, Jan 118, 119

Saint-Simon, Henri de xiii, 72, 82
Sapir, Edward 100–3, 106, 108, 110, 111, 135
Sartre, Jean-Paul 174, 186, 193
Saussure, Ferdinand de 104, 105, 115
Schelling, Friedrich W.J. 18
Schleiermacher, Friedrich 18, 29, 33, 114, 139
Schliemann, Heinrich 49
Schongauer, Martin 117, 119
Serres, Michel 32, 43, 55, 59, 82, 94, 95, 122, 181, 193, 201
Serres, Olivier de 81
Seznec, Jean 135, 138, 139, 144
Shakespeare, William 68, 70, 81, 82, 133, 158, 175
Sidney, Philip 73
Simon, Herbert 147
Simonides 64
Smith, Adam 24–5, 43, 206
Socrates 155, 184, 189
Spenser, Edmund 73, 74
Spinoza, Baruch 127, 186
Strauss, Leo 93

Tarde, Gabriel 19, 197
Tarkovsky, Andrei 147
Tasso, Torquato 129
Tertullian 175
Thode, Henri 67, 133–4
Thomassen, Bjørn xii, xiv, 26, 204

Tiberius 180
Tocqueville, Alexis de xiii
Tolkien, John R.R. 15, 159
Tolstoy, Lev 192
Toulmin, Stephen 38, 61, 82, 94, 95
Toynbee, Arnold 196
Tribe, Keith 16
Turnbull, Colin 32, 153, 194, 199–200
Turner, Victor 11, 29, 153, 193, 195
Turquet de Mayerne, Louis 81

Unamuno, Miguel de 159

Verrocchio, Andrea del 138, 147
Veyne, Paul 165, 168
Virgin Mary 131, 175, 193
Vitruvius 66
Voegelin, Eric xii, 9, 38, 61, 81, 82, 84, 93, 114, 153, 155, 159, 164, 165, 166, 167, 180, 192, 201, 208
Voltaire 167

Wahl, Jean 186
Warburg, Aby 64, 133–48, 201
Weber, Max xii, 5–6, 16, 21, 73–4, 81, 85, 86, 87, 95, 134, 150, 151, 153, 154, 155, 157, 163, 164, 179, 181, 184–5, 187, 192, 197, 208
Whimster, Sam 16
Whitehead, Lawrence 203
Whorf, Benjamin Lee 101, 103, 111, 114, 115, 145
Wiener, Norbert 127
Winckelmann, Johannes 143
Wind, Edgar 12, 64, 74–5, 135, 137–44 *passim*, 147, 153
Wittgenstein, Ludwig 38, 93, 94–5, 179
Wright brothers 145
Wydra, Harald xii, xiv, 95

Yates, Frances 38, 42, 61–74, 82, 95, 121, 126, 135, 141, 144, 153, 202
Yeats, W.B. 203

SUBJECT INDEX

absolute 101, 142, 209; certainty 29, 57, 171; life 190–1; start 29, 30
abstraction 15, 65, 87, 133, 202, 203
absurdity xiii, 5, 15, 27, 37, 38, 53, 73, 81, 84, 92, 95, 164, 167, 168, 173, 175, 205, 209
abyss 29, 61
academia 32, 200; *see also* academic(s)
academic(s): classicism 144; disciplines xii, 8, 151; enclaves 9; integrity 15; jetsetter 4; life 8–9, 14, 19, 22, 32, 37–8, 59; power 14, 19–20, 135 (*see also* university: politics); staff 8; world 87, 156; young 154
activist, utopian (Voegelin) 114, 171
actor(s) 21–5, 53, 118, 120, 169, 208
Advertisements from Parnassus (Boccalini) 82
advertising 37, 116; *see also* marketing
age: 'classical' (Foucault) 7, 112; Ecumenic (Voegelin) 159, 201, 208; Elizabethan 82; Golden 61, 69, 73, 118, 168; Present 133; Pyramid (Mumford) 208; Stuart 82
'agency of art' (Gell) 128
Aglaia 175
aksara (indestructible) 102–3
alchemy 10, 15, 30, 39, 47, 56, 57, 58, 59, 62–5 *passim*, 74, 115, 118, 120,121, 122, 125, 171, 206
Alexandria 81, 137, 141, 147
algorithms 5, 10, 11, 14; computer 10; *see also* scenario
allegorisation 138, 147
ambivalence 144, 162, 181, 184

Amsterdam 81, 147
'Anatomy of the World' (Donne) 161; *see also* 'Anniversary'
angel(s) 62, 69, 206
anguish *see* anxiety
'Anniversary' (Donne) 82; *see also* 'Anatomy of the World'
Antiquity 112, 115, 125, 126, 138, 141, 144, 167, 184; classical 49, 63, 64, 124, 139; decadent 139; late 139, 144, 147, 182
Antwerp 81, 118, 121, 147
anxiety 197, 200
Ape and Essence (Huxley) 58
apeiron 201; *see also* liminality
apocalyptic 121, 126, 134, 137, 164, 168; *see also* eschatological
Apollo 124
Appropriation (Heidegger) 99, 110–1
arbitrariness 21, 104–5, 113
archaeology 9, 49–50, 104, 106, 115, 159, 202; comparative xii; etymological 106
archetype(s) 91, 117, 131, 133, 150
arithmetic *see* mathematics
arrogance 30–1, 83, 94, 100, 127, 129, 156, 163, 175
art 63–5, 117–18, 131–2, 136, 138–9, 141, 143, 157–8, 202–3; contemporary rock 128; hermeneutics of 117; imitating 147; mechanical 42, 45; prehistoric 145; universal 67; visual 65, 136, 139, 198; works of 141, 157, 160, 203
Artemis 123–5; *see also* Isis

222 Subject Index

ascetic(ism) 185; ideal 164; medieval monastic 164
Asclepius 144, 148, 189
Asia(n) 74, 139, 186; imagery 119; techniques 96
Asia Minor 140
associations (disciplinary, professional) 33, 92, 150, 155
Astraea (Yates) 69, 73
astral 65, 131, 144
astrology 65, 137, 144
astronomy 8, 69
Atapuerca (cave) 41
atheism 83, 84, 95
Athens 137
attuning 109
audience 22–3, 73, 110, 187, 190
Aufhebung (Hegel) 18
authentication *see* truth
authenticity 104, 124, 141, 185
author(s) 6, 15, 149–56
authority 31, 44, 64, 76, 81, 89
autobiography 53, 146, 147; *see also* autobiographical
automatism 174
Aztecs 144

Babylon 81, 147
beauty 101, 133, 141, 175; unspeakable 133
Being Alive (Ingold) 202
belongingness 18, 32, 109, 110; *see also* participation
'best practice' (HR) 4, 151
betraying 15, 78–9, 95, 122
Beyond Good and Evil (Nietzsche) 149
Bible 11, 44, 70, 74, 119, 130, 165; criticism 114; *see also* Gospel(s), New Testament, Old Testament
biopolitics 183, 201
Birth of the Clinic (Foucault) 146
Birth of Tragedy, The (Nietzsche) 61, 163
Bleak House (Dickens) 8, 123, 157
Book of Genesis 127, 142, 192
Book of Martyrs (Foxe) 70
Book of Revelation 123
border(s) 66, 71, 95, 127, 128
boredom 6, 150, 156
boundaries 30, 82, 83, 130
bracketing (Husserl) 199
brainwashing 92, 152
bringing forth (Heidegger) 115
Buddhism 117
bureaucracy 92, 155, 156, 206
Burgundy 70

Byzantium 18, 43, 65, 70, 138, 177; *see also* Empire: Byzantine

Cabala 62, 63, 65, 67, 73–4; Christian 69, 73–4
calculus 67; infinitesimal 68
Cambridge 44, 94, 198, 199
capitalism 6, 74, 87, 164
Cappadocia 172
care: loving 47; of the self/soul 155, 182, 184; for truth 96, 185
carnival 121
Cartesian(ism): mathematics 55; method 54, 67; rationalism 19, 54–5
Çatalhöyük 48
Catholicism 70, 117
cave(s) 41, 45; art 101, 128; -dwellers 41; idols of (Bacon) 41, 45, 48; walls 128; *see also* individual caves
cenno (hint) (Castelli) 120, 122; *see also* hint(s)
chaos 30, 50, 61, 82, 105, 114, 115, 145; original 61
charis xii, 115, 123; logic 100, 173
charisma 184, 197
charlatans 94, 118, 121; *see also* trickster
Chauvet (cave) 128
child(ren) 8, 31, 45, 51, 103, 133, 151, 195, 197–8, 203
childhood 188, 198; early 103
choice: free 32, 174; rational 9, 22–4, 38, 147, 203
Christianity xiii, 63, 64, 70, 71, 115, 138, 147, 166–81, 184, 185, 187, 189, 199, 207; Augustinian 175; Eastern 127, 128, 147; medieval 119, 126, 165; Platonic 175
Christianity and Classical Culture (Cochrane) 165–80
chronotope (Bakhtin) 50
circle(s) 9, 21, 23–4, 44, 64, 73, 119, 128, 173, 178, 180; concentric (Elias) 26, 32; of recognition (Pizzorno) 21, 24, 173
circularity *see* circle(s)
City of God (Augustine) 168, 176
civilisation 41, 100–101, 145, 147, 161, 166, 168, 171, 185–6, 195–6; city-based 69; human 142; mad 48; modern 144–5; Western 10 (*see also* culture: European)
Civilizing Process (Elias) 59
Classical Greece 63, 68, 123
codification 42, 173, 199
cognitive(ism) 27, 79, 105, 108, 130, 150, 151, 152, 171, 172, 203
'coincidence of opposites' 82
collapse 30, 43, 69

Collège de France 123, 179, 181, 184
commerce 75–8, 80
common sense 5, 22, 24, 51
communication 21, 72, 99, 101, 103, 111, 114, 147; technology 198, 208 (*see also* technology: communication)
Communism 8, 84, 89, 156
Communist Manifesto (Marx and Engels) 73, 162
community 9, 30, 49, 106, 174, 195, 196, 197, 199; early Christian 166; of scientists 54
compartmentalisation 9, 15, 19, 152
complexity 5, 26, 102, 158
concept-building 4; *see also* theory building
conceptual history *see* history: conceptual
concreteness 55, 72, 116, 127, 129, 185, 193, 208; historical 171; indelible 207
condition(s): extreme 166; human 188, 192; normal 128; of possibility 29, 48, 79, 87, 103, 183; primordial 145; wartime 186
Confessions (Augustine) 175, 176
confusion 102, 117, 118, 129, 132, 136, 150, 197
conquest 12, 56, 126; concupiscential (Voegelin) 167; of Nature 58, 126
consciousness 29, 79, 102, 130, 132, 172, 175, 176; philosophy of 114, 171; self- 29, 44, 128, 129, 173–5, 180
consensus 79; disciplinary 155
consonants 103–4
conspiracy *see* plotting
Constantinople 81, 82, 147; sack of 65, 134
construction 124, 168, 182, 203; social 92
constructivism 114; Kantian 105; social 158
control 23, 28, 45, 46, 63, 89–91, 170, 184, 206; *Magi* 147; manipulative 91; power to 62; rational 144
conversion 166–7, 171, 175
convictions 9, 147; ideological 9
convincing 9, 71, 177
correlation 87, 91
corruption 43, 205; existential 173; intellectual 7
cosmos 8, 64, 145
court society (Elias) 18
COVID xii, 156
Cratylus (Plato) 104
creation 63, 112, 115, 126–7, 139–40, 191–2; artistic 142–3; conscious 142; original 109
creativity 88; artistic 142; *see also* destruction: creative
crisis 75, 143, 153, 173, 174, 183, 196, 197; environmental 17, 171; *see also* liminality

critique 39, 40, 42, 43, 58, 164, 184
crystal(s) 104, 130, 184
cult 127, 142, 144, 148, 156; religious 62
culture 6, 9, 41, 42, 100, 101, 143, 145, 195, 196, 197, 206, 208; classical 158 (*see also* Classical Greece); European 10
cunning 59, 124, 125, 126, 139; tricks 118, 125; *see also* trickster
cybernetics 91
cycles 28, 206; cosmic 28; eternal 178; geological 178
Cynics 184–5, 189

Dadaists 73
daemonic (Goethe) 136
data: analysis 84; collection 4, 92; empirical 4; hard 200; quantitative 88, 155, 205; sets 85, 91; statistical 85, 156
David Copperfield (Dickens) 60, 158, 175
Davos 81
'Death of Orpheus' (Dürer) 136, 137
decadence 139, 147; moral 139
deceit 120, 122, 128–30, 132; self- 129; *see also* trickster
deconstruction (Derrida) 163
decontextualisation 4, 90, 150
definition 4, 6, 23
degradation 74, 152, 188; *see also* decadence
deification 127
deity(ies) 30, 74, 124, 139, 148, 177, 178; *see also* gods/goddesses
democracy 6, 32, 81, 154, 156, 202
democratisation 9; hyper- 164
demon(s) 69, 118, 119, 122, 129, 131, 144, 178
demonic 71, 117–21 *passim*, 136, 137, 143, 144, 145, 148, 206
Demonic in Art, The (Castelli) 117–22
Demons (Dostoevsky) 131
denatured 119, 120, 121, 146; *see also* unnatural
dependence 18, 173, 189
depersonalisation (Weber) 79, 149, 151
design 113, 203; circular 64; genealogical 164
desire 120, 142; to know 54; mimetic (Girard) 159
destruction 55, 75, 81, 122, 148, 186; creative 15; systematic 42; technological 38
destructiveness 111; programmatic 15
devastation 43
devil 63, 121, 122
Devils of Loudun, The (Huxley) 17
dialectic(al) 40, 74, 114; master-serf (Hegel) 18, 39; materialism 95
Diana 124

dichotomies 39, 104, 202
dignity 64, 74
Dionysus, cult 144
diphthongs 102
discipline 92, 134, 150, 153, 183–4
Discipline and Punish (Foucault) 164, 208
Discourse on Method (Descartes) 51–8
Discourse on Trade (North) 76
disintegration 166, 175
distinction 104, 122, 138, 158, 176, 191, 207
Dits et écrits (Foucault) 182
divine 62, 63, 120, 171–2, 187, 201, 206, 207; love 138; names 65; persons 170; *see also* deity, gods, God
divinisation 62, 71
division 28, 54–6, 127, 187; as violence 55
dogmatism 83, 91, 150, 162, 180; extreme 94; infinite 147; religious 91; scientific 83, 91, 94
Dombey and Son (Dickens) 37, 39, 60
domination 81, 154
Don Quixote (Cervantes) 112, 159, 203
door(s) 11, 127, 128, 131, 187; *see also* liminality
dotti 125
doubting 57–8, 155, 176
dream(s) 54, 127–8, 142, 148; shamanistic initiatory 133; and waking 127, 142
Dream and Existence (Binswanger) 183
dualism(s) 39, 114, 138, 168, 176
duckspeak 49, 100
duplicity 142, 190

Earth xi, xii, 8, 26, 27, 28, 37, 40, 45, 46, 47, 60, 64, 68, 88, 90, 109, 112, 127, 146, 181, 209
earthquake 77
écart (gap) (Serres) 122
'Economic Ethic of World Religions' (Weber) 136
Economic Thought and Ideology in England (Appleby) 75–80, 99
economics 9, 25, 38, 49, 80, 84–5, 135, 147; mathematical 84; micro- 9, 203; modern 24, 82; neoclassical 147; positive 93
economy 32, 75–9, 84, 99, 164, 207; fairground 80, 82; modern 61, 68, 75, 80, 82, 118, 209; political 75–81, 208 (*see also* economics)
Economy and Society (Weber) 164
education 9, 13, 14, 15, 31, 37, 65, 71, 72, 84, 151–2, 166–7, 203; classical 158; of judgment 14, 16
Ego Dominus Tuus (Yeats) 157, 203

egoism 147, 149, 191
Egypt 71, 124, 127, 124, 208
emergency 156; *see also* liminality
empathy 52, 140, 147
Empire(s) 69, 70, 81, 167, 201, 208; British 69; -building 56; Byzantine 69; Holy 69, 70; Near-Eastern 180; Roman 55, 69, 166, 196
empiricist: positivism 87, 114; -rationalistic-constructivist 107
empowerment 61, 184
emptiness 29, 73, 129, 130, 131, 200; *see also* void
'Enchanted Forest' (Tasso) 129
enchantment 133, 152
encounter: with the abyss 29; face-to-face 108–10, 115
energy/ies 131, 133, 175, 180
England 42, 69, 71, 74–5, 82
Enlightenment 71–2, 74, 112, 125, 164, 168; thinking 164; vision: of history 165; of progress 165, 169
entrapment 120, 121, 129, 165, 168, 169, 189, 196, 197
enslavement 47, 61, 132, 208
entrepreneur xiii, 147
Ephesus 123, 124
epiphany 140
episteme (Foucault) 43, 92, 113, 114
epistemology 55, 170–1, 178–81, 201
ERC (European Research Council) 3, 37
erring 38, 40, 41, 45, 48, 52, 56, 189, 192
Eros 136, 137
eschatology 70, 73; 'intramundane' (Voegelin) 164
etymology 7, 11, 13, 31, 48, 51, 90, 92, 104–6, 108, 110, 116, 119, 140, 150; English 11, 40, 122, 146, 150, 203, 206; German 12, 95, 106, 107, 110, 150, 151; Greek xii, 10, 11, 44, 65, 90, 103, 117, 125, 150; Hungarian 11, 78–9, 90, 95, 102, 105, 121, 122, 123–4, 146, 150, 173; Latin 54, 55, 90, 92, 119, 146, 174; Russian 130, 146, 147; Sanskrit 103; *see also* language(s)
evil 81, 119, 122, 139, 149, 151–2, 188, 191, 197
exchange 76–9, 81, 99, 103, 208; bills of 69, 81; economy 78; gift 79
experience(s) 11–2, 18–9, 27, 29, 31, 48, 88, 90, 92, 96, 100, 103, 117, 129, 133, 134, 138, 139, 140, 147, 155, 171–2, 174–6, 178, 182–4, 190–2, 199–200, 202, 205, 206, 207, 209; aha- 106; conversion 165, 166, 170, 171, 175; creative 110; death

29; of home 26; with language 101, 103, 106, 107–11; liminal 153, 195, 200; limitlessness 206; mediated (Hegel) 18, 103, 207; mystical 140; original 108–9; participatory 18, 19, 48, 106, 200 (non- 57); personal 55, 94, 152, 156; reading 154, 182; recognitive 110; stamping 164; surprise 140; unified 175–6; void 29
experiment(s) 12, 40, 43–5, 89–90, 125–6, 155, 171; controlled 48, 89–90, 171, 178
experts 47, 156, 206
explanation 5, 20–4, 31, 47, 88, 94; universalistic 22
Exploratory Data Analysis 85

face 130–1, 147
face-to-face 90, 109–110, 115
fact(s) 27, 40, 50, 92, 158; social 58
fairground 118; permanentized 121; *see also* economy: fairground
fairs 80–1, 113, 118, 122; late Renaissance 80; permanent 80–1
faking 32, 150, 156, 158, 198
Fall 169, 173
falsification (Popper) 92–6, 158
familiarity 22, 41, 110, 150, 151, 158, 179, 200
'Fantasia of the Library' (Foucault) 117
fashion 156, 198
Faust (Goethe) 30, 137, 175
Fear and Trembling (Kierkegaard) 95, 119
fixate/ing 58, 81, 86, 152
fixer (trickster) 87
Flanders 118, 121
flow 76–7, 102, 103, 115, 118, 119, 146
fluidity 77, 80
flux 29, 61, 75–8, 102, 118, 124; limitless 118; vertiginous 121
fluxions 102, 170
fools 120
forces 81, 83, 89, 91, 129, 136, 144–5, 167–8, 169, 188, 189, 206; active 144; chthonic 144; demonic 137, 144–5; economic 76; external 136; guiding 110, 168, 209; history-forming 167, 177; irresistible 75; moving 186; physical 89; radiating 175; social 135
formalism 83, 87, 94, 106, 111, 114
forms of expression (*Pathosformeln*) (Warburg) 133, 136–42
foundations 19, 22, 23, 24, 39, 41, 44, 52, 165, 186; pre-reflexive 29
founding fathers 5, 18, 24, 198
fragmentation 9, 152

Franciscans 133, 134
Frankfurt School 164
freedom 132, 154, 174, 180
Freemasonry 72 127
fresh start 44, 46, 53, 55
friendship 26, 195

'Garden of Delights' (Bosch) 122
Gay Science (Nietzsche) 114, 179
gaze 24, 25, 131, 133; *see also* regard
gender 62, 124, 136, 157
genealogy xiii, 32, 41, 87, 153, 159, 162–4, 181, 182–4, 185, 194–5, 196, 199, 208; historical xiii; of power 164; *see also* sociology: historical
Genealogy of Morals (Nietzsche) 32, 41, 163–4
generations 6, 10, 41, 48, 93, 105, 106, 133, 203; World War 153, 186
genius 18, 87, 117, 156; *see also* talent
geometry 57, 68, 69, 121, 122, 126, 128
Germany 18, 20, 29, 101, 118, 132, 135
gift(s) 12, 58, 87–8, 100–101, 106, 109, 110, 111, 115, 173, 180, 191; exchange 79; logic 79
giftedness *see* talent
givenness xii, 28, 127, 172–3
'Glasgow lectures' (Smith) 24
Gnosticism 13, 30, 39, 40, 56, 62, 63, 64, 99, 114, 120, 125, 126, 150, 165, 166, 167, 168; modern (Voegelin) 9, 82
God 39, 63, 112–14, 161, 176–80, 186–7, 190–2, 207; creator 112, 114, 127; the Father 179, 187; image of (man) 42, 130; knowledge of 191; likeness of 112, 130; Mother of 131; Son of 178, 179, 180, 186, 190, 192; will of 63, 137, 173; Word of 70, 190–2
god(s) 71, 84, 177, 178; *see also* deities, divinity
goddess(es) 88; virgin 73, 123–6
Gospel(s) 44, 123, 186–92; John 11, 191–2; Luke 129, 187; Mark 187, 188; Matthew 119, 129, 187, 188
governmentality (Foucault) 182, 184
grace xii, 12, 87, 119, 121, 129–30, 138, 173, 175, 180
Graces (Three) 12, 175
gratitude xii, 14, 60, 100, 172–3
Great Expectations (Dickens) xi, 37
Great Instauration, The (Bacon) 44
Greek 11, 55, 63–4, 70, 90, 136, 159, 167, 201; classical 103; culture 143–4; deity 30, 74; episteme 150; law 178; logos 55; maenad 136; mythology 30, 74, 87–8; philosophers 42, 188, 201; sculpture 131; spirit 63, 136, 144

growth 66, 77–9, 87, 113, 123, 146, 169, 202–3; economic 77; exponential 6
guidance 6, 13, 47, 48, 129, 151, 152, 158, 169, 199
guide(s) xiii, 6, 13–5, 54, 55, 56, 68, 101, 151, 152, 154, 156, 159, 165, 168; -word (Heidegger) 107, 108, 109

Hamlet (Shakespeare) 159
'Happy the Man' (Dryden) 194
Hard Times (Dickens) 3, 17, 31, 60, 83
harmony 30, 39, 55, 78, 118, 122, 133, 145
Harvard 20, 151
hatred 84, 151, 188, 190
heart 151, 155, 161, 169, 172, 180, 182, 188–90, 192; reasons of (Pascal) 31, 92, 155, 205, 207, 209
Heaven xi, 45, 60, 71, 142, 194
Hebraism 74, 82; English 74
Hell 120
Hellenism 127, 139, 141, 185
hermeneutics 26, 28–30, 106, 112, 114, 152, 157, 177, 199
Hermes 30, 122, 125, 139, 148
Hermes Trismegistos 64, 139
Hermeticism 30, 58, 61–8, 71, 118, 125, 138; Renaissance 61, 65, 66, 67, 73, 74
hint(s) 14, 105, 120, 208
historiogenesis (Voegelin) 164, 201
history 11, 47, 49, 50, 51, 70, 71, 81, 94, 95, 133, 144, 157, 158, 160, 161–93, 195–6, 197, 199, 201, 208; art xii, 133–5; conceptual 48, 91, 110, 123–4; intellectual 63, 165; linear vision 164–5, 167–9, 180, 196; modern 29, 126, 197; natural 170; semantic 7, 55, 109, 116; world 172, 173
Holy Spirit 169, 179–80
home(land) 26, 32, 63, 100, 103, 125, 194; in the world 38, 104, 106, 110, 111, 145
Homeric Hymn to Hermes 125
homo clausus (Elias) 59
Hopi: language 115; ritual 144–4
horizon: background 29; of experiences' (Koselleck) 21
HR (Human Resources) 6, 59
hubris 30–1, 83, 91, 125, 156, 191; modern 30
Huguenots 68, 81
humanism: Renaissance 66; secular politicised 114; trans- 114, 126, 147
humbleness 30, 46, 100, 126
hybrid 102, 139
Hyperion (Hölderlin) 152
hypothesis 95, 187; -testing 64, 85, 86–9, 92

icon(s) 127, 130–4, 147
iconography 123, 124, 128, 138
iconology 135, 136, 142
Iconostasis (Florensky) 127–33
'iconymy' (Alinei) 104–6, 108
identification 21, 92; self- 17
identity/ies 20–1, 25, 163, 177, 183, 195, 199
ideology 7, 9, 14, 23, 38, 61, 81, 83, 91, 92, 93, 132, 167, 168
idol(s) 17, 142, 144; of Bacon 39–43, 45, 48, 99, 100, 102, 103, 116; methodology as 37–8; of scientific methodology 83–95
image(s) 56, 64, 66, 67, 70, 95, 104, 105, 116–147, 180, 201; of God (man) 42, 130
imagination 40, 45, 66, 67, 119, 120, 132, 142, 159, 206
imitation 4, 12, 19, 38, 73, 86, 128, 132, 134, 139, 158, 195, 197–8, 201, 205
immortality 51, 178
impassivity 119, 122
imperialism 68–70
imprisonment 45, 48, 61, 62, 121, 190
in-betweenness 127, 136, 142, 143, 198; *see also* liminality
incarnation 168, 171, 180
incision 117, 132
incommensurability 17, 27, 88, 150, 172, 178, 205–7, 209; *see also* liminality
indestructible 51, 54, 102, 103, 111, 115; *see also* soul
indoctrination 7, 8, 14, 84, 92, 167
infinity 113, 121, 158, 191, 198
information 13, 65, 99, 111, 150, 170, 200, 203
integrity 15, 145, 208
intellect 6, 40, 45, 66, 151, 166
intellectual(s) 84, 134, 186
intelligence 91, 177; artificial 114, 147, 150
intensification 126, 136, 138, 140–1, 147, 198, 208
intention(s) 21, 23, 24
interchangeability 78–80; *see also* substitutability
intermediary 113, 115, 127, 139, 143; *see also* liminality
International Political Anthropology (IPA) xii, xiv, 135
intimacy 59, 99, 100, 103, 109, 150–1
intrusion 6, 38, 39, 78, 99, 171
involvement-detachment (Elias) 21, 56, 59
irrationality 55, 118; *see also* incommensurable
irresistible 75, 77, 81, 91, 175, 180

Isis 123–7

Janus 74, 142
Jesuit(s) 52, 117, 138
joke(s) 8, 18, 196
joker 201; *see also* trickster
judgment 14, 23–5, 30–1, 156, 188; informed 88, 96; children's 31; sense of 31, 156

King Lear (Shakespeare) 175
Kingship and the Gods (Frankfort) 82
knowledge 39–43, 46–50, 63–8, 112–14, 120–2, 150–2, 169–73, 175–8, 181–3, 191; academic 9; common 94; concrete 183; of death 122; historical 170; human 46, 95, 202; of life 191; magical 62; scientific 43, 62, 83, 91, 122, 209; secret 120–2, 124; society 83; supernatural 133; transformative 47; tree of 191; true 52, 179, 183; universal 10, 49; will to 38, 183, 186
Kreuzlingen 134, 146, 148

language(s) 11, 13, 33, 40, 41, 48, 49, 99–115, 135–6, 170, 179, 190; agglutinating 105; essence of 103, 106–9, 114; experiencing 108, 109, 110; as gift 100–1, 106, 109–11; as 'house of Being' (Heidegger) 109, 111; Hopi 115; Hungarian 11, 78, 90, 102, 105, 121, 122, 124, 146, 150, 173; nature of 108, 111; as perfect 101; private 7, 18; referential 190; as unconscious 102–3; well-ordered 100, 101; *see also* etymology
'Language' (Sapir) 100–3
Laocoon 139, 144, 145, 148
larva (mask) 131
Lascaux cave 128
Latin 9, 11, 44, 70, 90, 102, 119, 146
law(s) 45, 63, 96, 178
'Letter on humanism' (Heidegger) 109, 115
Leviathan (Hobbes) 26
Le voile d'Isis (Hadot) 123–7
Life of Jesus (Schleiermacher) 33
liminal: conditions 178; crises 174, 196–7; events 196; experience 153, 200; field 194; incommensurable 209; situation 128, 198; space 142
liminality 11, 19, 28, 29, 30, 58, 60, 61, 66, 115, 142–3, 152–3, 174, 179, 194, 195–6, 197, 198, 199, 201; analysis 152–3; permanent 197; theory 177; *see also* crisis, door(s), emergency, in-betweenness, incommensurability, intermediary, liquidity, threshold, transition, uncertainty
'Liminality' (Turnbull) 199–200
limit 82, 127, 128, 187, 191, 205; *see also* measure
limitlessness 6, 118
lineal (Ingold) 59
linear vision of history *see* history: vision
linguistics 100, 104–6, 108, 114, 135–6, 140; anthropological 100–3
links: analysis-synthesis 37; Babylon-Alexandria-Constantinople 81, 147; *charis*-truth 184; cognitive-emotive 151, 152; data-facts 27, 92; Descartes-Kant 58, 59; Dionysian-Apollonian (Nietzsche) 145; face-mask 110, 115, 130–1, 133; flux-void 29, 61, 170; generation-creation 191; geometry-logic 121; gift-grace-beauty 101; grace-works (Aquinas) 87; historicity-scientificity 32, 161–3; hubris-rationalism 30–1; images-words 64, 70, 104–5, 116–7, 135–7, 201; inner-outside 91, 131, 177, 188–92, 199, 207; life-word 188–92; liminality-marginality 143, 148; limit-unlimited (Plato) 201; Nazi-Bolshevik 8, 89; order-chaos 30, 105, 114; poetry-philosophy 108–10; power-knowledge (Bacon) 30, 39, 46, 59, 91, 169; power/knowledge (Foucault) 113, 181–3; public sphere-theatricality 68, 73, 121, 198; Puritan-Enlightenment 73–4; reality-unreality 73; reason-emotion 51–2, 138, 151, 175–6, 200; religion-science (Yates) 62, 206–7; signifier-signified 104; social-individual liminality 153, 195; subject-truth (Foucault) 179–85; sublime-beauty 141; symbolic-expressive (Warburg) 101–2; truth-usefulness (Bacon) 46; Venice-Lyon-Antwerp-Amsterdam-London-New York 81, 147; words-things 13, 100, 104, 109, 112–3, 189
liquid(ity) 77, 102, 174, 179; *see also* liminality
literature review 4, 5, 6, 14
living dead 147
logic 4, 18, 25, 66, 68, 92, 94, 121–2, 132, 144, 156, 198; 'Aristotelian' 95; as *ars diaboli* 121; *charis* 100, 173; gift 79; iron 174; market 78; military 55; trickster 59, 78, 87, 197
Logic of Scientific Discovery, The (Popper) 93

228 Subject Index

logos 12, 30, 55, 109, 123, 145, 192
London 70, 81, 94, 134, 147
L'origine delle parole (Alinei) 104–6
love 123, 136, 137, 138, 150–1, 173, 175, 176, 180, 189, 190, 195; divine 138; *see also* Eros, *philia*
LSE *see* London
Lyon 81

machination 169
machine(s) 45, 47, 66, 124, 145, 148, 150, 203, 208; *see also* megamachine
madness 56, 66, 101, 121, 174
Magi 71, 91, 120, 126, 147; Byzantine 64, 82; misogyny 126; Renaissance 53, 62–3, 67, 69, 70, 118
magic 10, 58, 59, 63, 64, 69, 71, 120, 122, 125, 126, 144, 145, 206, 207; Renaissance 63, 66, 71
magician(s) 15, 121, 194
magus *see* Magi
mainstream 3, 4, 10, 20, 28, 116, 126, 151, 154, 155, 158, 167, 196, 199, 203
májá (Vedic) 146
Making (Ingold) 202
managerialism xiii, 92, 155
Manichaeanism 39, 165–6, 168
manipulation 48, 50, 65, 69, 90, 91, 92, 170
marginality 69, 72, 76, 143, 148
market(s) 49, 78–81, 162; calculations 79; economy 32, 75–7, 80; extension of 78–9, 81; stock- 80, 81, 118, 147, 198, 208
marketplace 41, 81, 99, 100; idols of 41, 99, 100, 102, 103, 116
Martin Chuzzlewit (Dickens) 75, 99, 181, 194, 205
masks 26, 120, 129–31, 133; funeral 131; obligatory 110
Master and Margarita (Bulgakov) 132
master of ceremonies 197
mathematics 9, 51, 52, 54, 55, 57, 63, 67, 69, 72, 77, 84, 95, 125–7
meaning 21–2, 24, 88, 89, 104–5, 136, 178, 187, 199, 207; of education 13; original 9, 11, 55, 90, 104, 108, 110, 123, 124, 136
measure 31, 46, 51, 68, 89, 114, 171; money as 206, 207; *see also* limit
mechanics 124–5, 169; ancient 125; quantum 91
mechanisation 56, 208; of the world 126; *see also* mechanics
mechanism 120, 203, 204; market 76; sacrificial 208

media 38, 92, 116, 150, 155–6, 198; gurus 47
mediation 49, 207
mediatisation 152
megamachine (Mumford) 208
memory 64–8, 88, 117, 137, 141, 177, 178, 206; art of 64–8; social 141; theatre (Camillo) 65, 66, 141
merchant(s) 79–81, 140
Mesopotamia 206
metalepsis 32; *see also* participation
metallurgy 47, 56, 125, 206
metaxy 201; *see also* liminality
methexis 32, 54; *see also* participation
method(s): anthropological 194–204; Cartesian 54, 67; ethnographic 194, 202, 204; genealogical 162–4, 182, 185, 195, 196; historical 161–93
method-logic 7, 9, 18, 25, 78, 100, 104, 106, 110, 115, 117, 119, 123, 124, 126, 130, 133, 135, 141, 146, 151, 153, 157, 160 164, 165, 177, 187, 192, 193, 194, 199, 201, 202
methodological individualism 24, 101
methodology 4, 7–10, 14, 37–9, 44–9, 63–8 *passim*, 71; scientific xiii, 4, 8, 10, 14, 17, 32, 33, 38, 39, 44–9, 54, 64–6, 69, 71, 82, 83–96, 112, 155, 156, 157, 200, 202, 203
microscope 88, 206; *see also* incommensurability
Middle Ages 9, 63, 64, 69, 70, 121, 126, 132, 138
military 55–6, 95, 202; *see also* soldier(s)
mime(s) 198
mimesis xiii, 150
mind 30, 40, 45–8, 52, 54, 87, 91, 92, 102, 103, 105, 109, 120, 155–6, 167, 176–7; alien frame of 83; archaic 19; control 62, 65; training 59; transcendental 105, 168
modelling 64; causal 85–6, 91–2
modernity 24, 27, 60, 149, 150, 151, 154, 158, 163, 164, 174, 181; absurdities xiii; destructiveness 15; diagnosis 73, 129, 181, 195, 199, 208; Gnostic 9; hyper- 32, 158; post- 164; Rabbinic (Calasso) 147; rise of 72, 109; *see also* world: modern
Moloch 17
monasticism 9, 164, 185
monotheism 144, 207
monster(s) 118, 119, 120, 122
Montpellier 186
Moses 144, 148
motivation (Alinei) 104–5
Mnemosyne 88
Mnemosyne atlas (Warburg) 136, 141–2

Muses 87–8, 141, 159
mutability 74; *see also* transformation
mystery 12, 80, 126, 149, 165
mysticism 58, 66, 140, 145; Eastern 13, 117; medieval 118–20, 129, 185
myth(s) 145, 168, 178, 196
mythology xii, 48, 83, 134, 138, 197; Greek 30, 74, 84, 87–8, 125, 137, 138

Natufian culture 48
nature xii, 8, 28, 39, 46, 58, 62, 68, 90, 112, 122, 123–7, 133, 145, 178, 188, 206–9; conquest of 39, 46, 58, 126; human 39, 40, 43, 45, 68; rape of 122, 125; servant of 46; of things 81
nearness (Heidegger) 108, 109–10, 111
negation 132; double 94–5
neo-Kantianism 4, 7, 11, 18, 20, 21, 84, 92, 134, 138, 140, 147, 153, 158, 159, 195
Neoplatonism 42, 56, 62, 63, 65, 70, 74, 138–9, 166
neutrality xii, 14, 17, 128
New Organon, The (Bacon) 38–51
New Atlantis, The (Bacon) 43
New Testament 155, 172, 185, 191; *see also* Gospels
New York 81, 147
Nicholas Nickleby (Dickens) 27, 149
'Nietzsche, Genealogy, History' (Foucault) 164
nihilism (Nietzsche) 114
Nobel prize 38, 147
normality 197, 199; return to 69
nothingness 29, 132
not-knowing (Ingold) 203
Nouveau Christianisme (Saint-Simon) xiii
novel(s) 31, 157–60, 197
nulla 119, 120, 122; *see also* zero

objectivity xi, 14, 22, 28, 85–6, 129, 130, 132, 176, 200
' "Objectivity" essay' (Weber) 155
observation: participant/ participatory 32, 194, 195, 199, 200
occult 65–73 *passim*, 125
Old Curiosity Shop, The (Dickens) 157
Old Testament 173, 192
On Learned Ignorance (Cusanus) 82
On the Origins of Cognitive Science (Dupuy) 37
On the Dignity of Man (Pico) 74
On the Sublime (Pseudo-Longinus) 141
On the Way to Language (Heidegger) 106–122
onomatopoeia 11, 105, 146
Open Society and Its Enemies, The (Popper) 93, 94

operationalisation 4, 13, 86
order xi, 30, 80, 113, 129, 197, 199; cosmic 146; dialectical (Ramus) 66; global world trade 76; natural 63, 76; new 23; old (European) 60, 75, 80; sequential 50, 57; of things 75; world 60
Order of Things (Foucault) 112
orientation 27, 33, 62, 67, 71, 129, 142, 147, 183
oscillation 29, 37, 141, 142, 143
Our Mutual Friend (Dickens) 157, 161
owning (Heidegger) 110–1; *see also* Appropriation
Oxford 20, 135, 152, 159

painting 117–22, 128, 131–4, 138, 142, 146, 147
Palaeolithic 51, 101, 197
pamphlet(s) 73, 76, 80
Pan 74
Panopticon 89
Papua New Guinea 198
Paradise 122; on Earth 45, 46, 133
Paradise Lost (Milton) xi, 3, 73, 161
parasite 99, 201; *see also* trickster
Parmenides (Plato) 74
Paroles du Christ (Henry) 185–92
parrhesia 85, 179, 80, 182, 184–5, 188, 193
participation xii, 6, 12, 15, 17–33, 48, 49, 54, 59, 145, 194, 202; total (Turnbull) 194, 199–200
Passages (Benjamin) 141
passion(s) 129, 136, 158
Passion 191
path 10–15, 16, 44, 45, 52, 57, 61, 91, 157, 188, 192, 203; analysis 91
pathogenesis (Koselleck) 164
pathos 11, 147
Pathosformeln see forms of expression
Patmos 123
patos (road) 11
pattern(s) 85, 91, 101, 103, 157
perfection 20, 101, 113, 126, 131, 175, 186
performative speech act 73, 190
personality 8, 47, 71, 155–6, 169–77, 180
perspectivism 132
Pharisee(s) 122, 129, 166, 188
PhD 3, 4, 9, 13, 14, 15, 37, 85, 151, 195
phenomenology 114, 117, 190
Phenomenology of the Spirit (Hegel) 18
Philebus (Plato) 201
philia 123
philology xii, 11, 123, 125, 189, 193
philosophy 42–3, 114, 159–60, 171, 186, 200–1; analytical 24, 49, 58, 193; classical

xii, 66, 173, 182, 188, 195, 200; of consciousness 114, 171; critical 58; Hermetic 62, 63, 66, 67, 118, 138; of history 165–72; idealist (German) 132, 134; of language 192; of life 147; of the other 193; presocratic 171; Renaissance 64, 73 (*see also* Hermeticism); of science 95; *see also* neo-Kantianism, Neoplatonism
'Philosophy as a way of life' (Hadot) 123
physics 59, 77, 94
physis 42, 111, 123, 124; *see also* Nature
plotting 186
poetry 108–9, 111–2, 137
Poetry and Truth (Goethe) 136
poiesis 108, 115
polemics 94
positivism 19, 24, 48, 50, 86, 87, 88, 114, 131, 155, 159; logical 93; neo- 18, 20, 21, 158
Poverty of Historicism, The (Popper) 95
power(s) 28, 63–4, 71, 76, 89, 91, 128, 146, 164, 169, 175, 184, 191, 196, 206; academic 14, 19–20, 135; beauty 175; to control 62; imaginative 66, 67, 143; images 70, 139; merchant 80–1; of method 12; mind 40, 52, 105, 155, 166; over Nature 62; over- 131; pastoral 184; of reason/ing 31–2, 51–2, 91, 189, 207 (*see also* ratiocination); transformative 30, 46, 71, 74, 143; unlimited 20
powerlessness 188, 189
Prague 70
praying 119, 129, 145
precondition 20 22, 32, 80, 170, 199; *see also* condition of possibility
prehistory 41, 145; *see also* Palaeolithic
presence 20, 21, 26, 109, 110, 115, 129, 144, 175, 202
press 46, 113; *see also* media
prevention 45, 89
pride 37, 129; *see also* arrogance, hubris
problematisation 24, 25, 32, 33, 38, 49, 75, 88, 139, 149, 162, 164, 181, 182, 190, 202, 203
profession 8, 9, 26, 143
professionalisation 8–10, 19, 152
progress 42, 44, 47, 50–1, 61, 80, 96, 113, 114, 126, 143, 163, 164, 165, 168, 169, 180, 181, 196; idea of 162, 181; linear 168–9
Prometheus 30, 84, 125, 126, 145, 173
Prometheus (Goethe) 30
Prometheus Bound (Aeschylus) 125

prophecy 137, 177, 190, 191, 193; self-fulfilling 73
proportionality 30, 55, 118
Protestantism 66, 69, 70, 127, 132, 148
Protestant Ethic (Weber) 5, 74, 81, 85, 87, 164, 187, 208
Proteus 74
Prussia 18, 19, 134
psychogenesis (Elias) 164
psychology 134, 140, 151, 180; ecological 202; historical 140
public 38, 121; interest 13; spectacle 118; sphere 66, 68, 72–3, 155, 175, 198, 208
Puritanism 70, 73–4, 159, 173
Pygmy/ies 199, 200
Pythagoreans 124, 201

quantification 4, 77
quantum mechanics 91

radiance 76, 175
radiation 62
ratio 30, 55, 118; *see also* harmony, proportionality
ratiocination 132, 158, 168
rationalism 19, 20, 22–3, 25, 28, 30–1, 32, 34, 38, 43, 51, 54, 59, 60, 61, 62, 64, 67, 71, 72, 75, 82, 101, 103, 107, 112, 116–7, 123, 131, 132, 134, 144, 146, 147, 160, 179, 197, 199, 202
rationality 20–5, 30, 31, 55, 61, 132, 142, 184, 189; instrumental 24, 25, 58
reality 32, 86, 88, 92, 103, 110, 113, 116, 128–33, 157–9, 167, 174, 188–91, 206, 208; -blind 93, 188; pseudo- 131; sense of 58; superior 128, 129, 189; vision of 157, 200, 203; *see also* unreality
reason 31, 51–2, 121, 132, 144, 175–6, 188; pure/mere 116, 121, 132, 168, 175, 188, 189; of state 68, 81, 82, 113, 146
reciprocity 21, 187
recognisability 147
recognition (Pizzorno) xii, 14, 20–4, 31, 38, 52, 108, 110, 130, 135, 150, 170–6, 180, 191, 202, 203
Redemption 169
reflexivity 5, 11, 158; self- 5, 164
reform(s) 70–2; educational 66, 67
Reformation 43, 70, 73, 118; Counter- 69, 70
regard (Florensky) 129–133, 199
religion 39, 72–3, 144, 206–7
Renaissance 49, 53, 60–74, 80, 81, 82, 112–3, 118, 126, 130–2, 133–4, 138–41, 144, 147, 163, 199; *Magi* 53, 62, 63, 67, 69, 70; Medici 138, 139, 141

representation (Foucault) 113–4
research: funding 3, 4, 5, 7, 14, 15, 37, 156; meaningful xiii, 14, 154, 156; personal 14, 153, 154, 156; project xiii, 3–6, 14, 37
resemblance (Foucault) 112–4
Resurrection 192
revelation 131; self-revelation of life (Henry) 188, 190
revolution(s) 28, 43–4, 74, 190; bourgeois 162; epistemological 178; French 127; industrial 58; moral 178; Puritan 73, 74; scientific 43, 62, 71
rhetorics 39, 42, 53, 65, 179
rhythm 28, 56, 59, 76, 165
rites of passage 19, 195
Rites of Passage (van Gennep) 28
ritual(s) 143, 206; of sacrifice 17, 208; serpent 137, 144–5, 146
road *see* path
Rome 70, 135, 147; sack of 168
Rosicrucians 67, 68, 71–4
Rosicrucian Enlightenment (Yates) 61–3, 71–4
ruse 124, 125, 126; *see also* trick

sacred 131, 181
sacrifice 17, 19, 144, 184, 207, 208; human 17, 206
sacrificial mechanism (Girard) 208
Salomé 136
salvation 122, 129
Samson 137, 176
Sattelzeit (Koselleck) 68; *see also* liminality
Saying (Heidegger) 12, 99, 108–11; *see also* speech
schism(s): Church 64, 196, 199
schismatic self 25
schismogenesis (Bateson) 59, 147, 148, 154, 174, 195, 198–9
scholasticism: medieval 18, 42, 65; modern 7, 87, 100
science(s): human xi, 12, 17, 38, 49, 83, 86, 122, 141, 183, 205; natural xiii, 4, 8, 13, 17, 38, 50, 77, 86, 135, 145, 158, 179, 202, 205, 206; of opposites 122; social xiii, 3, 17, 19, 20, 25, 28, 38, 48, 49, 50, 86, 88, 91, 93, 100, 135, 159, 160, 195; technologized 38, 64, 122, 150, 186; universal(istic) 30, 113, 206
scientificity 7, 8, 9, 32, 38, 85, 89
scientism 38, 68, 93
Scriptures 112, 169, 172, 179, 187, 190
Second Coming 169
secrecy 72–3, 124

secret(s) 62, 74, 82, 112, 118–26, 191; knowledge 120–6, 178; of nature 120–26; societies 66, 68, 72
secularisation 9, 70, 131, 139, 165, 167, 168, 171, 180, 181, 182, 184,
seduction 118, 120, 121, 128–9, 144
self-consciousness *see* consciousness
semantic history *see* history: semantic
sense: of discrimination 6; of judgement 31, 156; of reality 58
sensuals (Horvath) 65
serpent: bronze 148
'Serpent ritual' (Warburg) 133, 137, 143–5, 146
settlement 11, 41, 48, 56
'Seventh Letter' (Plato) 93
sexual/ity 74, 141, 151; history (Foucault) 182–3
Showing (Heidegger) 108–11
siderurgy 206; *see also* metallurgy
simplicity 10, 122, 143, 175, 193
sin 121, 129; original 168, 169, 173
situation 197–8; concrete 22, 25, 209; global 32; grammatic of 23; meaning of 22; *see also* liminality
sociability (Simmel) 101
socialism xiii, 84, 85, 208
sociality 24; *see also* sociability
sociogenesis (Elias) 164
sociology xiii, 5, 21, 52, 84, 138, 140, 158, 160, 199, 208; historical (reflexive) xii, 162, 163, 164
soldier(s) 53, 55, 208
solidarity 82
solidity 56, 77, 82, 166
Sophist(s) 42, 49, 64, 65, 101, 114, 117, 120, 121, 124, 125, 128, 167, 201
Sophist, The (Plato) 56
Sophistic: Second 64, 86
sophistry 7, 18, 77, 82, 100, 116, 167
sorcery 48, 131
soul(s) 47, 52, 64, 65, 87, 102–3, 109, 129–31, 144, 155, 182, 203; indestructibility 51, 54, 102–3
Spaccio della bestia trionfante (Bruno) 71
Spain 65, 69, 73
specialisation 50, 143, 206; hyper- 6, 8, 49, 152; *see also* expert(s)
spectacle(s) 104, 118
spectator 24, 25, 53, 63, 142; impartial 24, 25, 43; omnipotent 25
spectres 129
speech 72, 100–3, 110, 115, 178, 186
spirit(s) 110, 144, 149, 178, 194, 206; guiding 136, 166, 169

232 Subject Index

spirituality 83; Eastern 175
standardisation 8, 13, 208; *see also* streamlining
statistics 4, 8, 84–5, 91, 92, 156, 205
stealing 59, 89, 118
stock market *see* market(s): stock
Stoics 188
streamlining 8–10; *see also* standardisation
structuralism 50, 112, 113
substitutability 79–80, 207–9
subversion 80, 188, 191
super-real 128, 133, 178
syllable(s) 102–3, 115
symbol(s) 120, 131, 140, 143, 145, 189, 206
symbolism: of language 101–5
system: analysis 91; building 28, 71

tabula rasa 29, 31, 81
Tabula Smaragdina 43
talent 48, 87, 88, 173, 156
technocracy xiii
technology 10, 30, 38, 42, 47, 49, 58, 61, 62, 66, 69, 72, 78, 83, 91, 109, 125, 148, 153, 158, 161, 162, 196, 206, 208; alchemic 10, 47; bio- 182; of self (Foucault) 184; telecommunication 198
telegraph 145; *see also* incommensurability
telephone 145; *see also* incommensurability
telescope 88, 206; *see also* incommensurability
Tempest, The (Shakespeare) 70, 82
temptation 117–22 *passim*, 128–9, 146
'Temptation of Saint Anthony' (Schongauer) 117
terribility 119, 130, 146
terror 25, 119, 146
textbook(s) 6, 7, 80, 153
Theaetetus (Plato) 23, 64
Theatre of Envy, The (Girard) 37, 81
theatre 26, 42, 43, 65, 68, 69, 82, 113, 147, 158, 198; idols (Bacon) 42–3; memory (Camillo) 65, 66, 141
theatricalisation 23, 25, 121, 133, 158
theatrical/ity 23, 24, 25, 43, 51, 52, 53, 59, 73, 121, 157, 158; of Descartes 43
theology 18, 70, 114, 117, 118, 122, 123, 127, 128, 130, 137, 147, 150, 160, 165–73, 177, 181, 185, 186, 189, 191; anti-Trinitarian 171; economic 201; orthodox 127, 128; Trinitarian 170, 171, 172, 176–80
theoretical framework 4, 6, 13, 21, 110, 149, 150, 154
theory: building 4, 6, 48, 149; of continuity (Alinei) 106 (*see also* Palaeolithic); critical 164, 184; economic 9, 14, 79–81; of forms (Plato) 127; social 19, 20, 48, 93, 101, 116, 163
Theory of Moral Sentiments (Smith) 24
thinker(s) 7, 13, 93, 149–54, 159; maverick 7, 154, 197, 199, 202; as seismograph 145–6
threshold 11, 127–131 *passim; see also* liminality
totalitarianism xiii, 90, 208
tradition 28, 177
transcendental: mind 105, 168; phenomenology 114; subject 183
transformation 30, 39, 46, 47, 50, 56, 71, 73, 74, 75, 78, 81, 92, 106, 107, 122, 125, 129, 136, 150, 158, 171, 195, 196, 200
transition 19, 29, 142, 143, 148, 195, 196; between dreaming and waking up 127, 142; *see also* liminality
transmutation 58, 74
travel/ling 11, 53, 57, 107, 147
trial and error (Popper) 96, 99
tribe: idols (Bacon) 39–40
trick(s) 18, 32, 42, 64, 67, 91, 94, 99, 117, 118, 124, 125, 126, 147, 203; theatrical (Descartes) 51; *see also* ruse
trickster 30, 59, 78, 125, 139, 147, 148, 159, 195, 196–7, 198, 199, 201; confidence 196; logic 59, 78, 87, 197; *see also* illusionist, joker, *Magi*, magician, parasite
Trinity 176–80, 181, 207
Trinity (Augustine) 176–7
'Trinity' (Rublev) 131
'Triumph of Death' (Brueghel) 122
trust 6, 15, 21, 47, 121, 154, 156, 187, 197
truth 8, 10, 40, 94–5, 175, 178–80, 185–92, 209; authentication of 181 (historical 178–80; self- 185, 189–92); care for 96, 185; historical 168–9, 177–81; living 209; search for 29, 40, 45, 46, 186; -telling 178–9, 181–2, 184–5, 188–9

Ulysses 125
Unbearable Lightness of Being (Kundera) 162
uncertainty 29, 197; *see also* liminality
understanding xii, 12–3, 22, 33, 41, 48, 87–9, 100, 149–60, 163–4, 170, 203; quest for 150, 152, 153, 203; self- 164, 180
Untimely Meditations (Nietzsche) 95
universe xii, 26, 30, 46, 63, 68, 74, 111, 112, 113, 115, 162, 190, 192, 209
university 9, 42, 49, 52, 152; contemporary 5, 10, 15, 32, 123; politics 4, 19–20, 48 (*see also* academic: power); Prussian 134

unnatural 119, 120, 125, 171; *see also* denatured
unreality 24, 47, 73, 120, 173
unsustainability 27
unsubstitutability 133, 207–9; *see also* substitutability
Unworte 12, 108; Goethe's 136–7
Use of Pleasures, The (Foucault) 164
utility 46, 49, 50, 76, 78, 206
utilitarianism 42, 50, 144, 150, 170
utopia xiii, 71, 114, 171
Utrecht 104

validity 81, 122, 170
values 77, 79, 143, 188, 196; as gift 180; revaluation (Nietzsche) 28, 76, 113
Vedas 13, 103
Venice 65, 147
victim 129, 208
Vienna 20, 70, 159
Vietnam 186
violence 55, 89, 118, 125, 126, 141, 187
virtue(s) 60, 71, 175, 180
vision 69, 72, 91, 101, 129–30; of history 162, 166, 167 (Augustine's 167–77; dualist 168; cyclical 165; Enlightenment 165; linear 162, 164–5, 167–9, 180, 196; Marx's 181)
vowels 102; long 105
void 29, 61, 73, 155, 168, 170, 190, 198; liminal 30, 174, 197, 205, 209
vulnerability 128, 175

walking 10, 11, 59, 202, 203; culture 16, 41
wall(s) 45, 59, 128, 131
walling 45

war(s): civil 43; global 43; Thirty Years 196; Trojan 125; world 153, 196, 208 (First 134, 153; Second 29, 117, 153, 181, 186)
Warburg library 134, 143
Warburg school 64, 74, 117
way *see* path
will: free 132, 173; good 180; of God 63, 137, 173; to knowledge 38, 183, 186; to operate 62–3, 95; to truth 186
Will to Power, The (Nietzsche) 3
wisdom 7, 10, 15, 48, 49, 100, 112, 154, 170, 175, 180, 200, 203, 209; love of 96
witch 8, 68; *see also* magician
word(s) 7, 11, 12, 13, 41–2, 48, 55, 56, 64, 70, 99–115; of Christ 186–92; experiencing 106, 108, 140; of God 70, 190–2; primary *see Unworte*
'Word, The' (George) 108, 109
world: angelic 128; alien 114; closed 48; created 81, 123; global 80, 81; home- 38; modern 6, 18, 20, 25, 81, 82, 109, 157, 158, 161, 162, 180, 181, 196, 206; moving force 110, 209; medieval order 60, 80; other xi, 127, 128, 129, 189, 190; picture 63; spiritual 129, 131, 132; vision/view 6, 115, 124 (European 126; Greek (classical) 123; scientific 29, 67, 71, 80, 82, 118, 121, 171, 202)
'world's fourfold' (Heidegger) 109, 110
WWII *see* war(s), world

Yahweh 127

Zarathustra (Nietzsche) 26
zero 29, 31, 77, 87
zoon politikon (Aristotle) xii, 54
Zürau Aphorisms (Kafka) 117, 147

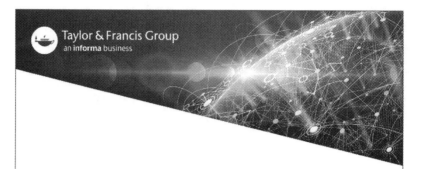

Taylor & Francis eBooks

www.taylorfrancis.com

A single destination for eBooks from Taylor & Francis with increased functionality and an improved user experience to meet the needs of our customers.

90,000+ eBooks of award-winning academic content in Humanities, Social Science, Science, Technology, Engineering, and Medical written by a global network of editors and authors.

TAYLOR & FRANCIS EBOOKS OFFERS:

- A streamlined experience for our library customers
- A single point of discovery for all of our eBook content
- Improved search and discovery of content at both book and chapter level

REQUEST A FREE TRIAL
support@taylorfrancis.com

Printed in the United States
by Baker & Taylor Publisher Services